Canadian Fiction

Recent Titles in
Genreflecting Advisory Series

Diana T. Herald, Series Editor

Canadian Fiction

A Guide to Reading Interests

Sharron Smith
and Maureen O'Connor

Foreword by Catherine Sheldrick Ross

Genreflecting Advisory Series
Diana Tixier Herald, Series Editor

A Member of the Greenwood Publishing Group

Westport, Connecticut • London

Library of Congress Cataloging-in-Publication Data

Smith, Sharron.
   Canadian fiction : a guide to reading interests / Sharron Smith and Maureen O'Connor
; foreword by Catherine Sheldrick Ross.
     p. cm. — (Genreflecting advisory series)
   Includes bibliographical references and index.
   ISBN 1-59158-166-4 (alk. paper)
   1. Canadian fiction—Bibliography—Handbooks, manuals, etc. 2. Books and reading—
English-speaking countries—Handbooks, manuals, etc. 3. Books and reading—Canada—
Handbooks, manuals, etc. I. O'Connor, Maureen, 1947- II. Title. III. Series.
Z1377.F4S65   2005
[PR9192.2]
016.813—dc22   2005016100

British Library Cataloguing in Publication Data is available.

Library of Congress Catalog Card Number: 2005016100
ISBN: 1-59158-166-4

First published in 2005

Libraries Unlimited, 88 Post Road West, Westport, CT 06881
A Member of the Greenwood Publishing Group, Inc.
www.lu.com

Printed in the United States of America

The paper used in this book complies with the
Permanent Paper Standard issued by the National
Information Standards Organization (Z39.48–1984).

10   9   8   7   6   5   4   3   2   1

To my mother, Pat Douglas, for nurturing my passion for reading;
my husband Al for knowing where I needed to be before I did;
and my daughter Heather, who has always seen her mother as a reader:
your guidance, patience, and support have made what seemed impossible,
a reality.

SS

To my Nana, Maggie McGinley: unschooled though she was,
she started me on my lifelong journey of books and reading, a journey that
has brought me to this point of being able to share the reading with others.

MO

Contents

Chapter 5—Genre Fiction (*Cont.*)

Foreword

Avid readers agree there is little they value more than a helpful suggestion for the "What do I read next?" question. When readers ask for a "good book," they mean a book that provides the special reading experience they are in the mood for. They might be looking particularly for fast-paced action or leisurely description; for a single strong character or the complex interweaving of many characters through several generations; for a well-realized setting so important to the story that it becomes a character in its own right; for a book that is soothing and comforting or else challenging and quirky; or possibly for a book in which the language is used so felicitously it sings.

Library catalogues and single alphabetical shelf arrangements in libraries and bookstores aren't much help in this regard. That's why readers and readers' advisors alike will welcome this book, which uses what Joyce Saricks has called "appeal characteristics" —setting, story, characters, and language—to provide access to recent Canadian fiction.

In *Canadian Fiction: A Guide to Reading Interests*, readers will encounter well-known friends such as Margaret Atwood, Joan Barfoot, Ann-Marie MacDonald, Yann Martel, Anne Michaels, and Timothy Findley, who have been celebrated internationally for their award-winning work. But readers are also guaranteed to discover unfamiliar books—fully 19 percent of the entries are first novels—and new Canadian voices. Readers aware of the strength of Canadian mainstream fiction may not know that Canadian writers have also excelled at popular genre fiction. They will be pleasantly surprised by the range of authors included in the genre fiction chapter, such as Julie Czerneda, Charles de Lint, Nalo Hopkinson, William Gibson, and Guy Gavriel Kay in the science fiction/fantasy category or Gail Bowen, Howard Engel, Lyn Hamilton, Kathy Reichs, Peter Robinson, and Medora Sale in mystery.

Whatever your reading interests, you will find that this book gives you a valuable tool to unlock the storehouse of Canadian fiction.

Catherine Sheldrick Ross

Faculty of Information and Media Studies
The University of Western Ontario

Acknowledgments

A project such as this can only become a reality if one has the support of many. I could never have given this work the attention required if my family had not taken on responsibility for all things domestic; you ensured that life went on while I sat at the computer and I thank you. I must also acknowledge the support and input I received from a number of my colleagues: Maureen Plomske, Mary Monteith, Natalie Gibbons, and Julie Najjar, the final work is all the better thanks to your thoughtful and insightful comments. And to Maureen: Thank you, the collaboration has been great, your diligence and organization kept us on track.

SS

I always read authors' acknowledgements with great interest, to see who helped, and how they helped. Now that I have shared in the writing of a book, I understand only too well just how important are those being acknowledged. For my own part, I could not have done this work without the generous gifts of time, practical help, and solid, unstinting encouragement from my three children, Beth, Kate, and Geoff. There have been several occasions when deadline pressures loomed and they jumped in to help, putting in many hours editing or inputting, or simply feeding me and making sure that life outside my study could go on. I truly could not have done this book without their help. Other family and friends cheerfully helped with various aspects of the project, especially my brother Greg O'Neill, my sister Mary Anne O'Neill and her husband Roger Ancel, and my grand-niece Rosie McCarthy. Chanda Gilpin gave me Excel-ent help, and the moral support I received from her and from my other library friends, my neighbourhood friends, my choir friends, and my extended family gave me much-needed encouragement. Thank you one and all! And finally, my heartfelt thanks to Sharron for inviting me along on this marvellous journey! And to the Lubuto Library Project I will be happy to donate any royalties I recieve from this book.

MO

Together we gratefully acknowledge the contribution and support provided by Nancy Pearl, who allowed us to include here a number of annotations from *Now Read This* and *Now Read This II*. Nancy, your work set a standard we hope we have continued. We both wish to thank also the various librarians, editors, authors, and award-granting agencies that answered our myriad questions related to their areas of expertise, but especially the Writers Guild of Alberta and Heritage Toronto for the extra kilometres they went to ensure that we had not only winners but also the nominees for all their awards.

And finally, of course we both want to express our great appreciation to Barbara Ittner and Diana Tixier Herald for getting this publication off the ground, through the process, and into print.

Introduction

A Profile of Canadian Fiction Writers and Readers

Interest in Canadian fiction, both in Canada and beyond, has never been higher, and as the recognition of Canadian authors has grown, so too has their readership. Canadian authors and their books are now read and enjoyed worldwide; for example, Margaret Atwood's *Alias Grace* is available in twenty-two countries worldwide;, Anne Michaels's *Fugitive Pieces* is available in more than thirty countries; the rights for *Deafening* by Frances Itani have been bought by twelve different publishers in countries ranging from Japan, to France, Holland, Germany, and beyond; and Yann Martel's *Life of Pi* and Ann-Marie MacDonald's *Fall on Your Knees* each sold more than one million copies worldwide. Statistics Canada, Canada's central statistical agency, reports that the sales of all trade books published in Canada in the last reporting period (2000–2001) was valued at $154.8 million.

The international acclaim of such authors as Margaret Atwood, Alice Munro, Mavis Gallant, and the late Mordecai Richler, Robertson Davies, and Carol Shields has grown so that their work is acknowledged as some of the best among that of the literary elite. In the last decade or so, a number of Canadian authors have garnered international recognition through the winning of the world's most prestigious literary prizes. In 1992, Michael Ondaatje was the first Canadian to win the Booker Prize, for *The English Patient,* followed by Margaret Atwood in 2000 for *The Blind Assassin* and Yann Martel in 2002 for *Life of Pi.* The 2001 International IMPAC Dublin Literary Award for the Novel was presented to Alistair MacLeod for *No Great Mischief.* Carol Shields's *The Stone Diaries* was awarded the 1995 Pulitzer Prize for Fiction, and in 1998 *Larry's Party* earned for her another international award, the Orange Prize for Fiction. The acknowledgement of Anne Michaels's novel *Fugitive Pieces* was a remarkable achievement: this work was awarded eleven literary prizes including the Orange Prize for Fiction, the Guardian Fiction Award, and the Giuseppe Acerbi Literary Award.

With this interest in and focus on the work of Canadian authors, the awards presented to Canadian authors in their own country have also gained global recognition. Through this recognition, the fiction of a new generation of authors including Ann-Marie MacDonald, Barbara Gowdy, Richard B. Wright, Guy Vanderhaeghe, Rohinton Mistry, and Jane Urquhart continues to gain in popularity, and the books of these authors are being widely collected and read beyond Canadian borders. (Oprah Winfrey selected novels by both Mac-Donald and Mistry for her popular Book Club.)

Further recognition of the interest in and importance of Canadian literature was highlighted in 2004 with the publication of *The Cambridge Companion to Canadian Literature,* edited by Eva-Marie Kröller. This work contains a number of essays focusing on the social, political, and economic developments that have affected literary events in this country, in chapters on fiction, drama, Aboriginal writing, francophone writing, writing by women, and urban writing. The work is particularly useful in providing an overview of the development and history of the body of literature that represents Canada.

The strength of Canadian literature can also be seen in the work of emerging authors such as Timothy Taylor (*Stanley Park*), Andrew Pyper (*Lost Girls* and *The Trade Mission*), and Mary Lawson, whose first novel, *Crow Lake*, was selected for the *Today's* Book Club. In a time when the publishing industry has experienced significant upheavals, Canadian writers are being widely read.

As a bilingual country, Canada has many authors who publish in both official languages. French-Canadian authors such as Gabrielle Roy, Marie-Claire Blais, Michel Tremblay, and Anne Hébert have also earned international acclaim; those who have translated their work into English have been recognized in their own right, most notably Sheila Fischman, who has won three Governor General's Literary Awards for Translation, including one for Michel Tremblay's *Bambi and Me*. As the number of translations in the mainstream grows, so too does the readership.

Beyond the recognition garnered by awards, Canadian writers also receive active support from their Canadian readers. The Canadian reading public demonstrates a commitment to the literary work its best writers produce, and they eagerly await new fiction from both the well known and the lesser known. Across the country, more than a dozen well-attended literary festivals celebrate the work of both international and Canadian authors. To name a few:

> Eden Mills Writers' Festival (http://www.edenmillswritersfestival.ca)
>
> The Harbourfront Reading Series and International Festival of Authors (http://www. readings.org)
>
> Ottawa International Writers Festival (http://www.writersfest.com)
>
> Thin Air—Winnipeg International Writers Festival (http://www. winnipegwords.com/index.html)
>
> Vancouver International Writers & Readers Festival (http://www.writersfest.bc.ca/)
>
> WordFest: Banff-Calgary International Writers Festival (http://www.wordfest.com)

While Canadians enjoy "home-grown" literature, they avidly read the work of authors from around the world, with particular emphasis on titles from the United States and Great Britain. It must be noted that mass-market publishing is limited in Canada, with most genre titles being released in a trade-paperback format; most mass-market titles come in as the bestseller releases from the United States. Notable exceptions to this are the works of Joy Fielding (*Whispers and Lies* and others) and Charlotte Vale Allen (*Sudden Moves* and others), whose books are published in hardcover and mass-market paperback in both Canada and the United States. The other exception is the Canadian publisher Harlequin, a leading global publisher of women's fiction, selling 144 million books in 2003 in the mass-market format (http://www.eharlequin.com).

In 2002, the Association of Canadian Studies commissioned a survey on the reading habits of Canadians. The survey reported that 84 percent of Canadians indicated that they read at least one book a month, and 46 percent reported reading six or more per month. This survey illustrates that reading is a viable activity within the Canadian culture.

In recent years, Canadian literature has immensely diversified. As Canada's changing demographics have begun to reflect a more urban reality, authors who set their stories within the context of an urban environment have emerged. For the most part, these young edgy authors, such as Russell Smith (*Muriella Pent* and others), use their work to depict and respond to life and living in Canadian cities. Other authors use an urban setting as a venue to comment on environmental issues: in Luanne Armstrong's *The Bone House* the city of Vancouver is a ravaged landscape where people struggle to survive.

Earlier, writers such as George Bowering (*Burning Water*), Rudy Wiebe (*The Temptations of Big Bear*), and Frederick Philip Grove (*Over Prairie Trails* and *Settlers of the Marsh*) focused on themes of "creating Canada." Although the dominant setting of novelists continues to be Canada, it is not exclusively so. Confidence, curiosity, and the realities of the global village have risen, causing authors to move beyond Canada's borders and write about Canadians in the world (for example, Marnie Woodrow's *Spelling Mississippi* or Dennis Bock's *The Ash Garden*).

The increasing multicultural nature of Canadian society is reflected in the writings of notable authors who have immigrated to Canada. There are many first- and second- generation immigrants (Josef Škvorecký and three-time Governor General's Literary Award winner Michael Ondaatje), whose success has encouraged the emergence of other writers in Canada, originally from all over the world, to write about their experiences in Canada or in their own countries before arriving here. A few representative parts of the world and their authors are Italy (Nino Ricci), China (Sky Lee, Judy Fong Bates), Japan (Joy Kogawa, Hiromi Goto, and Kerri Sakamoto), Southeast Asia (Rohinton Mistry, Shyam Selvadurai, and Anita Rau Badami), Kenya (M.G. Vassanji), and the Caribbean (Rabindranath Maharaj, Austin Clarke, Dany Laferrière and André Alexis). Their work is recognized as international literature in setting and topic as well as in prize-winning, and Canada is proud to call them Canadian. For an amplification of this topic, you may want to consult Marta Dvorak's article in *The Cambridge Companion to Canadian Literature* (2004, 173–175).

Canadian writers are spread across the country. While we have many from the cities—Toronto, Vancouver, or Montreal—so too do we have stories from Vancouver Island by Jack Hodgins and Gail Anderson-Dargatz; from the Prairies by Sandra Birdsell and Greg Hollingshead; from small-town Ontario by Matt Cohen and Timothy Findley; from Quebec by Roch Carrier, Jacques Poulin, and Yves Beauchemin; from Atlantic Canada by David Adams Richards, David Helwig, and Sheldon Currie; and from Newfoundland by Michael Crummey and Donna Morrissey. And this is just a sampling. The stories of Aboriginal writers, such as Eden Robinson (Haisla), Jeannette C. Armstrong (Okanagan), and Thomas King (Cherokee), and of Métis writers such as Lee Maracle and Beatrice Culleton Mosionier are also part of the Canadian milieu, and they continue to gain in readership.

Themes of and Influences on Canadian Fiction

The history of Canada has been and continues to be the basis of much of Canadian fiction, chronicling national, regional, and local events, characters, and periods. Historical fiction frequently combines a number of elements—history, biography, and story—in presenting the tale. Prominent Canadians figure large in historical fiction, in works by such writers as Rudy Wiebe (Louis Riel), Richard Rohmer (Sir John A. Macdonald), and John Wilson (Sir John Franklin). There is also interaction between fictional characters and historical figures, as in Timothy Findley's *Famous Last Words* (Wallis Simpson) or Katherine Govier's *Creation* (John James Audubon).

The vast distances of the country have created a solid tradition of regional fiction that can be traced from the East in L. M. Montgomery's *Anne of Green Gables* to Hugh MacLennan's Quebec in *The Watch That Ends the Night*, to Hugh Garner's *Ontario in Cabbagetown,* to the Prairie world in Sinclair Ross's *As for Me and My House* and Ethel Wilson's British Columbia novel, *Swamp Angel*. However, the common thread in all of these works tends to be our shared values, which include tolerance and understanding. This rich tradition continues today as it informs the writing of such authors as Kevin Major, Bernice Morgan and Joan Clark, David Homel and David Macfarlane, Sharon Butala, Robert Kroetsch, and Anne Cameron.

In attempting to identify what is unique within the Canadian literary scene, one should look at the proliferation and stature of Canadian women writers and the fact that they share equal space with men. This has long been the case and was demonstrated most clearly in 2001 when *Quill & Quire* ("Canada's Magazine of Book News and Reviews") compiled a list of "Who's taught, who's not" (Smith 2001, 17). Of the twenty top Canadian authors taught by university English departments across the country, the list was evenly divided between women and men, with Margaret Atwood being the highest, followed by Michael Ondaatje.

As previously noted, Canada is very much a multicultural nation, and the voices of those who have come from somewhere else and now call Canada home have been blended into the literary landscape. Statistics indicate that the greatest percentage of immigrants have settled into Canada's urban areas, and their writers tell of the urban immigrant experience: Michael Ondaatje set his novels in Toronto, and H. Nigel Thomas sets his *Behind the Face of Winter* in Montreal. Yet the immigrants' stories are not exclusively urban: in *Midnight at the Dragon Café* by Judy Fong Bates, a young Chinese girl tells the story of her family and their Chinese restaurant in a small town in Ontario.

Conflict and tension have been created in novels through setting, not only urban versus rural, but also man versus nature. The work of Margaret Laurence (*The Stone Angel* and others) depicts life in small-town Manitoba, and as the stories unfold, the reader comes to see this place as having as much race and class conflict as any novel set in the Southern United States. The most obvious conflict of man versus nature is of course the struggle to survive the elements. Early frontier life and the challenge to survive were chronicled in *Roughing It in the Bush, or Life in Canada* by Susanna Moodie (1852); this struggle is also evident in Merilyn Simonds's contemporary story *The Holding* (2004). The reader can feel Joey Smallwood's pain as he endures the harshness of winter in Newfoundland in Wayne Johnston's *The Colony of Unrequited Dreams* or suffer from the drought of the Prairies as conveyed in Elizabeth Hay's *A Student of Weather*.

Canadian literature also reveals the Canadian sense of humour, and while from first impressions one might conclude that much of the fiction published has a sombre tone (e.g., David Adams Richards's Miramichi trilogy), Canadian authors often blend humour and satire to discuss difficult subjects. For example, Miriam Toews lightens her chronicling of the lives of two single mothers on welfare in *Summer of My Amazing Luck,* with touches of humour that still communicate the challenges these women face. This approach is not without precedent. Canadian authors in the past frequently used humour and satire, from the very early *Sunshine Sketches of a Little Town* by Stephen Leacock, to the black humour of Douglas Coupland (*All Families Are Psychotic*), to the satire of Mordecai Richler's *Barney's Version* or Will Ferguson's *Generica*, to the sentimental humour of Stuart McLean's Vinyl Cafe stories and Bill Richardson's Bachelor Brothers' Bed and Breakfast stories. Regardless of the form the humour takes, it is most often set out as a way to say, "don't take things too seriously and remember to laugh."

Coming-of-age stories are not unique to Canadian fiction, but they do have a strong representation in the Canadian literary output, peopled by the quintessential Canadian hero: a quiet, unassuming, everyday person. Charles Taylor, in *Six Journeys: A Canadian Pattern* (1977, 1–2), remarked, "More than most peoples, Canadians are prejudiced in favour of the ordinary. . . . It might almost be said that something in us hates a hero." Linda Little's Jackson Bigney (*Strong Hollow*) struggles to overcome life's challenges, doing the best he can with what he has. It is within the context of these individual struggles that the author introduces issues and ideas of social importance such as child abuse, the environment, physical and mental disabilities, AIDS, gender identity, and Native rights, and in doing so creates tension and heightens awareness. In Tomson Highway's *Kiss of the Fur Queen*, the author combines two difficult issues in telling the story of two Cree brothers who struggle to overcome the impact of relocation to a residential home and the abuse suffered there.

The number of emerging voices and the breadth of Canadian genre fiction writing also continue to expand. Already, each of the main genres has its "superstars." Romance novelists Mary Balogh and Jo Beverley consistently delight readers with their wonderfully romantic stories that—of course!—feature that all-important happily-ever-after. For years now, Robert J. Sawyer and Charles de Lint have garnered awards both in Canada and beyond for their work in science fiction and fantasy. Many consider Nalo Hopkinson to be a voice to watch, and fantasy writer Guy Gavriel Kay so successfully blends the genres of fantasy and historical fiction that readers from both genres eagerly await his next book.

The mystery genre has a long-standing tradition of story in Canada, beginning in the late nineteenth century with Grant Allan's *An African Millionaire*, growing in the 1970s with works by Hugh Garner and Sara Woods, and flourishing in the present with such internationally recognized authors as Peter Robinson and the late L. R. Wright. Within the genre, women authors are strongly represented by writers such as Suzanne North, Medora Sale, Gail Bowen, Sparkle Hayter, Nora Kelly, Rosemary Aubert, Michelle Spring, and Mary Jane Maffini, whose novels of detection continue to gain readership.

Ultimately, the literature, like the country, has adapted to embrace the storytelling of all those who consider themselves a part of the community. The result is that the profile of the literature has increased worldwide, so that not only are the works of established authors (Atwood and Ondaatje) being sold worldwide, but so too are first novelists such as Mary Lawson (*Crow Lake*) and John Bemrose (*The Island Walkers*), with rights being sold in the United States, the United Kingdom, Australia, and South Africa.

Why a Guide to Canadian Fiction?

We have already noted that Canadian literature has grown in readership and recognition both at home and beyond. In the past, other resources created to assist readers in making reading selections have included some Canadian titles. This is certainly the case in the Nancy Pearl guides, *Now Read This* and *Now Read This II*, and other guides in the Genreflecting Advisory Series. Naturally, size restrictions in those publications have limited the number of Canadian titles included, and therefore the emphasis was placed on well-known award-winning titles or, in the case of *Genreflecting: A Guide to Reading Interests in Genre Fiction* by Diana Tixier Herald, select Canadian titles were simply included along with other titles from around the world.

The proximity of Canada to the United States and the shared language of English have increased the North American readership of Canadian literature beyond just the well known. Indeed, today readers around the world can enjoy a wealth of Canadian literature. Canadian literature offers readers a culturally distinctive experience, as we have described, but as of this date no other readers' advisory guide to Canadian literature that spans the breadth and depth of the literature has been published. This guide seeks to help readers and those who work with readers in finding Canadian authors and titles, both well known and obscure, that they will enjoy. It is meant to give readers a sense of the qualities of Canadian literature, as well as an understanding of the sometimes subtle differences between the literature of Canada and other countries. It is also intended to define the nuances found within Canada's own writings. Our hope is that this guide will also promote the identity of Canadian literature and cultivate its readership.

Process and Scope of This Guide

In looking to define the scope of what is Canadian literature and therefore which authors and titles to include in this volume, we decided to be as broad as possible in definition. The announcement of the shortlist for the 2002 Man Booker Prize sparked discussion in literary circles regarding the "nationality" of three names on the list (Yann Martel, Carol Shields, and Rohinton Mistry), as none of them was born in Canada. Charles Foran, in an article in *The Globe and Mail* (2002), responded to the controversy by noting that in the case of Martel, although he was born in Spain, his parents were Canadian diplomats on posting at the time, and Shields did and Mistry does call Canada home, and so they are considered part of the literary community. Therefore, if an author's work were eligible for consideration for a Canadian literary award (Governor General's Literary Award, Giller Prize, Arthur Ellis Mystery Award, etc.) that author was considered for inclusion. Thus our list includes authors such as Nancy Huston (*The Mark of the Angel* and others) and Charlotte Vale Allen (*Fresh Air, Sudden Moves,* and others), both of whom divide their time between Canada and elsewhere. Our list also includes those who, from time to time, have called Canada home, writers such as Brian Moore (*The Magician's Wife* and others) and Paulette Jiles (*Enemy Women*), who holds dual U.S. and Canadian citizenship. As we began the selection of titles for this volume, we knew we wanted to include books that had some level of familiarity to a broad base of librarians and readers. That seemed to indicate the inclusion of the major award winners; therefore we looked at and considered the following arenas: international (Man Booker Prize, Pulitzer, etc), national (Governor General's Literary Awards and Giller

Prize), provincial (Trillium, Saskatchewan Book Awards, and Atlantic Writing Awards, etc.), and municipal (Toronto Book Awards, Regina Book Award, Vancouver Book Award, and others). We have included winning and shortlisted titles, believing these were books readers might have read and could thus lead to other titles. We also looked at reviewing sources such as *Quill & Quire* and *Books in Canada;* National Writers' associations; genre associations (The Crime Writers of Canada and Canadian Romance Authors Network); and the holdings of both public and academic libraries, most notably the University of Toronto Library and the Vancouver Public Library. In addition, we surveyed the collections of four U.S. libraries (New York Public Library, Hennepin County Library, San Antonio Public Library, and Los Angeles Public Library), to ensure that a broad representation of the titles included in the volume was available in the United States. Titles not found in these libraries were checked in *Global Books in Print* to verify their availability to the U.S. market. With few exceptions, they are available, and librarians interested in developing the Canadian content of their collections should be able to do so.

Although Canada's national newspapers, *The Globe and Mail* and *The National Post*, both have book review columns, we chose to rely on the reviewing journals noted above. We should also mention that we did not rely on bestseller lists, as we felt that any title that achieved that status would have already appeared in the reviewing sources.

To keep the present volume at a manageable size and lend a focus to the work, we have limited its coverage to novels published between 1990 and 2004. We chose this period partly because it is during these years that Canadian fiction truly came into its own. This is clearly demonstrated by the significant number of first novels published during this period. Of the list we initially gathered, first novels accounted for 19 percent of the total. These newer releases are also more likely to be in library collections, and if not, are usually still in print so that they can be added to collections.

Even within these parameters, we quickly realized that it would be impossible to be all-inclusive; hence the idea that this is simply a "guide" to some of the best or most popular work that has been produced within the time period. This realization forced us to make an arbitrary wholesale exclusion. While recognizing that some of the best fiction produced in Canada has been in the form of short stories (most notably but not exclusively by Mavis Gallant and Alice Munro)—indeed the short story collections made up 13 percent of the entire original list—we made the decision to exclude these collections in this guide except as possible read-alikes.

Inclusion is not based on literary credentials or on the intrinsic value of the work. Instead, we have tried to offer a broad sampling that represents the wide spectrum of reading possibilities and enjoyment in Canadian literature. We have included both mainstream and genre fiction, and, of course, ensured our personal favourites were there as well, stories that appeal to us on a number of levels: the humour of Joan Barfoot in *Getting Over Edgar*, the intriguing story of an astrologer and amateur sleuth in Ottawa (Karen Irving), the spirit of an elderly woman in Dorothy Speak's *The Wife Tree,* or the beauty of the language of Elizabeth Hay's *A Student of Weather*. With few exceptions, we have either read or dipped into most titles listed here, and in the case of titles not read, we have solicited the input of a group of selected colleagues.

Because ours is a bilingual country, with a rich tradition of French-Canadian literature, we have included some novels in translation as well, primarily based on the stories they tell, unique, interesting, and with broad-based appeal.

The bibliographic information noted is based on the Canadian edition of the work. Whenever possible, we took the information from the actual work itself; in those instances where that was not possible, we used the bibliographic data primarily from the University of Toronto Library catalogue and the Vancouver Public Library catalogue. In cases where a title was released in the United States with a variant title, we have noted that title, when known.

How to Use This Book

The guides in the <u>Genreflecting Advisory Series</u> are written to assist those who help readers navigate what can be perceived as dangerous waters. In "Reinventing Readers' Advisory" in *The Readers' Advisor's Companion* (2001), Duncan Smith notes that an understanding of readers is necessary in order to meet the needs of readers. Therefore, considering why a person reads, thinking about the motivation that brings a reader to look for a book to read for pleasure, and what that reader hopes to gain from the experience can make the task less daunting and the outcome more successful. Also worth considering is the work of Dr. Catherine Sheldrick Ross, the dean of the faculty of information and media studies at The University of Western Ontario. Ross has conducted research into the role mood plays in the selection of a reading choice, and her model for the process of choosing a book for pleasure should be considered by those engaged in readers' advisory work. Ross presented her work in an issue of *Library Journal* in 2001 (Ross and Chelton 2001, 52–55). Librarians are equipped to handle even the most esoteric request for information, but when faced with a request for a "good book," the first response is often a sense of dread. For anyone who works with readers, whether librarian or bookseller, connecting readers to books they will enjoy is the most satisfying and rewarding part of what we do. The idea that reading suggestions can flow from a book the reader has enjoyed in the past has been clearly articulated by Joyce Saricks and Nancy Brown in *Readers' Advisory Service in the Public Library* (1997). Saricks and Brown suggest that by encouraging readers to describe books they have read and enjoyed, the "appeal characteristics" will be revealed. Nancy Pearl took the theory of appeal characteristics further and applied it to mainstream fiction in her guides *Now Read This* and *Now Read This II*. When talking about books, readers will often mention four primary or dominant appeal elements: setting, story, character, and language. Once the advisor understands the most important appeal for readers, the process of suggesting other books with similar characteristics can begin.

While these four appeal characteristics are the dominant traits that draw a reader to a work, rarely do they stand alone. Often, during what has been called the readers advisory conversation, a reader will articulate a number of elements that should be present in the ideal read. Understanding this, and realizing that most of the titles to be included in this volume fall into the category of mainstream fiction, we decided to organize the chapters following the pattern set out in Nancy Pearl's *Now Read This* and *Now Read This II*. You will find, therefore, that the titles included in this volume are organized into chapters according to those same appeal characteristics, indicating secondary appeals if appropriate. Some entries do not indicate secondary appeals. In assessing our choices of primary appeal, it must be remembered that in the words of Edmund Wilson in 1971, "No two persons read the same book" (2005). There may be cases of disagreement with our categorizations; we believe that this questioning is a positive thing and that it will only increase the dialogue about the books found here and the read-alikes, a conversation we encourage. Finally, we have also gone beyond the scope of mainstream literary fiction and added a fifth chapter, to include examples of genre titles from Canadian authors.

The Main Entry

We briefly annotated each entry in the appeal chapters to describe the work itself and to articulate its theme. We then assigned subject headings to each title, taking them from a variety of sources, so that through the subject index a number of works could be grouped together, providing the reader with the widest possible access to books on that topic. We have used the subject indexes from both of Nancy Pearl's volumes as our guide in creating the subject terms here.

The following icons appear on some of the entries:

 award

Book Groups 📖 Book Groups

The final major portion of the individual entry is the signpost for further reading, to intrigue a new reader, or to lead a familiar reader from a favourite author/title to the possible discovery of a new author/title. To provide a wider basis for appeal and to make connections for librarians and readers across both Canada and the United States, we have not limited read-alikes to solely Canadian authors and titles, but have included a combination of authors from Canada, the United States, and beyond. In addition, we have made connections (where appropriate) to collections of short stories; in this way an author such as Alice Munro, Canada's premier short story writer, can be included in this guide, despite not meeting the selection criterion for a main entry. At times, we have noted non-fiction titles if we felt readers might be interested in enhancing their reading experience by learning more about a particular topic.

The genre fiction chapter is organized by genre: mystery, science fiction, fantasy, romance, thriller, and horror. The entries include author, title, and imprint information, and, understanding the desire of readers to enjoy a series in its entirety, the entry includes, where appropriate, the entire series regardless of publication date. Series main entries by the same author are listed in chronological order. The books within a series have been listed in series order, regardless of the dates of publication of re-issues or translations. In some cases this may appear confusing, but keep in mind that the order in which you see the titles listed is the order in which the action takes place, so that if a prequel was written after several volumes were already published, it is listed first. In addition, some series titles and all stand-alone titles have been annotated, following the same format as in the appeal chapters.

Conclusion

The history of Canadian fiction, like the history of the country, is in fact a short one, and the identity of both country and literature is still developing. To explain how Canadian literature differs from "English literature" or "American literature," Dr. Glen Lowry of Coquitlam College has said, ""Perhaps the one most salient trait of study of Canadian Literature is that, from the outset, it has focused primarily on living writers and their significance to the development of Canadian culture in the present. Throughout the short history of Canadian literature [sic], readers have looked for ways of imagining ourselves in relation to the cultures around us" (Lowry 2005). And so while surely unique, both Canadian fiction and its readers are still part of the wider North American experience.

Perhaps the most exciting thing about Canadian fiction is the strength of its future, as seen in the voices of such authors as Eden Robinson, Miriam Toews, Colin McAdam, Russell Smith, Edeet Ravel, David Macfarlane, and others, who continue to garner interest at home and beyond, ensuring the development of the Canadian literary scene. Add to this the fact that Canada's genre writers (Robert J. Sawyer, Guy Gavriel Kay, Peter Robinson, Lyn Hamilton, Medora Sale, Claire Delacroix, and others) are constantly extending their reach with their wonderful storytelling. The literary awards that now exist are not only an indicator of a strong future for Canada's literature but are also a demonstration of the intense feeling Canadians have for the work created by their authors.

The number of prizes for writing in Canada has grown steadily, including significant prizes for poetry and non-fiction—prizes such as the Charles Taylor Prize for Literary Non-fiction. Although the Governor General's Literary Award and the Giller Prize are considered by many to be Canada's most prestigious awards, most provinces, regions, and even cities have their own awards. These awards (as well as other prizes for which Canadian authors have been the winners) are listed in Appendix 2. The winners and nominees of these awards would be solid additions to any library collection.

For libraries interested in establishing a collection or further developing their Canadian fiction collections, a number of resources are listed in Appendix 1, along with a selected number of Web sites. In addition to the texts listed in the Appendix, two primary reviewing journals are essential selection tools. *Quill & Quire* is a monthly periodical featuring articles, interviews, industry news, and reviews of fiction, non-fiction, and children's materials (http://www.quillandquire.com); and *Books in Canada* (http://www.booksincanada. com), in nine issues/year, publishes over 400 reviews, essays, and author interviews. We have taken a very brief look at Canadian publishing through an annotated list of Canadian publishers in Appendix 3.

Chapter 1

Setting

For the reader who longs for the experience of being transported to another place or time, the primary reading appeal is setting. When place or time is well crafted the reading experience is a profoundly satisfying one. Settings range from large urban centres such as Vancouver, Toronto, and Montreal to small towns across a vast, diverse country from the West Coast to the Prairies to Southern Ontario, Quebec, and the Atlantic Provinces. This chapter is divided into two sections: setting as a place, and setting as a time period.

When an author succeeds in rendering the power of a landscape, that setting plays a significant role in the story. Wayne Johnston's *The Colony of Unrequited Dreams*, for example, fully realizes the power of Newfoundland and the landscape becomes a major force, almost a character in the story. Nino Ricci's *Lives of the Saints* paints a realistic picture of a small Italian village in the 1960s, and in this case, setting means both where and when. Setting can also be the mood or ambience an author creates; in Aritha van Herk's *Restlessness*, the reader is drawn right into the room with a woman and the assassin she has hired to end her life.

These place-related annotations are then followed by titles in which setting becomes the historical time period of the story. In selecting titles for this section, we followed the definition used in Diana Tixier Herald's *Genreflecting: A Guide to Reading Interests in Genre Fiction*, "historical fiction is considered [to be] stories that begin prior to the middle of the twentieth century" (2000, 1). These stories take the reader back in time to visit and experience both the exotic and the familiar: travelling to thirteenth-century Venice with Mark Frutkin in *The Lion of Venice,* or walking the streets of a small Manitoba town in *The Red-headed Woman with the Black Black Heart* by Birk Sproxton. Canadian authors, like others the world over, also chronicle the events that have shaped the history of their country. Events found here include the 1759 Siege of Quebec (Daniel Poliquin's *The Straw Man*), the 1837 Mackenzie Rebellion (Sidney Allinson's *Jeremy Kane)*, and the 1917 Halifax Explosion (Robert MacNeil's *Burden of Desire*). Historical novels are not just about events but are also about the people, famous and infamous, whose lives had an impact on shaping the country that is Canada today. The reader can meet Canada's first prime minister, Sir

John A. Macdonald, and Louis Riel, or be invited to share the innermost thoughts of explorer Marco Polo, or Josephine Bonaparte, the woman who became the wife of one of Europe's most famous rulers.

The advisor working with the reader seeking books whose primary appeal is setting will want to consider that for some readers this type of novel allows them to see themselves in the stories and experience along with the characters the events of the time, perhaps participating as the protagonist works through his or her own destiny. Setting-based fiction takes the reader to other times, places, and experiences, all from the comfort and safety of one's own reading space, making it possible to experience, for example, the horrors of wartime with none of the dangers. When introducing elements of the horrific, the advisor is reminded to refer again to the aspects of mood discussed in Ross and Chelton's article in *Library Journal* (2001, 52–55).

For anyone who reads for the setting, as well as for the reader of historical fiction, it may be possible to suggest titles in areas beyond mainstream fiction. Such a reader may be very open to reading suggestions from genre fiction, open to titles in which the author has been able to craft a truly believable world. For example, the reader may enjoy novels with an alternative view of history such as those by Dave Duncan, whose books ask the question "What if . . . " . Or the reader may want to experience (or be forewarned by) the world created in Margaret Atwood's speculative novel, *The Handmaid's Tale*, a novel in which the author presents a view of a futurist society. Perhaps the reader may want to indulge in the fantasies of Guy Gavriel Kay (*Sailing to Sarantium* and others), in which the author puts his protagonist in a historical setting of the author's own creation.

Regardless of the time or the place, the authors of the following titles will take the reader on a journey, turning their books into travel tickets to the world and beyond, allowing a reader to discover new places or times.

Ackerman, Marianne.

Jump. McArthur, 2000. 349pp. Book Groups 📖

Freelance journalist Myra Grant struggles with her ex-husband's nervous breakdown and her near-adult children's decision to live independent lives, all the while keeping a close eye on the political fervour surrounding the vote over independence for Quebec in 1995.

Subjects: Beckett, Samuel • First Novels • Montreal • Quebec • Quebec Referendum • Single Mothers • Teenagers • Theatre • Women Journalists

Read On: Ackerman is the author of numerous plays, including *L'affaire Tartuffe*, *Celeste*, and *Venus of Dublin*. Samuel Beckett's influence and writings also form part of the plot in James McManus's *Going to the Sun*. Quebec politics provides the backdrop for François Gravel's *Ostend*. Claude Fournier's *René Lévesque: Portrait of a Man Alone* tells the story of a key player in the drive for Quebec's independence.

Anderson-Dargatz, Gail.

A Recipe for Bees. Alfred A. Knopf Canada, 1998. 311pp. Book Groups 📖

Augusta Olsen looks back on a rugged and difficult life on a farm in British Columbia —a life as multifaceted as her beehives, and sometimes as sweet as the honey within them. This novel was shortlisted for the Giller Prize.

Second Appeal: Character

Subjects: Aging • Beekeeping • British Columbia • Family Relationships • Farm Life • Male–Female Relationships

Read On: Other novels about feisty Canadian women are Margaret Laurence's *The Stone Angel*, Elizabeth Hay's *A Student of Weather*, and Constance Beresford-Howe's *The Book of Eve*. For another story featuring a long-married couple, try Katherine Govier's *The Truth Teller*. Beekeeping is an added storytelling element in Sue Monk Kidd's *The Secret Life of Bees*.

Bartlett, Wayne.

Louder Than the Sea. Cormorant Books, 2001. 342pp. Book Groups 📖

As part of a government resettlement program, insecure fourteen-year-old Martin Bellam and his family are moved from their island home to mainland Newfoundland in the mid-1960s. Unable to accept this change easily, Martin and his father clash. When Martin returns to their deserted village following a disastrous seal hunt and becomes trapped there, he and his father come to realize the depth of their relationship.

Second Appeal: Language

Subjects: 1960s • Family Relationships • Fathers and Sons • First Novels • Land Settlement • Newfoundland and Labrador • Relocation • Small-town Life • Survival

Read On: Other novels with a strong sense of place that are also set in Newfoundland are Annie Proulx's *The Shipping News* and Wayne Johnston's *The Colony of Unrequited Dreams*. Kevin Major's *Gaffer: A Novel of Newfoundland* and Patrick Kavanagh's *Gaff Topsails* are novels featuring young boys in small Newfoundland villages and their coming-of-age struggles.

Basilières, Michel.

🎗 *Black Bird.* Alfred A. Knopf Canada, 2003. 311pp.

In 1970 Montreal, the divisions in an eccentric family are reflected in the current political situation of French- versus English-language speakers. It is during the October Crisis in Quebec that events spiral out of control and the family teeters on the edge of destruction. *Black Bird* won the Amazon.ca/*Books in Canada* First Novel Award, and was shortlisted for the Commonwealth Writers Prize for Best First Book in the Caribbean and Canada, and for The Stephen Leacock Memorial Medal for Humour.

Subjects: Dysfunctional Families • Family Relationships • First Novels • Humorous Fiction • Montreal • October Crisis • Quebec

Read On: The irreverent style of storytelling here is similar to the style of Christopher Moore (*Lamb: The Gospel According to Biff, Christ's Childhood Pal* and others) and Tom Robbins (*Skinny Legs and All* and others). A classic Canadian tale of the divisions between French and English speakers in Quebec is Hugh MacLennan's *Two Solitudes*. The political tension between Quebec separatists and Quebec federalists during the 1970 October Crisis is also present in Aimée Laberge's *Where the River Narrows*.

Bemrose, John.

The Island Walkers. McClelland & Stewart, 2003. 498pp. Book Groups 📖

In the mid-1960s, the acquisition of a local knitting mill in a small Ontario town by a large Quebec company is viewed through the lives of the Walker family. Each of them struggles with the tremendous changes this brings to them personally and to the community. Bemrose was longlisted for the Man Booker Prize and was also a Finalist for the Giller Prize.

Second Appeal: Character

Subjects: 1960s • Class Consciousness • Family Relationships • First Novels • Labour Unions • Ontario • Small-town Life • Textile Workers

Read On: Richard Russo's *Empire Falls* and *We Were the Mulvaneys* by Joyce Carol Oates both focus on working-class families. Life in small-town Ontario is realistically created in the work of Alice Munro (*Runaway* and others) and Bonnie Burnard (*A Good House*).

Currie, Sheldon.

The Glace Bay Miners' Museum. Breton Books, 1995. 130pp.

Margaret McNeil, a coal miner's daughter, falls in love with a wandering musician, but even their passion cannot keep them from the tragedies of the coal mines.

Second Appeal: Character

Subjects: Cape Breton Island • Death of a Spouse • Labour Unions • Mental Illness • Mining • Nova Scotia

Read On: Currie is also the author of *The Company Store*, another tale about the hard life of labourers. His short-story collection, *The Story So Far*, includes many of the themes of both of these novels. For other stories set in Cape Breton, try Ann-Marie MacDonald's *Fall on Your Knees,* D. R. MacDonald's *Cape Breton Road,* and Alistair MacLeod's *Island: The Collected Short Stories of Alistair MacLeod.* Other novels about labour unrest in North American mining towns include Denise Giardina's *Storming Heaven*, Robert Houston's *Bisbee '17*, Donald McCaig's *The Butte Polka,* and Mary Lee Settle's *The Scapegoat.*

Foran, Charles.

🎗 *Butterfly Lovers*. HarperCollins, 1996. 308pp. Book Groups 📖

David, a divorced man coming to terms with his epilepsy, his uncaring mother, and the deterioration of his AIDS-stricken best friend, abandons his unfulfilling life in Montreal to teach English in post-Tiananmen Square Beijing. Foran received the Alcuin Society Design Award for Excellence in Canadian Book Design and the Hugh MacLennan Prize for Fiction for this work.

Subjects: AIDS • China • Communism • Epilepsy • Identity • Men's Friendships • Men's Lives • Middle-aged Men • Mothers and Sons • Teachers

Read On: Foran's first novel is *Kitchen Music*; he also wrote *Sketches in Winter*, a non-fiction account of the Tiananmen Square massacre, as well as a literary thriller, *House on Fire. Butterfly Lovers* appears to be highly autobiographical, not unlike

Martha McPhee's *Bright Angel Time* and Reeve Lindbergh's *The Names of the Mountains*. Peter Hessler's *River Town: Two Years on the Yangtze* is a non-fiction account of the author's experiences teaching in a small town in China.

Helm, Michael.

The Projectionist. Douglas & McIntyre, 1997. 299pp. Book Groups 📖

The decline of teacher Toss Raymond's drought-ravaged small Saskatchewan town reflects the disintegration of his life. In his attempts to cope with his wife's departure and the potential loss of job, lover, and reputation, he emerges as a man in search of belonging. *The Projectionist* was shortlisted for the Giller Prize.

Second Appeal: Character

Subjects: 1980s • First Novels • High School Teachers • Saskatchewan • Small-town Life

Read On: The prairie landscape is clearly evoked in Elizabeth Hay's *A Student of Weather*, Alissa York's *Mercy,* and W. O. Mitchell's *Who Has Seen the Wind*. Small towns in decline are found in Larry McMurtry's *Texasville* and Sharon Butala's *The Fourth Archangel*. Men attempting to come to terms with their lives are found in André Alexis's *Childhood* and Charles Foran's *Butterfly Lovers*. In his subsequent novel, *In the Place of Last Things*, Helm's protagonist is again in turmoil, this time following the death of his father.

Hunter, Aislinn.

Stay. Raincoast Books, 2002. 269pp. Book Groups 📖

Abbey, a young Canadian woman, has come to a village in Ireland near Galway, hoping to move beyond feelings of grief over her father's recent death and her mother's abandonment years earlier. While there she becomes involved with Dermot, an older man, as the village copes with secrets from the past. This novel was shortlisted for the Amazon.ca/*Books in Canada* First Novel Award, as well as the ReLit Award.

Second Appeal: Character

Subjects: Abandoned Children • Canadians in Ireland • Death of a Parent • Dublin • Fathers and Daughters • First Novels • Galway • Ireland • Love Stories • Older Men–Younger Women • Rural Life

Read On: Hunter won the Gerald Lampert Award in 2002 for her poetry collection, *Into the Early Hours*. Niall Williams's *Four Letters of Love* also chronicles the intertwining of relationships in an Irish town. Another young Canadian woman travels to a small Irish village in Dana Bath's *Plenty of Harm in God*. In the novels by Maeve Binchy (*Scarlet Feather* and others), the residents of Irish towns are vividly drawn, as are the connections among the characters. Michael Redhill's *Martin Sloane* offers a Dublin setting for a relationship between an older man and a younger woman.

Huston, Nancy.

🎗 *The Mark of the Angel.* **Steerforth Press, 1999. 222pp. Book Groups** 📖

A young German woman who lost her innocence in World War II goes to Paris in 1957, where she marries an aristocratic musician. It is only her relationship with a Hungarian Jewish refugee, however, that enables her to regain her soul. The French version of this novel won the Prix des Lectrices d'ELLE (France) and the Prix des Librairies (Canada) and was nominated for the Prix Goncourt in France. The English version received a Torgi award and was nominated for the Giller Literary Prize. Written originally in French [*L'empreinte de l'ange*] by Nancy Huston.

Second Appeal: Character

Subjects: 1950s • Adultery • Algeria • Colonialism • France • Love Stories • Musicians • Paris • Translations • World War II

Read On: Born in Canada, but living and writing in France for the last twenty-five years, Huston has won various literary awards in both countries. Her other novels available in English include *Prodigy*, *Dolce Agonia*, *An Adoration*, *The Goldberg Variations*, *Instruments of Darkness*, and *Plainsong*. Paris in the dozen or so years after the end of World War II provides the setting for Arthur Koestler's *The Age of Longing*, Piers Paul Read's *Polonaise*, and Boris Vian's *Mood Indigo*. Other novels dealing with the effects of French colonialism in Algeria are Albert Camus's *The First Man*, Robert Irwin's *Mysteries of Algiers*, Djanet Lachmet's *Lallia*, Claire Messud's *The Last Life*, and Brian Moore's *The Magician's Wife*.

Kidd, Monica.

Beatrice. **Turnstone Press, 2001. 210pp**

The local grain elevator in Beatrice, Alberta, becomes a symbol for the residents of the small town when corporate farm management decides to take it down.

Second Appeal: Character

Subjects: Alberta • Farm Life • First Novels • Grain Elevators • Prairies

Read On: Richard Russo's *Empire Falls* explores the realities of life in a small town when industry fails, as does John Bemrose's *The Island Walkers*. The connections among the struggling residents of a small town are also forged in Bonnie Burnard's *A Good House*, David Bergen's *A Year of Lesser*, and Sandra Birdsell's *The Chrome Suite*. An entire town vanishes following the government resettlement of the residents in Wayne Bartlett's *Louder Than the Sea*.

King, Thomas.

Green Grass, Running Water. **HarperCollins, 1993. 360pp. Book Groups** 📖

Nothing in Blossom, Alberta, will ever be the same after Trickster Coyote decides to assist a motley group of Blackfoot men and women who are searching for the middle ground between their traditions and the modern world. King's novel was shortlisted for the Governor General's Literary Award for Fiction.

Second Appeal: Character

Subjects: Aboriginal Peoples • Alberta • Blackfoot Nation • Coyote (Legendary Character) • Culture Clash • Humorous Fiction • Magic Realism

Read On: King's other books include *Medicine River, Truth & Bright Water,* and a short-story collection, *One Good Story That One.* He also edited *All My Relations: An Anthology of Contemporary Native Fiction.* Sherman Alexie's fiction and poetry (*Indian Killer* and *The Summer of Black Widows*) also combine humour and sadness as the characters try to understand their lives both on and off the reservation. Another novel in which Trickster Coyote plays a part is Melinda Worth Popham's *Skywater.* E. Donald Two-Rivers's collection of stories, *Survivor's Medicine*, is also about contemporary Native life.

Lynch, Gerald.

Troutstream. **Random House of Canada, 1995. 243pp.**

The residents of an Ottawa suburb offer a glimpse of life in their community until their real stories, which include adultery, racism, abuse, and murder, are revealed.

Second Appeal: Character

Subjects: First Novels • Ontario • Ottawa • Satire • Serial Murders • Suburbia • Troutstream (Imaginary Place)

Read On: Lynch returns to the suburb of Troutstream in *Exotic Dancers.* Rick Moody's *The Ice Storm* and Ann Beattie's *Falling in Place* feature suburban lives dotted with tragic moments. Like Mordecai Richler (*Solomon Gursky Was Here*) or the more contemporary Russell Smith (*How Insensitive*), Lynch portrays this community in a satirical way.

Macfarlane, David.

🎗 *Summer Gone.* **Alfred A. Knopf Canada, 1999. 266pp. Book Groups** 📖

Bay Newling, divorced and estranged from his son, tries to understand the losses in his life through his memories of summers past. Macfarlane received the Chapters/*Books in Canada* First Novel Award for this work, which was also shortlisted for the Giller Prize.

Second Appeal: Language

Subjects: Canoeing • Cottages • Divorce • Fathers and Sons • First Novels • Ontario • Summer • Wilderness

Read On: Macfarlane is also the author of a memoir, originally entitled *The Danger Tree; Memory, War and the Search for a Family's Past.* It was republished with a new title, *Come from Away.* A collection of stories by Andrew Sean Greer, *How It Was for Me*, mines the memories of childhood and the facets of loss in much the same way that *Summer Gone* does. Macfarlane's treatment of time and memory is reminiscent of Dermot Healy's *A Goat's Song.* Wallace Stegner's *Crossing to Safety* explores with the same quiet intensity the toll that living takes on two couples.

Maillard, Keith.

Gloria. Soho Press, 1999. 643pp.

In the summer after her college graduation in 1957, Gloria Cotter, having grown up in a wealthy family in a small town in West Virginia, tries to balance her family's expectations with her love of literature and her desire to go to graduate school. *Gloria* was shortlisted for the Governor General's Literary Award for Fiction.

Second Appeal: Story

Subjects: 1950s • Class Consciousness • Family Chronicles • Mothers and Daughters • Older Men–Younger Women • Raysburg (Imaginary Place) • Small-town Life • Upper Classes • West Virginia • Young Women

Read On: Other novels that portray an era and the coming of age of the main character as beautifully as *Gloria* does are Herman Wouk's *Marjorie Morningstar,* Mona Simpson's *Off Keck Road,* and Mary McCarthy's *The Group.* Since 1980 Maillard has set seven of his novels in the fictional landscape of Raysburg, West Virginia: *Alex Driving South, The Knife in My Hands, Cutting Through, Light in the Company of Women, Hazard Zones, Gloria,* and *The Clarinet Polka.*

Miller, Almeda Glenn.

Tiger Dreams. Polestar, 2002. 363pp. Book Groups 📖

Following her father's death, documentary filmmaker Claire Spencer travels from Canada to India with her boyfriend David. Determined to discover why he turned his back on his Indian heritage, she uncovers her grandparents' history and their connection with Gandhi.

Second Appeal: Language

Subjects: Canadians in India • Family Chronicles • First Novels • Gandhi, Mahatma • Grandmothers • India • Women Filmmakers

Read On: Other novels with a very strong sense of place set in India are Indira Ganesan's *The Journey,* Meena Alexander's *Nampally Road,* and Rohinton Mistry's *Family Matters.* Another young female filmmaker who journeys back to India is the protagonist in Leslie Forbes's *Bombay Ice.* The search for roots and family history is recounted in Thomas King's *Medicine River* (set on the Canadian Prairies).

Nattel, Lilian.

🎗 *The River Midnight.* Alfred A. Knopf Canada, 1999, c.1998. 414pp. Book Groups 📖

A portrait of life in a small Jewish village in Poland at the end of the nineteenth century is depicted first through the recollections of the women and then through those of the men in their lives. Nattel won the Martin & Beatrice Fischer First Novel Award for this book.

Second Appeal: Character

Subjects: First Novels • Jewish Families • Magic Realism • Male–Female Relationships • Nineteenth Century • Poland • Village Life • Women's Friendships

Read On: The hope expressed here is also found in Anne Michaels's *Fugitive Pieces.* A portion of Sandra Birdsell's *The Russländer* is set in a small Eastern European village prior to World War I. The works of Isaac B. Singer (*The Death of Me-*

thuselah and Other Stories) and Sholom Aleichem (*Adventures of Mottel, the Cantor's Son,* and others) vividly describe the Jewish experience. Nattel's addition of folklore elements to her story is reminiscent of the work of Gabriel García Márquez (*Love in the Time of Cholera* and others). It is also found in Nattel's novel *The Singing Fire.*

Needles, Dan.

With Axe and Flask: The History of Persephone Township from Pre-Cambrian Times to the Present. **Macfarlane Walter &Ross, 2002. 250pp.**

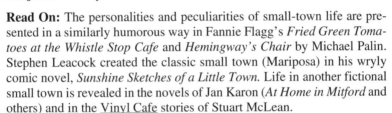

The history of a small Ontario town comes alive through the stories of the town's colourful residents, from farmers to shady land speculators. There are even visits from some of Canada's most celebrated historical figures, including Sir John A. Macdonald, Wilfred Laurier, and the future King Edward VII. This work received The Stephen Leacock Memorial Medal for Humour.

Second Appeal: Character

Subjects: Country Life • Farm Life • Humorous Fiction • Small-town Life

Read On: The personalities and peculiarities of small-town life are presented in a similarly humorous way in Fannie Flagg's *Fried Green Tomatoes at the Whistle Stop Cafe* and *Hemingway's Chair* by Michael Palin. Stephen Leacock created the classic small town (Mariposa) in his wryly comic novel, *Sunshine Sketches of a Little Town.* Life in another fictional small town is revealed in the novels of Jan Karon (*At Home in Mitford* and others) and in the <u>Vinyl Cafe</u> stories of Stuart McLean.

Norman, Howard.

The Bird Artist. **Farrar, Straus & Giroux, 1994. 289pp. Book Groups** 📖

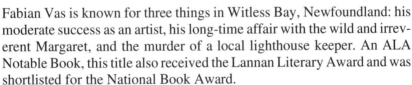

Fabian Vas is known for three things in Witless Bay, Newfoundland: his moderate success as an artist, his long-time affair with the wild and irreverent Margaret, and the murder of a local lighthouse keeper. An ALA Notable Book, this title also received the Lannan Literary Award and was shortlisted for the National Book Award.

Second Appeal: Language

Subjects: Adultery • Artists • Birds • Male–Female Relationships • Mothers and Sons • Murder • Newfoundland and Labrador • Small-town Life • Trilogies

Read On: This novel is the first in Norman's <u>The Canadian Trilogy</u>. The other two titles are *The Museum Guard* and *The Haunting of L.*, both of which display the same economy of writing that is found in *The Bird Artist.* Katherine Govier also writes of a bird artist in *Creation*, a biographical novel about John James Audubon. Other novelists who emphasize setting include Beryl Bainbridge in *The Birthday Boys*, Sandra Benítez in *A Place Where the Sea Remembers*, and Shena Mackay in *The Orchard on Fire.*

Quaife, Darlene A.

Days and Nights on the Amazon. Turnstone Press, 1994. 197pp. Book Groups ▢

The Amazon River links two women, each on her own personal quest: Acacia Aranha is a plant collector who travels the Amazon by boat searching for both a ghost tribe and new plant species; Liberty "Libby" Hall is an Alberta farm woman on a journey to find the man responsible for her husband's death.

> **Second Appeal:** Language

> **Subjects:** Amazon River • Brazil • Journeys • Quests

> **Read On:** Quaife's first novel, *Bone Bird,* collected the 1989 Commonwealth Writers Prize for Best First Book in the Caribbean and Canada. Quaife is also the author of an ecological thriller, *Polar Circus,* written under the name D. A. Barry. Tension exists elsewhere on the Amazon in Andrew Pyper's *The Trade Mission. Gerontius* by James Hamilton-Paterson is the account of a journey down the Amazon by the English composer Edward Elgar. In Sharon Butala's *The Garden of Eden*, a farm wife embarks on an African odyssey.

Quarrington, Paul.

The Spirit Cabinet. Random House of Canada, 1999. 341pp.

Magicians and lovers Jurgen and Rudolfo honed their craft in the seedy clubs of Europe and are now at the top of the circuit in Las Vegas. Jurgen, however, is disillusioned with life on and off the stage. Believing he can discover "real magic," he becomes obsessed with a recently acquired collection of books, props, and artifacts (including a large box known as a spirit cabinet) once owned by The Great Houdini. This obsession will tragically test the limits of the lovers' faith.

> **Second Appeal:** Character

> **Subjects:** Las Vegas • Magicians • Nevada • Spiritual Journeys

> **Read On:** Although much more graphic, John O'Brien's *Leaving Las Vegas* shares the landscape of the Las Vegas found here. Katherine Dunn's *Geek Love*, John Updike's *The Witches of Eastwick,* and John Irving's *The Hotel New Hampshire* all have a similar combination of quirky characters and humour. This novel shares the offbeat style of Timothy Findley's *Pilgrim.* Quarrington won the Governor General's Literary Award for Fiction for *Whale Music* and The Stephen Leacock Memorial Medal for Humour for an earlier novel, *King Leary.*

Ricci, Nino.

❦ *Lives of the Saints.* Cormorant Books, 1990. 238pp. Book Groups ▢

Seven-year-old Vittorio Innocente must endure the scorn and gossip of his entire small Italian village when his mother becomes pregnant while his father is away working in "America." *Lives of the Saints* won the Governor General's Literary Award for Fiction, the Betty Trask Prize, the F. G. Bressani Prize, the W. H. Smith/*Books in Canada* First Novel Award, and the Winifred Holtby Memorial Prize.

> **Second Appeal:** Story

Subjects: Coming of Age • Family Relationships • First Novels • Immigrants and Refugees • Italy • Mothers and Sons • Trilogies • Village Life • Young Boys

Read On: *Lives of the Saints* was published in the United States with the title *The Book of Saints*. The story of Vittorio and his family continue in *In a Glass House* and *Where She Has Gone*. His other novel is *Testament*, a story of Jesus's life. Other novels in which a child watches helplessly as her world falls apart are Sheila Bosworth's *Almost Innocent* and Donna Morrissey's *Kit's Law*.

Scott, Gail.

My Paris. Mercury Press, 1999. 165pp.

On a sabbatical leave in Paris, an author records her fragmented reflections on life, literature, and the residents of the "City of Light." She discovers the personal isolation that is possible even in a contemporary metropolis populated with minority communities and ongoing arrivals of refugees.

Second Appeal: Language

Subjects: Benjamin, Walter • Canadians in France • Diaries • France • Lesbians • Paris • Women

Read On: Two of Scott's other books are the novel *Heroine* and a collection of short stories, *Spare Parts*. Paris is the setting for a lesbian love affair in Naomi Holoch's *Off Season*. Two major Canadian writers, Morley Callaghan (*That Summer in Paris*) and John Glassco (*Memoirs of Montparnasse*) chose to write about their memories of Paris. E. L. Doctorow similarly characterizes a city (New York) in *The Waterworks*. Robert Majzels has a unique narrative style in *City of Forgetting* (another story of personal isolation), in which he inserts characters from other times into a present-time narrative. Canada's *Quill & Quire* magazine called *My Paris* one of 1999's ten best books.

Smith, Michael V.

Cumberland. Cormorant Books, 2002. 296pp. Book Groups 📖

In the small Ontario town of Cumberland, the lives of five people intersect as they struggle to understand the confusion brought on by personal loss, loneliness, disappointment, and, ultimately, their need for each other. *Cumberland* was shortlisted for the Amazon.ca/*Books in Canada* First Novel Award.

Second Appeal: Character

Subjects: Alcoholism • First Novels • Friendship • Gay Men • Interpersonal Relations • Ontario • Saint Lawrence River • Small-town Life

Read On: Life in small Ontario towns is eloquently portrayed in the work of Alice Munro (*Friend of My Youth* and others). Other books set in small towns where people are faced with personal challenges include Russell Banks's *The Sweet Hereafter*, David Bergen's *See the Child,* and Christiane Frenette's *Terra Firma*. Michael Cunningham in *A Home at the*

End of the World and Caroline Adderson in *A History of Forgetting* write about gay and straight friends coming together to help each other.

Smith, Ray.

The Man Who Loved Jane Austen. **Porcupine's Quill, 1999. 233pp.**

Six months after his wife's accidental death, Frank Wilson, a Montreal professor with two young boys, is struggling to keep his life together as his wife's side of the family threatens to take custody of his children by ruining his career, finances, and reputation.

Subjects: 1990s • Austen, Jane • Family • Montreal • Quebec • Widowers

Read On: Among Smith's other books are *Lord Nelson's Tavern*, *A Night at the Opera* (winner of the Hugh MacLennan Prize for Fiction), and a collection of short stories, *Cape Breton Is the Thought-control Centre of Canada*. Smith returns to the streets of Montreal in *The Man Who Hated Emily Brontë*, a novel referred to as the "comic counterpart" of *The Man Who Loved Jane Austen,* in which another man is taken in unexpected directions by the developments in his life. Mary Soderstrom's *Endangered Species* is also about families and politics in Montreal, specifically in Outremont. Quebec's political situation in the 1990s is described in Marianne Ackerman's *Jump*.

Smith, Russell.

How Insensitive. **Porcupine's Quill, 1994. 258pp.**

Newly arrived in Toronto, Ted Owen is drawn into the urban twenty-something scene of parties, nightclubs, sex, and drugs. As he slowly becomes disillusioned with his savvy new friends, who lead less than perfect lives, he finds himself becoming almost as jaded and confused as they are. *How Insensitive* was shortlisted for the Governor General's Literary Award for Fiction, The Smithbooks/*Books in Canada* First Novel Award, and the Trillium Book Award.

Second Appeal: Story

Subjects: 1990s • First Novels • Music Halls • Satire • Toronto

Read On: Smith explores the young, urban scene in his short-story collection *Young Men: Stories* and in his second novel, *Noise*. In *Muriella Pent*, Smith brings young urbans and an upper-class maven together as he examines the contemporary social scene. He has also written a modern-day fable, *The Princess and the Whiskheads*. Other authors who also examine the urban scene in their fiction are Bret Easton Ellis (*American Psycho*, *Less Than Zero,* and *Glamorama*), Jay McInerney (*Bright Lights, Big City,* and *Brightness Falls*), and Mike Tanner (*Acting the Giddy Goat*).

Stachniak, Eva.

Necessary Lies. **Simon & Pierre, 2000. 265pp. Book Groups** 📖

Ten years earlier, when a research scholarship took her from a Poland about to overthrow communism to a Montreal teeming with an abundance of life, Anna had been seduced by Montreal and by William in Montreal. His sudden death leads to her discovery of his long-term affair with a German woman, knowledge that sends her back to Europe to search for the truth behind his betrayal. Stachniak won the Amazon.ca/*Books in Canada* First Novel Award for this novel.

> **Second Appeal:** Character

> **Subjects:** Adultery • First Novels • Forgiveness • Love Stories • Marriage • Montreal • Poland • Quebec • Reconciliation

> **Read On:** Other novels set in Montreal include *The Night Travellers* by Elizabeth Spencer and *Voice-over* by Carole Corbeil. In Jane Urquhart's *The Stone Carvers* a woman searches for the redemption needed to overcome lost love. In Anne Tyler's *Ladder of Years* a woman abandons her former life.

Teleky, Richard.

🎗 *The Paris Years of Rosie Kamin.* **Steerforth Press, 1998. 218pp. Book Groups** 📖

Rosie Kamin, a forty-year-old American, has worked to build herself a life of self-imposed exile in Paris. Following the sudden death of her long-time lover, she is forced to examine her feelings and reactions to this horrific event. When her sister arrives from the United States, and they travel to their mother's homeland in Budapest, Rosie finally gains the understanding she needs to move forward in her life. Teleky won the Harold U. Ribalow Prize for this work.

> **Second Appeal:** Character

> **Subjects:** Children of Holocaust Survivors • Death of a Parent • Jewish Women • Love Stories • Mothers and Daughters • Obsession • Paris • Sisters • Suicide

> **Read On:** Teleky is the author of the novel *Pack up the Moon* and the short-story collection, *Goodnight, Sweetheart and Other Stories*. Lily Brett's *Too Many Men* also recounts the story of a daughter returning to her mother's homeland to understand her own legacy. The woman in Eva Stachniak's *Necessary Lies* also flees her homeland, in this case from Europe to North America (Montreal), and finds herself captivated by a city. In a very different environment, Pat Conroy's *Beach Music* shares several themes, including the suicide of a loved one, self-exile, and subsequent self-discovery through learning about his mother.

Tremblay, Lise.

🎗 *Mile End.* **Talonbooks, 2002. 142pp. Book Groups** 📖

In Montreal, a grossly overweight young woman, despondent and filled with self-loathing, isolates herself from her family and neighbourhood, and as her depression deepens, she embarks on a journey to connect with her father's estranged family in a futile attempt to belong. Tremblay won the Governor General's Literary Award for Fiction (French) for the original version of this work. Translated from the French [*La danse juive*] by Gail Scott.

Subjects: Depression, Mental • Dysfunctional Families • French Canadian • Overweight Women • Translations

Read On: Diane Baker Mason's *Last Summer at Barebones* looks at the subject of obesity, as does Wally Lamb's *She's Come Undone*, the story of an obese woman who looks for her place in the world. Like the character in *Mile End*, the woman in Christiane Frenette's *The Whole Night Through* also isolates herself, creating her own world within a small village, despite an almost desperate need to belong. Hélène Rioux's *Reading Nijinsky* and Louise Dupré's *The Milky Way* are both first-person narratives of Montreal women.

Vassanji, M. G.

🔖 *The Book of Secrets.* **McClelland & Stewart, 1994. 337pp. Book Groups** 📖

When an old diary of a British colonial administrator is unearthed in the walls of a dusty shop in Dar es Salaam in the 1980s, retired schoolteacher Pius Fernandes attempts to unravel the mystery it presents. Vassanji's novel was awarded the inaugural Giller Prize and the F. G. Bressani Prize.

Second Appeal: Story

Subjects: 1980s • Africa • Colonialism • Culture Clash • Diaries • East Africa • Research Novels • Tanzania • World War I

Read On: Vassanji became the first author to win the Giller Prize a second time for his novel *The In-Between World of Vikram Lall.* His other books of fiction include *The Gunny Sack*, *No New Land,* and the short-story collection *Uhuru Street.* The plot of Lee Langley's *Persistent Rumours* also involves a British colonial mystery, with tantalizingly few clues. In *The Holding* by Merilyn Simonds, when a young woman discovers a century-old diary, she begins to delve into the life of the author.

Historical Fiction

Allinson, Sidney.

Jeremy Kane: A Canadian Historical Adventure Novel of the 1837 Mackenzie Rebellion and Its Brutal Aftermath in the Australian Penal Colonies. **Xlibris Corp., 1998. 364pp.**

Following the failure of the Rebellion of 1837, Mackenzie supporter Jeremy Kane and 100 others are transported to a penal colony in Tasmania. Young Jeremy's hope and determination enable him to overcome the horrors of nineteenth-century transportation.

Second Appeal: Story

Subjects: Australia • Convicts • Nineteenth Century • Penal Colonies • Prisons • Rebellion of 1837 • Tasmania

Read On: The Australians series by William Stuart Long begins with *The Exiles,* which chronicles the journey of another young convict deported to the penal colonies. *Morgan's Run* (Colleen McCullough) tells the tale of a convict who is among the first to test this experiment in justice and punishment. Although set in the era of the American Revolution, <u>The Kent Family Chronicles</u> by John Jakes, beginning with *The Bastard,* is similar in its style of storytelling.

Assiniwi, Bernard.

 *The Beothuk Saga.* **McClelland & Stewart, 2000. 341pp. Book Groups** 📖

This story of the now-extinct Beothuk Nation opens during the time of the Vikings with young initiate Anin's coming of age as he establishes his own clan. The saga continues through 500 years of history to the arrival of John Cabot and the subsequent annihilation of the Nation. This novel, published in French in 1996, won the Prix Littéraire France-Québec Jean-Hamelin. Translated from the French [*La saga des Béothuks*] by Wayne Grady.

> **Second Appeal:** Story

> **Subjects:** Aboriginal Peoples • Beothuk Nation • Cabot, John • French Canadian • Newfoundland and Labrador • Translations • Treatment of First Nations • Vikings in Newfoundland and Labrador

> **Read On:** Michael Crummey's *River Thieves* is a vivid account of the last days of the Beothuk Nation. *All Gone Widdun* by Annamarie Beckle is also a fictionalized account of life among the Beothuk Nation. "Widdun" is the Beothuk word for sleep, meaning death.

Bouzane, Lillian.

In the Hands of the Living God. **Turnstone Press, 1999. 308pp.**

The intrigues of fifteenth-century Venice come to life in the diaries and correspondence of musician and cartographer Mathye. In these documents she recounts her life, travels, and inner struggle with husband Giovanni's decision to switch his loyalties from Venice to England, a move that ultimately leads to the European settlement of Newfoundland, as he sails for the king under the name John Cabot.

> **Second Appeal:** Story

> **Subjects:** Epistolary Novels • Explorers • Italy • Newfoundland and Labrador • Venice • Women Cartographers • Women Musicians

> **Read On:** Dorothy Dunnett vividly re-creates historical details of fifteenth-century Venice in <u>The House of Niccolò</u> series. Another woman with an unusual vocation (that of physician) in the fifteenth century can be found in C. L. Grace's <u>Kathryn Swinbrooke</u> mysteries (*The Book of Shadows* and others). Bernard Assiniwi in *The Beothuk Saga* tells the story of life in Newfoundland both before and after the arrival of Cabot.

Bowering, George.

Shoot! **Key Porter Books, 1994. 297pp.**

A band of socially outcast brothers, led by their Métis half-brother Alex, meet a tragic end in traditional Western style when they are hunted and caught by a posse after their petty crimes escalate to murder.

Subjects: Aboriginal Peoples • British Columbia • Frontier and Pioneer Life • McLean Family • Métis • Murderers • Outlaws • Westerns

Read On: Bowering's *Burning Water* won the Governor General's Literary Award for Fiction in 1980. The story of the McLean Gang is told in Mel Rothenburger's non-fiction work *The Wild McLeans*. Bowering's historical Western is similar to those told by Richard S. Wheeler (*Second Lives, Sun Mountain,* and others). Other examples of non-formula Westerns are Thomas Berger's *Little Big Man*, Michael Blake's *Marching to Valhalla,* and Sandra Dallas's *The Diary of Mattie Spenser.*

Cruise, David, and Alison Griffiths.

Vancouver: A Novel. HarperFlamingoCanada, 2003. 756pp. Book Groups 📖

Beginning with the Ice Age and moving forward in time, the dynamic life and history of Vancouver unfold in the stories of the people who make up its history.

Subjects: British Columbia • First Nations • First Novels • Vancouver

Read On: For another fictional telling of Vancouver's history, read *Vancouver!* by Linda Wikene Johnson. Other epic historical novels include Bernard Assiniwi's *The Beothuk Saga* and works by James Michener (*Hawaii* and others), John Jakes (*Charleston* and others), James Clavell (*Shogun* and others), and Edward Rutherfurd (*London* and others).

Crummey, Michael.

🎗 *River Thieves*. Doubleday Canada, 2001. 335pp. Book Groups 📖

Naval officer David Buchan returns to Bay of Exploits, Newfoundland, to investigate the kidnapping of a Beothuk woman and the murder of her husband. He must also determine whether an influential settler, John Peyton, and his son were justified in their actions against the Aboriginal inhabitants. *River Thieves* won the Thomas Head Raddall Atlantic Fiction Award, the Torgi Literary Award, the Winterset Award, and the Atlantic Independent Booksellers' Choice Award. It was shortlisted for the Amazon.ca/*Books in Canada* First Novel Award, the Giller Prize, and the Commonwealth Writers Prize for Best First Book in the Caribbean and Canada.

Second Appeal: Language

Subjects: Aboriginal Peoples • Bay of Exploits • Beothuk Nation • Fathers and Sons • First Novels • Frontier and Pioneer Life • Newfoundland and Labrador • Nineteenth Century • Treatment of First Nations

Read On: Bernard Assiniwi's *The Beothuk Saga* is another account of events that led to the extinction of the Beothuk Nation in Newfoundland. The <u>Seven Dreams Series</u> by William Vollmann describes the colonization of North America by European settlers and their interactions with the Aboriginal peoples. The harsh landscape of Newfoundland is also depicted in Wayne Johnston's *The Colony of Unrequited Dreams* and Annie Proulx's *The Shipping News. Blood Red Ochre* by Kevin Major is a young adult novel that explores the tragic plight of Newfoundland's Beothuk Nation.

Frutkin, Mark.

The Lion of Venice. Beach Holme Publishers, 1997. 213pp.

In a prison cell in Genoa, Marco Polo relates tales of his travels. His stories begin as he embarks on a journey to the Orient pursued by an assassin sent by the Venetian Doge, and continue into his time in the land of Kublai Khan.

Second Appeal: Story

Subjects: China • Explorers • Italy • Kublai Khan • Polo, Marco • Venice

Read On: Frutkin is the author of *Invading Tibet, In the Time of the Angry Queen*, *Slow Lightning*, and others. John Banville's fictional biographies *Kepler* and *Doctor Copernicus* are both set in the same time period. Gary Jennings's *The Journeyer* chronicles a journey by Polo to the Orient at the age of seventeen. Paul Griffiths's *Myself and Marco Polo* recounts the travels of Polo as dictated to, and embellished by, his scribe. Frutkin's blending of storytelling elements such as history, quests, and magic realism is also found in the work of Guy Gavriel Kay (*The Lions of Al-Rassan* and others).

Gedge, Pauline.

Lords of the Two Lands.

The titles in this series blend elements of revenge, espionage, and rebellion to recount the struggle for reunification of ancient Egypt.

The Hippopotamus Marsh. Viking, 1998.

The Hyksos, invaders from Asia, have fiercely ruled Egypt for more than 200 years. Finally, the Tao family, hereditary rulers of Egypt, begin their struggle to reclaim their birthright.

The Oasis. Soho Press, 1999.

The Horus Road. Viking, 2000.

Subjects: Ahmose I, King of Egypt • Ancient Egypt • Princes • Rulers

Read On: Gedge's *The Eagle and the Raven* shares a similar depth of the strong historical detail found in this series. Judith Tarr's *The Shepherd Kings* and Christian Jacq's Ramses Quintet (*Ramses: The Son of the Light* and others) are also set in ancient Egypt.

Glover, Douglas.

🎗 *Elle*. Goose Lane, 2003. 205pp. Book Groups 📖

Promiscuous behaviour leads to the exile of a young sixteenth-century French woman, along with her lover and her childhood nurse, to an isolated island in the Gulf of St. Lawrence. In this harsh and isolated new world the lover and the nurse perish, and so begins a hallucinatory account of Elle's fantastical adventures among the Natives as she resolves to survive. *Elle* was awarded the Govenor General's Literary Award for Fiction and was shortlisted for the International IMPAC Dublin Literary Award.

Subjects: Cartier, Jacques • Discoveries in Geography • French Canada • Magic Realism • Sexuality • Survival • Women Pioneers

Read On: Douglas Glover's previous works include *A Guide to Animal Behaviour*, which was a finalist for the Governor General's Literary Award for Fiction; *The Life and Times of Captain N.*, which was selected as a *Globe and Mail* top-ten paperback of 2001; and *16 Categories of Desire*, which was a finalist for the Rogers Writers' Trust Fiction Prize. The loneliness conveyed here is also present in Margaret Atwood's *Surfacing*. But then there's the raucous, carnal side of this novel, and that aspect is also a part of Terry Griggs's *Rogues' Wedding*. Yann Martel's *Life of Pi* is another richly imagined tale of survival. A novel with fantastical elements chronicling contact between the Inuit and early Europeans is John Steffler's *The Afterlife of George Cartwright*.

Gulland, Sandra.

The Many Lives & Secret Sorrows of Josephine B. HarperCollins, 1995. 439pp.

The diary of Rose, a young woman who will become known to the world as Josephine, wife of Napoleon Bonaparte, describes her early life, including a first marriage, children, imprisonment, and finally her courtship and marriage to the future Emperor of France.

Second Appeal: Story

Subjects: Empresses • First Novels • France • French Revolution • Josephine, Empress • Kings and Queens • Napoleon I • Trilogies

Read On: Gulland continues Josephine's story in *Tales of Passion, Tales of Woe*, and *The Last Great Dance on Earth*. Antonia Fraser's *Marie Antoinette: The Journey* shares the story of another Queen of France, while Rosalind Miles tells the story of a strong English female ruler in *I, Elizabeth*. Sharon Kay Penman's *Time and Chance* describes the marriage of a ruler (Henry II) and his queen (Eleanor of Aquitaine).

Holdstock, Pauline.

Beyond Measure. Cormorant Books, 2003. 355pp. Book Groups 📖

Chiara is a young, piebald slave girl working for a series of artists in Renaissance Italy. As her experiences are chronicled, they reveal a world that, while revering beauty, is also both decadent and sadistic to those who are less than perfect. Holdstock was shortlisted for the Giller Prize for this work.

Subjects: Artists • Beauty • Cruelty • Italy • Renaissance • Sixteenth Century • Slaves

Read On: Holdstock is the author of a number of other works of fiction including *The Blackbird's Song*, *The Burial Ground,* and *House*. Other novels that blend both art and history in a similar way include Tracy Chevalier's *Girl with a Pearl Earring* and Sarah Dunant's *The Birth of Venus*. Sheri Holman's *The Dress Lodger* also contains elements of the macabre, as does Iain Pears's *An Instance of the Fingerpost,* which has the same pacing and blend of drama and history that are found here.

Houston, James A.

The Ice Master: A Novel of the Arctic. McClelland & Stewart, 1997. 372pp.

In 1875 two ships voyage to a remote whaling port on the Inuit shore of
Baffin Island, one commanded by an American, Captain Caleb Dunston,
the other captained by Newfoundlander Tom Finn. Over the winter the
two compete against each other as they look toward spring and their journey home with a cargo of whale oil and bone.

Second Appeal: Story

Subjects: Arctic Expeditions • Baffin Island • Inuit • Nunavut • Seafaring
Life • Whaling

Read On: Houston's trilogy of memoirs (*Confessions of an Igloo Dweller*,
Zigzag: A Life on the Move, and *Hideaway: Life on the Queen Charlotte Is-
lands*) is an example of non-fiction that reads like fiction. A clear picture of
the Arctic is also painted in such novels as *The Broken Lands* by Robert
Edric, *A Discovery of Strangers* by Rudy Wiebe, *North with Franklin: The
Lost Journals of James Fitzjames* by John Wilson, and *The Navigator of
New York* by Wayne Johnston.

Humphreys, C. C.

The French Executioner. McArthur & Co., 2001. 371pp.

Summoned by Henry VIII to behead his second wife, Anne Boleyn, Jean
Rombaud begins an adventurous journey across Europe after he grants
the doomed queen's final request that he bury her six-fingered hand in
the Loire Valley.

Second Appeal: Story

Subjects: Anne Boleyn, Queen • Executioners • French in England • Kings
and Queens • Relics • Rombaud, Jean

Read On: Humphreys continues the adventures of Rombaud in *Blood
Ties*. He has two other historicals to his credit: *Jack Absolute* and its
prequel, *The Blooding of Jack Absolute*. Anne Boleyn is the subject of Jean
Plaidy's *The Lady in the Tower*, Robin Maxwell's *The Secret Diary of
Anne Boleyn*, and Mollie Hardwick's *Blood Royal*. Humphreys's style of
historical fiction will appeal to readers of Bernard Cornwell's series featur-
ing Thomas of Hookton (*The Archer's Tale*, *Vagabond*, and *Heretic*). For
a treatment of twentieth-century executions and executioners, read Tim
Binding's *A Perfect Execution*, or Colin McDougall's *Execution*, set in the
Canadian arena in World War II.

Jack, Donald Lamont.

The Bandy Papers.

This series chronicles the adventures of small-town boy Bart Bandy from
the early days of World War I through to his participation in the events of
World War II. Originally published in the early 1970s, this humorous series was reissued by McClelland & Stewart.

🎗 *Three Cheers for Me.* McClelland & Stewart, 2001.

Awarded The Stephen Leacock Memorial Medal for Humour.

🎗 *That's Me in the Middle.* McClelland & Stewart, 2001.

Awarded The Stephen Leacock Memorial Medal for Humour.

It's Me Again. McClelland & Stewart, 2002.

🎗 *Me Bandy, You Cissie.* McClelland & Stewart, 2002.

Awarded The Stephen Leacock Memorial Medal for Humour.

Me Too. McClelland & Stewart, 2004.

Hitler Versus Me: The Return of Bartholomew Bandy. McClelland & Stewart, 2004.

In the early 1940s, determined to participate in the war effort, forty-five-year-old Flight Lieutenant Bart Bandy lands a chance to appeal directly to the prime minister to let him fight in the war. Once in Europe, Bart begins a series of adventures that culminate when he is shot down over France and is pursued by the Allies, the Resistance, and the Gestapo because he knows the date of D-Day.

Subjects: Bandy, Bartholomew (Fictional Character) • Humorous Fiction • Pilots • World War I Veterans • World War II

Read On: The same light touch of gentle humour in this series can also be found in the work of P. G. Wodehouse (*The World of Jeeves* and others) and Jerome K. Jerome (*Three Men in a Boat* and others). Robert Crichton also manages to put humour in a wartime story, *The Secret of Santa Vittoria*. To stay in Europe, try the <u>Don Camillo Stories</u> by Giovanni Guareschi.

Jiles, Paulette.

🎗 *Enemy Women.* HarperFlamingo, 2002. 321pp. Book Groups 📖

Branded an enemy woman and imprisoned by the Union army, strong-willed Adair Colley falls in love with one of her jailors, a Union officer. She escapes with his help and begins a perilous journey from St. Louis back to her home and life in the Ozark Mountains during the Civil War. *Enemy Women* received the Rogers Writers' Trust Fiction Prize.

Second Appeal: Character

Subjects: Civil War • Farmers • First Novels • Missouri • War • Young Women

Read On: Jiles won the Governor General's Literary Award for Poetry in 1984 for her collection *Celestial Navigation*. The "enemy women" in Jiles's novel are created in a style similar to that of other writers' works (Margaret Mitchell's *Gone with the Wind* and Charles Frazier's *Cold Mountain*) whose heroines are strong-willed women facing the hardship of survival during the American Civil War. Other novels set during the Civil War include Howard Bahr's *The Black Flower* and Miriam Grace Monfredo's *Sisters of Cain*. A book that presents the story of ordinary people in extraordinary times is Geraldine Brooks's *Years of Wonder*.

King, Ross.

Domino. Sinclair-Stevenson, 1995. 439pp. Book Groups 📖

In 1770s London, aspiring artist George Cautley's life takes a number of twists: he becomes caught in a maze of masquerades and the darker side of society when he learns the story of a castrato from fifty years earlier.

Second Appeal: Story

Subjects: Artists • Castrati • Eighteenth Century • England • First Novels • Italy • London • Masquerades • Venice

Read On: King has written a second historical novel, *Ex-libris*, set in London and Europe. Stories about the castrati have a mysterious angle in *Scherzo: A Venetian Entertainment,* by Jim Williams; *The Last Castrato* by John Spencer Hill; and *Cry to Heaven* by Anne Rice. Rosalind Laker's *The Venetian Mask*, also set in Venice, a city renowned for its masquerades, is rich in details of the eighteenth century.

Koch, Eric.

Earrings: A Novel. Mosaic Press, 2002. 222pp.

Jeweller Robert Koch is in Baden-Baden, the summer playground of the rich and famous in the nineteenth century, seeking to make his mark. While there, he is caught up in the intrigues surrounding the mysterious disappearance of a pair of earrings.

Second Appeal: Story

Subjects: Baden-Baden • Europe • Germany • Jewellers • Nineteenth Century

Read On: Koch is also the author of the historical fiction novels *Icon in Love: A Novel about Goethe* and *The Man Who Knew Charlie Chaplin: A Novel about the Weimar Republic*. A pair of earrings creates a pivotal moment in Tracy Chevalier's *Girl with a Pearl Earring*. Artisans figure prominently in the novels of Rosalind Laker (*Banners of Silk*, *The Golden Tulip*, and *The Silver Touch*).

Kroetsch, Robert.

The Man from the Creeks. Vintage Canada, 1998. 307pp. Book Groups 📖

Fourteen-year-old Peek and his mother stow away on a ship to Dawson City in the late 1890s. Along the way they connect with Benjamin Reed who, like them and many others, is on a quest to the North hoping to make his fortune during the gold rush.

Second Appeal: Story

Subjects: Klondike Gold Rush • Klondike River Valley • Mothers and Sons • Prospecting • Yukon Territory

Read On: Poet Robert Service's work *The Shooting of Dan McGrew* provided the inspiration for Kroetsch's story. Kroetsch is also the author of *The Puppeteer*, *Alibi*, and *The Studhorse Man*, which won the Governor General's Literary Award for Fiction in 1969. To enjoy the sense of adventure found here, read Jack London's *Call of the Wild*. Other books that chronicle the lure of the Klondike gold rush include Tim Champlin's *By Flare of Northern Lights*, Dan Cushman's *In Alaska with Shipwreck Kelly*, and James Michener's *Journey*.

MacNeil, Robert.

🎗 *Burden of Desire*. N. A. Talese/Doubleday, 1992. 466pp. Book Groups 📖

Following the 1917 Halifax explosion, a sexually explicit diary is found in the debris. Clergyman Peter Wentworth and psychologist Stewart MacPherson become obsessed with uncovering its author's identity and then compete for the recently widowed woman's affections. *Burden of Desire* won the Dartmouth Book Award for Fiction.

Second Appeal: Story

Subjects: 1910s • Clergy • Diaries • Explosions • First Novels • Halifax • Nova Scotia • Obsessive Love • Psychologists • World War I

Read On: MacNeil is the author of the novels *The Voyage* and *Breaking News*; his other books include *The People Machine: The Influence of Television on American Politics*, *The Story of English,* and two memoirs, *The Right Place at the Right Time* and *Wordstruck*. Hugh MacLennan's *Barometer Rising* originally immortalized the devastating 1917 explosion. Al Purdy's *A Splinter in the Heart* tells the tale of Trenton, Ontario, another town torn by an explosion.

Major, Kevin.

No Man's Land. Doubleday Canada, 1995. 251pp. Book Groups 📖

In the hours prior to the Battle of the Somme in July 1916, the young men of the doomed Newfoundland Regiment go about the tasks of everyday living as they await their orders to go over the top of the trenches into certain death.

Second Appeal: Story

Subjects: Battle of the Somme • France • Newfoundland and Labrador • Royal Newfoundland Regiment • War Stories • World War I

Read On: In Timothy Findley's *The Wars*, the horrors of war are graphically detailed as he clearly articulates that it is not only the enemy that inflicts harm. Frederic Manning has written two novels on the Battle of the Somme, *Her Privates, We*, and *The Middle Parts of Fortune: Somme & Ancre, 1916*. There are several non-fiction accounts of the Royal Newfoundland Regiment; one is a personal memoir, *Memoirs of a Blue Puttee: The Newfoundland Regiment in World War One* by A. J. Stacey. To read about the ill effects of this war on women participants, try *Strangers and Sojourners* by Michael D. O'Brien. *The Stone Carvers* by Jane Urquhart also poignantly captures the impact of the war to end all wars.

Morgan, Bernice.

Random Passage. Breakwater, 1992. 269pp. Book Groups 📖

Propelled initially by loneliness, Lavinia Andrews begins to record her family's story. She begins with their journey from England to Canada and then documents a fifteen-year period of hardships they and the other residents of a remote village in Newfoundland endured in the early 1800s.

Second Appeal: Story

Subjects: Family Chronicles • First Novels • Fishing Villages • Frontier and Pioneer Life • Newfoundland and Labrador • Nineteenth Century • Poverty • Women Pioneers

Read On: Morgan continues the story of life in Cape Random in *Waiting for Time*. *Random Passage* was published in the United States as *Cape Random*. Morgan is also the author of a short-story collection, *The Topography of Love*, which was shortlisted for the Winterset Award and the Atlantic Booksellers' Choice Award in 2001. Other novels set in Newfoundland and Labrador, in the nineteenth century, include Joseph Schull's *The Jinker* and Gordon Rodgers's *A Settlement of Memory*. To compare *Random Passage* with nineteenth-century life on Canada's West Coast, look at Jack Hodgins's *Innocent Cities*.

Mowat, Farley.

The Farfarers: Before the Norse. Key Porter Books, 1998. 377pp.

Blending fact and fiction, Mowat tells the story of a tenth-century tribe of sailors and hunters who flee the British Isles and settle in Newfoundland. There, they establish a village and live peaceably amongst the Aboriginal peoples until the arrival of the Europeans.

Second Appeal: Story

Subjects: Aboriginal Peoples • Alba (Kingdom) • Exploration • Newfoundland and Labrador • Pre-Columbian America

Read On: Bernard Assiniwi's *The Beothuk Saga* chronicles 500 years of First Nations history in Newfoundland. W. Michael and Kathleen O'Neal Gear's <u>First North Americans Series</u> (*People of the Wolf* and others) explores life in precolonial North America. The history of Newfoundland continues in Joan Clark's *Eiriksdottir* with the Norse arrival; the Europeans, as seen in Alan Fisk's *Forty Testoons*, later usurp these settlers. Mowat tells the stories of Aboriginal peoples in the Arctic in *The Snow Walker*.

Oatley, Keith.

A Natural History. Viking, 1998. 405pp. Book Groups 📖

In 1838, Dr. John Leggate, obsessed with discovering the origins of cholera, meets and then marries Marian Brooks, a young musician in Middlethorpe, England. Striving for personal success, each clashes with Victorian society and with one another; this conflict drives them to Canada, where they discover professional and personal happiness.

Second Appeal: Story

Subjects: England • Love Stories • Nineteenth Century • Physicians • Women Musicians

Read On: Oatley's first novel, *The Case of Emily V.*, a historical mystery in which he brought together Sigmund Freud and Sherlock Holmes, won the Commonwealth Writer's Prize for Best First Book. Other authors who have written intensely interior novels include J. M. Coetzee (*The Master of*

Petersburg) and Jane Hamilton (*The Short History of a Prince*). George Eliot's *Middlemarch* inspired Oatley's novel. Literary allusions also appear in Timothy Findley's *Headhunter,* John Fowles's *The French Lieutenant's Woman*, and Francesca Marciano's *Rules of the Wild.*

Poliquin, Daniel.

☗ *The Straw Man*. Douglas & MacIntyre, 1999. 238pp.

In the final days of the 1759 Siege of Quebec, the fortune of a troupe of struggling French actors takes a sudden and mysterious turn for the better when a murderous mercenary befriends them. This novel, in its original French, was the winner of the Prix Trillium. Translated from the French [*L'homme de paille*] by Wayne Grady.

Second Appeal: Story

Subjects: Battle of the Plains of Abraham • French Canadian • Plains of Abraham • Quebec • Translations

Read On: Set in contemporary Quebec, Mordecai Richler's *Barney's Version* also takes a satirical look at the political situation in Quebec. To revisit the historical setting found here, read Thomas Wharton's *Salamander*. Marianne Ackerman's *Jump* and Hubert Aquin's *Next Episode* both use Quebec politics to propel the story. The Shakespearean elements of this satire appear again in Jane Smiley's *Moo*, Will Self's *Great Apes*, and James Hynes's *The Lecturer's Tale*.

Richards, David Adams.

☗ *River of the Brokenhearted*. Doubleday Canada, 2003. 381pp. Book Groups 📖

The sheer will and determination of Irish Catholic Janie McLeary King prove to be a legacy for her son and grandchildren against small-town prejudices. Ostracized in her small New Brunswick town, initially for marrying an older English man and then for her determination after his death to continue running the movie theatre they developed together, she is befriended by Lord Beaverbrook. This novel won the Atlantic Independent Booksellers' Choice Award.

Second Appeal: Character

Subjects: 1920s • Irish Canadians • Mothers and Sons • Motion Picture Theatre Managers • New Brunswick • Prejudice • Small-town Life • Trilogies • Widows

Read On: This is the concluding volume of Richards's the <u>Miramichi Trilogy</u>, which begins with *Nights Below Station Street*, followed by *Mercy Among the Children*. Jennifer Johnston's *The Old Jest* is another novel set in the 1920s about the conflict between Irish and English factions. Like Colum McCann (*Fishing the Sloe-black River* and others), Richards writes about the Irish outcast. Irish immigrant culture is also explored in Brian Moore's *The Luck of Ginger Coffey*, Margaret Atwood's *Alias Grace,* and Jane Urquhart's *Away*.

Richler, Nancy.

☗ *Your Mouth Is Lovely*. HarperFlamingoCanada, 2002. 357pp. Book Groups 📖

Imprisoned in Siberia for her part in the Russian Revolution of 1905, Miriam records her life in a journal for the daughter she was forced to give up at birth; her daughter, now in Canada, is growing up away from her mother, just as Miriam had done. Richler received the Canadian Jewish Book Award for Fiction for this novel.

Second Appeal: Character

Subjects: Abandoned Children • Death of a Child • Diaries • Jewish Women • Political Prisoners • Russia • Women Prisoners

Read On: Richler's first novel, *Throwaway Angels,* was shortlisted for the Arthur Ellis Award for Best First Novel. A young woman, abandoned by her mother at an early age, narrates Helen Humphreys's *The Lost Garden,* sharing her struggles to come to terms with feelings of longing and loss. Lilian Nattel's *The River Midnight* is another novel that paints a clear picture of life in a small Jewish village. Sandra Birdsell's *The Russländer* chronicles the life of a woman and her family, who escape Russia, immigrating to Canada following the Russian Revolution.

Rohmer, Richard.

John A.'s Crusade. Stoddart, 1995. 259pp.

Canadian Prime Minister John A. Macdonald travels between London, Paris, and St. Petersburg on a secret mission meant to change the balance of power in North America by thwarting the Americans' Alaskan purchase.

Subjects: Alaska • Fenians • Macdonald, Sir John A. • Prime Ministers of Canada

Read On: Rohmer's *Death by Deficit: A 2001 Novel* also explores Canadian political history, only this time by looking forward. He is also the author of *Caged Eagle*, the biographical novel of a ruthless World War II fighter reconnaissance pilot. Frederick Forsyth's *The Day of the Jackal* is another historical novel whose well-known outcome does not affect the reader's enjoyment of the storytelling. For stories about Alaska's history, try *Quest for Empire: The Saga of Russian America* by Kyra Petrovskaya Wayne, or *The Last New Land: Stories of Alaska, Past and Present*, edited by Wayne Mergler. Claude Fournier's *René Lévesque: Portrait of a Man Alone* is a fictionalized account of another prominent Canadian politician.

Silver, Alfred.

Lord of the Plains. Ballantine, 1990. 406pp.

In 1885, settlers and Aboriginals band together in rebellion when the government begins to sell off their occupied land. Gabriel Dumont, his wife, and Louis Riel lead this fight against the government, a rebellion that ends disastrously.

Second Appeal: Story

Subjects: Cree Nation • Dumont, Gabriel • Manitoba • Métis • Nineteenth Century • Riel, Louis • Riel Rebellion • Saskatchewan • Trilogies

Read On: Silver begins the <u>Red River Trilogy</u> with *Red River Story* and concludes with *Where the Ghost Horse Runs*, which returns again to Riel and the Rebellion. His other titles include *Acadia* and *The Haunting of*

Maddie Prue. Rudy Wiebe's *The Scorched-wood People* also looks at Dumont, Riel, and the Great Rebellion, as do books by Byrna Barclay (*Summer of the Hungry Pup*) and Giles A. Lutz (*The Magnificent Failure*). Jordan Zinovich tells Gabriel Dumont's story in *Gabriel Dumont in Paris: A Novel History.*

Sproxton, Birk.

The Red-headed Woman with the Black Black Heart. Turnstone Press, 1997. 188pp.

Mickey Marlowe, dubbed by the Royal Canadian Mounted Police as "the red-headed woman with the black, black heart," leads the women of a northern Manitoba mining town during the 1934 General Strike. In so doing, she changes the town and becomes one of its heroes; nonetheless, she still ends up in prison for her actions.

Second Appeal: Story

Subjects: First Novels • Flin Flon • Manitoba • Mining • Strikes and Lockouts

Read On: Sproxton's other works include *The Hockey Fan Came Riding* and *Headframe*. Margaret Sweatman's *Fox* chronicles Winnipeg's 1919 General Strike and depicts the women of that time. The harsh reality of the miner's life comes to light in Alistair MacLeod's *No Great Mischief* and in Sheldon Currie's *Down the Coaltown Road.*

Steffler, John.

♟ *The Afterlife of George Cartwright.* McClelland & Stewart, 1992. 296pp. Book Groups 📖

George Cartwright, explorer, soldier, and adventurer, died almost 170 years ago. His soul lives on, however, wandering through the world he had explored in the eighteenth century, reviewing things left unfinished in his lifetime. In his post-mortem travels he has the opportunity to witness the impact of his actions on the land and the people of Labrador both in his time and thereafter. Steffler won the Smithbooks/*Books in Canada* First Novel Award and the Thomas Head Raddall Atlantic Fiction Award, and was shortlisted for the Governor General's Literary Award for Fiction and the Commonwealth Writers Prize for Best First Book in the Caribbean and Canada.

Second Appeal: Story

Subjects: Aboriginal Peoples • Cartwright, George • First Novels • Frontier and Pioneer Life • Ghost Stories • Inuit • Newfoundland and Labrador

Read On: Michael Crummey's *River Thieves* also explores the European impact on the Aboriginal populations of Newfoundland and Labrador. The main protagonist in Joan Clark's *Latitudes of Melt* revisits episodes from her life and evaluates their impact on those who came after her. Annalita Marsigli's *The Written Script* is another story of life after death.

Stenson, Fred.

♟ *The Trade.* Douglas & McIntyre, 2000. 344pp. Book Groups 📖

A Hudson's Bay Company clerk, a fur trader, and the Métis son of a former governor are forever changed by a doomed journey into unmapped Indian Territory to discover new sources of beaver pelts in 1822. *The Trade* won the Grant MacEwan Author's Award, the Georges Bugnet Award for Best Novel, and the City of Edmonton Book Prize; it was also nominated for the Giller Prize.

Second Appeal: Story

Subjects: Canadian Northwest • Fur Trade • Hudson's Bay Company • Métis • Pioneers • Rowland, John

Read On: Stenson is the author of several works of fiction as well as books about the RCMP in the West and the Rocky Mountain House Trading Post. He won the Canadian Authors Association Award for Fiction for *Lonesome Hero*. Rudy Wiebe's *A Discovery of Strangers* and Brian Moore's *Black Robe* both explore the theme of European/Native conflict during the days of the fur trade. Stenson's episodic style of connecting his characters' lives to history and events is similar to Willa Cather's (*My Antonia* and others).

Suthren, Victor.

Edward Mainwaring Series.

These are the eighteenth-century seafaring adventures of Captain Edward Mainwaring, a colonial officer in the British Royal Navy. This series, originally published beginning in the late 1980s, was reissued by Hodder & Stoughton in the 1990s.

Royal Yankee. Hodder & Stoughton, 1996.

Golden Galleon. Hodder & Stoughton, 1997.

Admiral of Fear. Hodder & Stoughton, 1995.

Captain Monsoon. Hodder & Stoughton, 1995.

In 1744, following what appears to be a successful attack against the French, Captain Edward Mainwaring of the British Royal Navy is kidnapped and imprisoned. Escaping, he heads into battle on an ill-equipped ship against his nemesis, the Chevalier Rigaud de la Roche-Bourbon.

Subjects: Eighteenth Century • England • Mainwaring, Edward (Fictional Character) • Naval History • Sea Stories • War

Read On: Suthren's <u>Paul Gallant Series</u> features the exploits of a French-Canadian naval officer serving during the war with Great Britain. Suthren's stories portray eighteenth-century naval life and action on the high seas in the same storytelling style found in the novels of C. S. Forester, Alexander Kent, and Richard Woodman.

Sweatman, Margaret.

When Alice Lay Down with Peter. **Alfred A. Knopf Canada, 2001. 459pp. Book Groups** 📖

An epic spanning 100 years of Manitoba history, this is the humorous story of Alice and Peter, their descendants, and the prairie they live on. This novel received a number of prizes, namely the Carol Shields Winnipeg Book

Award, the Margaret Laurence Award for Fiction, the McNally Robinson Book of the Year, the Rogers Writers' Trust Fiction Prize, and the Sunburst Award.

Second Appeal: Language

Subjects: Aboriginal Peoples • Family Sagas • Frontier and Pioneer Life • Manitoba • Métis • Multi-generational Fiction • Revolutionaries

Read On: This award-winning author has also written other novels: *Fox* and *Sam and Angie*. Alistair MacLeod offers another multi-generational family story in *No Great Mischief*. Works set in Manitoba include the historical novels *The Red-headed Woman with the Black Black Heart* by Birk Sproxton, *Red River Story* by Alfred Silver, and the Aboriginal story *Kiss of the Fur Queen* by Tomson Highway.

Thomas, Audrey.

Isobel Gunn. Viking, 1999. 230pp. Book Groups 📖

A young Scottish woman, disguised as a man, works for the Hudson's Bay Company in 1806 until the birth of her son reveals her secret. After giving up the child for adoption and returning to Scotland, she spends the rest of her life longing for the child.

Second Appeal: Story

Subjects: Disguise • Gender Identity • Gunn, Isabel • Hudson's Bay Company • Manitoba • Mothers and Sons • Nineteenth Century • Pregnant Women

Read On: Thomas's other works include *Songs My Mother Taught Me*, *Graven Images*, *Coming Down from Wa*, and two collections of short stories, *The Wild Blue Yonder* and *The Path of Totality*. Another telling of the Isabel Gunn story is in Steven Scobie's long narrative poem, *The Ballad of Isabel Gunn*. *Climates of Our Birth* by Stuart James Whitley features Isabel Gunn's son. Stories of strong women living in the early days of Canadian history come alive in Margaret Atwood's *Alias Grace*, Jane Urquhart's *Away,* and Susanna Moodie's classic *Roughing It in the Bush, or, Life in Canada*. Fred Stenson recounts the role of the Hudson's Bay Company in Canadian history in *The Trade*.

Wiebe, Armin.

🎗 *Tatsea.* Turnstone Press, 2003. 249pp. Book Groups 📖

A young Dogrib woman and her husband find themselves on parallel journeys of survival in the Northwest Territories in the 1700s when Tatsea is taken captive during a raid on their village by a rival tribe, and Ikotsali, her husband, then searches for her. *Tatsea* won the Margaret Laurence Award for Fiction and the Manitoba Book of the Year Award.

Subjects: 1700s • Aboriginal Peoples • Dogrib Nation • Love Stories • Northwest Territories • Survival

Read On: Novels by both Bernard Assiniwi (*The Beothuk Saga*) and Michael Crummey (*River Thieves*) recount stories of Native contact with Europeans in the early days of Canada's exploration. The spiritual undertones and strong, well-drawn characters in this novel are also found in Eden Robinson's *Monkey Beach*. Wiebe's first novel, *The Salvation of Yasch Siemens,* was nominated for the Amazon.ca/ *Books in Canada* First Novel Award and The Stephen Leacock Memorial Medal for Humour.

Wiebe, Rudy.

A Discovery of Strangers. **Alfred A. Knopf Canada, 1994. 317pp. Book Groups** 📖

In the 1820s, on an ill-fated expedition in search of the Northwest Passage, Robert Hood, a member of Sir John Franklin's crew, has an affair with a young Yellowknife Native. Wiebe won the Governor General's Literary Award for Fiction for this title as well as for an earlier novel, *The Temptations of Big Bear*.

Second Appeal: Story

Subjects: Aboriginal Peoples • Arctic Regions • Exploration • Franklin, Sir John • Northwest Passage • Yellowknife Nation

Read On: Among Wiebe's other works are the historical fiction titles *The Scorched-wood People* and *The Mad Trapper*. Franklin's expedition to find the Northwest Passage is also chronicled in John Wilson's *North with Franklin: The Lost Journals of James Fitzjames* and Robert Edric's *The Broken Lands*. *Frozen in Time: The Fate of the Franklin Expedition* by Owen Beattie and John Geiger and *Ice Blink: The Tragic Fate of Sir John Franklin's Lost Polar Expedition* by Scott Cookman are non-fiction accounts of this tragic expedition.

Chapter 2

Story

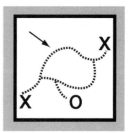

The reader who likes a good story is generally more interested in novels that emphasize situations or events over the people who are experiencing them, being pulled through the story by the events or storytelling, wondering what the impact on or consequences for the characters will be. That said, of course a well-told story will combine several of the appeal factors, intriguing characters, interesting place or time, and finely wrought sentences that draw the reader along, such as in Margaret Atwood's *The Blind Assassin*. However, in the case of story, events and "action" will take precedence over individual characters. This is certainly the case in Alistair MacLeod's *No Great Mischief*, where the reader keeps turning the pages to learn the fate of a family over many years, and experiences their joys, tears, and tragedies.

One appeal for the reader of novels that are story-driven is that there is usually a high degree of action; events tend to unfold swiftly, with the plot quickly revealed, drawing the reader into the tale. In Will Ferguson's *Generica* the reader cannot wait to learn what will happen to the book editor who publishes the self-help book that actually works. In Mary Lawson's *Crow Lake*, as the tale of a family of orphans unfolds, the reader moves through the story to discover how four children will "survive" tragically losing their parents. Another characteristic of this type of novel is that it often features more dialogue than lengthy descriptive passages of thoughts, feelings, or emotions. The dialogue does not always need to take the form of direct conversation; in fact authors can be quite creative and imaginative in the ways their characters interact. In his <u>Griffin & Sabine Series</u>, Nick Bantock's characters correspond via beautifully illustrated postcards, a correspondence that is clearly a love story. Diaries and letters are another way in which authors allow the voices of characters to be heard. These are quickly read and yet provide depth to the reader's understanding of the characters and events unfolding. In Joe Fiorito's *The Song Beneath the Ice* or John Miller's *The Featherbed* the story is revealed through notebooks and diaries, providing both the characters in the novels and the reader an insight into what has happened to those whose words they are reading. The illustrated novels of Barbara Hodgson (*Hippolyte's Island* and others) draw the reader in through beautifully wrought illustrations and maps.

When discussing a book read and enjoyed in the past, the reader will often first describe or articulate what happens in the story before telling who the characters are. For this reader it is clearly what happens that takes precedence, not to whom it happens. Therefore, the advisor working with a reader whose preference is for story will want to listen to how the reader details previous reading experiences.

Adams, Sylvia.

This Weather of Hangmen. General Store Publishing House, 1996. 268pp.

After the charred remains of the Luckey family are discovered in their Eastern Ontario farmhouse, Charlie Luckey is tried, convicted, and executed. The question remains however: Was he guilty or was this a copycat crime of the Lizzie Borden killings of just months before?

Subjects: 1890s • Borden, Lizzie • Murder • Ontario • Trials (Murder)

Read On: Meet Lizzie Borden again as the subject in Elizabeth Engstrom's *Lizzie Borden* and Walter Satterthwait's *Miss Lizzie*. To witness the investigation and unravelling of another Victorian crime, read Margaret Atwood's *Alias Grace*. James King tells the story of another Canadian woman (Evelyn Dick) convicted of murder in *Blue Moon*.

Allen, Charlotte Vale.

Grace Notes. Mira, 2002. 220pp.

Author Grace Loring, a survivor of wife abuse, corresponds via e-mail with a young woman claiming to be in an abusive relationship. When the messages suddenly stop, Grace, fearing the worst, investigates and discovers things are not always as they seem.

Subjects: Abusive Relationships • Battered Women • Electronic Mail Messages • Mothers and Daughters • Runaway Wives • Women Authors

Read On: Women's capacity to survive and overcome adversity is a theme Allen revisits in both *Painted Lives* and *Leftover Dreams*. Elizabeth Forsythe Hailey's *Home Free*, Judith Guest's *Errands,* and Beth Gutcheon's *Domestic Pleasures* all feature women striving to do their best in difficult times. The psychological suspense in *Grace Notes* is also present in Joy Fielding's *Missing Pieces*. Stephanie D. Fletcher's *E-mail: A Love Story* unfolds in electronic messages. Allen's autobiography, *Daddy's Girl,* is a personal telling of the impact incest had on her life as an adult and parent.

Amernic, Jerry.

Gift of the Bambino. Boheme Press, 2002. 219pp. Book Groups 📖

Young dreams and old memories bring together Stephen Slack and his grandfather, Lazo Slackowicz, who, as a young boy in 1914, witnessed Babe Ruth's first professional home run.

Subjects: Baseball • Baseball Players • Coming of Age • Fathers and Sons • Grandfathers • Prohibition • Ruth, Babe • Toronto

Read On: The Babe has appeared in other fictional works, including Bernard Malamud's *The Natural* and Heywood Broun's *The Sun Field*. Baseball is at the heart of hopes and dreams in W. P. Kinsella's *Shoeless Joe*, which was the basis for the movie *Field of Dreams*.

Appignanesi, Lisa.

Kicking Fifty. McArthur & Co., 2003. 348pp.

Jude Brautigan, divorced mother and bookstore owner, has used the art of letter writing to cope with the demands of an aging parent and an often-rebellious teenage daughter. Now approaching fifty, Jude finds herself rebelling in totally unexpected ways against her loss of youth.

> **Subjects:** Alzheimer's Disease • Bookstores • Divorced Women • Humorous Fiction • Love Stories • Middle-aged Women • Mothers and Daughters • Single Mothers

> **Read On:** Appignanesi has written a number of thrillers, including *Sanctuary and The Dead of Winter*. Her non-fiction title *Losing the Dead* was nominated for the Charles Taylor Prize for Literary Non-fiction in 2000. The mid-life plight of women is both poignantly and humorously examined in Joan Barfoot's *Getting Over Edgar*, Mary Sheepshanks's *Picking up the Pieces,* and Maeve Binchy's *Tara Road*.

Arnopoulos, Sheila.

Jackrabbit Moon. Ronsdale Press, 2000. 425pp.

Montreal Tribune journalist Maggie MacKinnan questions whether the justice system applies to everyone equally as she covers the trial of a biker and a stripper accused of murdering their infant.

> **Subjects:** Child Abuse • First Novels • Journalists • Montreal • Murder • Quebec • Women Journalists

> **Read On:** Harper Lee examines injustice in *To Kill a Mockingbird* when a black man accused of raping a white woman is put on trial. Questions concerning the justice system are raised in Don Carpenter's *The Dispossessed* and *The Sabbathday River* by Jean Hanff Korelitz. Arnopoulos co-authored *The English Fact in Quebec,* which won a Governor General's Literary Award for Nonfiction.

Atwood, Margaret.

¶ *The Blind Assassin*. McClelland & Stewart, 2000. 521pp. Book Groups 📖

Now nearing the end of her life, eighty-two-year-old Iris, hoping to leave a written legacy for her estranged granddaughter, chronicles the often-tragic events that shaped the lives of her sister Laura and herself. As the past reflects on the present, Laura's novel "The Blind Assassin," posthumously published by Iris following her sister's death at age twenty-five, tells a fantastical tale of a society and love lost, a tale that often mirrors their own lives. Atwood was awarded the Booker Prize and the Dashiell Hammett Award for Best Literary Crime Novel for this work; she was also nominated for several other prizes, namely the Toronto Book Award, the CBA Libris Award: Fiction Book of the Year, the

Governor General's Literary Award for Fiction, the Orange Prize, the International IMPAC Dublin Literary Award for the Novel, and the Alcuin Society Design Award. *The Blind Assassin* was also an ALA Notable Book.

Second Appeal: Language

Subjects: Death of a Sibling • Elderly Women • Love Affairs • Mothers and Daughters • Novels-within-Novels • Ontario • Sisters • Toronto • Widows • Women's Lives

Read On: Atwood is also the author of *Oryx and Crake*, *Lady Oracle*, *The Robber Bride,* and *Cat's Eye*, among many other novels and short-story collections. She explored the theme of the role of women in society in *The Handmaid's Tale* and *Alias Grace*; this is also the topic of Edith Wharton's *The House of Mirth*. The layered story-within-a-story structure is also used in Kate Atkinson's *Emotionally Weird*, Ellen Gilchrist's *The Anna Papers,* and Carol Shields's *Swann*. Elderly women narrate their life stories in distinctive voices in Jessica Anderson's *Tirra Lirra by the River*, Angela Carter's *Wise Children*, Margaret Laurence's *The Stone Angel,* and Carol Shields's *The Stone Diaries*. In *Three Junes*, Julia Glass also skilfully explores the tragic events of a family over the course of a number of years.

Baldwin, Shauna Singh.

The Tiger Claw. Alfred A. Knopf Canada, 2004. 570pp. Book Groups 📖

Noor is a Sorbonne-educated Muslim woman in Nazi-occupied France. She works there as a radio operator and resistance agent, hoping to reunite with her Jewish lover Armand, a musician. Betrayed, Noor is imprisoned, and as she awaits execution she records an account of the events of her life and the consequences of the decisions she made in her pursuit of love. Baldwin was shortlisted for the Giller Prize for this novel.

Second Appeal: Character

Subjects: France • Inayat Khan, Noor-un-Nisa • Jewish Men • Love Stories • Muslims • Resistance Movement • War • Women Spies

Read On: Baldwin's short-story collection *English Lessons and Other Stories*, and her earlier novel *What the Body Remembers,* both examine the relationship between women and men. *The Tiger Claw* was inspired by the life of Noor Inayat Khan, a Muslim woman who worked against the Nazi occupation of France and who was awarded a George Cross, the Croix de Guerre, and an MBE for her war efforts. Khan's activities are recorded in William Stevenson's *A Man Called Intrepid*. Nancy Richler's protagonist in *Your Mouth Is Lovely* is another woman who records her life story in a prison journal. Wayne Johnston's *The Colony of Unrequited Dreams* and David Adams Richards's *River of the Brokenhearted* are other novels that create a relationship between a real-life hero and a fictional character.

Bantock, Nick.

Griffin & Sabine Series.

A series of illustrated letters chronicles the relationships between London artist Griffin Moss and a mysterious South Pacific Island woman, Sabine Strohem.

Subjects: Archaeologists • Artists • Epistolary Novels • Imaginary Histories • Imaginary Places • Letters • Love Stories • Moss, Griffin (Fictional Character) • Strohem, Sabine (Fictional Character)

Griffin and Sabine. Chronicle Books, 1991.

The arrival of a postcard from a woman he has never met begins a unique relationship, through illustrated letters, between London artist Griffin Moss and a mysterious South Pacific Island woman, Sabine Strohem. This unusual work was nominated for a Locus Non-fiction Award, as well as a Crawford Award.

Sabine's Notebook. Chronicle Books, 1992.

The Golden Mean. Chronicle Books, 1993.

The Gryphon. Chronicle Books, 2001.

Alexandria. Chronicle Books, 2002.

The Morning Star. Chronicle Books, 2003.

> **Read On:** *Postcard Fictions* is a collaborative work between writer Michelle Berry and artist Andrew Valko. He creates a series of paintings, each one like a postcard, while she weaves a short story about two people in a motel. Other examples of epistolary novels include *Alice's Tulips* by Sandra Dallas, *The Love Letter* by Cathleen Schine, and *Clara Callan* by Richard B. Wright. *The Jolly Postman, or, Other People's Letters* by Janet Ahlberg and Allan Ahlberg (a work for children) is similar to Bantock's work in its use of letters that must be removed from envelopes to reveal the story.

Bates, Judy Fong.

Midnight at the Dragon Café. McClelland & Stewart, 2004. 315pp. Book Groups 📖

> While recounting her family's difficult life running a restaurant in a small Ontario town, a young Chinese girl is burdened by family secrets as she attempts to understand her place in two worlds—one Chinese and the other Canadian.
>
> **Second Appeal:** Character
>
> **Subjects:** Chinese Canadians • Chinese in Ontario • Culture Clash • Family Secrets • First Novels • Immigrants and Refugees • Ontario • Small-town Life
>
> **Read On:** The children in Wayson Choy's *The Jade Peony* also struggle with the conflict between the old Chinese ways of their parents and the values and practices of a life in Canada. The immigrant experience is further explored in Bharati Mukherjee's *Jasmine*, Anita Rau Badami's *Tamarind Mem*, and Neil Bissoondath's *The Worlds Within Her*, to name but a few. Nino Ricci's *Lives of the Saints* is another first novel featuring a young person struggling to understand family dynamics.

Bath, Dana.

Plenty of Harm in God. DC Books, 2001. 215pp.

> Twenty-year-old Clare, despondent and pregnant, travels from Newfoundland to Ireland to fulfill a five-year–old suicide pact but discovers that there are people from the past who believe in her potential.

Second Appeal: Character

Subjects: Canadians in Ireland • First Novels • Ireland • Newfoundland and Labrador • Pregnant Women • Suicide

Read On: The sense of desperation and loneliness evoked here emerges in Aritha van Herk's *Restlessness*, in which an older woman contemplates suicide. Maeve Binchy also makes her readers feel right at home in the villages of Ireland that provide the setting for her novels (*Circle of Friends* and others). Faith, family secrets, and the past all connect in Priscila Uppal's *The Divine Economy of Salvation*. A suicide pact ends tragically in *The Pact* by Jodi Picoult.

Bergen, David.

🎗 *A Year of Lesser*. **HarperCollins, 1996. 215pp. Book Groups** 📖

Bergen's debut novel recounts a year in the life of Lesser, a small Canadian town, according to Johnny Fehr, his wife Charlene, and his pregnant mistress, Loraine. This novel was the McNally Robinson Book of the Year and a *New York Times* Notable Book.

Second Appeal: Character

Subjects: Adultery • Country Life • First Novels • Love Affairs • Male–Female Relationships • Manitoba • Prairies • Single Parents • Small-town Life

Read On: Bergen has also published a collection of short stories, *Sitting Opposite My Brother,* and the novels *See the Child* and *The Case of Lena S.* In Richard B. Wright's *Adultery*, a man must confront the implications of his actions when he engages in an adulterous affair. Small-town life is also nicely portrayed in Judy Troy's *West of Venus*, Jonis Agee's *South of Resurrection*, and Tom Drury's *The End of Vandalism.*

Blackbridge, Persimmon.

Prozac Highway. **Press Gang Publishers, 1997. 267pp. Book Groups** 📖

Lesbian performance artist Jane, moving deeper into depression, self-mutilation, and self-destruction, reaches out to an Internet listserv, connecting with others who are also struggling with mental illness and the drugs commonly used as remedies. Blackbridge was nominated for the Lambda Literary Award for Best Lesbian Fiction and the American Library Association's Gay, Lesbian and Bisexual Book Award (now called the ALA Stonewall Book Award).

Second Appeal: Character

Subjects: Black Humour • Depression, Mental • Humorous Fiction • Lesbians • Mental Illness • Performance Arts

Read On: Blackbridge's first novel, *Sunnybrook: A True Story with Lies,* also explores the theme of mental illness and coping with society, as does Madelyn Arnold's *Bird-Eyes*. The main character in Robert Majzels's *Hellman's Scrapbook* shares the despair found here and is ultimately institutionalized in an attempt to stop his spiralling self-destruction. The characters in Leslie Edgerton's short-story collection *Monday's Meal* live on the fringe of society. Middle-aged lesbians are characters in Helen Hodgman's *Passing Remarks* and Edith Konecky's *A Place at the Table.*

Burke, Martyn.

Ivory Joe. Bantam Books, 1991. 303pp.

Young sisters Christie and Ruthie scheme to reunite their divorced parents Leo and Tina, respectively the owner of a New York garment factory with possible Mafia ties and a sometime political activist and manager of the black rock group Ivory Joe and the Classics. This story unfolds against the backdrop of the early days of rock and roll in the 1950s.

Subjects: 1950s • Bands • Coming of Age • Dressmakers • Fathers and Daughters • Mothers and Daughters • Musicians • New York City • Sisters • Women Promoters

Read On: Burke continues Christy and Ruth's story in *The Shelling of Beverly Hills.* His other novels include *Laughing War, The Commissar's Report,* and *Tiara.* Dave Margoshes's *I'm Frankie Sterne* is another novel with musical connections set in a similar time period. Two sisters learn the value of family bonds in *Sometimes I Dream in Italian* by Rita Ciresi. To meet more sisters coming of age in the 1950s, read *Night of Many Dreams* by Gail Tsukiyama and *Delia's Way* by Olga Berrocal Essex.

Butala, Sharon.

The Garden of Eden. HarperFlamingoCanada, 1998. 387pp. Book Groups 📖

Following the death of her husband Barney, a grieving Iris travels from Saskatchewan to Ethiopia to search for her estranged niece Lannie and to discover an identity apart from wife. *The Garden of Eden* was shortlisted for two Saskatchewan Book Awards: the Book of the Year and the award for Fiction.

Second Appeal: Character

Subjects: Canadians in Ethiopia • Ethiopia • Farmers' Spouses • Married Women • Prairies • Saskatchewan

Read On: Butala, who won the Marian Engel Award in 1998, tells Iris and Lannie's story before they became estranged in *Country of the Heart.* Bette Ann Moskowitz's *Leaving Barney* features another newly widowed woman who is seeking a new future for herself, and in Lolly Winston's *Good Grief* a young woman must leave her life behind as she works through a widow's grief after only three years of marriage. Butala's exploration of prairie life parallels Elizabeth Hay's in *A Student of Weather.*

Caple, Natalee.

Mackerel Sky. Thomas Allen, 2004. 254pp.

After almost twenty years Guy travels to a remote area north of Montreal to meet his adult daughter and to try to renew his relationship with his daughter's mother Martine. Instead of the family reunion he had hoped for, Guy finds himself involved in Martine's family business, the counterfeiting of U.S. dollars.

Second Appeal: Language

Subjects: Birth Fathers • Counterfeiting • Family Relationships • Fathers and Daughters • Mothers and Daughters • Quebec • Triangles

Read On: Caple is the author of a collection of poetry, *A More Tender Ocean*, and two earlier works of fiction, *The Heart Is Its Own Reason* and *The Plight of Happy People in an Ordinary World*. Andrew Pyper's *Lost Girls* and Mark Sinnett's *The Border Guards* are also vividly created crime stories filled with eccentric characters. Alice Hoffman (*Practical Magic* and *The Probable Future*) also features strong matriarchs in her novels.

Choyce, Lesley.

Sea of Tranquility. Dundurn Press, 2003. 311pp.

When the Nova Scotia government decides to discontinue ferry service to their island, the residents of Ragged Island, including eighty-year-old, four-time widow Sylvie Young, look for ways to save their home in order to safeguard their way of life.

Second Appeal: Character

Subjects: Acadia • Humorous Fiction • Island People • Nova Scotia • Small-town Life

Read On: Earlier novels by Choyce include *The Ecstasy Conspiracy* and *The Republic of Nothing*. He has also written a short-story collection, *Trapdoor to Heaven*, as well as numerous young adult titles. Readers will be reminded of the personal struggles facing the characters in Carol Shields's *Unless*. The gentle humour expressed here by Maritimers is at the heart of Alistair MacLeod's *No Great Mischief*. The eccentricities of everyday life in a small town are portrayed in the novels of Jan Karon (*At Home in Mitford* and others) and Adriana Trigiani (*Big Stone Gap* and others).

Clark, Joan.

Latitudes of Melt. Alfred A. Knopf Canada, 2000. 332pp. Book Groups 📖

Discovered in a basket on an ice floe as an infant and then adopted by her rescuer, Aurora, always considered a changeling by the residents of her small Newfoundland fishing village, becomes an accepted member of the community. It is only when Aurora is an old woman that her granddaughter solves the mystery of her heritage. Clark was awarded the 1991 Marian Engel award, and *Latitudes of Melt* was a finalist for the International IMPAC Dublin Literary Award for the Novel and the Commonwealth Writers Prize for Best Book in the Caribbean and Canada.

Second Appeal: Character

Subjects: Fishing Villages • Foundlings • Lighthouse Keepers • Newfoundland and Labrador • *Titanic* (Steamship) • Women

Read On: The spirit-like characters found in this novel resemble those in Kim Echlin's *Dagmar's Daughter*. Donna Morrissey explores the dynamics of a family in a small Newfoundland fishing village in *Kit's Law* and *Downhill Chance*. The passion of the residents of Newfoundland for their home is also portrayed in Wayne Johnston's *The Colony of Unrequited Dreams*. Clark's *Eiriksdottir* describes an earlier ill-fated voyage, that of the Greenlanders and Icelanders to Vinland in the early 1010s.

Conlin, Christy Ann.

Heave. Doubleday Canada, 2002. 322pp. Book Groups

When twenty-one-year-old Serrie leaves her groom at the altar, she reflects on how a life of excess has brought her to this moment and questions the connections among generations of a small-town family. *Heave* was nominated for the Amazon.ca/*Books in Canada* First Novel Award, the Dartmouth Book Award for Fiction, and the Thomas Head Raddall Atlantic Fiction Award.

> **Second Appeal:** Character
>
> **Subjects:** Coming of Age • Family Chronicles • Family Relationships • First Novels • Mental Illness • Nova Scotia • Self-discovery • Small-town Life
>
> **Read On:** Lynn Coady's *Saints of Big Harbour* and Donna Morrissey's *Kit's Law* both explore family life in small Maritime towns. The young women in Kaylie Jones's *Celeste Ascending* and Angie Day's *The Way to Somewhere,* reflecting on the past, realize they must learn how to move beyond it.

Corey, Deborah Joy.

Losing Eddie. Algonquin Books of Chapel Hill, 1993. 222pp. Book Groups

A rural New Brunswick family struggles after the death of their eldest child, while nine-year-old Laura, watching and listening, acquires an understanding far beyond her years. Corey was awarded the Chapters/*Books in Canada* First Novel Award for this work.

> **Subjects:** Alcoholics • Brothers and Sisters • Coming of Age • Death of a Child • Dysfunctional Families • First Novels • Girls • New Brunswick • Poverty
>
> **Read On:** Other novels that explore the effect of the loss of a child on other family members include Anne Tyler's *The Tin Can Tree*, Luanne Rice's *Home Fires*, two of Jane Hamilton's novels, *The Short History of a Prince* and *A Map of the World*, Linda Gray Sexton's *Points of Light,* and Ian McEwan's *The Child in Time*.

Coupland, Douglas.

Microserfs. HarperCollins, 1995. 371pp.

Dan Underwood and his housemates spend their days and nights as slaves to the software industry, breaking from work only occasionally to consume junk food and contemplate pop culture. But when they begin to search for some meaning in their lives, they enter unfamiliar emotional territory.

> **Second Appeal:** Character
>
> **Subjects:** 1990s • Family Relationships • Friendship • Generation X • Humorous Fiction • Male–Female Relationships • Microsoft Corporation

Read On: Coupland's other books include *Life After God, Shampoo Planet, Generation X,* and *Girlfriend in a Coma.* Nick Hornby's *High Fidelity* and Andrew McGahan's *1988* are other books about life and love from a Generation X point of view. Julio Cortázar's *Hopscotch* is a novel about alienation and existential dilemmas.

Courtemanche, Gil.

A Sunday at the Pool in Kigali. **Alfred A. Knopf Canada, 2003. 258pp. Book Groups** 📖

Courtemanche, a journalist, has given witness to one of the more recent occurrences of man's humanity to man, the genocide in Rwanda. He has woven a tender love story between a French-Canadian journalist and a Hutu waitress who looks like a Tutsi into the dreadful fabric of mass murder by machete or grenade. But he does not allow the reader to forget that other killer, AIDS, which in 1994 in Rwanda became the preferable way to die. Many characters in the novel are real, and Courtemanche has given the fictional characters the names of friends he knew. This debut novel was awarded the Prix des Libraires du Québec for the original French and was a Canada Reads winning title. The English version was nominated for the Governor General's Literary Award for Translation and for the Rogers Writers' Trust Fiction Prize. Translated from the French [*Un dimanche à la piscine à Kigali*] by Patricia Claxton.

> **Second Appeal:** Character
>
> **Subjects:** 1994 • AIDS • First Novels • French Canadian • Genocide • Interracial Romance • Journalists • Love Stories • Massacres • Rwanda • Translations
>
> **Read On:** There are various facets to the prism of the Rwanda genocide, and several works have been written to explore them. *Shake Hands with the Devil* (Roméo Dallaire) recounts the experience of the Canadian Force Commander of UNAMIR, the United Nations Peacekeeping Force. Dallaire appears in Courtemanche's novel but is never mentioned by name. *We Wish to Inform You That Tomorrow We Will Be Killed with Our Families: Stories from Rwanda* (Philip Gourevitch) focuses on the victims themselves, corralled into churches and slaughtered, completely abandoned by all members of the Western world. But the Western world arrives after the fact, as witnessed in part by forensic anthropologist Clea Koff. In *The Bone Woman: A Forensic Anthropologist's Search for Truth in Rwanda, Bosnia, Croatia and Kosovo*, she writes about her experiences trying to identify the victims forensically, thereby bringing them some form of justice.

Cumyn, Alan.

Losing It. **McClelland & Stewart, 2001. 365pp. Book Groups** 📖

Ottawa-based Poe scholar Bob Sterling and his wife Julia struggle to survive a particularly stressful week. In New York at a conference with one of his students, Bob risks everything when she encourages him to fulfill a sexual fetish fantasy; his wife at home must cope with her mother's Alzheimer's. *Losing It* was shortlisted for the Ottawa Book Award.

> **Second Appeal:** Character
>
> **Subjects:** Alzheimer's Disease • Humorous Fiction • Male–Female Relationships • Marriage • Middle-aged Men • Poets • Teacher–Student Relationships • University Professors • Women Poets

Read On: Jonathan Franzen's family-driven novel, *The Corrections,* is definitely more humorous when compared to Cumyn's dark work. In a similar vein, *It's a Slippery Slope* by Spalding Gray ponders aging and the sometime vagaries of family life. Cumyn's other books include *Man of Bone,* winner of the Ottawa-Carleton Book Award and a finalist for the Trillium Book Award; *Burridge Unbound,* winner of the Ottawa Book Award and a finalist for the Giller Prize; and *Sojourn,* a novel set during World War I that explores the war through one soldier as he takes leave before an upcoming offensive.

Currie, Sheldon.

Down the Coaltown Road. **Key Porter Books, 2002. 279pp. Book Groups** 📖

During World War II, while Italian members of his parish are interned, Father Rod MacDonald attempts to work through his own theological doubts. This novel was shortlisted for the Dartmouth Book Award for Fiction.

Second Appeal: Character

Subjects: Cape Breton Island • Italian Canadians • Nova Scotia • Priests • Prisoners of War • World War II

Read On: *Gaff Topsails* by Patrick Kavanagh is also set in a small town on the East Coast and includes in its cast a lonely priest. Mary Doria Russell's *The Sparrow* features a priest who experiences a crisis of faith. The internment experience is related in Joy Kogawa's *Obasan,* Julie Otsuka's *When the Emperor Was Divine,* and Ernest Finney's *California Time.*

Daigle, France.

🎗 *Just Fine.* **House of Anansi Press, 1999. 148pp. Book Groups** 📖

A successful writer has been asked to travel to France for an interview, something she would love to do. Unbeknownst to her family and friends, however, she is agoraphobic, and has no idea how she will succeed in leaving her house and getting on a plane. Telling those she loves about her illness will prove to be even more difficult for her. In addition to being awarded a Governor General's Literary Award for Translation, this work also received the Prix France-Acadie and Prix Littéraire Antonine Maillet-Acadie-Vie. Translated from the French [*Pas pire*] by Robert Majzels.

Second Appeal: Character

Subjects: Acadia • Agoraphobia • French Canadian • Translations • Writers

Read On: Daigle's *A Fine Passage* shares characters with *Just Fine*; she also wrote *1953: Chronicle of a Birth Foretold.* Agoraphobic women suffer in Marjorie Reynolds's *The Starlite Drive-in,* Michael Lee West's *American Pie,* and Cris Mazza's *How to Leave a Country.* Other experimental novels include Hazard Adams's *Many Pretty Toys,* Hiber Conteris's *Ten Percent of Life,* and Christine Brooke-Rose's *Amalgamemnon.*

Dearing, Sarah.

🎗 *Courage My Love.* Stoddart, 2001. 196pp. Book Groups 📖

Philipa, feeling trapped as an ad executive's trophy wife, throws off her old life in Yorkville and starts over with a lifestyle change in Kensington Market, under a new name. This novel received the Toronto Book Award.

Subjects: Marriage • Ontario • Runaway Wives • Toronto

Read On: Constance Beresford-Howe's *The Book of Eve*, Prue Leith's *Leaving Patrick*, Anne Tyler's *Ladder of Years,* and Elizabeth Berg's *The Pull of the Moon* all tell a woman's story when she abandons her family to find herself.

den Hartog, Kristen.

Water Wings. Alfred A. Knopf Canada, 2001. 225pp. Book Groups 📖

Darlene Oelpke is marrying for the second time. Her daughters Hannah and Vivian, her sister Angie, and her niece Wren all take turns revisiting the events of their common past in small-town Ontario as they prepare for the wedding.

Second Appeal: Character

Subjects: Coming of Age • Death of a Parent • Divorce • First Novels • Mothers and Daughters • Remarriage • Sisters • Small-town Life • Young Women

Read On: Alice Munro's stories are filled with characters from small-town Ontario. Other novels in which the story and characters are painted with a "delicate hand" are Bonnie Bluh's *The Eleanor Roosevelt Girls*, Lorna Landvik's *Your Oasis on Flame Lake*, and Brenda Jernigan's *Every Good and Perfect Gift*. The novels of T. Coraghessan Boyle (*The Tortilla Curtain*) and Barbara Kingsolver (*The Poisonwood Bible*) are told from shifting points of view.

Denoon, Anne.

Back Flip. Porcupine's Quill, 2002. 323pp.

In the insular world of the Toronto art community of 1967, various artists, all at different points in their artistic lives, present their own versions of the disappearance of a painting by emerging artist Eddie O'Hara.

Subjects: 1960s • Art Collectors • Art Galleries, Commercial • Art Museums • Artists • First Novels • Ontario • Satire • Toronto

Read On: Greg Kramer's *The Pursemonger of Fugu* is another story set within the Toronto art world, as are Ursula Pflug's *Green Music* and Roxane Ward's *Fits Like a Rubber Dress*. Joseph Geary's *Spiral* is set in the New York art world of the sixties. Tension and suspense are created around a missing painting in Peter Watson's *Landscape of Lies*.

Dickinson, Don.

Robbiestime. HarperFlamingoCanada, 2000. 324pp. Book Groups 📖

When his mother and brother suddenly journey to England during the summer of 1958, eleven-year-old Robbie attempts to understand the events that have shaped his family, including the lingering impact of World War II on his parents, a veteran and an English war bride.

Second Appeal: Character

Subjects: 1950s • Boys • Children of World War II Veterans • Coming of Age • Family • Mothers Deserting Their Families • Saskatchewan • World War II

Read On: Young boys try to come to terms with the changes in their lives and families in Nino Ricci's *Lives of the Saints*, Frederick Reuss's *Henry of Atlantic City,* and Peter Hedges's *An Ocean in Iowa*. Dickinson's style of storytelling is reminiscent of Roddy Doyle's *Paddy Clarke, Ha Ha Ha*. For another coming-of-age story set on the prairies, read W. O. Mitchell's *Who Has Seen the Wind*.

Dohaney, Myrtis T.

A Fit Month for Dying. **Goose Lane Editions, 2000. 213pp. Book Groups**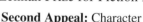

Tess Corrigan, Newfoundland's first female member of the House of Assembly, is a woman who believes in commitment. It is this standard of conduct that drives her to seek out the father she never knew and to insist that her twelve-year-old son fulfill his commitment as an altar boy at their church, a decision that will have tragic consequences.

Second Appeal: Setting

Subjects: Catholics • Child Abuse • Family Relationships • Newfoundland and Labrador • Politicians • St. John's • Suicide • Trilogies • Women Politicians

Read On: Dohaney began her trilogy focusing on women of Newfoundland with *The Corrigan Women* and *To Scatter Stones*. Bernice Morgan's *Random Passage* and *Waiting for Time* provide the Protestant perspective of life in traditional Newfoundland. The young title character in *The Confessions of Nipper Mooney* (Patrick Kavanagh) also comes under the influence of the Church when his mother sends him off to a school run by the Christian Brothers. Wayne Johnston's *The Story of Bobby O'Malley* is a humorous coming-of-age story about a young Newfoundland Catholic boy.

Ferguson, Trevor.

🎗 *The Timekeeper.* **HarperCollins, 1995. 241pp. Book Groups**

Young Martin Bishop begins a journey toward manhood when he joins an Alberta railway-section gang as the timekeeper and finds he must face both moral and physical challenges. Ferguson received the Hugh MacLennan Prize for Fiction for this novel.

Second Appeal: Character

Subjects: Coming of Age • Northwest Territories • Railroad Construction • Railroads • Young Men

Read On: The railroad and its construction are the source of a variety of stories throughout North America, including Ferguson's other work, *The Fire Line*. More examples are William Hauptman's *The Storm Season*, in which a boy journeys to manhood along the railroad; and *Short Lines*, a collection of stories edited by Rob Johnson about differing aspects of the railroad. *The Road* by John Ehle also describes the building of the railroad, this time in North Carolina.

Ferguson, Will.

♥ *Generica.* **Penguin Books, 2001. 309pp. Book Groups** 📖

A satirical look at what can happen when a self-help book actually works, this novel received The Stephen Leacock Memorial Medal for Humour and the CAA Literary Award for Fiction.

Second Appeal: Character

Subject: 1990s • Authors • Book Publishing • Editors • First Novels • Happiness • Humorous Fiction • Satire • Self-help Books

Read On: *Generica* was later reprinted with the title *Happiness*. In *Men in Black*, Scott Spencer's character must also deal with the consequences of writing a best-selling novel. To read more about the publishing world look at Steve Martini's *The List*, which features a female novelist. In *Mount Misery*, Samuel Shem takes a satirical look at mental illness and its treatment, discovering that the cure may be worse than the disease.

Fielding, Joy.

Grand Avenue. **Doubleday Canada, 2001. 392pp.**

Four women become close friends when they meet in a park with their small children. Later one of the four looks back on their lives together, remembering the good and the bad, including the murder of one of the women.

Second Appeal: Character

Subjects: Cincinnati • Murder • Ohio • Women's Friendships

Read On: For stories about groups of women who join together in friendship you may want to look at *The Book Club* by Mary Alice Monroe, *Friendship Cake* by Lynne Hinton, or *The Last Girls* by Lee Smith. Joy Fielding is the author of several other stories about women, including *Lost* and *Whispers and Lies*.

Fiorito, Joe.

♥ *The Song Beneath the Ice.* **McClelland & Stewart, 2002. 347pp. Book Groups** 📖

Journalist Joe Serafino's childhood friend, an acclaimed concert pianist, mysteriously disappeared more than a year ago when he walked off the concert stage mid-performance. When Joe receives a package of tapes and notebooks from the Northwest Territories, he attempts to understand his friend's motive for seeking a new life in the North. Fiorito won the Toronto Book Award for this novel.

Second Appeal: Setting

Subjects: Baffin Island • Diaries • First Novels • Gould, Glenn • Musicians • Nunavut • Pianists • Toronto

Read On: Fiorito has also written a family memoir, *The Closer We Are to Dying*. In Thomas Bernhard's *The Loser*, Glenn Gould is the object of the narrator's obsession.

Cat's Eye by Margaret Atwood and *Courage My Love* by Sarah Dearing are both set within the context of the Toronto art community. Other novels that vividly re-create Toronto are Michael Ondaatje's *In the Skin of a Lion* and Katherine Govier's *Hearts of Flame*.

Foster, Cecil.

Slammin' Tar. **Random House of Canada, 1998. 434pp. Book Groups** 📖

Johnny is one of a group of Barbadian migrant farm labourers who have been coming to Canada every year for twenty-five years to work on tobacco farms. Living in squalor, the displaced men struggle to earn a living to support the families they have left behind, while dreaming of a better life in Canada.

> **Second Appeal:** Character
>
> **Subjects:** Barbadians in Canada • Barbados • Migrant Workers • Ontario • Tobacco Workers
>
> **Read On:** The Black-Canadian experience is the subject of Foster's *Sleep On, Beloved*. His non-fiction work *A Place Called Heaven*, a study on racism in Canada, won the Gordon Montador Award for the Best Canadian Non-fiction Book on Social Issues. John Steinbeck's *The Grapes of Wrath* is a classic novel that relates the experience of the migrant worker. *Luck* by Eric Martin features the migrant tobacco worker, while *The Dark Side of the Dream* by Alejandro Grattan-Dominguez is about migrant fruit workers.

Fraser, Sylvia.

The Ancestral Suitcase. **Key Porter Books, 1996. 247pp.**

The discovery of an old suitcase containing family photos and mementos is the catalyst that transports professor of English literature Nora Locke from the present-day home of her deceased mother in Hamilton, Ontario, to the English village of Barrow in 1913, just prior to her grandmother's immigration to Canada. This journey back in time allows Nora the opportunity to come to terms with events of her own past as well as those of her mother and grandmother.

> **Subjects:** 1910s • England • Family Relationships • Hamilton • Mothers and Daughters • Travel • University Professors • Women Teachers
>
> **Read On:** Fraser's other novels include *Pandora, A Casual Affair, The Emperor's Virgin,* and *Berlin Solstice*. Fraser's repressed memories of abuse surfaced while she was writing *Berlin Solstice* and subsequently became the basis for her non-fiction work *My Father's House: A Memoir of Incest and Healing*—one of the first published memoirs that focused on the sexual abuse of children. Personal possessions spark an investigation into the past in Genni Gunn's *Tracing Iris*, Barbara Sapergia's *Secrets in Water,* and Merilyn Simonds's *The Holding*. The time travel element here is similar to that in Barbara Erskine's novels (*Whispers in the Sand* and others).

Gadd, Ben.

Raven's End: A Tale from the Canadian Rockies. McClelland & Stewart, 2001. 347pp.

Colin, an injured young raven with no memory, is rescued and taken in by the Raven End flock at Yamnuska, east of Banff. As he recovers and gains strength he discovers his power of second sight, a gift that will allow him to revisit his past and see his future.

Second Appeal: Setting

Subjects: Animals as Characters • First Novels • Ravens • Rocky Mountains, British Columbia and Alberta

Read On: Birds or animals embark on journeys of self-discovery in Richard Bach's *Jonathan Livingston Seagull* and Richard Adams's *Watership Down*. R. D. Lawrence personifies a family of pumas in *The White Puma*. For another unique story told by a non-human, try *Mrs. Chippy's Last Expedition* by Caroline Alexander. It is a first-hand account by a cat aboard the ship of Sir Ernest Shackleton's expedition when they spent the winter trapped in the ice in the Antarctic.

Gardiner, Scott.

The Dominion of Wyley McFadden. Random House of Canada, 2000. 337pp.

Wyley McFadden, former fertility doctor, is an urban trapper on a mission. He has set out from Toronto in his camper, intent on restoring the non-existent rat population to Alberta. Along the way he picks up a young woman hitchhiker, who eventually shares her own reasons for being on the road. This debut novel was shortlisted for the Amazon.ca/*Books in Canada* First Novel Award.

Second Appeal: Character

Subjects: Car Accidents • First Novels • Hitchhiking • Humorous Fiction • Prostitution • Quests • Road Novels • Trappers • Travel

Read On: Robert Kroetsch's *Gone Indian* features a character who embarks on a journey west and is drawn into a series of bizarre events. Charles Portis's *Norwood* is another road novel filled with eccentric characters. Like Louis de Bernières (*Birds Without Wings* and others), Gardiner blends moments of hilarity with the horrific to tell his story.

Giangrande, Carole.

A Forest Burning. Cormorant Books, 2000. 334pp.

When Vietnam vet and journalist Lorne Winter jumps from a helicopter into a raging forest fire, his suicide is caught on TV. This act brings his adopted son Gabe and friend Sally Groves together as they try to understand the past's influence on this very public death, and what it means for them.

Subjects: Aircraft Accidents • First Novels • Forest Fires • Ontario • Photographers • Suicide • Vietnamese Conflict • Women Pilots

Read On: In Nelson DeMille's *Up Country* a Vietnam vet returns to Vietnam and confronts the images of the war while investigating the death of a soldier during the conflict. The imagery of a forest fire underlies an emotional story of love and conflict in Pearl Luke's *Burning Ground.* Characters who travelled to Canada to avoid the Vietnam War appear in Tim O'Brien's *July, July* and Don Metz's *Catamount Bridge.* Giangrande's other works include a collection of short stories, *Missing Persons,* and a novel, *An Ordinary Star,* the story of an elderly woman reflecting on the events of her childhood, which began in the 1920s.

Gom, Leona.

Hating Gladys. **Sumach Press, 2002. 272pp. Book Groups** 📖

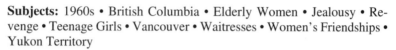

Events from a summer spent waitressing at a Yukon resort became for Kendy and Elke the genesis of a lifelong obsession. A chance encounter thirty-five years later with Gladys, their tyrant boss, leads them on a path toward revenge.

Subjects: 1960s • British Columbia • Elderly Women • Jealousy • Revenge • Teenage Girls • Vancouver • Waitresses • Women's Friendships • Yukon Territory

Read On: Gom is the author of the <u>Vicky Bauer Mystery Series</u> and the futurist novel *The Y Chromosome.* Janet Appleton's *That Summer* is also a story of a young woman working the summer before college. Aritha van Herk's protagonist works in the Yukon as a bush-cook in *The Tent Peg.*

Goto, Hiromi.

🎗 *Chorus of Mushrooms.* **NeWest Press, 1994. 222pp. Book Groups** 📖

Past and present clash as three generations of Japanese-Canadian women find themselves in conflict while each adapts to life in small-town rural Alberta. Grandmother Obachan Naoe speaks no English, her daughter Keiko Tonkatsu refuses to speak Japanese, and Muriel/Murasaki is the granddaughter caught between two cultures. Goto received a number of awards for this work, namely the Canada-Japan Literary Award, the Commonwealth Writers Prize for Best First Book in the Caribbean and Canada, and the Grant MacEwan Author's Award.

Second Appeal: Character

Subjects: Culture Clash • First Novels • Grandmothers • Japanese Canadians • Mothers and Daughters • Multi-generational Fiction • Small-town Life

Read On: Goto's other works include a novel (*The Kappa Child*), a young adult novel (*The Water of Possibility*), and a short-story collection (*Hopeful Monsters*). In Sky Lee's *Disappearing Moon Café,* another grandmother attempts to influence her child. Nora Okja Keller's *Comfort Woman* explores the universal conflict between mothers and daughters. Anita Rau Badami's *Tamarind Mem* is also about the collision of cultures within a family of three generations of women. The story of four generations of Japanese American women unfolds in Julie Shigekuni's *A Bridge Between Us.* The family in Judy Fong Bates's *Midnight at the Dragon Café* must deal with similar issues of conflict in a small-town setting.

Gould, Richard.

Lake of Gulls. Canadian Publishing Co., 2002. 401pp.

While on an end-of-summer fishing trip, childhood friends Patrick and Ken decide to bring media attention to the fact that twenty-five years earlier their childhood hometown was essentially dismantled to preserve the area for sportsmen. Their decision will bring them into conflict with politicians, Aboriginal peoples, corporate executives, and a police tactical unit, all of whom are willing to do whatever it takes to stop them.

> **Subjects:** Environmentalists • Expropriated Land • Friendship • Journalists • Kiosk • Northern Ontario • Ontario

> **Read On:** Gould's first novel *Red Fox Road* also explores environmental issues. Jessie Dearborn, a character created by Karen Hood-Caddy (*Tree Fever*, *Flying Lessons*), takes an interest in the environmental health of her part of Northern Ontario. In Louis Hamelin's *Cowboy*, a consortium buys a small Quebec town with the intention of turning it into a hunting-and-fishing paradise. Like the friends in Leona Gom's *Hating Gladys*, the characters in this novel are attempting to right past wrongs.

Gowdy, Barbara.

The White Bone. HarperFlamingoCanada, 1998. 330pp. Book Groups 📖

A family of elephants suffer tragedy as they travel in search of a home where they can be free from their human predators. This novel was shortlisted for the Giller Prize, the Rogers Writers' Trust Fiction Prize, and the Governor General's Literary Award for Fiction.

> **Second Appeal:** Character

> **Subjects:** Africa • Animals as Characters • Elephants • Family Relationships • Nature • Quests

> **Read On:** For other elephant stories, read Sara Cameron's *Natural Enemies*, Kim Echlin's *Elephant Winter*, or Catherine Palmer's *Sunrise Song*. Animals appear as characters in *Raven's End: A Tale from the Canadian Rockies* by Ben Gadd and most famously in *Animal Farm* by George Orwell. In 1996 Barbara Gowdy won the Marian Engel Award for her work, which includes *Falling Angels*, *Mister Sandman*, and *The Romantic*.

Green, Terence M.

Shadow of Ashland. Forge, 1996. 223pp.

Leo Nolan's dying mother claims that her brother, who mysteriously disappeared during the Depression, has visited her. Initially skeptical, Leo is pulled into the past to solve this family mystery when letters postmarked fifty years earlier begin to arrive from Ashland, Kentucky. *Shadow of Ashland* was shortlisted for the Prix Aurora Award and the World Fantasy Award.

> **Subjects:** Family Relationships • Kentucky • Missing Persons • Mothers and Sons • Small-town Life • Time Travel • Trilogies

Read On: Green continues this story in a prequel, *A Witness to Life,* and a sequel, *St. Patrick's Bed.* Green's method of magically connecting present and past are reminiscent of W. P. Kinsella's *Shoeless Joe,* Jack Finney's *Time and Again,* and Sylvia Fraser's *The Ancestral Suitcase.*

Greer, Darren.

Tyler's Cape. Algonquin Press, 2001. 263pp. Book Groups 📖

Luke Conrad, who thought he had escaped his family and life in their Nova Scotia fishing village, must confront secrets from the past and face his relationship with his two brothers when he returns home to care for his elderly mother.

Second Appeal: Setting

Subjects: Brothers • Family Relationships • Family Secrets • First Novels • Gay Men • Memory • Mothers and Sons • Nova Scotia

Read On: To acquire a strong sense of the Maritimes, read fiddler Ashley MacIsaac's memoir, *Fiddling with Disaster* and Annie Proulx's *The Shipping News.* In Andrew Solomon's *A Stone Boat* a son reflects on family relationships during his mother's illness. Characters connect with intense sensitivity in Greer's second novel, *Still Life with June,* a story in which a young gay man comes to a better understanding of himself through his friendship with a young woman suffering from Down syndrome.

Griggs, Terry.

Rogues' Wedding. Random House of Canada, 2002. 292pp.

In 1898, timid Griffith Smolders is certain that the ball of lightning chasing him around his hotel room on his wedding night is an omen. Consequently, he leaves his bride Avice by jumping out the window, thus beginning a fantastical circuitous journey, with his bride in close pursuit. *Rogues' Wedding* was shortlisted for the Rogers Writers' Trust Fiction Prize.

Second Appeal: Language

Subjects: Humorous Fiction • London • Marriage • Ontario • Rogues and Vagabonds • Runaway Husbands • Spouses

Read On: Griggs's style parallels John Irving's in *The World According to Garp,* Peter Carey's in *Bliss,* and Douglas Glover's in *Elle,* with its use of language, fantastic situations, and metaphors. Avice is a strong female protagonist who resembles Margaret Laurence's Hagar Shipley (*The Stone Angel*) and Margaret Mitchell's Scarlett O'Hara (*Gone with the Wind*).

Hill, Lawrence.

Any Known Blood. HarperCollins, 1997. 512pp. Book Groups 📖

Recently fired political speechwriter Langston Cane V embarks on a journey to discover his family roots. His search will trace his family from slavery in nineteenth-century Virginia to the present day in Oakville, Ontario, a town that was once a final destination on the Underground Railway.

Subjects: Black Families • Blacks in Ontario • Coming of Age • Family Relationships • Fathers and Sons • Identity • Oakville • Race Relations • Segregation • Underground Railroad

Read On: This second work by Lawrence Hill is loosely connected to his first novel, *Some Great Thing*. Julius Lester's *Do Lord Remember Me* is another story that traces the Black-American family experience from slavery forward. Lori Lansens's *Rush Home Road* is another novel that is set at a Canadian stop on the Underground Railway. Beginning in Africa, Alex Haley's family biography *Roots* traces the story of one African-American family over seven generations. Hill is also the author of *Black Berry, Sweet Justice*, a non-fiction work in which he discusses racial identity in a Canadian context.

Hodgson, Barbara.

🎗 *Hippolyte's Island.* **Raincoast Books, 2001. 282 pp**

Learning that the Aurora Islands, originally discovered and mapped in the sixteenth century, no longer appear on maps, writer-adventurer Hippolyte Webb decides he will rediscover the islands and use his journey as the basis of a book. This work received the Alcuin Society Award for Excellence in Canadian Book Design.

Subjects: Adventurers • Discoveries in Geography • Exploration • South Atlantic Ocean

Read On: Hodgson's novels *The Lives of Shadows, The Tattooed Map,* and *The Sensualist* are other examples of illustrated novels. Although not so highly illustrated as the <u>Griffin & Sabine Series</u> by Nick Bantock, this work has a similar graphic style. G. Garfield Crimmins creates an island-discovery journey, illustrated with maps and accompanying materials, in *The Republic of Dreams*.

Hogg, Peter.

🎗 *Crimes of War.* **McClelland & Stewart, 1999. 232pp. Book Groups** 📖

The horrors of the past are resurrected in the present as the story of Friedrich Reile, Nazi war criminal and retired architect, unfolds. Now living in Canada, Reile's anonymity is threatened as Dennis Connor, a member of Canada's Special Prosecutions Unit, works to expose him before the unit is shut down. Hogg won the Chapters/*Books in Canada* First Novel Award for this work, which was also shortlisted for the Arthur Ellis Award for Best First Novel.

Subjects: First Novels • Historians • Holocaust • Multiple Points of View • Nazi Hunters • Ottawa • Revenge • War Crimes • Winnipeg • World War II

Read On: In Alan Dershowitz's *Just Revenge* a Holocaust survivor discovers the man responsible for atrocities against his family and takes justice into his own hands. A victim's memories of the Holocaust and how it affected his life haunt Herman Broder in Isaac B. Singer's *Enemies, a Love Story*. Barbara Fradkin's mystery *Once upon a Time* features a man who spent many years hiding his identity and the role he played in the war. The suspense created in this novel will appeal to readers of Jack Higgins (*The Eagle Has Landed* and others). For other stories told from multiple points of view, try Barbara Kingsolver's *The Poisonwood Bible*, Amanda Hale's *Sounding the Blood,* or Barbara Lockhart's *Requiem for a Summer Cottage*.

Hospital, Janette Turner.

Oyster. Alfred A. Knopf Canada, 1996. 402pp.

Two parents searching for their lost children arrive in a remote opal-mining town in Queensland and spark the destruction of the town, a willing partner in the work of a charismatic and evil cult leader. *Oyster* was shortlisted for the Miles Franklin Literary Award (Australia).

Second Appeal: Setting

Subjects: Australia • Cults • Mining • Missing Children • Queensland

Read On: Georgia Savage's *The House Tibet* also uses Queensland as the setting for her story of a group of young runaways who seek refuge with a cult leader. The Australian outback is the setting of Colleen McCullough's *The Thorn Birds*, Susan Webster's *Small Tales of a Town*, and Nevil Shute's *A Town Like Alice*. The Australian landscape is vividly described in Richard Flanagan's *The Sound of One Hand Clapping* and Delia Falconer's *The Service of Clouds. The Last Magician*, one of Hospital's earlier novels, is also set in Australia.

Hough, Robert.

The Final Confession of Mabel Stark. Random House of Canada, 2001. 430pp. Book Groups 📖

A former tiger trainer with the Ringling Brothers circus, Mabel Stark recounts her lifelong obsession with her tigers, an obsession that ultimately cost her everything important to her. This novel was shortlisted for the Commonwealth Writers Prize for Best First Book in the Caribbean and Canada and also for the Trillium Book Award.

Second Appeal: Character

Subjects: First Novels • Marriage • Obsession • Stark, Mabel • Tigers • Women Animal Trainers • Women Circus Performers

Read On: Animal obsession is at the core of *Animal Acts* by Rhoda Lerman, *Bear* by Marian Engel, and *After Roy* by Mary Tannen. *Masters of Illusion* by Mary-Ann Tirone Smith is a novel about the Ringling Brothers Barnum and Bailey Combined Shows. The circus is also a setting in *Visible Worlds* by Marilyn Bowering.

Hunter, Catherine.

In the First Early Days of My Death. Signature Editions, 2002. 141pp. Book Groups 📖

When Winnipeg librarian Wendy Li realizes she is dead and floating among her loved ones, she is determined to ensure that her murderer is brought to justice in spite of a family and a police force not fully focused on the crime. Hunter was nominated for the McNally Robinson Book of the Year, as well as the Margaret Laurence Award for Fiction.

Second Appeal: Language

Subjects: Ghost Stories • Librarians • Manitoba • Murder • Murder Victims • Winnipeg

Read On: Hunter has written other suspense titles: *Where Shadows Burn* and *The Dead of Midnight*. Alice Sebold's *The Lovely Bones* is a poignant story about a victim of violent crime who watches her family in the aftermath of her death and, like Wendy Li, wants to point them in the right direction in apprehending her murderer. *The Time Traveler's Wife* by Audrey Niffenegger is also a unique story featuring a librarian. Like Larissa Lai's *When Fox Is a Thousand*, this novel is based on Chinese legend.

Kertes, Joseph.

Boardwalk. ECW Press, 1998. 253pp.

The differences between two brothers emerge on a road trip from Toronto to Atlantic City.

Subjects: Atlantic City • Brothers • Humorous Fiction • New Jersey • Road Novels

Read On: Kertes's first novel, *Winter Tulips,* won The Stephen Leacock Memorial Medal for Humour. Cary Fagan's title character Felix Roth and his brother prove to be quite different as they travel together to New York City. Kertes's characters and humour will appeal to readers of David Sedaris's work. Paul Quarrington's *The Spirit Cabinet* is set in the gambling world of Las Vegas and has an equally eclectic cast of casino-based characters.

King, James.

Blue Moon. Simon & Pierre, 2000. 361pp.

In her memoirs, celebrated author Elizabeth Delamere reveals the secret of her past life as a young prostitute and murderess in Hamilton in the late 1940s. Despite her conviction and subsequent twelve years in prison, she portrays herself as a victim.

Second Appeal: Character

Subjects: Dick, Evelyn MacLean • Hamilton • Murder • Trials (Murder) • Vancouver • Women Murderers • Women Novelists • Women Prisoners

Read On: In his first novel, *Faking*, King fictionally chronicles another real life, that of forger and supposed serial killer Thomas Wainewright. He also blends fictional and historical characters in *Transformations*. King's main forte, however, is non-fiction biography: *The Life of Margaret Laurence* and *The Last Modern: A Life of Herbert Read* are two of his works. For factual biographies of Evelyn Dick read Marjorie Campbell's *Torso: The Evelyn Dick Case* or Brian Vallee's *The Torso Murder: The Untold Story of Evelyn Dick*. Equally intriguing is the question of guilt or innocence in *Alias Grace* by Margaret Atwood.

Kinsella, W. P.

If Wishes Were Horses. HarperCollins, 1996. 216pp.

Ex-major league pitcher Joe McCoy, on the run and wanted by the FBI for kidnapping and other crimes, relates his story to fellow Iowans Ray Kinsella and Gideon Clarke.

Subjects: Baseball Players • Fugitives from Justice • Iowa • Unidentified Flying Objects

Read On: Kinsella's other books include *The Iowa Baseball Confederacy*, *Dance Me Outside: More Tales from the Ermineskin Reserve*, *Box Socials*, and *Magic Time*. Ray Kinsella first appears in Kinsella's *Shoeless Joe*. Bernard Malamud's *The Natural* and Mark Harris's *Bang the Drum Slowly* are other novels that hit on baseball. Kinsella's style of blending humour into his storytelling will appeal to readers of Garrison Keillor (*Lake Wobegon Days* and others).

Krueger, Lesley.

Drink the Sky. Key Porter Books, 1999. 351pp.

Holly, wife and mother of two, hopes her husband's posting to Brazil will allow her the time she needs to return to her painting, thereby enabling her to reclaim her sense of self.

Second Appeal: Language

Subjects: Aboriginal Peoples • Amazon River • Brazil • Canadians in Brazil • Environmentalists • Identity • Marriage • Motherhood • Rainforest Ecology • Women Artists

Read On: Krueger's other works include the novel *The Corner Garden*, a short-story collection entitled *Hard Travel*, and a book of travel writing, *Foreign Correspondences: A Traveller's Tales*. Sergio Kokis's *Funhouse* features an artist whose story is also set in Brazil, and another woman takes a journey up the Amazon in Eva Ibbotson's *A Company of Swans*. Krueger's novel shares both setting and intensity with Andrew Pyper's *The Trade Mission*, in which a group of Canadians travel to Rio on Internet business and take a trip up the Amazon.

Lawson, Mary.

🎗 *Crow Lake*. Alfred A. Knopf Canada, 2001. 294pp. Book Groups 📖

Kate Morrison approaches her nephew's eighteenth birthday with a painful review of her tragic childhood in Northern Ontario. She remembers her parents' deaths and her two elder brothers' subsequent adoption of parental roles at the expense of their own dreams. *Crow Lake* received a number of awards and accolades: the ALA Alex Award, the Amazon.ca/*Books in Canada* First Novel Award, and the McKitterick Prize. It was shortlisted for the CBA Libris Award: Fiction Book of the Year and the Torgi Award, and was also a *Today's* Book Club Selection, a *New York Times* Notable Fiction choice, and was included on the *Publishers Weekly* and the *Washington Post* Best Fiction lists.

Second Appeal: Character

Subjects: Brothers and Sisters • Canadian Shield • Car Accidents • Family Relationships • First Novels • Orphans • Reminiscing • Small-town Life • Toronto • Women Zoologists

Read On: Wayne Curtis's *One Indian Summer* also features a young man who sets aside his dreams to take on family responsibilities beyond his years. *A Good House* by Bonnie Burnard looks at the life of a family spanning several decades. For other outstanding first novels, try Lauren B. Davis's *The Stubborn Season*, Lori Lansens's *Rush Home Road*, Ann-Marie MacDonald's *Fall on Your Knees*, or Anne Michaels's *Fugitive Pieces*.

Livingston, Billie.

Going Down Swinging. **Random House of Canada, 1999. 326pp. Book Groups** 📖

A threat by the Children's Protection Society to remove her young daughter Grace forces Eileen, former teacher-turned-prostitute, to re-examine her life choices—a dependency on alcohol and drugs, a series of bad relationships, and a decline into poverty—and pushes both of them to confront their life situation if there is to be any hope of staying together.

Subjects: Alcoholics • Child Welfare • Drug Abuse • First Novels • Mothers and Daughters • Prostitution

Read On: Mother-and-daughter relationships reach a crisis in Janet Fitch's *White Oleander* and Mona Simpson's *Anywhere but Here*. The mothers in Sue Miller's *The Good Mother* and Jessica Auerbach's *Catch Your Breath* are in danger of losing custody of their children. The child's voice is also heard in Sandra Campbell's *Getting to Normal* and Nino Ricci's *Lives of the Saints*.

MacDonald, Ann-Marie.

🎗 *Fall on Your Knees*. **Alfred A. Knopf Canada, 1996. 566pp. Book Groups** 📖

The sudden return of opera singer Kathleen Piper to her family's home on Cape Breton Island, Nova Scotia, provides the focal point for this multi-generational saga that encompasses race relations, incest, birth, death, marriage, and the insidiousness of family secrets. MacDonald received a number of awards for this work: the Commonwealth Writers Prize for Best First Book, the Dartmouth Book Award for Fiction, the CAA Literary Award for Fiction, the CBA Libris Award: Fiction Book of the Year, and the Torgi Literary Award. *Fall on Your Knees* was also one of two Canadian novels selected by Oprah Winfrey for her book club. In addition, MacDonald's novel was shortlisted for the Chapters/*Books in Canada* First Book Award, the Giller Prize, the Trillium Book Award, the Orange Prize, and the International IMPAC Dublin Literary Award for the Novel.

Second Appeal: Character

Subjects: 1920s • Cape Breton Island • Family Secrets • Fathers and Daughters • First Novels • Incest • Marriage • Multi-generational Fiction • Musicians • New York City • Sisters

Read On: Mysteries are unwoven in another tale of family tragedy in Jeffrey Eugenides's *The Virgin Suicides*. For similar richness of language and complexity of human relationships, try Rohinton Mistry's *A Fine Balance*. Toni Morrison's *Jazz*, also a gem of language, is set in the same time period as MacDonald's book and deals in depth with Harlem jazz, an important discovery for Kathleen Piper in *Fall on Your Knees*.

🎗 *The Way the Crow Flies*. **Alfred A. Knopf Canada, 2003. 720pp. Book Groups** 📖

A young girl's murder poisons the optimism and idyllic life of the 1960s on a Canadian Air Force base. Nine-year-old Madeleine and her father Jack are each forced to keep secrets related to the murder and more. These secrets serve to betray both their idealism and their innocence. This novel was the winner of the CBA Libris Award: Fiction Book of the Year. The author was also selected for the *Today's* Book Club and nominated for the Giller Prize, as well as the Commonwealth Writers Prize for Best Book in the Caribbean and Canada.

> **Second Appeal:** Setting
>
> **Subjects:** 1960s • Child Sexual Abuse • Cold War • Coming of Age • Family Relationships • Girls • Historical Fiction • Military Bases • Murder
>
> **Read On:** MacDonald first explored the theme of the power of secrets in her novel *Fall on Your Knees*. Elizabeth Berg (*The Art of Mending*) and Julia Glass (*Three Junes*) are authors whose novels share this theme. Doris Lessing's *The Sweetest Dream* and Joyce Carol Oates's *I'll Take You There* both paint portraits of the 1960s. MacDonald's creation of a childhood world will remind readers of Donna Tartt's *The Little Friend*.

MacIntyre, Linden.

The Long Stretch. **Stoddart, 1999. 252pp. Book Groups** 📖

During the course of a long evening spent drinking, cousins John Gillis, a Cape Bretoner, and Sextus, home from Toronto after a thirteen-year absence, reminisce about their shared family past, their own fractured relationship, and other long-buried secrets. In chronicling the past, they are able to discover their own truths and to dispel the resentment that has plagued them both. This first novel was shortlisted for the Dartmouth Book Award for Fiction.

> **Second Appeal:** Setting
>
> **Subjects:** Cape Breton Island • Cousins • Family Chronicles • Family Relationships • First Novels • Nova Scotia
>
> **Read On:** *Robbiestime* by Don Dickinson also addresses the need to reconcile with past events in order to move forward. There are several similarities between *The Long Stretch* and Alistair MacLeod's *No Great Mischief*, from the Cape Breton/Toronto settings to the family histories that leave lasting legacies. *The Long Stretch* also parallels *Fall on Your Knees* by Ann-Marie MacDonald, not just for its Cape Breton setting but also for its portrayal of serious family problems.

MacLeod, Alistair.

🎗 *No Great Mischief*. **McClelland & Stewart, 1999. 283pp. Book Groups** 📖

This story is the saga of one family over several generations, beginning with their emigration to Cape Breton, Nova Scotia, from Scotland in 1779 up to the mid-1980s in Southern Ontario. Told through family

memoirs and anecdotes, it is a story of loss and loyalty, but most of all a story of love. MacLeod's *No Great Mischief* won the International IMPAC Dublin Literary Award for the Novel, the Trillium Book Award, the Thomas Head Raddall Atlantic Fiction Award, the Dartmouth Book Award for Fiction, the CAA Literary Award for Fiction, the CBA Libris Award: Fiction Book of the Year, the Atlantic Independent Booksellers' Choice Award, and the Lannan Literary Award.

Second Appeal: Character

Subjects: Alcoholics • Brothers • Cape Breton Island • Clans • Coming of Age • Family Relationships • First Novels • Grandparents • Loyalty • Mining • Nova Scotia • Scotland

Read On: MacLeod is the author of *Island: The Collected Short Stories of Alistair MacLeod*, *As Birds Bring Forth the Sun and Other Stories*, and *The Lost Salt Gift of Blood*. *Oatmeal Ark* by Rory MacLean, similarly set on Cape Breton Island, also includes Scottish history and touches on its influence on Nova Scotian families. *After the Angel Mill*, a collection of short stories by Carol Bruneau, is set on the Island, as are novels by Darren Greer (*Tyler's Cape*), D. R.. MacDonald (*Cape Breton Road*), and Linden MacIntyre (*The Long Stretch*).

Marom, Malka.

Sulha. Key Porter Books, 1999. 566pp. Book Groups 📖

Her son's decision to follow in his father's footsteps and enlist in the Israeli Air Force sends Lenora, an Israeli war widow, to the site of her husband's death in the Sinai Desert. There she moves into a Bedouin encampment and attempts to confront the conflicting loyalties she feels between her life in Canada and the country she left behind twenty years earlier.

Subjects: Arab–Israeli Conflict • Bedouins • Culture Clash • Egypt • First Novels • Israel • Mothers and Sons • Sinai • Toronto • War Widows

Read On: Kazuo Ishiguro's *A Pale View of Hills* looks at two war widows and their relationships with their children. Sharon Butala's *The Garden of Eden*, Muriel Spanier's *Staying Afloat,* and Hilma Wolitzer's *Hearts* all look at widows searching for life beyond grief.

Martel, Yann.

🎗 *Life of Pi.* Alfred A. Knopf Canada, 2001. 352pp. Book Groups 📖

Sixteen-year-old Pi, embracer of three different religions, is cast adrift for 227 days on a lifeboat with four animals from his parents' erstwhile zoo in India: a hyena, an orangutan, a zebra, and a Bengal tiger. *For Life of Pi*, Martel won the Man Booker Prize and the Hugh MacLennan Prize for Fiction; he was also shortlisted for the Governor General's Literary Award for Fiction and the Commonwealth Writers Prize for Best Book in the Caribbean and Canada.

Second Appeal: Character

Subjects: Castaways • Coming of Age • Human–Animal Relationships • India • Odysseys • Pacific Ocean • Shipwrecks • Teenage Boys • Survival • Tigers • Toronto

Read On: Martel's first novel was an autobiographical work, *Self*, which was shortlisted for the Amazon.ca/*Books in Canada* First Novel Award. For another story about a shipwreck, try *Motoo Eetee: Shipwrecked at the Edge of the World* by Irv C. Rogers. *Life of Pi* is about more than a shipwreck, however, and *Red Earth and Pouring Rain* by Vikram Chanda shares both storytelling and fantastic and mystical elements with Martel's novel.

McCormack, Eric

First Blast of the Trumpet Against the Monstrous Regiment of Women. Viking, 1997. 272pp.

The tragic events of Andrew Halfnight's life form the basis of nightmares that continually confront him: the death of his twin sister on their christening day, his parents' early demise, a murdering aunt, the destruction of an entire island village, and more. On Halfnight's journey from Canada back to the place of his birth, the mystery of his existence is revealed and the nature of happiness uncovered. McCormack was nominated for the Governor General's Literary Award for Fiction for this novel.

Second Appeal: Language

Subjects: Death of a Parent • Death of a Sibling • Erotic Fiction • Gothic Fiction • Men's Lives

Read On: Other books by McCormack include *The Dutch Wife* and *The Mysterium*. The dark, somewhat nightmarish tone of this novel shares horrific elements with the storytelling of Thomas Ligotti (*The Nightmare Factory* and others). Joseph Skibell writes a very different surreal novel with similar elements of magic realism in *A Blessing on the Moon*.

Melnyk, Eugenie.

My Darling Elia. St. Martin's Press, 1999. 277pp.

At a Montreal flea market, Holocaust survivor Elia Strohan discovers a locket he had made for his wife Anna fifty years earlier, renewing his hope of finding the woman from whom he has heard nothing since he was sent to a concentration camp in 1941.

Second Appeal: Language

Subjects: Concentration Camps • Holocaust Survivors • Husbands and Wives • Jewish Canadadians • Poland • Treblinka • Ukraine • War-torn Lovers • World War II

Read On: Love withstands the horrors of the Nazi camps in the story of *Marek and Lisa* by Henia Karmel-Wolfe. James Michael Pratt's *The Last Valentine* is another story of undying love set against the backdrop of World War II. Terry Kay explores enduring love in two separate novels, *To Dance with the White Dog* and *Shadow Song*. Charles Frazier's *Cold Mountain* tells the story of lovers separated by war, whose love lives on after death.

Miller, John.

The Featherbed. Simon & Pierre, 2002. 352pp. Book Groups 📖

After more than fifty years of being estranged, two elderly sisters reunite at their mother's funeral. There they reconnect, reading through the pages of their mother's diary as the details of her life in 1900s New York emerge.

> **Second Appeal:** Character
>
> **Subjects:** 1900s • Diaries • Family Relationships • First Novels • Mothers and Daughters • New York City • Separation • Sisters • Toronto
>
> **Read On:** Miller's novel is multi-layered, but the theme of sisters reuniting after a bitter separation because of a parent's illness or death is particularly prominent. This theme appears again in *Wild Apples* by Lucinda Franks and in *Daughters of Memory* by Janis Arnold. In *The Properties of Water* by Ann Hood, sisters also reunite, but not because of a parent's death. Miller skilfully weaves the hidden lives of people involved in same-sex relationships into this novel. Another author whose work includes this story element is Lilian Nattel (*The River Midnight*).

Moore, Brian.

The Magician's Wife. Alfred A. Knopf Canada, 1997. 215pp.

Emmeline and her husband, renowned magician Henri Lambert, travel to Algeria in 1856 on a mission for Napoleon III. Once there, the exotic landscape and culture seduce Emmeline, resulting in her betrayal of husband and country.

> **Subjects:** Algeria • France • Love Stories • Magicians • Married Women • Napoleon III • Nineteenth Century • Politics
>
> **Read On:** Set in Algeria, Malika Mokeddem's *The Forbidden Woman* tells the story of another woman's rebellion within the Muslim world. The effects of French colonialism in Algeria are explored in Albert Camus's *The First Man*, Robert Irwin's *Mysteries of Algiers*, and Nancy Huston's *The Mark of the Angel*. Jeanette Winterson's *The Passion* is set in Napoleon's Europe. Moore won the Governor General's Literary Award for Fiction for *The Great Victorian Collection* and *The Luck of Ginger Coffey*; he has also been shortlisted for the Booker Prize three times.

Moritsugu, Kim.

The Glenwood Treasure. The Dundurn Group, 2003. 268pp.

Twenty-eight-year old Blithe Morrison returns to her parents' Toronto home after her marriage fails, intending to wallow for the summer until she resumes teaching in the fall. Instead, she becomes drawn into the search for a supposedly long-buried treasure and in the process discovers a new love and truths about herself and her family.

> **Subjects:** Divorced Women • Family Secrets • Sibling Rivalry • Toronto • Treasures • Women Teachers
>
> **Read On:** Moritsugu is also the author of the novels *Looks Perfect* (shortlisted for the Toronto Book Award) and *Old Flames*. Women must resolve issues underlying failed relationships in order to move on in Joan Barfoot's *Getting Over Edgar* and Jennifer Webber's *Defying Gravity*. Barbara Sapergia's protagonist in *Secrets in*

Water is a woman who returns home and discovers buried family secrets that allow her to put family relationships into perspective.

Nickson, Elizabeth.

The Monkey-Puzzle Tree. **Alfred A. Knopf Canada, 1994. 277pp. Book Groups** 📖

Catherine, back with her family following her brother's suicide attempt, begins to work with a legal team seeking damages from the government for victims of brainwashing experiments at a CIA-funded institute during the 1950s and 1960s. It is this work that will help her to come to terms with the past and move forward.

Second Appeal: Language

Subjects: Allan Memorial Psychiatric Institute • Brainwashing • Central Intelligence Agency • First Novels • Human Experimentation • Montreal • Mothers and Daughters • Quebec

Read **On:** In *Itsuka* by Joy Kogawa another daughter fights for justice for her family because of the treatment they endured at the hands of the government. Brainwashing is the subject of *Mindfield* by William Deverell, *The Manchurian Candidate* by Richard Condon, and *The Kill Zone* by David Hagberg. *In the Sleep Room* by Anne Collins is an account of these experiments based on interviews with actual patient survivors.

Oliva, Peter.

🎗 *The City of Yes.* **McClelland & Stewart, 1999. 336pp. Book Groups** 📖

A modern-day English-language teacher, longing for home in Canada, attempts to understand the subtle nuances of Japanese life and custom. In support, his friend Hideo Endo shares the story of Ranald MacDonald, a nineteenth-century Canadian adventurer and one of Japan's first English teachers, who faked his own shipwreck off Hokkaido in 1848 and whose experiences seem to mirror the Canadian teacher's. This work by Oliva received a number of awards: the F. G. Bressani Prize, the Georges Bugnet Award for Best Novel, and the Rogers Writers' Trust Fiction Prize. It was also shortlisted for the City of Calgary W. O. Mitchell Book Award.

Subjects: Adventurers • Canadians in Japan • English Teachers • Japan

Read On: David Galef's *Turning Japanese*, Holly Thompson's *Ash*, and Matthew Kneale's *Whore Banquets* all include English-language teachers working in Japan. Novels with parallel stories are Patrick Gale's *Rough Music* and Ahdaf Soueif's *The Map of Love*. Yann Martel's *Life of Pi* tells the fantastical story of a young man who survives a shipwreck.

Pearson, Patricia.

Playing House. **Random House of Canada, 2003. 280pp.**

Frannie MacKenzie's unplanned pregnancy sends her on a humorous journey toward a major life change when she decides to keep the child. A

Toronto native, working as a magazine editor in New York, Frannie chooses to build a relationship with the father, a Cape Breton musician, despite the fact that she barely knows him.

Second Appeal: Character

Subjects: City and Town Life • First Novels • Humorous Fiction • Motherhood • New York City • Pregnant Women • Single Women • Women Editors

Read On: *Baby, Baby* by Liz Nickles, *Dating Big Bird* by Laura Zigman, *From Here to Maternity* by Kris Webb, and *Motherhood Made a Man out of Me* by Karen Karbo are all humorous depictions of motherhood. Thirty-something women attempt to cope with life's challenges in Helen Fielding's *Bridget Jones's Diary* and Allison Pearson's *I Don't Know How She Does It*.

Poloni, Philippe.

🎗 *Olivo Oliva.* **Stoddart, 1999. 197pp.**

Olivo Oliva, whose life began as a trick of fate, spends many years wandering throughout the world, even working as a hit man in America. Eventually he returns to Sicily, the country of his birth, to uncover the truth about his heritage. This work received an Alcuin Society Award for Excellence in Canadian Book Design. Translated from the French [*Olivo Oliva*] by David Homel.

Second Appeal: Language

Subjects: Allegories • Family • First Novels • French Canadian • Illegitimate Children • Italy • Mafia • Murderers • Olive Industry • Translations

Read On: This book's fantastical elements resemble Mark Dunn's in *Ella Minnow Pea*; Poloni's style of magic realism is reminiscent of Salman Rushdie's *The Satanic Verses*. Men journey in search of truth in Timothy Findley's *Pilgrim* and Daniel Quinn's *Ishmael*.

Poulin, Jacques.

Autumn Rounds. **Cormorant Books, 2002. 164pp. Book Groups** 📖

A bookmobile driver and a woman unexpectedly discover love late in their lives as they meet time and again on his route along the north shore of the St. Lawrence. Translated from the French [*La tournée d'automne*] by Sheila Fischman.

Second Appeal: Language

Subjects: Bookmobiles • Elderly Men • Elderly Women • French Canadian • Love Stories • Musicians • Quebec • Translations

Read On: A number of Poulin's earlier novels received critical acclaim in their original French language; he won a Governor General's Literary Award for Fiction (French) for *Les grandes marées* and the Prix France-Amérique for *Le vieux chagrin*. *Volkswagen Blues*, *Mr. Blue,* and *Wild Cat* are all Poulin titles that Sheila Fischman has translated into English. Love comes late in life in *Julie and Romeo* by Jeanne Ray. In *Love in the Time of Cholera*, Gabriel García Márquez describes, with similar lyrical prose, an older man's quest to woo the woman he desires. Gabrielle Roy's *The Cashier* paints a vivid portrait of an ordinary man and his life.

Quarrington, Paul.

Galveston. **Random House of Canada, 2004. 256pp. Book Groups** 📖

An eclectic group of travellers arrives on a small Caribbean island hours before the forecast landfall of a hurricane. As they look into the face of possible death and destruction, they ultimately realize how their actions in the past have brought them to this pivotal moment. Quarrington was shortlisted for the Giller Prize for this novel.

> **Subjects:** Guilt • Humorous Fiction • Redemption • Weather

> **Read On:** Quarrington won the Governor General's Literary Award for Fiction for *Whale Music* in 1989 and The Stephen Leacock Memorial Medal for Humour in 1988 for *King Leary*. Other novels that focus on the guilt and confusion that follow horrific events include *Half a Heart* by Rosellen Brown and *A Map of the World* by Jane Hamilton. William Styron's *Sophie's Choice* is a novel that explores survivors' guilt, although with much more intensity than is found here.

Rehner, Jan.

🎗 *Just Murder*. **Sumach Press, 2003. 252pp. Book Groups** 📖

Lily Ross is a news photographer who has taken upon herself the investigation of an unsolved murder. This investigation, however, soon makes her a target for murder. She has heard about a network that may help her, but she doesn't know if they are a solution or part of the problem. This network has helped women at risk before—can it help her, or are their methods too much beyond the law? Rehner won the Arthur Ellis Award for Best First Novel for this title.

> **Subjects:** Murder • New Identities • News Photographers • Relocation Agents • Stalking • Violence Against Women • Women Photographers

> **Read On:** Thomas Perry's Jane Whitefield (*The Face-Changers* and others) is perhaps the best-known relocation agent for women and children in abusive situations; Allen Carmichael in Laurie R. King's *Keeping Watch* is another. Anna Quindlen's *Black and Blue* and Nancy Price's *Sleeping with the Enemy* also tell the story of women who change their identities and relocate to escape abusive relationships. But often the road to relocation has serious moral issues. To read other mysteries that raise difficult moral questions, try Thomas Cook's *The Chatham School Affair* or Dennis Lehane's *Gone, Baby, Gone*.

Ruth, Elizabeth.

Ten Good Seconds of Silence. **Dundurn Group, 2001. 414pp. Book Groups** 📖

Lilith Boot, a clairvoyant child-finder for the Metropolitan Toronto Police, and her daughter Lemon must work through Lilith's past in order to heal and move on. Issues on the table include time spent at a Vancouver mental institution, an abusive mother and father, confused sexual orientation, and rape. This debut novel was shortlisted for the Rogers Writers'

Trust Fiction Prize, the Amazon.ca/*Books in Canada* First Novel Award, and the Toronto Book Award.

> **Subjects:** First Novels • Identity • Lesbians • Memory • Mothers and Daughters • Psychics • Toronto

> **Read On:** The heroine in Timothy Findley's *Headhunter* must also deal with mental illness. In Nora Okja Keller's *Comfort Woman* a daughter comes to understand her mother and face the truth about her family history. A woman searches for her identity in A. Manette Ansay's *Vinegar Hill.* Iris Johansen's *Body of Lies* features Eve Duncan, a forensic sculptor, who assists in the search for missing children.

Sakamoto, Kerri

🎗 *The Electrical Field.* **Alfred A. Knopf Canada, 1998. 305pp. Book Groups** 📖

Thirty years after her family was interned in a camp for Japanese Canadians, Asako Saito finds the past brought vividly to the present when a beautiful woman is found murdered. This work was awarded the Commonwealth Writers Prize for Best First Book and the Canada-Japan Lterary Award, and was shortlisted for the Chapters/*Books in Canada* First Novel Award, the Governor General's Literary Award for Fiction, the Kiriyama Pacific Rim Book Prize, and the Arthur Ellis Award for Best First Novel.

> **Subjects:** Brothers and Sisters • Fathers and Daughters • First Novels • Internment Camps • Japanese Canadians • Middle-aged Women • Murder

> **Read On:** Sakamoto followed this novel with *One Hundred Million Hearts*, the story of a young woman who travels to Japan following her father's death. She meets her half-sister and learns of her father's wartime experiences as a kamikaze pilot. In Susan Dodd's *No Earthly Notion,* a daughter is forced to care for her father and brother. Joy Kogawa's *Obasan* is the story of one Japanese-Canadian family and their experience in an internment camp during World War II. Stewart David Ikeda's *What the Scarecrow Said* examines a man's life following his release from an internment camp during World War II. Terry Watada provides a glimpse of life in an internment camp in the collection of stories *Daruma Days: A Collection of Fictionalised Biography*.

Silvera, Makeda.

The Heart Does Not Bend. **Random House of Canada, 2002. 264pp. Book Groups** 📖

Raised in Jamaica by her loving yet merciless matriarchal grandmother Maria, Molly shares the stories of five generations of her family's women as she struggles to come to terms with Maria's final act of rejection.

> **Second Appeal:** Language

> **Subjects:** First Novels • Grandmothers • Immigrants and Refugees • Inheritance and Succession • Jamaica • Love Stories • Mothers and Daughters • Toronto

> **Read On:** *Sleep On, Beloved* by Cecil Foster tells the story of a Jamaican woman who leaves her daughter and immigrates to Canada, adjusting later when her child finally joins her. Matriarchs dominate in Isabel Allende's *Portrait in Sepia* and Kate Atkinson's *Behind the Scenes at the Museum.* Nancy Freedman's *The Seventh Stone* and Ursula Hegi's *The Vision of Emma Blau* share multi-generational stories.

Silvera is the author of two collections of short stories, *Remembering G.* and *Her Head a Village and Other Stories*. *The Heart Does Not Bend* has also been published as *Maria's Revenge*.

Simonds, Merilyn.

The Holding. McClelland & Stewart, 2004. 313pp. Book Groups 📖

In alternating chapters, Simonds reveals the lives of two women living on the same farm a century apart, both of whom must come to terms with their secrets and the repercussions of lives lived in isolation. Alyson's discovery of settler Margaret's long-buried secret ultimately allows her to move beyond her own personal tragedy.

> **Subjects:** Farm Life • Frame Stories • Frontier and Pioneer Life • Journals • Marriage • Ontario • Small-town Life • Women

> **Read On:** Simonds is also the author of the non-fiction work *The Convict Lover*, based on correspondence in 1919 between a young village schoolgirl and a convict in the Kingston Penitentiary that was discovered in the attic of a Kingston home in 1987. Simonds weaves this story in a manner reminiscent of Margaret Atwood in *Alias Grace*. Women connect between the past and present in *Sisters of Grass* by Theresa Kishkan, and A. S. Byatt's *Possession* also features the parallel lives of its characters.

Simpson, Anne.

Canterbury Beach. Penguin Group, 2001. 312pp.

As Verna and Allister prepare to celebrate forty years of marriage, they make the annual pilgrimage with their children to the family cottage in Maine. All the family members have their own stories to tell and thus reveal their individual perceptions of their family's truth. Simpson was shortlisted for the Thomas Head Raddall Atlantic Fiction Award for this novel.

> **Second Appeal:** Character

> **Subjects:** Cottages • Family Relationships • Family Reunions • Maine • Marriage • Vacations

> **Read On:** Various family members tell their stories in Barbara Kingsolver's *The Poisonwood Bible* and Rahna Reiko Rizzuto's *Why She Left Us*. Emma Richler's *Sister Crazy* is also an intimate examination of a family. Elyse Friedman writes from various perspectives to offer the reader a quirky look at a family reunion and family relationships in *Then Again*.

Škvorecký, Josef.

Two Murders in My Double Life. Key Porter Books, 1999. 183pp. Book Groups 📖

Against the backdrop of a murder investigation on a Toronto university campus, an unnamed professor and his wife unsuccessfully and tragically attempt to disprove her supposed collaboration with the Communist-era secret police.

Subjects: Czechoslovakia • Immigrants and Refugees • Murder • University Professors • Women Publishers

Read On: *The Cowards* and *The Engineer of Human Souls* are two of Škvorecký's novels that have been translated into English. The novels of Czech writer Milan Kundera (*The Unbearable Lightness of Being, Immortality,* and *The Book of Laughter and Forgetting*) also intertwine politics and personal relationships. In Lynn Coady's *Saints of Big Harbour*, rumour has a significant impact on a young man's life. Škvorecký's approach to mystery writing resembles the traditional English-village style of Agatha Christie's mysteries.

Smith, Brad.

All Hat. Penguin Canada, 2003. 308pp.

Despite his best intentions to stay out of trouble, newly paroled Ray Dokes cannot resist the temptation to exact revenge against local bully Sonny Stanton, the man Ray assaulted for raping his sister. When Ray discovers the location of Stanton's recently stolen race horse, he and an eclectic cast of characters set in motion a plan that ultimately puts an end to Sonny's nasty schemes.

Second Appeal: Character

Subjects: Ex-convicts • Horse Racing • Humorous Fiction • Men's Friendships • Revenge • Swindlers • Women Jockeys

Read On: Kate Sterns's *Down There by the Train* is another humorous novel featuring a recently paroled man. The works of both Dick Francis and John Francome are set in the world of horse racing. Like Brad Smith, Jane Smiley taps into the humour of the horse-racing world in *Horse Heaven*. The fast-paced storytelling and plot twists in this novel will appeal to readers of John Grisham (*The Firm* and others) and Thomas Perry (*Blood Money* and others).

Spalding, Esta, and Linda Spalding.

Mere. HarperFlamingoCanada, 2001. 211pp.

Twelve-year-old Mere has lived her entire life aboard *The Persephone* with her mother Faye. One day they dock for supplies in the Toronto Harbour and find Mere's father waiting there. Finally Faye must confront a past she has been running from for the past twelve years.

Second Appeal: Language

Subjects: Coming of Age • First Novels • Fugitives from Justice • Mothers and Daughters • Sailing • Toronto

Read On: Linda Spalding's isolated, solitary women first appeared in her earlier novels *Daughters of Captain Cook* and *The Paper Wife*. Kim Echlin's *Dagmar's Daughter*, Jacquelyn Mitchard's *The Most Wanted*, and Kathleen Hill's *Still Waters in Niger* also evoke the myth of Demeter and Persephone.

Taylor, Kate.

Madame Proust and the Kosher Kitchen. Doubleday Canada, 2003. 432pp.
Book Groups 📖

The intertwining stories of three women reveal connections based on the
power of memory and remembering. Marie, a Proust scholar and transla-
tor in Paris, hopes to escape an unrequited passion for Max Segal by connecting to Proust through his mother Jeanne's diaries. These diaries
reveal an anxious, protective mother facing the challenges of European
war-era politics. Max's own mother, Sarah Bensimon, escaped the Holocaust as a twelve-year-old girl when her family sent her to Canada. Marie
begins to wonder about her life when she is faced with the truth of what
Sarah must have suffered as her family's sole survivor. Taylor won the
Commonwealth Writers Prize for Best First Book for this work, as well
as the Toronto Book Award.

> **Second Appeal:** Character

> **Subjects:** Diaries • First Novels • Holocaust • Jewish Cooking • Jewish
> Women • Mothers • Paris • Proust, Jeanne Weill • Proust, Marcel • Women
> Translators

> **Read On:** Michael Cunningham's *The Hours* is also an acclaimed novel
> whose story weaves three lives together, including one of a literary lion.
> Literary figures are also integrated into Julian Barnes's *Flaubert's Parrot*
> and A. S. Byatt's *Possession*.

Tisseyre, Michelle.

Divided Passions. Key Porter Books, 1999. 351pp.

During World War I, sixteen-year-old Jeanne Langlois's parents, one a
Quebec politician and the other an extremely religious woman, send her
to a Carmelite convent in Manitoba. Unable to cope with the austere life
of a nun, she returns to Montreal and promptly marries, a decision that
proves disastrous. She eventually turns away from family, religion, and
country in her search for independence. Translated from the French [*La
passion de Jeanne*] by the author.

> **Subjects:** Coming of Age • Depressions, 1929– • French Canadian • Nuns •
> Quebec • Religious Life • Translations • Women • World War I

> **Read On:** A young woman runs away from a convent in search of inde-
> pendence in *The Love of Women* by Jenifer McVaugh. Hugh MacLennan
> shares Tisseyre's setting of time and place in *The Watch That Ends the
> Night*. Although set in the 1970s, Marianne Ackerman's *Jump* also tells the
> story of a woman struggling to find her place against the backdrop of a
> Quebec in crisis.

Toews, Miriam.

Summary of My Amazing Luck. Turnstone Press, 1996. 192pp. Book Groups 📖

Life in a welfare housing project is examined through the experiences of single moms Lucy and Lish. They follow regulations and endure the challenges of making ends meet until they decide to take to the road in search of Lish's twins' father, a fire-eating busker. Toews won the John Hirsch Award for the most promising Manitoba writer, and was shortlisted for the McNally Robinson Book of the Year and The Stephen Leacock Memorial Medal for Humour for this novel.

Subjects: First Novels • Humorous Fiction • Journeys • Road Novels • Single Mothers • Welfare Recipients • Women's Friendships

Read On: Toews's other work includes *A Boy of Good Breeding*, *A Complicated Kindness* (winner of the Governor General's Literary Award for Fiction), and the memoir of her father, *Swing Low: A Life*. *Mad Cows* by Kathy Lette is another comic take on the plight of a single mother. *Pink Slip* by Rita Ciresi makes room for humour while tackling issues of trauma and family relationships. Tim Sandlin's humorous GroVont Trilogy (*Skipped Parts*, *Sorrow Floats*, and *Social Blunders*) features characters embarking on a quest or journey.

Torgov, Morley.

The War to End All Wars. Malcolm Lester Books, 1998. 311pp.

In 1917, Russian Jew Eliezer Pinsky is reluctantly conscripted into the Tsar's army. Through a quirk of fate he is the only member of his regiment to survive the assault on the Austrian front. After immigrating to the United States, he opens a store in a small Michigan town, competing directly with another Jew he faced on the battlefield.

Second Appeal: Character

Subjects: Humorous Fiction • Jewish Men • Michigan • Small-town Life • World War I

Read On: Torgov is a two-time winner of The Stephen Leacock Memorial Medal for Humour for *A Good Place to Come From* and *The Outside Chance of Maximilian Glick*. Stuart McLean and Jack Boyd capture the humour of small-town life in *Home from the Vinyl Cafe*, and *If It Ain't Broke*, respectively. The legacy of war is seriously explored in Barbara Fradkin's *Once upon a Time*, David Guterson's *Snow Falling on Cedars*, and D. M. Thomas's *Pictures at an Exhibition*.

Tulchinsky, Karen X.

Love Ruins Everything. Press Gang Publishers, 1998. 267pp.

Young lesbian Nomi Rabinovitch, heartbroken after her lover unexpectedly dumps her for a man, returns to Toronto for her mother's wedding. Here, through her gay cousin who is living with AIDS and convinced that the U.S. government created the virus as a weapon, she reconnects with a former acquaintance and finds love once again.

Subjects: AIDS • First Novels • Gay Men • Government Conspiracies • Humorous Fiction • Jewish Women • Lesbians • Love Stories • San Francisco • Toronto

Read On: Tulchinsky continues Nomi's story in *Love and Other Ruins*. She is also the author of the short-story collection *In Her Nature*. Lesbian love stories unfold with a similar element of humour in Rita Mae Brown's *Alma Mater*, Sylvia Brownrigg's *Pages for You*, and Edith Forbes's *Alma Rose*. In John Casey's *The Half-life of Happiness* a man's wife leaves him for another woman.

Webber, Jennifer.

Defying Gravity. Coteau Books, 2000. 361pp. Book Groups 📖

When Miranda's fiancé abandons her at the top of a mountain in Jasper National Park, she cannot bear to face her friends and colleagues again as a jilted woman. Instead she embarks on a road trip with a young South Asian man who will soon be entering a Catholic seminary in Vancouver. For both Miranda and Indrin their travels become a platonic journey of discovery. This novel was shortlisted for a Saskatchewan Book Award: First Book (Brenda MacDonald Riches Award).

Second Appeal: Character

Subjects: British Columbia • First Novels • Jasper National Park • Male/Female Relationships • Religious Life • Road Novels • Self-discovery • Single Women • Vancouver • Women Television Producers and Directors

Read On: *Getting Over Edgar* is Joan Barfoot's novel about a woman on a journey of self-discovery. In Billie Letts's *Where the Heart Is* another young woman's life takes an ultimate turn for the better after she is dumped by her boyfriend. Other road novels include *Chinchilla Farm* by Judith Freeman, *The Floating World* by Cynthia Kadohata, and *Northern Exposure* by Ann duMais McCormick.

Wiebe, Rudy.

Sweeter Than All the World. Alfred A. Knopf Canada, 2001. 438pp. Book Groups 📖

A father's search for his missing daughter takes him on a journey into his Mennonite past, where he rediscovers his family stories and feels the enduring love that ties families together.

Second Appeal: Character

Subjects: Family History • Fathers and Daughters • Love Stories • Mennonites

Read On: Wiebe also writes about Mennonite traditions in *Peace Shall Destroy Many, First and Vital Candle,* and *The Blue Mountains of China.* Sandra Birdsell's *The Russländer* is another intensely written saga about a Mennonite family and their journey to a life in Canada. John Weier's *Steppe* is the story of Mennonites in the Ukraine, before they travel to Canada. For novels about missing people and the impact of their disappearance on those left behind, read Tim O'Brien's *In the Lake of the Woods* and Jacquelyn Mitchard's *The Deep End of the Ocean.*

Wynveen, Tim.

Sweeter Life. Random House of Canada, 2002. 426pp. Book Groups 📖

Orphaned as children, Cyrus Owen and his brother and sister have followed very different life paths. Cyrus, a young man with limited musical talent but great passion, is looking to escape a rural farming life. He joins a touring rock band and begins a tumultuous journey that brings him full circle toward self-awareness.

Second Appeal: Character

Subjects: Bands • Brothers and Sisters • Family • Musicians • Orphans

Read On: Wynveen also explored the theme of homecoming in his novel *Balloon*. Mary Lawson's *Crow Lake* is another story about the different choices a family of orphans makes. In Madison Smartt Bell's coming-of-age novel, *Anything Goes,* a young man's experiences in a rock band enable him to understand his past and move on. In Gail Anderson-Dargatz's *A Rhinestone Button*, the main protagonist also embarks on a journey of self-discovery, without ever leaving his small Prairie town. Wynveen's first novel, *Angel Falls,* won the Commonwealth Writers Prize for Best First Book.

Chapter 3

Character

The reader who enjoys novels with the primary appeal of character is usually looking for strong, realistic portraits. If a character is well crafted, it is this strength that can create a connection between the reader and the character, and as the reader learns the details of the character's life, an understanding develops. This discovery, through the pages of a book, is for many readers the ultimate reading experience.

When an author is able to create a complete portrait of those who tell the story, the characters will stay with the reader for a long time to come. Richard B. Wright does just this in *Clara Callan,* making Clara an unforgettable woman. To accomplish this he lets the reader into the thoughts and feelings, revealed through their letters, of two very different yet connected sisters. The appeal of character is not necessarily limited to novels focusing on a single individual; there can in fact be several voices, each of whom participates in the telling of the story, such as in Wayson Choy's *The Jade Peony,* a novel in which the adult siblings of a Chinese-Canadian family recall childhood memories. In Bonnie Burnard's *A Good House* the lives of the members of a family in small-town Ontario come to life. As the family faces and moves on from tragedy, the reader is brought into their lives and home.

In this chapter the reader will become intimately acquainted with a variety of characters through their coming-of-age stories. The coming-of-age story is not restricted to just the very young; there are stories of individuals who come into their own at a number of stages of life, including the middle-aged and the elderly (Dorothy Speak's *The Wife Tree*), and featuring both men (Yves Beauchemin's *The Second Fiddle*) and women (Joan Barfoot's *Getting Over Edgar*).

Readers' advisors are reminded by Joyce Saricks (1997, 45) that point of view can be extremely important to some readers: there are those who find first-person narratives too intimate and may not want to be that close to a character, like Barney Panofsky in Mordecai Richler's *Barney's Version*. These readers prefer stories told from a distance.

It is often the case that authors will provide strong supporting characters, individuals whose presence in the story moves the narrative and helps the main protagonist tell the story; look to the novels of Emma Richler (*Sister Crazy*) or Edward Riche (*Rare Birds*) for examples of this.

So, whether the character is a gay hairdresser, an Aboriginal artist, a teenage stripper, a World War II survivor, or a six-year-old boy, the reader should expect to develop an attachment to the people found on the pages of these novels as they share their stories.

Adderson, Caroline.

A History of Forgetting. Patrick Crean Editions, 1999. 359pp. Book Groups 📖

Malcolm, an aging gay man, is struggling with the loss of his life partner to Alzheimer's disease. Now he must also face the murder of a fellow hairdresser by neo-Nazis. Hoping to make sense of this murder, he and his salon apprentice Alison make a journey to the Auschwitz museum. Adderson was shortlisted for the Ethel Wilson Fiction Prize and the Rogers Writers' Trust Fiction Prize for *A History of Forgetting*.

Second Appeal: Story

Subjects: Alzheimer's Disease • Auschwitz • Canadians in Poland • First Novels • Gay Men • Hairdressers • Holocaust Survivors • Neo-Nazism • Vancouver • Young Women

Read On: Peter Robinson's *Dead Right* features Inspector Alan Banks investigating a murder for which a group of neo-Nazis are the suspected killers. For another look at Auschwitz, try *Pictures at an Exhibition* by D. M. Thomas. The subject of Alzheimer's disease is sensitively dealt with in a collection of stories by Sandra Sabatini, *The One with the News*. Adderson also provides a glimpse into the thoughts and lives of her characters, a husband and wife, in *Sitting Practice*, as the couple struggles to cope with personal tragedy.

Aitken, Will.

A Visit Home. Simon & Schuster, 1993. 285pp. Book Groups 📖

While in therapy to deal with the sudden death of a colleague, Daniel Kenning recalls repressed childhood memories of sexual abuse. Making two visits home to confront his parents, he must deal with the consequences of this early abuse by his father.

Subjects: Abuse • Adult Child Abuse Victims • Architects • Fathers and Sons • Incest • Repressed Memory

Read On: Aitken's other novels discuss very different issues. *Terre Haute* is the coming-of-age story of a young gay man, and *Realia* chronicles the experiences of a brash woman in the pop culture of Japan in the mid-1980s. A family in crisis because of abuse can be found in Ann-Marie MacDonald's *Fall on Your Knees*. In Elizabeth Berg's *The Art of Mending*, a young woman's repressed memories of abuse surface and must be confronted by her surprised siblings, whose lives are very different from the victim's. The main character in Janice Galloway's *The Trick Is to Keep Breathing* also seeks therapy in an attempt to cope as life spirals out of her control. Sylvia Fraser was one of the first Canadian authors to write about incest, in her memoir *My Father's House: A Memoir of Incest and Healing*. In *What Birds*

Can Only Whisper, Julie Brickman leads a young woman through repressed memories of incest.

Alexie, Robert.

Porcupines and China Dolls. Stoddart, 2002. 286pp. Book Groups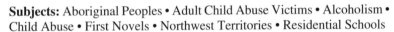

After Jake Nolan sees on television the former priest who abused him and many other Native children in a Christian residential school, he and his best friend James report the abuse to the authorities. This confrontation begins a healing journey for Jake, James, and their community.

Second Appeal: Story

Subjects: Aboriginal Peoples • Adult Child Abuse Victims • Alcoholism • Child Abuse • First Novels • Northwest Territories • Residential Schools

Read On: The intensity in Alexie's work is similar to that in James Welch's *Winter in the Blood* and Sherman Alexie's *The Lone Ranger and Tonto Fistfight in Heaven.* A young Aboriginal who seeks to come to terms with past abuse is the subject of Richard Van Camp's *The Lesser Blessed.* Like the characters in Larry Watson's *Montana 1948* and Henry Denker's *The Retreat*, those here possess the strength needed to resolve their personal crises.

Alexis, André.

🎗 *Childhood.* McClelland & Stewart, 1998. 265pp. Book Groups

After the death of his mother, middle-aged Thomas reflects on his childhood and the three people who most shaped his life: the grandmother who raised him until her death, the mother he first met at the age of ten, and Henry Wink, the man who may or may not have been his father. This novel won the Trillium Book Award and the Chapters/*Books in Canada* First Novel Award, and was shortlisted for the Giller Prize and the Rogers Writers' Trust Fiction Prize.

Second Appeal: Language

Subjects: 1950s • 1960s • Coming of Age • Death of a Parent • First Novels • Forgiveness • Mothers and Sons • Ottawa • Race Relations • Small-town Life

Read On: Alexis's collection of short stories, *Despair*, was shortlisted for the Commonwealth Writer's Prize for Best Book in the Caribbean and Canada. Neil Bissoondath's *The Worlds Within Her* features an adult child reflecting on the relationship of parent and child following the parent's death. The central figure in Eden Robinson's *Monkey Beach* reflects on her childhood (although she is still a young woman) as her family copes with tragedy. In his autobiography *This Boy's Life*, a narrative that reads very much like fiction, Tobias Wolff re-creates his childhood and those who shaped his life.

Anderson-Dargatz, Gail.

🔖 *The Cure for Death by Lightning*. **Alfred A. Knopf Canada, 1996. 294pp. Book Groups** 📖

Family life in remote British Columbia during World War II is seen through the eyes of fifteen-year-old Beth Weeks, as she and her best friend, Nora, learn to survive the daily trials of living as they strive for independence and their place in the world. This novel received a number of awards: the Betty Trask Prize, the Ethel Wilson Fiction Prize, and the VanCity Women's Book Prize. It was also nominated for the Giller Prize and the Chapters/*Books in Canada* First Novel Award..

Second Appeal: Setting

Subjects: Aboriginal Peoples • British Columbia • Coming of Age • Farm Life • First Novels • Friendship • Teenage Girls • World War II

Read On: Anderson-Dargatz is also the author of *A Recipe for Bees* as well as *The Miss Hereford Stories*, which revolve around the life of a young boy in a fictitious Canadian town. Ella Leffland's *Rumors of Peace* is also about the coming of age of a young girl during World War II. Anderson-Dargatz weaves both legend and the mystical into her novel in a way that is reminiscent of Louise Erdrich (*Four Souls* and others) and Eden Robinson (*Monkey Beach*). Other novels with rural settings include Barbara Kingsolver's *Prodigal Summer*, Jane Smiley's *Good Will,* and Susie Moloney's *A Dry Spell.*

A Rhinestone Button. **Alfred A. Knopf Canada, 2002. 319pp. Book Groups** 📖

The solitary world of Job, an Alberta farmer with a rare condition that causes him to see sounds in colour, is shaken up when his out-of-work pastor brother and family move in. This intrusion into his home and life begins Job's journey of discovery as he struggles with faith, love, and his place within his small town.

Second Appeal: Setting

Subjects: Alberta • Baptists • Farm Life • Farmers • Small-town Life • Synesthesia

Read On: Anderson-Dargatz also explores rural farm life and marriage in *A Recipe for Bees*. Mark Salzman's *Lying Awake* blends spirituality and a neurological disorder to examine faith. Other novels with characters suffering from synesthesia are Clare Morrall's *Astonishing Splashes of Colour*, Michele Jaffe's *Lover Boy,* and Jeffrey Moore's *The Memory Artists*. Like Alistair MacLeod (*No Great Mischief*), Anderson-Dargatz displays a notable depth of understanding for her characters and their lives. Betty Wilson's *The Book of Sarah* shares the setting of small-town Alberta, while Christina Kilbourne's *Day of the Dog-tooth Violets* offers another view of life in a rural community.

Armstrong, Jeannette C.

Whispering in Shadows. **Theytus Books, 2000. 296pp. Book Groups** 📖

Aboriginal artist Penny Jackson abandons both painting and family following her agent's request that her work become less politically graphic. What follows is a spiritual journey of global activism as she faces the challenges of being an Aboriginal woman in a modern world.

Second Appeal: Language

Subjects: Aboriginal Peoples • Art • Cancer • Coming of Age • Environmentalists • Okanagan Nation • Single Mothers • Women Artists

Read On: The young Aboriginal woman in Eden Robinson's *Monkey Beach* also embarks on a journey of self-discovery. The artist in Diane Glancy's *The Mask Maker* is a woman of mixed heritage who works to understand her identity. Anne Tyler's *Ladder of Years* tells the story of a woman who abandons her family and responsibilities looking for a new life, but ends up taking on a different set of responsibilities. Art and activism combine as another woman embarks on a journey of self-discovery in Lesley Krueger's *Drink the Sky*. Armstrong incorporates letters and diary entries to reveal her character's journey in a similar style to that found in *Clara Callan* by Richard B. Wright. The gentle poetic quality of this novel is reminiscent of Helen Humphreys's *The Lost Garden*.

Atkinson, Diana.

Highways and Dancehalls. Alfred A. Knopf Canada, 1995. 235pp.

While living the life of a stripper, seventeen-year-old Sarah, known as Tabitha on the British Columbia strip-club circuit, records her thoughts in a diary and ultimately comes to find the inner strength needed to move on with her life. This novel was shortlisted for the Governor General's Literary Award for Fiction and the Chapters/*Books in Canada* First Novel Award.

Subjects: Abusive Relationships • British Columbia • Drugs • Fathers and Daughters • First Novels • Strippers • Teenage Girls

Read On: Eliza Clark's *What You Need* is another novel that depicts the life of the stripper, while *Nerve* by Barbra Leslie is an exploration of a woman's sexuality from adolescence to middle age. Chris Bruckert's *Taking It Off, Putting It On: Women in the Strip Trade* is a collection of interviews with strippers that provides a glimpse into their lives. Another first novel that captures the gritty underbelly of the lives of street teens is *After Nirvana* by Lee Williams; this novel also shares elements of the horrific seen in novels by Bret Easton Ellis (*Glamorama* and others).

Atwood, Margaret.

 Alias Grace. McClelland & Stewart, 1996. 470pp. Book Groups 📖

In 1843, sixteen-year-old Grace Marks and her supposed lover are convicted of murdering Grace's employer and his housekeeper-lover. Sixteen years later a fledgling psychologist visits Grace in prison to probe her lost memories of the event, hoping to prove her innocent and secure her release from prison. *Alias Grace*, an ALA Notable Book, won the Giller Prize and received the Heritage Toronto Award of Merit and the Premio Mondello. *Alias Grace* was also shortlisted for the Booker Prize, the Orange Prize for Fiction, the International IMPAC Dublin Literary Award for the Novel, the Governor General's Literary Award for Fiction, the Arthur Ellis Award for Best Novel, and the Alcuin Society Award for Excellence in Canadian Book Design.

Second Appeal: Story

Subjects: 1840s • Domestic Workers • Irish Canadians • Male–Female Relationships • Marks, Grace • Murder • Trials (Murder) • Women Murderers • Women Prisoners

Read On: Like Sheri Holman in *The Dress Lodger* and Sarah Waters in *Fingersmith*, Atwood has written a novel that examines the victimization of working-class women in Victorian culture. Emma Donoghue's *Slammerkin* is another fictional biography of a young woman who is convicted of murder. Susan Musgrave's main character in *Cargo of Orchids* is a woman on death row for murder. *The Convict Lover* by Merilyn Simonds, the true story of a clandestine correspondence between a young girl and a convict in the Kingston Penitentiary in the early 1900s, is an excellent companion piece to this novel. Atwood's other works include *The Handmaid's Tale*, *Cat's Eye*, and *The Edible Woman.*

Babiak, Todd.

🎖 *Choke Hold.* **Turnstone Press, 2000. 237pp.**

Teenage Jeremy Little eventually learns how violence and a desire for revenge have shaped his life, after he returns to the small town he left following an incident at a high school party that drove him away. This work received the Henry Kreisel Award for Best First Book and was shortlisted for the Rogers Writers' Trust Fiction Prize.

Subjects: Alberta • Anger • Coming of Age • First Novels • Martial Arts • Small-town Life • Teenage Boys

Read On: The coming-of-age story of young males is told in Robert Cormier's *The Chocolate War* and in John Knowles's *A Separate Peace*. The violence Babiak explores is intensely portrayed in Chuck Palahniuk's *Fight Club*. In *Affliction* by Russell Banks a young man returns to his small-town home to reconcile with the past.

Badami, Anita Rau.

🎖 *The Hero's Walk.* **Alfred A. Knopf Canada, 2000. 359pp. Book Groups** 📖

Following the death of her parents in a car accident, seven-year-old Nandana arrives in India to live with her mother's estranged family. In alternating voices Nandana, her grandfather Sripathi, and other relatives struggle to come to terms with tragedy and move toward reconciliation. Badami, winner of the Marian Engel Award in 2000, won the Commonwealth Writers Prize for Best Book in the Caribbean and Canada for this novel; she was also shortlisted for the Ethel Wilson Fiction Prize and the Kiriyama Pacific Rim Book Prize.

Second Appeal: Story

Subjects: Bengal • Canadians in India • Car Accidents • Death of a Parent • Family Relationships • Grandfathers • India • Orphans • Resentment • Young Girls

Read On: Badami also explored the complexity of family relationships in her first novel, *Tamarind Mem*. Other titles dealing with family in India are Chitra Banerjee Divakaruni's *Sister of My Heart* and Indira Ganesan's *Inheritance*. The children in Mary Lawson's *Crow Lake* must learn to live without their parents following a car accident. Barbara Kingsolver's *The Poisonwood Bible* is another novel whose story is told in the alternating voices of a family in crisis; the family in John Bemrose's *The Island Walkers* is also in crisis although for very different reasons.

Baillie, Martha.

Madame Balashovskaya's Apartment. **Turnstone Press, 1995. 118pp. Book Groups** 📖

Ninety-year-old Eugenie gives visitors to her Parisian apartment glimpses of a long life as she reflects on the events of her past, including her marriage to a Russian musician and the death of her daughters.

> **Subjects:** Elderly Women • Family Relationships • Grandmothers • Mothers and Daughters • Reminiscing in Old Age

> **Read On:** In Baillie's first novel, *My Sister, Esther,* the title character's sister attempts to understand what has driven Esther toward anorexia and suicide. Susanna Tamaro's *Follow Your Heart* and Mark Helprin's *Memoir from Antproof Case* centre on characters reflecting on their lives. For another examination of long lives, try Wendy McGrath's *Donovan's Station* or Carol Shields's *The Stone Diaries.*

Baldwin, Shauna Singh.

🎗 *What the Body Remembers.* **Doubleday, 1999. 475pp. Book Groups** 📖

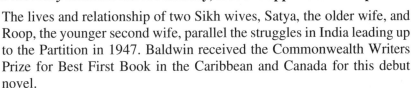

The lives and relationship of two Sikh wives, Satya, the older wife, and Roop, the younger second wife, parallel the struggles in India leading up to the Partition in 1947. Baldwin received the Commonwealth Writers Prize for Best First Book in the Caribbean and Canada for this debut novel.

> **Second Appeal:** Setting

> **Subjects:** First Novels • India • Marriage Customs and Rites • Older Men–Younger Women • Partition, 1947 • Sikh Women in India

> **Read On:** Baldwin's other work includes a short-story collection, *English Lessons and Other Stories,* and a novel, *The Tiger Claw.* In Nahid Rachlin's *Married to a Stranger* a wife struggles with the role society demands she play. Joanna Trollope's *The Men and the Girls* and Anita Shreve's *Fortune's Rocks* both explore the relationship between younger women and older men. Other authors who set their novels in the same time period in India include Vikram Seth (*A Suitable Boy* and others), Rohinton Mistry (*Family Matters* and others), and Salman Rushdie (*Midnight's Children*).

Barfoot, Joan.

Critical Injuries. **Key Porter Books, 2001. 336pp. Book Groups** 📖

Wanting to escape small-town life, seventeen-year-old Roddy plans a robbery that goes horribly wrong. He shoots a local woman, making her a paraplegic; each then alternately shares the impact of this life-changing event. This novel was shortlisted for the Trillium Book Award.

> **Second Appeal:** Language

> **Subjects:** Coming of Age • Juvenile Delinquents • Middle-aged Women • Paraplegia • Small-town Life • Teenage Boys • Violence

Read On: Teens involved with violence are forced to come to terms with the consequences of their actions and seek redemption in David Small's *The River in Winter* and Scott Spencer's *Endless Love.* A spur-of-the-moment decision has life-changing results for the characters in Scott Smith's *A Simple Plan.* In *Sitting Practice* by Caroline Adderson, a husband and wife struggle to find a way to move on following a serious accident that leaves the wife paralysed. The lives of another couple are devastated by a random act of violence in a convenience store in Richard Bausch's *Violence.* Novels that feature alternating points of view include Maxine Chernoff's *A Boy in Winter* and Russell Banks's *The Sweet Hereafter.*

Getting over Edgar. **Key Porter Books, 1999. 270pp. Book Groups** 📖

When Gwen Stone finds herself forced to endure her husband Edgar's funeral after he had left her only a few weeks before, she questions why she must conform to the expectations of society, and embarks on a journey of self-discovery. Along the way she has two relationships: one with a younger man and one with an older man. Ultimately Gwen matures and finds the fulfillment she has been seeking.

Second Appeal: Story

Subjects: Death of a Spouse • Grief • Older Men–Younger Women • Older Women/Younger Men • Runaway Husbands • Self-discovery • Widows

Read On: Other novels by Barfoot include *Abra, Duet for Three,* and *Some Things About Flying.* Readers encounter women coping with grief in *Staying Afloat* by Muriel Spanier and *Leaving Barney* by Bette Ann Moskowitz's . In *Ladder of Years* by Anne Tyler, a woman leaves her life behind and embarks on a journey of self-discovery. Constance Beresford-Howe's *A Serious Widow* and David Doucette's *Strong at the Broken Places* both follow recently widowed women as they seek to gain a sense of their own identity.

Beauchemin, Yves.

The Second Fiddle. **Stoddart, 1998. 442pp.**

Forty-five-year-old journalist Nicolas, clearly headed for a mid-life crisis, has abandoned his wife, children, and career. He is certain he can gain the literary fame he so desperately seeks by writing an exposé of the corrupt practices of a minister in the National Assembly. Translated from the French [*Le second violon*] by David Homel.

Second Appeal: Setting

Subjects: Abandoned Children • French Canadian • Journalists • Marriage • Mid-life Crisis • Montreal • Politics • Quebec • Runaway Husbands • Translations

Read On: Beauchemin's *The Alley Cat* also features a man whose life spirals out of control and who risks everything to maintain control of his life and sanity. Martin Amis's *The Information* introduces a similar writer hero struggling through a mid-life crisis. For more about political corruption, try an early Leon Rooke title, *Who Goes There.* In *Adultery* by Richard B. Wright, a man's mid-life crisis has disastrous consequences for more than just himself. Politics and Montreal combine in Marianne Ackerman's *Jump*; also set in Montreal are Mordecai Richler's *Barney's Version*, Ray Smith's *The Man Who Loved Jane Austen,* and Eva Stachniak's *Necessary Lies.*

Bergen, David

The Case of Lena S. McClelland & Stewart, 2002. 286pp. Book Groups 📖

As his parents' marriage breaks apart, sixteen-year-old aspiring poet Mason Crowe begins to experience the angst of teenage love, first with Seeta, an older girl headed for an arranged marriage, and then with Lena, a girl who battles both her family and manic depression with ultimately tragic results. Bergen received the Carol Shields Winnipeg Book Award for this novel and was shortlisted for the McNally Robinson Book of the Year, the Margaret Laurence Award for Fiction, and the Governor General's Literary Award for Fiction.

Second Appeal: Language

Subjects: Coming of Age • Depression, Mental • First Love • Love Stories • Manitoba • Teenage Boys • Young Men

Read On: Bergen is also the author of *See the Child*, a compassionate tale of a father mourning the loss of his son. Bergen's use of footnotes as a storytelling device appears in Mordecai Richler's *Barney's Version* and in Dave Eggers's *A Heartbreaking Work of Staggering Genius*. The descriptive language here parallels Richard Ford's writing in *Independence Day*. To read a coming-of-age love story, look at Robert Bell's *Of Water & Wine*. A young man struggles within his dysfunctional family and finds a relationship with a young woman who is facing her own demons in *Into the Great Wide Open* by Kevin Canty.

Berry, Michelle.

What We All Want. Random House of Canada, 2001. 239pp. Book Groups 📖

When three eccentric adult siblings gather for their mother's funeral, they each have differing views regarding the handling of this occasion. The result is a unique response to the celebration of a life.

Second Appeal: Language

Subjects: Agoraphobia • Black Humour • Brothers and Sisters • Death of a Parent • Family Relationships • First Novels • Funerals

Read On: Quirky characters dealing with life are met in Barbara Gowdy's *Mister Sandman* and Lynn Coady's *Strange Heaven,* as well as in the novels of Anne Tyler (*Back When We Were Grownups*). Black humour and quirky characters also appear in Katherine Dunn's *Geek Love*, John Irving's *The Hotel New Hampshire,* and Lewis Nordan's *The Sharpshooter Blues*. Joan Barfoot's *Getting over Edgar* is another novel with a humorous, non-traditional response to death.

Birdsell, Sandra.

🎗 *The Chrome Suite.* McClelland & Stewart, 1992. 364pp. Book Groups 📖

On a trip from Toronto to Winnipeg with her lover Piotr, scriptwriter Amy Barber looks back over the years since the summer in her childhood when her older sister's death was followed by the breakup of her family, the loss of a friend, and a search for both love and self. This novel was the McNally Robinson Book of the Year and was shortlisted for the Governor General's Literary Award for Fiction.

Second Appeal: Story

Subjects: Black Humour • Child Abuse • Coming of Age • Death of a Child • Family Relationships • Manitoba • Reminiscing in Old Age • Self-acceptance • Small-town Life • Women

Read On: Birdsell also wrote *Agassiz: A Novel in Stories* and *The Two-Headed Calf. The Chrome Suite*, a claustrophobic, interior novel, shares a sense of the difficulties of childhood with the works of other Canadian writers, including Diane Schoemperlen (*In the Language of Love: A Novel in 100 Chapters*) and Margaret Atwood (*Cat's Eye* and others). Two people search for love and find it in Carol Shields's *The Republic of Love*.

🎗 *The Russländer.* McClelland & Stewart, 2001. 350pp. Book Groups 📖

Elderly Katya Vogt, now living in Winnipeg, recounts the story of her life, beginning in pre-Revolutionary Russia through World War I to the pivotal event that led to her immigration to Canada. Birdsell, winner of the 1993 Marian Engel Award, also garnered three Saskatchewan Book Awards for this novel: Book of the Year, the Fiction Award, and City of Regina Book Award. She was also shortlisted for the Giller Prize.

Second Appeal: Setting

Subjects: Elderly Women • Immigrants and Refugees • Manitoba • Mennonites • Reminiscing in Old Age • Russia • Women Immigrants

Read On: Carol Shields's *The Stone Diaries* and Mary Lee Settle's *Celebration* explore women's long lives. In Martha Blum's *The Walnut Tree,* another woman relates significant memories of the past, including her journey from Europe to Western Canada. *My Darling Dead Ones* by Erika de Vasconcelos traces generations of family connections from Europe to North America. This title was released in the United States in 2004 with the title *Katya*.

Bissoondath, Neil.

🎗 *Doing the Heart Good.* Cormorant Books, 2002. 328pp. Book Groups 📖

When a fire destroys his home, seventy-five-year-old Alistair Mackenzie moves in with his daughter and her family. Fearing that his life may disappear in much the same way that fire destroyed his home and possessions, Alistair begins to record the stories, events, and people that helped to create the landscape of his life. Bissoondath won the Hugh MacLennan Prize for Fiction for this novel.

Second Appeal: Language

Subjects: Elderly Men • Fathers and Daughters • Fires • Memory

Read On: Elderly men reflect on their lives in Mark Helprin's *Memoir from Antproof Case*, Ethan Canin's *Carry Me Across the Water,* and Robertson Davies's *The Cunning Man. Family Matters* by Rohinton Mistry is another deeply moving story of an elderly man who is forced to move into his daughter's home. Bissoondath's earlier novel *The Worlds Within Her* was nominated for the Governor General's Literary Award for Fiction.

Bock, Dennis.

The Ash Garden. **HarperFlamingoCanada, 2001. 281pp. Book Groups**

The bombing of Hiroshima intimately connects the lives of three people: Emiko, a Japanese filmmaker and Hiroshima survivor; Anton, a German physicist who worked on the atomic bomb; and Anton's wife Sophia, a German refugee in the final stages of lupus. Emiko discovers the connection when she visits them to view films Anton made following this life-changing historical event. Bock won the Canada-Japan Literary Award for *The Ash Garden*; he was also nominated for the Amazon.ca/*Books in Canada* First Novel Award, the Kiriyama Pacific Rim Book Prize, the CBA Libris Award Fiction Book of the Year, the Commonwealth Writers Prize for Best First Book in the Caribbean and Canada, and the International IMPAC Dublin Literary Award for the Novel.

Second Appeal: Story

Subjects: Atomic Bomb • First Novels • Hiroshima • Japan • Los Alamos • Lupus • New Mexico • Women Refugees • World War II

Read On: Bock's book of short fiction, *Olympia* won the Betty Trask Award, the CAA Jubilee Award, and the Danuta Gleed Literary Award. John Hersey's *Hiroshima* is considered to be the definitive non-fiction work on Hiroshima. James Thackara's *America's Children* is another novel about the scientists involved with the creation of the atomic bomb and the human stories related to the bombing of Japan. Through a series of richly described flashbacks, the author weaves his story back through time in a style similar to that of Michael Ondaatje in *Anil's Ghost*. Like Bock, Kerri Sakamoto in *One Hundred Million Hearts* also explores the rippling effects of war. Although it does not share the same time period as this novel, the destruction felt in this novel can also be found in Gaétan Soucy's *Vaudeville!*

Buday, Grant.

A Sack of Teeth. **Raincoast Books, 2002. 269pp. Book Groups** 📖

The lives of the Klein family unravel with dreadful results on a September day in the mid-1960s: six-year-old Jack is off for his first day of school, his father Ray is off having an affair, and his mother Lorraine discovers that their boarder has committed suicide.

Subjects: 1960s • Black Humour • Dysfunctional Families • Love Affairs • Mothers and Sons • Older Men–Younger Women • Suicide

Read On: Buday has written a number of other novels, including *White Lung* and *Under Glass*, and the short-story collection *Monday Night Man*. The black comedy here parallels the humour of James Ellroy or Irvine Welsh, although the subjects they cover are divergent. Another story that unfolds over the course of a single day is Patrick Kavanagh's *Gaff Topsails*. Michael Holmes's *Watermelon Row* also spans a single day, but is very different in its subject matter: it chronicles a day in the life of three self-destructive men, all of whom frequent a neighbourhood strip joint.

Burnard, Bonnie.

🎗 *A Good House.* **HarperFlamingoCanada, 2000. 283pp. Book Groups** 📖

Three generations of the Chambers family live out their ordinary lives in their small Canadian hometown near London, Ontario. Burnard, the 1995 recipient of the Marian Engel Award, won the Giller Prize for this first novel, *A Good House*.

Second Appeal: Setting

Subjects: Death of a Parent • Death of a Sibling • Family Relationships • First Novels • Multi-generational Fiction • Remarriage • Small-town Life • Veterans • World War II

Read On: Burnard's other books include two collections of stories, *Casino & Other Stories* and *Women of Influence*. For more about small-town life read David Bergen's *A Year of Lesser* and Sandra Birdsell's *The Chrome Suite*. In her loving and detailed descriptions of the lives of men and women, adults and children, Burnard's novel is reminiscent of *The Stone Diaries* and *Larry's Party* by Carol Shields. Meet a family facing a mother's death from cancer in Alexandra Marshall's *Gus in Bronze*.

Bush, Catherine.

Claire's Head. **McClelland & Stewart, 2004. 323pp. Book Groups** 📖

Toronto cartographer and migraine-sufferer Claire Barber sets out on a journey to search for her missing sister, who also suffers from migraine headaches. This quest becomes an inner exploration of Claire herself. As she travels from within Canada to Europe, the United States, and ultimately Mexico, she is finally able to make decisions about the future directions of her life.

Subjects: Migraine • Missing Persons • Road Novels • Sisters • Women Cartographers

Read On: Bush's earlier work includes *Minus Time* and *The Rules of Engagement*. The characters in *The Hours* by Michael Cunningham are faced with a struggle between inner conflict and illness. There is a character in Joanne Harris's *Five Quarters of the Orange* who also suffers with migraines. *In the Place of Last Things* by Michael Helm recounts a man's journey initially in search of his missing brother that ultimately becomes a journey toward self-understanding.

Cameron, Anne.

Hardscratch Row. **Harbour Publishing, 2002. 378pp. Book Groups** 📖

When a member of a large family dies, the siblings reunite and attempt to resolve their past and present problems with both humour and tenderness even as conflicts arise at this stressful time.

Second Appeal: Story

Subjects: British Columbia • Brothers and Sisters • Death of a Sibling • Family • Funerals • Violence

Read On: Cameron shares a style of writing with Lynn Coady (*Saints of Big Harbour*) and David Adams Richards (*River of the Brokenhearted* and others). Cameron has included the theme of family violence in other novels, such as *Aftermath* and *The Whole Fam Damily*. Douglas Coupland's *All Families Are Psychotic* also features a family that remains connected despite their unconventional relationships. Another realistic portrayal of a middle-class Canadian family desperately trying to survive can be found in John Bemrose's *The Island Walkers*. Although *Hardscratch Row* is a sequel to an earlier work by the author, *Wedding Cakes, Rats and Rodeo Queens*, it can be read as a stand-alone work.

Campbell, Sandra.

Getting to Normal. Stoddart, 2001. 244pp. Book Groups 📖

Following her mother's desertion, seven-year-old Alice, hospitalized with a mysterious illness and injury, is able to overcome her illness with the care and love of Irma, a Serbian immigrant woman.

Subjects: Coming of Age • Dysfunctional Families • Family Relationships • First Novels • Illness • Immigrants and Refugees • Mothers and Daughters • Mothers Deserting Their Families • Serbians • Sisters

Read On: C. E. Poverman's *Solomon's Daughter* and Joanne Greenberg's *I Never Promised You a Rose Garden* are novels that confront emotional disability. Jane Finlay-Young's *From Bruised Fell* is another novel in which young girls must cope with the harm parents can inflict on their children. Other novels told from a child's perspective include Nino Ricci's *Lives of the Saints*, Penelope Trevor's *Listening for Small Sounds,* and Helen Dunmore's *A Spell of Winter*.

Caple, Natalee.

The Plight of Happy People in an Ordinary World. House of Anansi Press, 1999. 248pp. Book Groups 📖

The arrival of the widower Josef forever changes the lives of Irma and Nadja, teenage sisters working in their parents' bakery; he charms one and seduces the other.

Second Appeal: Language

Subjects: Coming of Age • Family Relationships • First Novels • Older Men–Younger Women • Seduction • Sisters • Teenage Girls

Read On: Caple is the author of a collection of short stories, *The Heart Is Its Own Reason,* and the novel *Mackerel Sky*. Elizabeth Hay writes lyrically about the lives of two sisters in *A Student of Weather*. Richard B. Wright's *Clara Callan* also features a sister seduced by a man who comes into her life. Catherine Simmons Niven's *A Fine Daughter* and Maureen Medved's *The Tracey Fragments* are stories told from the daughter's perspective. Another novel that conveys a similar sense of family tragedy is *The Island Walkers* by John Bemrose.

Carpenter, David.

◆ *Banjo Lessons.* **Coteau Books, 1997. 281pp. Book Groups** 📖

Shy, sensitive Timothy "Fishy" Fisher, unable to compete with his popular, athletic, older brother, struggles to learn how to become a man as he pursues his dream of being a writer. Carpenter won the City of Edmonton Book Prize for *Banjo Lessons* and was nominated for the Book of the Year and the Fiction Award in the Saskatchewan Book Awards competition.

> **Subjects:** 1960s • Alberta • Banjo • Coming of Age • First Novels • Fishing • Teenage Boys • Writers

> **Read On:** Carpenter's other novel, *Courting Saskatchewan,* includes some of the same incidents that are covered in this novel. W. O. Mitchell is the author of some classic stories of Prairie childhood, including *Who Has Seen the Wind* and *How I Spent My Summer Holidays*, and Rick Book's *Necking with Louise* is a collection of Prairie coming-of-age stories. *The Story of Bobby O'Malley* by Wayne Johnston features another equally sensitive young man who is struggling with the decisions made by his often-warring parents regarding his life choices.

Carrier, Roch.

The Lament of Charlie Longsong. **Viking, 1998. 260pp. Book Groups** 📖

Recently separated Montreal history professor Robert, traveling in the southern United States to research the life of a nineteenth-century French-Canadian farmer, meets Charlie, a Native American. Charlie is a man consumed with the memory of a wartime liaison with a French-Canadian nurse, and it is the story of their relationship that will help Robert to understand what is most important in his own life. Translated from the French [*Petit homme tornade*] by Sheila Fischman.

> **Second Appeal:** Language

> **Subjects:** Aboriginal Peoples • French Canadian • Historians • Love Affairs • Love Stories • Translations

> **Read On:** Carrier is a prolific writer of stories for both adults (*The Man in the Closet*, *Prayers of a Young Man,* and others) and children, including the Canadian classic, *The Hockey Sweater and Other Stories*. A man begins a journey of self-discovery on the basis of another story in Michael Kaufman's *The Possibility of Dreaming on a Night Without Stars*. Michael Ondaatje's *The English Patient* relates the tale of a wartime romance with a nurse. Carrier weaves his story together with a magical style reminiscent of Gabriel García Márquez.

Charney, Ann.

Rousseau's Garden. **Véhicule Press, 2001. 206pp. Book Groups** 📖

With the help of a group of women, her friends and those who knew her mother, thirty-seven-year-old photographer Claire searches for the truth behind her mother's death to resolve her childhood feelings of abandonment.

> **Subjects:** Abandoned Children • Death of a Parent • France • Married Women • Mothers and Daughters • Rousseau, Jean-Jacques • Suicide • Women Photographers

Read On: *Dobryd*, Charney's first novel, is the memoir of a young Jewish girl's experiences at the end of World War II. A child seeks answers following a mother's suicide in Kevin Chong's *Baroque-a-nova*. Gail Scott's *My Paris* chronicles a woman's experiences while in Paris. Powerful images of the past are created through the lives of the women in Erika de Vasconcelos's *My Darling Dead Ones* in a way that allows the past and present to connect.

Choy, Wayson.

The Jade Peony. **Douglas & McIntyre, 1995. 238pp. Book Groups**

Jook-Liang, Jung-Sum, and Sek-Lung, three children of an immigrant Chinese family living in Vancouver in the 1940s, are torn between their parents' ways of Old China and their desire to be true Canadians. This novel was awarded both the City of Vancouver Book Award and the Trillium Book Award and was selected as an ALA Notable Book. It was also shortlisted for the Chapters/*Books in Canada* First Novel Award.

Second Appeal: Story

Subjects: 1940s • Boxing • British Columbia • Brothers and Sisters • Chinese Canadians • Culture Clash • Family Relationships • First Novels • Immigrants and Refugees • Vancouver • World War II

3

Read On: Choy returns to the home of the Chen family in 1940s Vancouver in his follow-up novel, *All That Matters*, this time allowing First Son Kiam-Kim to tell his story. Like Jung-Sum in Choy's novel, the main character in Gus Lee's *China Boy* gains acceptance and self-respect by learning to box. In Amy Tan's *The Bonesetter's Daughter,* Ruth is the daughter of Asian parents; as a child her mother's grip on the past embarrassed her. Ivy Huffman and Julia Kwong draw a portrait of the difficult lives of Chinese immigrants in Canada in *The Dream of Gold Mountain*. Choy's memoir *Paper Shadows: A Chinatown Childhood*, was shortlisted for the Governor General's Literary Award for Nonfiction, The Charles Taylor Prize for Literary Nonfiction, and the Writers' Trust of Canada Drainie-Taylor Biography Prize.

Coady, Lynn.

Saints of Big Harbour. **Doubleday Canada, 2002. 416p. Book Groups**

When sixteen-year-old Guy Boucher becomes a victim of teenager rumours, he must come to terms with community outrage while dealing with an overworked mother and an alcoholic uncle in small-town Nova Scotia.

Second Appeal: Story

Subjects: 1980s • Acadia • Adolescence • Alcoholics • Coming of Age • Dysfunctional Families • Fathers Deserting Their Families • Nova Scotia • Teenage Boys • Violence

Read On: David Adams Richards in *Mercy Among the Children* also captures the sometime bleakness of the Maritime experience. In *Fall on Your Knees*, Ann-Marie MacDonald examines a dysfunctional family in Nova

Scotia. Guy Boucher, as a teenager in a dysfunctional family, is reminiscent of Hezekiah Sheehand in Melinda Haynes's *Chalktown*. Randall Hunsucker, in *Goodnight, Nebraska* by Tom McNeal, faces the challenges of adolescence in small-town Nebraska.

Cohen, Matt.

🎗 *Elizabeth and After.* **Alfred A. Knopf Canada, 1999. 370pp. Book Groups** 📖

In a small Ontario town, Elizabeth McKelvey affects the lives of several men (her husband, her lover, and her son); this influence still exerts power decades after her death and alters personalities, characters, and destinies. Cohen's novel won the Governor General's Literary Award for Fiction.

> **Subjects:** Car Accidents • Death of a Parent • Death of a Spouse • Estranged Families • Fathers and Daughters • Forgiveness • Marriage • Mothers and Sons • Small-town Life

> **Read On:** Cohen authored more than twenty books, including novels (*The Bookseller*, *Last Seen,* and others), short stories (*Getting Lucky*), and poetry, as well as two books for children. Other novels set in small Canadian towns include Alice Munro's *Lives of Girls and Women*, Sandra Birdsell's *Agassiz: A Novel in Stories*, David Bergen's *A Year of Lesser,* and W. O. Mitchell's *Who Has Seen the Wind*.

Cole, Trevor.

Norman Bray in the Performance of His Life. **McClelland and Stewart, 2004. 367pp. Book Groups** 📖

Aging actor Norman Bray has lived a life of total self-absorption. Now perched on the edge of both personal and financial ruin, he must look beyond himself if he is to have any hope of personal salvation. *Norman Bray in the Performance of His Life* was shortlisted for the Governor General's Literary Award for Fiction.

> **Subjects:** Actors • First Novels • Toronto

> **Read On:** Kingsley Amis creates a flawed protagonist in *Lucky Jim*, introducing readers to a man who becomes his own worst enemy in a time of crisis. In David Gates's *Jernigan* we again meet a man whose life is filled with failures. Cole's humour is reminiscent of Daniel Pearlman's in *Black Flames,* in which the main character, unlike Cole's, is frantically attempting to right the wrongs of his life. Norman Bray's level of narcissism is rivalled by that of a character in Tim O'Brien's *July, July.*

Cooper, Douglas.

Amnesia. **Random House of Canada, 1992. 214pp. Book Groups** 📖

The characters, including a librarian, a mentally ill young woman, and the narrator, Izzy Barlow, tell and retell stories that intersect, diverge, contradict, embellish, and ultimately lay bare each life. *Amnesia* was shortlisted for the Smithbooks/*Books in Canada* First Novel Award.

> **Subjects:** Dysfunctional Families • First Novels • Librarians • Magic Realism • Memory • Mental Illness • Obsessive Love • Sexual Violence • Young Men

---

Read On: The relationship between Izzy and Katie is reminiscent of the relationship between the lovers in Scott Spencer's *Endless Love*. Steve Martin's *The Pleasure of My Company* paints a portrait of a lonely, reclusive neurotic who ultimately finds the courage needed to move outside his personal isolation. Cooper is credited with publishing the first novel to be serialized on the World Wide Web—*Delirium*.

Corbeil, Carole.

🏵 *Voice-over.* **Stoddart, 1992. 288pp. Book Groups** 📖

When their mother remarried in the mid-1980s, Claudine, a Toronto-based documentary filmmaker, and her sister Janine, now a mother herself, were forced to reinvent themselves into anglophones in order to fit into the home and family of their stepfather. As memories of the past resurface into the present, they reveal demons the women must confront. This novel received the Toronto Book Award.

Second Appeal: Language

Subjects: Child Abuse • Documentary Filmmakers • Dysfunctional Families • First Novels • Incest • Montreal • Motherhood • Sisters • Toronto

Read On: Corbeil's second novel, *In the Wings,* also looks at the past resurfacing in the present. An equally intense novel in which the events of the past are revealed is Ann-Marie MacDonald's *Fall on Your Knees.* The family in Michel Basilières's *Black Bird* is also a blend of francophone and anglophone. Hugh MacLennan's *Two Solitudes* is a Canadian classic about the French-English question. The protagonist in Wendy Hornsby's <u>Maggie MacGowen Mystery Series</u> is a documentary filmmaker.

Coupland, Douglas.

All Families Are Psychotic. **Random House of Canada, 2001. 279pp.**

The launching of the space shuttle is the occasion that reunites the Drummonds, a family plagued by drugs, alcohol, AIDS, cancer, suicide, and more. Their chaotic reunion provides an opportunity for them to experience both the horrific and the miraculous together.

Subjects: AIDS • Dysfunctional Families • Family Reunions • Florida • Humorous Fiction • Middle-class Families • Suicide • Women Astronauts

Read On: Coupland has authored a number of novels, including *Hey Nostradamus!* and *Miss Wyoming.* Eccentric families depicted with Coupland's brand of dark humour are featured in Jonathan Franzen's *The Corrections* and Jean Ferris's *Love Among the Walnuts.* Coupland creates characters and situations in a style reminiscent of Chuck Palahniuk (*Choke, Diary,* and others).

Girlfriend in a Coma. **HarperCollins, 1998. 284pp. Book Groups** 📖

In December 1979 Karen Ann MacNeil goes into an eighteen-year coma after ingesting a drug-and-alcohol cocktail. When she awakes to find she has a daughter, delivered nine months into her coma, she also discovers that the lives of her friends have had little or no meaning through the decades of excess. The world is now in danger of destruction unless the self-indulgence and self-pity can be stopped.

Second Appeal: Story

Subjects: British Columbia • Coma Patients • Friendship • Ghosts • Millennium • Television Programs • Vancouver • Viruses • Visions

Read On: In his novel *Miss Wyoming*, Coupland's characters piece together a life following crisis. A man, comatose because of an accident, awakens after eight years in Charles Mathes's *The Girl in the Face of the Clock,* and the character in *The Coma* by Alex Garland struggles to put his life back together after awakening from a coma. Other writers who chronicle the Gen X experience include Persimmon Blackbridge (*Prozac Highway*), Michael Chabon (*Wonder Boys*), and Jay McInerney (*Brightness Falls* and others). Marie-Claire Blais in *These Festive Nights* sets her characters and their story on the edge of the millennium.

Cumyn, Alan.

🎗 *Burridge Unbound.* **McClelland & Stewart, 2000. 342pp. Book Groups** 📖

Two years after Canadian diplomat Bill Burridge was kidnapped, raped, and tortured by a rebel group while posted in a small underdeveloped country, he is separated from his wife and suffering from severe post-traumatic stress syndrome. In an attempt to confront the events of the past, he returns to the country as part of a commission to investigate human rights atrocities. This novel received the Ottawa Book Award.

Subjects: Diplomats • Human Rights Workers • Kidnapping Victims • Politics • Torture • Victims of Terrorism

Read On: Cumyn began Burridge's story in *Man of Bone*, which also won the Ottawa Book Award. Cumyn tells another sad story in *Losing It* but speckles it with touches of humour. Men struggling with post-traumatic stress syndrome related to past violent experiences appear in Frederick Busch's *Closing Arguments* and Scott Anderson's *Triage*. The characters found here are reminiscent of those in *Smokey Joe's Café* by Bryce Courtenay.

Curran, Colleen.

Something Drastic. **Goose Lane, 1995. 213pp.**

Considering it a form of therapy, Lenore Rutland, a thirty-something Montreal waitress, writes unanswered letters to her ex-boyfriend Fergie, recounting her daily adventures (dog-sitting and befriending feminists, firemen, and theatre performers), after Fergie leaves her the day after Christmas.

Second Appeal: Story

Subjects: Epistolary Novels • First Novels • Humorous Fiction • Male–Female Relationships • Montreal • Quebec • Single Women • Waitresses

Read On: Curran continues Lenore's story in her second novel, *Overnight Sensation*. Other novels featuring sassy female characters are Amy Jenkins's *Honeymoon: A Romantic Rampage*, Raffaella Barker's *Hens Dancing*, Marian Keyes's *Last Chance Saloon,* and Helen Fielding's *Bridget Jones's Diary*. Jennifer

Webber's *Defying Gravity* chronicles a young woman's journey as she moves on after her fiancé leaves her.

Davies, Paul.

The Truth. Insomniac Press, 1999. 206pp.

An unnamed narrator recounts his life from birth to middle age and the characters he encountered as he journeyed through Canada, Britain, and the United States.

Subjects: Coming of Age • Fate and Fatalism • Lobsang Rampa, T. (Tuesday) • Male Psychology • Men's Lives • New Age

Read On: *Gelignite Jack* and *Pig Iron* are two of Davies's many other works. Sofia Shafquat's *The Shadow Man* recounts one woman's journey of self-discovery. In Clark Blaise's *If I Were Me*, a man reflects on and recounts his life journey. An unnamed narrator tells the story in *The Book of Jamaica* by Russell Banks and in Leonard Chang's *Dispatches from the Cold*.

Davies, Robertson.

The Cunning Man. McClelland & Stewart, 1994. 468pp. Book Groups 📖

Asked by a reporter to recall the story of a priest's strange death twenty years earlier, holistic physician Dr. Jonathan Hullah reflects on his long, extraordinary life. He recounts his observations and opinions of those who had been part of his life or on whom he had had an impact.

Subjects: Alternative Medicine • Elderly Men • Holistic Medicine • Humorous Fiction • Intellectuals • Physicians

Read On: Davies's other books, written with the same wit and intelligent prose, include *Fifth Business, The Manticore*, and <u>The Cornish Trilogy</u> (*The Rebel Angels*, *What's Bred in the Bone,* and *The Lyre of Orpheus*). Elderly men reflect on their lives in Mark Helprin's *Memoir from Antproof Case*, Ethan Canin's *Carry Me Across the Water,* and Alan Isler's *Clerical Errors*. Like Margaret Atwood's *The Blind Assassin*, this novel blends intriguing characters and a mystery to reveal a long life.

Davis, Lauren B.

The Stubborn Season. HarperFlamingoCanada, 2002. 339pp. Book Groups 📖

With his family's farm failing during the Depression, young David Hirsch takes to the rails to find his own way. Thus begins a journey that will ultimately connect him with Irene, the daughter of a middle-class family in Toronto, who also suffers from the effects of the stock market crash and more.

Second Appeal: Setting

Subjects: 1930s • Coming of Age • Depressions, 1929– • Dysfunctional Families • First Novels • Ontario • Toronto

Read On: Shirley Ann Grau's *Roadwalkers* tells of a wandering child during the Depression era. Depictions of families and the Depression are the focus of Camilla Bittle's *Dear Family* and Frederick Buechner's *The Wizard's Tide*. In this novel, Davis creates a portrait of the Great Depression. Another author who also vividly re-creates another time period is John Grisham, in *A Painted House*.

Endicott, Marina.

Open Arms. Douglas & McIntyre, 2001. 248pp.

Through a series of recollections at ages seventeen, twenty, and twenty-four, Bessie Smith Connolly links the various women her father Patrick Connolly has abandoned over the years. *Open Arms* was shortlisted for the Amazon.ca/*Books in Canada* First Novel Award.

Subjects: Coming of Age • Dysfunctional Families • Fathers Deserting Their Families • First Novels • Grief • Missing Persons • Mothers and Daughters • Saskatchewan

Read On: Strong bonds among women are forged in Elizabeth Berg's *Talk Before Sleep* and Jo-Ann Mapson's *Bad Girl Creek,* as well as in Robert Harling's play *Steel Magnolias*. Kent Haruf's *Eventide* relates the impact of a husband's desertion of his wife and children. Gail Godwin's *A Mother and Two Daughters* explores the connections among a man, his wife, and two daughters following his death.

Findley, Timothy.

❦ *The Piano Man's Daughter*. HarperCollins, 1995. 461pp. Book Groups 📖

Charlie Kilworth reconstructs the life of his mother Lily, the piano man's daughter, who—because of her inherited "spells"—is cast out of her family, kept away from society, and sent away to school; she never stops running from the shadows that pursue her. This novel won the Torgi Literary Award and was shortlisted for the Giller Prize and the Toronto Book Award.

Second Appeal: Story

Subjects: Epilepsy • Mental Illness • Mothers and Daughters • Mothers and Sons • Multi-generational Fiction • Ontario • Toronto

Read On: Among Findley's many novels are *The Last of the Crazy People*, *The Wars,* and *Famous Last Words*. Children deal with mentally ill mothers in *A Star Called Henry* by Roddy Doyle, *Sights Unseen* by Kaye Gibbons, *In Another Country* by Susan Kenney, *The Butcher Boy* by Patrick McCabe, and *My Old Sweetheart* by Susanna Moore.

Pilgrim. HarperFlamingoCanada, 1999. 485pp. Book Groups 📖

In 1912, Pilgrim is delivered to Carl Jung's clinic in Zurich after another successful suicide attempt and another successful revivification. Is Pilgrim immortal, having inhabited many personalities, or merely disturbed? *Pilgrim* was shortlisted for the Giller Prize.

Second Appeal: Story

Subjects: 1910s • Immortality • Jung, Carl • Mental Illness • Psychiatric Hospitals • Psychiatrists • Psychotherapy Patients • Suicide • Switzerland

Read On: Findley often weaves historical and literary figures into his fiction, as seen in his novels *Not Wanted on the Voyage* and *Headhunter.* Other novels populated with real people include E. L. Doctorow's *Ragtime* and *Billy Bathgate, The Old Gringo* by Carlos Fuentes, *Nevermore* by William Hjortsberg, and *Los Alamos* by Joseph Kanon. Novels adopting upper-class psychiatric hospitals as a frame include T. Coraghessan Boyle's *Riven Rock*, Robertson Davies's *The Manticore*, Mark Helprin's *Memoir from Antproof Case*, and Roderick MacLeish's *The First Book of Eppe.*

Flood, Cynthia.

Making a Stone of the Heart. Key Porter, 2002. 342pp. Book Groups 📖

During the autopsy of elderly Dora Dow, a sixty-year-old calcified fetus is discovered. Dora's lifelong secret is just one of many connections between her, Owen Jones (her sometime lover), and Jonathan Smyth, a Vancouver doctor. As other secrets are revealed, these three lives connect back through the early days of the development of Vancouver. This novel was shortlisted for the City of Vancouver Book Award.

Second Appeal: Setting

Subjects: Dysfunctional Families • First Novels • Friendship • Miscarriage • Poverty • Racism • Sexism • Vancouver

Read On: Flood's title story in her collection of short stories, *My Father Took a Cake to France,* won the Journey Prize in 1990. Other novels featuring stone babies include Russell T. Davies's *Damaged Goods* and Will Self's *How the Dead Live.* Dora Dow's pregnancy story is in total contrast to Karen Ann MacNeil's when she gestates and gives birth to a baby while in a coma (Douglas Coupland's *Girlfriend in a Coma*). David Cruise and Alison Griffiths's *Vancouver: A Novel* chronicles the history of this British Columbia city.

Friedman, Elyse.

Waking Beauty. Three Rivers Press, 2004. 244pp.

Living what is possibly one of the dreariest of lives, Allison Penny, an overweight and depressed twenty-two-year-old, wakes up one morning to the miraculous discovery that she is now super-model gorgeous. It is during the process of exacting revenge on family and friends for years of abuse that she finally comes to realize the importance of finding the balance between inner and outer beauty.

Subjects: Beauty • Coming of Age • Humorous Fiction • Male–Female Relationships • Metamorphosis • Overweight Women • Revenge • Self-acceptance • Single Women

Read On: Friedman also uses humour in her earlier novel, *Then Again,* the story of three siblings who come together to revisit their dysfunctional childhood. Single, overweight young women in search of their true inner selves are found in Helen Fielding's *Bridget Jones's Diary* and the sequel, *Bridget Jones: The Edge of Reason* and in *Jemima J.* by Jane Green. Sherri S. Tepper's fantasy *Beauty* is also a retelling of the classic fairy tale *Sleeping Beauty* in which a young woman awakens to find her life has changed drastically.

Gabriele, Lisa.

Tempting Faith DiNapoli. **Doubleday Canada, 2002. 291pp.**

Faith DiNapoli, the eldest daughter of a Catholic Italian family, is an angry teenage girl who breaks every one of her promises to be good. She clashes with her mother, she smokes, she shoplifts, and she swears, all in her journey through adolescence toward the life she hopes will one day be hers.

> **Subjects:** 1980s • Catholics • Coming of Age • Dysfunctional Families • First Novels • Italian Canadians • Mothers and Daughters • Teenage Girls

> **Read On:** Rita Ciresi's *Sometimes I Dream in Italian* is another reflection of the experience of growing up as an Italian Catholic girl, while Binnie Kirshenbaum describes the experience from a Jewish girl's point of view in *An Almost Perfect Moment*. Jane Gardam's *Bilgewater* and *A Long Way from Verona* share the theme of an adolescent girl seeking to find her way.

Galloway, Steven.

Finnie Walsh. **Raincoast Books, 2000. 165pp.**

From their first meeting in grade three, Paul Woodward and Finnie Walsh have been best friends. This friendship develops despite the fact that Finnie's family owns almost everything in their small town of Portsmouth, including the sawmill where Paul's father is employed. It is a shared love of hockey that binds these two friends together through success, tragedy, and death. *Finnie Walsh* was nominated for the Amazon.ca/*Books in Canada* First Novel Award.

> **Subjects:** Coming of Age • Family • First Novels • Hockey Players • Magic Realism • Men's Friendships • Teenage Boys

> **Read On:** In his second novel, *Ascension*, Galloway writes about a family of circus performers. Roch Carrier's *The Hockey Sweater* is a Canadian hockey classic. *The Last Season* by Roy MacGregor is another sports-based novel that displays a depth of knowledge about hockey. A hockey-obsessed boy is the central figure in Pete McCormack's *Understanding Ken*. As in John Irving's *A Prayer for Owen Meany*, a quirky boy's best friend narrates his story in Galloway's novel. To read a similar family story, try Wayne Johnston's *The Divine Ryans.*

Ghatage, Shree.

Brahma's Dream. **Doubleday Canada, 2004. 422pp. Book Groups** 📖

Suffering from a rare hereditary blood disease, thirteen-year-old Mohini is gifted with a perception of life that makes her wise beyond her years. As she and her extended family live through the turbulent years leading up to India's independence in the late 1940s, Mohini continues to live life to its fullest despite her increasingly diminished physical strength.

> **Second Appeal:** Language

> **Subjects:** Anemia in Children • Bombay • Coming of Age • Family • First Novels • Hinduism • India • Teenage Girls

> **Read On:** Ghatage's first book, a short-story collection entitled *Awake When All the World Is Asleep*, won the Thomas Head Randall Atlantic Fiction Award. Other au-

thors whose characters' lives unfold in pre- and post-colonial India include Salman Rushdie (*Midnight's Children*) and Anita Rau Badami (*Tamarind Mem*). Rohinton Mistry's *Family Matters* also describes intricacies in the life of a family in India. Other novels featuring young protagonists wise beyond their years include *Ellen Foster* by Kaye Gibbons and *The Little Friend* by Donna Tartt.

Gibb, Camilla.

The Petty Details of So-and-so's Life. **Doubleday Canada, 2002. 318pp. Book Groups**

Throughout their childhood, siblings Emma and Blue have only each other to rely on as they struggle to overcome an extremely difficult childhood with a deserting father and an unloving mother. Though each one responds differently to the past, they both find resolution with the help of friends and each other.

> **Subjects:** Abandoned Children • Abuse • Brothers and Sisters • Coming of Age • Dysfunctional Families • Family Relationships • Tattoo Artists

> **Read On:** Gibb's first novel, *Mouthing the Words,* which won the Toronto Book Award, is another disturbing portrait of a dysfunctional family. Gibb was named to the Orange Futures List. Difficult childhoods are further explored in Sandra Birdsell's *The Chrome Suite,* Lynn Coady's *Strange Heaven,* and Diane Schoemperlen's *In the Language of Love: A Novel in 100 Chapters.* Intense sibling relationships unfold in Helen Dunmore's *A Spell of Winter* and Arundhati Roy's *The God of Small Things.*

Gilmour, David.

Sparrow Nights. **Random House of Canada, 2001. 217pp. Book Groups**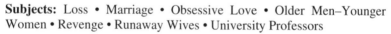

After his young lover, a former student, breaks off their affair, Darius Halloway's life spirals out of control toward madness as he commits acts of revenge and murder.

> **Subjects:** Loss • Marriage • Obsessive Love • Older Men–Younger Women • Revenge • Runaway Wives • University Professors

> **Read On:** Gilmour's earlier novel, *How Boys See Girls,* also details the mid-life crisis of an older man whose obsession with a much younger woman calls his sanity into question. The complexities of obsessive love are explored in Lawrence Osborne's *Ania Malina* and Josephine Hart's *Damage.* Gilmour's ability to take the reader into the mind of his character has been compared to Jerzy Kosinski (*The Painted Bird* and others).

Goodman, Joanna.

Belle of the Bayou. **Porcupine's Quill, 1998. 165pp.**

At forty, Arabella takes her son with her as she leaves her husband in Montreal. She moves in with her mother in Louisiana, makes friends with a motorcycle-riding, palm-reading gypsy, and falls in love with an aging jazz musician, ultimately finding the independence she has been seeking.

Second Appeal: Story

Subjects: Coming of Age • First Novels • Louisiana • Mothers and Daughters • Odysseys • Single Mothers • Voodoo

Read On: Joan Barfoot's *Getting Over Edgar* is another coming-of-age novel with eccentric characters featuring an older woman. Goodman's story unfolds in a similar fashion to Eliza Clark's *Miss You Like Crazy*. Louisiana provides the setting for another woman's search for peace and direction in Marnie Woodrow's *Spelling Mississippi*. Similar rocky mother–daughter relationships are the basis for *Divine Secrets of the Ya-Ya Sisterhood* by Rebecca Wells and *Anywhere but Here* by Mona Simpson.

Govier, Katherine.

Angel Walk. Little Brown Canada, 1996. 416pp. Book Groups 📖

Having agreed to a retrospective of her photographs, eighty-five-year-old Corinne "Cory" Ditchburn embarks on a journey of self-discovery as she and Tyke, the son she left behind to pursue a wartime career, sort through the pictures. Each photo evokes memories of her long life, from its beginnings in the Canadian North, through World War II London, and to the present.

Subjects: Elderly Women • England • London • Mothers and Sons • Mothers Deserting Their Families • Reminiscing in Old Age • Women Photographers • World War II

Read On: Govier's other novels include *Creation*, *The Truth Teller*, *Hearts of Flame*, and *Random Descent*. Strong female characters are central to novels by Margaret Atwood (*The Handmaid's Tale* and others), Margaret Laurence (*The Diviners*), and Paulette Jiles (*Enemy Women*). The artist in Atwood's *Cat's Eye* finds herself reflecting on the past when she returns home for a retrospective of her work. Caroline Bridgwood's *Trespasses* features a female photojournalist during World War II.

The Truth Teller. Random House of Canada, 2000. 403pp. Book Groups 📖

While Dugald Laird begins to question his fifty-year marriage to Francesca Morrow, students at their exclusive girls' school find in their midst a clairvoyant young woman who becomes a truth teller for them all on the annual school trip to Greece.

Second Appeal: Language

Subjects: 1990s • Classical Studies • Coming of Age • Girls' Schools • Greece • Marriage • Mythology • Teenage Girls • Toronto

Read On: The theme of illusion also appears in Govier's earlier novels, *Hearts of Flame*, *Random Descent,* and *Angel Walk*. Like Frances Mayes in *Under the Tuscan Sun*, Govier, winner of the 1997 Marian Engel award, conveys a strong sense of place. For elements of Greek mythology, read *Dagmar's Daughter* by Kim Echlin, a novel of mothers and daughters, and *Ariadne's Dream* by Tess Fragoulis. *Pilgrim* by Timothy Findley also explores the theme of mysticism. The voices of teenage girls so strongly heard here are echoed in Judy MacDonald's *Jane,* a novel about young girls removed from their parents' world.

Gowdy, Barbara.

Mister Sandman. Somerville House, 1995. 268pp. Book Groups 📖

An idiosyncratic middle-class family copes with raising the oldest daughter's illegitimate child, a strange, silent girl with remarkable musical talent, who becomes the repository for the family's secrets and deceptions. *Mister Sandman* was shortlisted for the Giller Prize, the Governor General's Literary Award for Fiction, and the Trillium Book Award.

> **Subjects:** Eccentrics • Family Relationships • Family Secrets • Gay Men • Lesbians • Musicians

> **Read On:** Gowdy also wrote *Through the Green Valley* and *The White Bone*. *Even Cowgirls Get the Blues* by Tom Robbins prominently features a character deemed a "freak." Tim Winton's *Cloudstreet* portrays relationships in a family filled with quirky characters. Another family with many secrets, including the parentage of an illegitimate child, is the Piper family in Ann-Marie MacDonald's *Fall on Your Knees*.

Gunn, Genni.

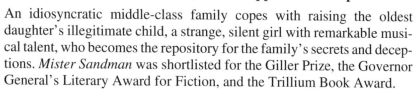

Tracing Iris. Raincoast Books, 2001. 268pp. Book Groups 📖

Kate Mason, a thirty-something social anthropologist, back home to attend her stepmother's funeral, embarks on a difficult journey to discover the truth behind her mother's disappearance years earlier. In cataloguing her mother's possessions she is able to understand the past and trust those closest to her.

> **Subjects:** Abandoned Children • Early Memories • Family Relationships • Missing Persons • Mothers and Daughters • Mothers Deserting Their Families • Women Anthropologists • Women Ethnologists

> **Read On:** The themes of family, childhood memory, and reconciliation are echoed in Margaret Atwood's *Surfacing* and Karen Lawrence's *Springs of Living Water*. The impact of love and loss emerges in Jane Urquhart's *The Stone Carvers* and in Claudia Casper's *The Reconstruction*. Two daughters reconnect to their mother through her diary following her death in John Miller's *The Featherbed*.

Harvor, Elisabeth.

Excessive Joy Injures the Heart. McClelland & Stewart, 2000. 344pp. Book Groups 📖

Having had no success with traditional treatment methods for her insomnia, Claire Vornoff turns to holistic healer Declan Farrell. She becomes obsessed with him but ultimately learns the danger of such emotional attachments.

> **Second Appeal:** Language

> **Subjects:** Alternative Medicine • Erotic Fiction • First Novels • Love Stories • Male–Female Relationships • Obsessive Love • Toronto

Read On: Greg Hollingshead's novel *The Healer* focuses on another kind of healer—a faith healer. *Waiting* by Ha Jin is a story of obsessive love, in which both main characters must wait for each other. Readers interested in the ethics of the doctor/patient relationship may want to read *Love in the Time of Cholera* by Gabriel García Márquez. Included among Harvor's work is a collection of short stories, *Let Me Be the One,* and novel, *All Times Have Been Modern,* in which another woman must begin again, following a divorce.

Hébert, Anne.

🎗 *A Suit of Light.* **House of Anansi Press, 2000. 103pp. Book Groups** 📖

When a stranger provides the means for a struggling Spanish immigrant family to realize their dreams of a better life, the result is disastrous for Pedro, his wife Rose-Alba, and their son Miguel. Hébert won Le Prix Littéraire France-Québec Jean-Hamelin for this work in the original French. Translated from the French [*Un habit de lumière*] by Sheila Fischman.

Second Appeal: Language

Subjects: Family Relationships • France • French Canadian • Immigrants and Refugees • Mothers and Sons • Paris • Translations

Read On: This is Anne Hébert's last work. Her earlier novels include *The First Garden, Burden of Dreams*, and *Am I Disturbing You?*, the first work in translation to appear on the Giller Prize shortlist. Families disintegrating under their discontent are found in Ann Beattie's *Falling in Place* and Rick Moody's *The Ice Storm.*

Helwig, David.

The Time of Her Life. **Goose Lane, 2000. 259pp.**

Jean, of no given family name, dies alone and unknown in Canada, but only after a life spent as an actress, married to a count, living on two continents, and suffering through a world war. Jean seems to resemble the pearl in the oyster: With every abrasion inflicted on her by life, she becomes more and more lucent. The reader can finally see her as she really is: a woman who has suffered pain and loss, but who perseveres through it all.

Subjects: Actresses • Montreal • Older Women • Photographers • Quebec

Read On: David Helwig is perhaps best known for his significant role as editor of the <u>Coming Attractions</u> series of short stories as well as the annual <u>Best Canadian Stories</u> series. He has also written several novellas and several collections of poetry. For other novels dealing with women and loss, you may want to try *Purple for Sky* by Carole Bruneau or *Martin Sloane* by Michael Redhill. Helwig's understated style in creating Jean's life resembles the style of Richard B. Wright in portraying the title character in *The Weekend Man.*

Hennessey, Michael.

The Betrayer. **The Acorn Press, 2003. 220pp. Book Groups** 📖

When two Islanders are arrested for the murder of a shopkeeper in Charlottetown, Prince Edward Island, they insist that there was a third person involved. But their code of honour will not allow them to reveal the culprit. The two men are convicted and executed, and Mickey Casey finally confesses his role in the murder to the only woman he has ever loved. His confession leads him to recognize his own culpability and the depth of this betrayal of his friends. This debut novel was shortlisted for the Best Atlantic Published Book Award.

Second Appeal: Story

Subjects: 1930s • 1940s • Betrayal • Charlottetown • Murder • Orphans • Prince Edward Island

Read On: This novel is based on a crime that actually occurred in Charlottetown, which was the last crime for which anyone would be executed there. Other novels based on real crime events are *True History of the Kelly Gang* (Peter Carey), *Aiding and Abetting* (Muriel Spark), and *The Way the Crow Flies* (Ann-Marie MacDonald). *The Garden of Martyrs* (Michael C. White), also about an event that took place in earlier days, portrays as well the execution of innocent men for the crime.

Highway, Tomson.

Kiss of the Fur Queen. Doubleday Canada, 1998. 310pp. Book Groups 📖

Two Cree brothers, Jeremiah and Gabriel, share a horrific bond forged in residential schools for Aboriginal children. Together they struggle to overcome the abuse—physical and psychological—that has shaped their lives. This novel was shortlisted for the Chapters/*Books in Canada* First Novel Award and the CBA Libris Award for Fiction Book of the Year.

Second Appeal: Setting

Subjects: Aboriginal Authors • Aboriginal Peoples • Abuse • Brothers • Coming of Age • Cree Nation • First Novels • Manitoba • Race Relations • Residential Schools

Read On: The impact of residential schools on Aboriginal children is a theme revisited in Eden Robinson's *Monkey Beach*. In Robert Alexie's *Porcupines and China Dolls*, two grown men, abused during their time in a residential school, confront their abuser. Russell Banks's *Rule of the Bone* offers a different account of teenage boys struggling to overcome abuse. Paullina Simons creates a character in *Tully* whose abuse as a teenager prompts her to make poor decisions regarding sexual partners in her adult life.

Hodgins, Jack.

🎗 *Broken Ground*. McClelland & Stewart, 1998. 359pp. Book Groups 📖

Veterans of World War I, the settlers of Portuguese Creek on Vancouver Island share the challenges, both comedic and tragic, of moving past the terrors of war and working to clear their land-grant stump farms in 1922. *Broken Ground* was awarded the British Columbia Book Award for Fiction, the Ethel Wilson Fiction Prize, and the Torgi Literacy Award, and was shortlisted for the International IMPAC Dublin Literary Award for the Novel.

Second Appeal: Setting

Subjects: 1920s • British Columbia • Community Life • Farms • Vancouver Island • Veterans • World War I

Read On: Hodgins populates another novel, *Distance,* with characters whose lives are shaped by the landscape; he is also the author of a number of short-story collections, including *Damage Done by the Storm.* Annie Proulx's *Bad Dirt* also pits the characters in her stories against the harshness of the landscape. Anne Michaels's *Fugitive Pieces* is the story of a man who works to build a new life after the destruction of war. The horror of soldier life is vividly described in Timothy Findley's *The Wars,* in Kevin Major's *No Man's Land,* and in Farley Mowat's personal account, *And No Birds Sang.* Hodgins's characters and story are reminiscent of Alistair MacLeod's in *No Great Mischief.*

The Macken Charm. McClelland & Stewart, 1995. 294pp.

In 1956 as the Macken clan gathers for the funeral of Glory Macken, young Rusty Macken, looking forward to leaving Vancouver Island for university, listens to stories rich with family history and finds himself a participant in the family's response to Glory's passing.

Second Appeal: Setting

Subjects: 1950s • British Columbia • Eccentric Families • Family Chronicles • Family Relationships • Funerals • Vancouver Island

Read On: An earlier novel by Hodgins, *The Resurrection of Joseph Bourne, or, a Word or Two on Those Port Annie Miracles,* won the Governor General's Literary Award for Fiction. The humour found here surfaces in a number of the author's other works, including *Spit Delaney's Island* and *Innocent Cities.* Another large family gathers for a funeral in Anne Cameron's *Hardscratch Row,* where they attempt to work through their relationships. Douglas Coupland's *All Families Are Psychotic* is another humorous story of an eccentric family, although these authors differ greatly in their sense of humour.

Holz, Cynthia.

Semi-detached. Patrick Crean Editions, 1999. 271pp. Book Groups 📖

When, after thirty-two years of marriage, Barbara and Elliot decide to separate but still live in the same house, each begins a personal journey toward new fulfillment.

Subjects: Marriage • Middle-aged Persons • Separation

Read On: Holz's other novels all feature relationships undergoing some type of turmoil (*A Good Man, Onlyville,* and *The Other Side*). Carol Shields's *Happenstance* also introduces a couple who learn about themselves by spending time apart. Katherine Govier's *The Truth Teller* offers another examination of a long-married couple. Evan Connell's two novels, *Mr. Bridge* and *Mrs. Bridge,* and David Gates's *Preston Falls* all present both sides of a marriage. The humour in the relationship between husband and wife in Anne Tyler's *Breathing Lessons* is mirrored in the relationship of Holz's couple.

Hood-Caddy, Karen.

Tree Fever. **Rendezvous Press, 1997. 240pp.**

When a developer moves in to cut down a stand of century-old trees, widowed psychotherapist Jessie Dearborn finds herself united with other older women in an effort to stop the destruction. Her social action ultimately helps her discover her life's meaning.

Second Appeal: Story

Subjects: Coming of Age • Dearborn, Jessie (Fictional Character) • Elderly Women • Environmentalists • First Novels • Forest Ecology • Logging • Northern Ontario • Psychotherapists • Widows

Read On: Hood-Caddy continues Jessie's story in *Flying Lessons.* Although lighter in tone, H. Mel Malton's Polly Deacon (*Down in the Dumps* and others) is another proactive woman who works for environmental health. Richard Gould's *Red Fox Road* also concerns itself with logging in Northern Ontario. In *The Bean Trees*, Barbara Kingsolver creates a feisty woman who tackles contemporary social issues.

Huston, Nancy.

Instruments of Darkness. **Little, Brown, 1997. 317pp. Book Groups** 📖

While researching the story of an eighteenth-century servant who was executed, Nadia, a divorced American writer, exorcises her personal demons and brings her own history into harmony. [English version of her French novel *Instruments des ténèbres*]

Subjects: Alcoholics • Family Relationships • Research Novels • Women Authors

Read On: Huston's other books include *An Adoration*, *Dolce Agonia*, *Slow Emergencies,* and *Plainsong*; *Cantiques des plaines* (Huston's French version of *Plainsong*) won the Governor General's Literary Award for Fiction (French) in 1993. Other research novels include A. S. Byatt's *Possession* and Cathleen Schine's *Rameau's Niece.*

Ireland, Ann.

The Instructor. **Doubleday Canada, 1996. 208pp. Book Groups** 📖

When nineteen-year-old Simone Paris's art teacher invites her to travel with him to Mexico, it is the beginning of a journey of self-discovery that will see her mature from an obsessed student into a young woman who has outgrown her first love. *The Instructor* was nominated for the Trillium Book Award.

Subjects: Artists • Coming of Age • Love Affairs • Maturation • Mexico • Obsessive Love • Older Men–Younger Women • Young Women

Read On: Ireland explored the notion of the younger woman–older accomplished man in her first novel, *A Certain Mr. Takahashi.* She is also the author of *Exile*, a story about a Latino writer in Vancouver. A young woman is drawn to her art instructor in Michael Redhill's *Martin Sloane.*

Philip Roth also writes about a similar obsessive relationship in *The Dying Animal*. *A Mixture of Frailties* by Robertson Davies is the story of another woman who grows into a greater maturity.

Ireland, Sally.

Fox's Nose. Cormorant Books, 1997. 308pp. Book Groups 📖

Fourteen-year-old Julie discovers her grandmother's diary in her family's attic. As she reads about her grandmother's survival during the Second World War in Leningrad, she compares the present-day details of her family life (a paraplegic father, an estranged mother, her first sexual experience, a rift with her best friend, and a death) to the past she is discovering. This novel was nominated for the Ethel Wilson Fiction Prize.

Subjects: Coming of Age • Diaries • Family Relationships • First Novels • Grandmothers • Immigrants and Refugees • Russia • Teenage Girls • Violence • World War II

Read On: In *The Blood Libel,* Allan Levine also explores the lasting effects of events in Eastern Europe on shaping the experience of Canadians. Granddaughters learn about their grandmothers' lives through diaries in Marianne Fredriksson's *Hanna's Daughters* and Sue Miller's *The World Below*. A granddaughter uncovers her family history through her grandfather's diaries in Tessa McWatt's *Out of My Skin*. Gail Anderson-Dargatz's *The Cure for Death by Lightning* is another story told from the perspective of a teenage girl.

Johnston, Wayne.

🏅 *The Colony of Unrequited Dreams.* Alfred A. Knopf Canada, 1998. 562pp. Book Groups 📖

This fictionalized biography of Joey Smallwood chronicles the path of Newfoundland's entry into Canada through the eyes of Smallwood and the fictional Sheilagh Fielding, the woman with whom the character Joey has a lifelong love-hate relationship. This novel won the CAA Literary Award for Fiction and the Thomas Head Raddall Atlantic Fiction Award. It was also shortlisted for the Governor General's Literary Award for Fiction, the Giller Prize, the Rogers Writers' Trust Fiction Prize, and The Stephen Leacock Memorial Medal for Humour.

Second Appeal: Setting

Subjects: Newfoundland and Labrador • Newfoundland Confederation, 1949 • Provincial Premiers • Reporters • Smallwood, Joseph Roberts

Read On: *Midnight's Children* by Salman Rushdie is another novel that characterizes the setting (India), and in *The Shipping News* by Annie Proulx, Newfoundland is also a character. Peter Carey draws a similar heroic portrayal of the main character in *True History of the Kelly Gang*. Another provincial premier provides the subject of a book in Claude Fournier's *René Lévesque: Portrait of a Man Alone*, and Richard Rohmer takes us back to the original Confederation of 1867 in *John A.'s Crusade*.

🎗 *The Navigator of New York.* **Alfred A. Knopf Canada, 2002. 486pp. Book Groups** 📖

Seeking the truth about his parents, Devlin Stead travels from Newfoundland to New York to meet Frederick Cook, who has claimed to be his biological father. Stead becomes Cook's protégé and assistant as Cook competes with Robert Peary to be the first to reach the North Pole. Johnston's work was awarded the Alcuin Society Award for Excellence in Canadian Book Design and the Atlantic Independent Booksellers' Choice Award and was shortlisted for the Commonwealth Writers Prize for Best Book in the Caribbean and Canada, the Giller Prize, the Governor General's Literary Award for Fiction, and the Winterset Award.

> **Second Appeal:** Story
>
> **Subjects:** Cook, Frederick • Explorers • Newfoundland and Labrador • New York City • North Pole • Orphans
>
> **Read On:** Johnston's early novels include *The Divine Ryans* and *The Story of Bobby O'Malley*. The lure of Arctic exploration is the basis of many historical novels, including *The Broken Lands* by Robert Edric and *A Discovery of Strangers* by Rudy Wiebe. Kenneth McGoogan is a novelist who has written a non-fiction account of Arctic exploration in *Fatal Passage: The Untold Story of John Rae, the Arctic Adventurer Who Discovered the Fate of Franklin*. The characters created in Johnston's novel are similar to those in the novels of Guy Vanderhaeghe (*The Last Crossing* and others).

3

Keefer, Janice Kulyk.

Thieves. **HarperFlamingoCanada, 2004. 303pp. Book Groups** 📖

Monty Mills, a failed academic, intercepts a letter inviting his father, a writer obsessed with New Zealand author Katherine Mansfield, to access new Mansfield materials. Perceiving this to be an opportunity to redeem his own career, Monty begins a journey into Mansfield's life that ultimately brings him a better understanding of his relationship with his father.

> **Subjects:** Authors • Fathers and Sons • Mansfield, Katherine • Obsession • Researchers • Women's Lives • Writers
>
> **Read On:** Both A. S. Byatt's *Possession* and Michael Cunningham's *The Hours* are novels that look inside the troubled lives of literary figures and blend them with contemporary lives. Claire Tomalin's *Katherine Mansfield: A Secret Life* is a biographical account of the famed short-story writer. Keefer is also the author of both poetry (*White of the Lesser Angels* and *Marrying the Sea*) and short stories (*The Paris-Napoli Express, Transfigurations,* and *Travelling Ladies*). She was shortlisted for the Governor General's Literary Award for Fiction for her novel *The Green Library* and the Governor General's Literary Award for Nonfiction for *Under Eastern Eyes: A Critical Reading of Maritime Fiction*.

Kelly, M. T.

Save Me, Joe Louis. Stoddart, 1998. 214pp. Book Groups 📖

Robbie Blackstone, a young fatherless boxer, demonstrates inner strength as he struggles to take control of his life and future from the hands of those seeking to exploit his talents for their own advantage, including his trainers, his mother's boyfriend, and even his mother.

Second Appeal: Language

Subjects: Aboriginal Authors • Boxers • Coming of Age • Fatherless Sons • Fathers and Sons • Mothers and Sons • Toronto • Young Men

Read On: Kelly won the Governor General's Literary Award for Fiction for his novel *A Dream Like Mine*. He shares an intense writing style with Martin Amis (*The Information* and others). Kevin Canty's *Into the Great Wide Open* is another novel with powerful prose featuring a young man struggling with isolation and a dysfunctional family. Young men also struggle in Lynn Coady's *The Saints of Big Harbour* and in John Bemrose's *The Island Walkers*.

King, Thomas.

🎗 *Truth & Bright Water.* HarperFlamingoCanada, 1999. 266pp.

Teenager Tecumseh's summer is filled with mysteries and wonderment. Why must his cousin Lum suffer his father's beatings with no one to help him? Why has his aunt Cassie returned home? What project has Monroe Swimmer, the town's most famous native son, planned? Will Tecumseh's parents get back together? This novel was selected as an ALA Notable Book.

Second Appeal: Setting

Subjects: Aboriginal Authors • Aboriginal Peoples • Abusive Relationships • Coming of Age • Cousins • Dogs • Fathers and Sons • Montana • Small-town Life • Teenage Boys

Read On: King is also the author of *Green Grass, Running Water*, set in a small town not far from the towns of Truth and Bright Water. Both Sherman Alexie (*Reservation Blues* and *The Lone Ranger and Tonto Fistfight in Heaven*) and Susan Power (*The Grass Dancer*) are Aboriginal writers whose works are set on Native reservations.

Kogawa, Joy.

Itsuka. Viking, 1992. 288pp. Book Groups 📖

Middle-aged teacher Naomi, the child of a Japanese-Canadian family that was deported from their Vancouver home to an internment camp in Alberta, becomes caught up in a campaign to redress the wrongs of the past; in doing so, she discovers passion in her relationship with another activist.

Second Appeal: Language

Subjects: Internment Camps • Japanese Canadians • Japanese Evacuation and Relocation • Racism • World War II in Canada

Read On: *Itsuka* is the sequel to Kogawa's first novel, *Obasan*. Gretel Ehrlich's *Heart Mountain* and Julie Otsuka's *When the Emperor Was Divine* tell different stories about Japanese people interned during World War II. Rahna Reiko Rizzuto's *Why She Left Us* focuses on the theme of interned families and raises questions related to this event, asking whether any amount of reparation can compensate for such acts of government.

Lansens, Lori.

Rush Home Road. Alfred A. Knopf Canada, 2002. 547pp. Book Groups 📖

Living in a trailer park near Chatham, Ontario, in the late 1970s, seventy-year-old Addy Shadd reminisces about the challenges she has faced in her life as she now takes on the responsibility of her neighbour's five-year-old child. Despite having been raped and then shunned at a young age, Addy is able to demonstrate decency and honour as she raises Sharla. This debut novel was shortlisted for the Rogers Writers' Trust Fiction Prize.

Second Appeal: Story

Subjects: 1970s • Abandoned Children • Black Women • First Novels • Girls • Mothers Deserting Their Families • Ontario • Racially Mixed Children • Reminiscing in Old Age • Underground Railroad

Read On: Other novels that feature ordinary women doing extraordinary things are Alice Munro's *Lives of Girls and Women* and Sue Monk Kidd's *The Secret Life of Bees*. The power of the relationship between Addy and Sharla is reflected in another strong relationship in Janet Fitch's *White Oleander*. Charles Long's *Undefended Borders* is another novel that features present-day characters who grew up near a stop on the Underground Railway.

Lee, Sky.

🏆 *Disappearing Moon Café.* Douglas & McIntyre, 1990. 237pp. Book Groups 📖

After giving birth to her first child, Kae Ying Woo tries to find her own place among four generations of women, whose courage and determination help an immigrant Chinese family find a home in Vancouver, British Columbia. Lee's novel won the City of Vancouver Book Award, and was shortlisted for the Governor General's Literary Award for Fiction and the Ethel Wilson Fiction Prize.

Second Appeal: Language

Subjects: British Columbia • Chinese Canadians • Family Relationships • First Novels • Immigrants and Refugees • Vancouver

Read On: Wayson Choy's *The Jade Peony* shares the immigrant experience as seen through the eyes of three children growing up in Vancouver's Chinatown. The main character in *Picture Bride* by Yoshiko Uchida comes to California from Japan to marry a man who has chosen her from her photograph; she discovers that her expectations differ greatly from the reality. Like Amy Tan in *The Bonesetter's Daughter*, Lee also combines magic realism with lyrical language to tell her story of three generations of

Asian Canadians. The main character in Pearl S. Buck's *The Three Daughters of Madame Liang* possesses both strength and courage as she operates a business and raises her daughters in the face of communism. Denise Chong's *The Concubine's Children* is a memoir of her mother's difficult role as second wife in Canada, while her father's first wife remained in China.

Little, Linda.

🏆 *Strong Hollow.* Goose Lane, 2001. 280pp. Book Groups 📖

Following the discovery of his father's body in a Nova Scotia roadside ditch, nineteen-year-old Jackson Bigney seeks to escape an unruly family by building a cabin, starting a bootlegging business, and falling in love. Although he turns to alcohol for solace when his lover abandons him, the art of carving introduces him to a group of people who demonstrate the true meaning of family. Little's novel received the Cunard First Book Award and was shortlisted for the Amazon.ca/ *Books in Canada* First Novel Award, the Dartmouth Book Award for Fiction, and the Thomas Head Raddall Atlantic Fiction Award.

Second Appeal: Setting

Subjects: Adult Children of Alcoholics • Alcoholics • Coming of Age • Fathers and Sons • First Novels • Gay Men • Nova Scotia • Woodcarving

Read On: Woodcarving provides solace and redemption in Jane Urquhart's *The Stone Carvers*. Michael Carson's *Brothers in Arms* and Jamie O'Neill's *At Swim, Two Boys* are also first novels that share stories about gay teens. Just like Jackson Bigney, the central character in Edmund White's *A Boy's Own Story* feels isolated because of his homosexuality.

Luke, Pearl.

🏆 *Burning Ground.* HarperFlamingoCanada, 2000. 249pp. Book Groups 📖

As she spends her seventh summer in a forest service station, Percy Turner reflects on her sexuality, the effects of her childhood in a trailer park, and a mother who tried to sell her as a baby on the side of the road, considering her the spawn of Satan. This novel won the Commonwealth Writers Prize for Best First Book in the Caribbean and Canada and was shortlisted for the Georges Bugnet Award for Fiction and the CBA Libris Award: Fiction Book of the Year.

Second Appeal: Language

Subjects: Coming of Age • First Novels • Forest Rangers • Lesbians • Mothers and Daughters • Unrequited Love • Wilderness • Young Women

Read On: Obsessive love is the theme of Elisabeth Harvor's *Excessive Joy Injures the Heart*. The first novel by Laisha Rosnau, *The Sudden Weight of Snow*, explores the angst of adolescent love. A teen in search of himself, his sexuality, and an understanding of his past appears in *The Man Who Fell in Love with the Moon* by Tom Spanbauer. The haunting language of longing found in *Burning Ground* is reminiscent of Helen Humphreys's *Wild Dogs* and Christiane Frenette's *The Whole Night Through*.

MacDonald, D. R.

Cape Breton Road. Doubleday Canada, 2000. 280pp. Book Groups

A series of car thefts explain nineteen-year-old Innis Corbett's deportation from Boston to his uncle's remote Cape Breton farm. Hoping to fund an escape, he cultivates a marijuana crop. However, it is his fascination with his uncle's live-in lover that brings violence into an already tenuous existence.

Second Appeal: Story

Subjects: Cape Breton Island • Coming of Age • Fatherless Sons • First Novels • Marijuana • Mothers and Sons • Nova Scotia • Uncles

Read On: MacDonald won the Pushcart Prize for *Eyestone*, his debut collection of short fiction, and he has one other collection of short stories, also set in Nova Scotia, *All the Men Are Sleeping*. The people of Nova Scotia are painted here in a style similar to Alistair MacLeod's in *No Great Mischief*. In Lynn Coady's *Saints of Big Harbour*, another novel set in Nova Scotia, a young man deals with both the violence in his life and a rocky relationship with an uncle. A teenage boy faces the consequences of his actions in Joan Barfoot's *Critical Injuries*.

MacDonald, Laura, and Alex Pugsley.

Kay Darling. Coach House Press, 1994. 212pp.

Friendship, rivalries, and ambition are all explored as three young people living in Toronto—screenwriter Kay Darling, her sister Claire, and gay actor Will—struggle to find direction and purpose in their adult lives.

Subjects: Coming of Age • Epistolary Novels • First Novels • Friendship • Generation X • Maturation • Ontario • Relationships • Sisters • Toronto

Read On: Douglas Coupland chronicles the experiences of Generation Xers, who search for meaning in their lives in *Miss Wyoming*, *Microserfs*, *Generation X*, and *Shampoo Planet*. Lev Grossman's *Warp* is a humorous story about Gen Xers. Although the main character in Nicholson Baker's *A Box of Matches* is not the age of Generation Xers, the story is told in a similar style, that is, stream-of-consciousness, with elements of humour.

MacNeil, Beatrice.

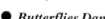 *Butterflies Dance in the Dark*. Key Porter, 2002. 331pp. Book Groups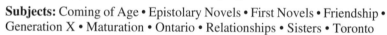

In a small 1950s Catholic village on Cape Breton Island, illegitimate Mari-Jen Delene, a child whose learning disability results in her being labelled as "retard," journeys toward adulthood in spite of her mother's death, her older brother's abandonment, and a cruel Mother Superior. This novel won the Dartmouth Book Award for Fiction.

Second Appeal: Setting

Subjects: Cape Breton Island • Coming of Age • Dysfunctional Families • Dyslexia • Family Relationships • First Novels • Illegitimate Children • Nova Scotia

Read On: MacNeil's short-story collection, *The Moonlight Skater,* also won the Dartmouth Book Award for Fiction. Another coming-of-age story set on Cape Breton Island is Lynn Coady's *Strange Heaven,* the story of a teenage girl who gives birth to an illegitimate child. Jean McNeil's novel, *Hunting Down Home*, tells the story of another outcast child living in Cape Breton. The characters in Camilla Gibb's *The Petty Details of So-and-so's Life* face childhood struggles similar to those described here, including abandonment by a parent.

Manners, Steven.

Ondine's Curse. **Porcepic Books, 2000. 208pp. Book Groups** 📖

Robert Strasser, a television documentary producer, becomes involved with Ondine, a historian researching the extermination of the Beothuk Nation. Robert's work on a film about the director of the psychiatric institution where she is attempting to work through her repressed memories of the violence she witnessed during the Montreal Massacre in 1989 complicates their relationship.

Second Appeal: Story

Subjects: Beothuk Nation • First Novels • Montreal • Montreal Massacre • Psychiatrists • Quebec • Repressed Memory Witnesses • Women Historians

Read On: Manners is also the author of a collection of short stories, *Wound Ballistics*. A psychiatrist probes repressed memories in Margaret Atwood's *Alias Grace*. Lisa Appignanesi's mystery *The Dead of Winter* begins immediately following the 1989 massacre at L'Ecole polytechnique, where she explores the motives for this real-life horrible event. Bernard Assiniwi's *The Beothuk Saga* and Michael Crummey's *River Thieves* are accounts of the now-vanished Beothuk Nation.

Maracle, Lee.

Daughters Are Forever. **Polestar, 2002. 250pp. Book Groups** 📖

Marilyn, an Aboriginal social worker and once a neglected child, counsels Elsie, a young Aboriginal mother. This encounter forces Marilyn to face her own neglectful behaviour as a mother, and finally, by listening to the wind in the traditional manner, to begin healing.

Second Appeal: Language

Subjects: Aboriginal Authors • Aboriginal Peoples • Child Abuse • Motherhood • Mothers and Daughters • Social Workers

Read On: *Prairie Rose* by Fred Smith is the story of an Aboriginal child who grows up without her mother. Some other Aboriginal writers to look for are Ruby Slipperjack, Lorne Joseph Simon, and Leslie Silko. Penny, the woman in Jeannette Armstrong's *Whispering in Shadows* also goes on a spiritual journey as she works to reconcile being an Aboriginal woman in a modern world. The creation of a spiritual transformation of Maracle's character will remind readers of the novels of Louise Erdrich (*Four Souls* and others). Sue Miller's *The Good Mother* concerns a mother accused of being unfit. In Janet Fitch's *White Oleander,* a young girl proves herself ultimately to be a survivor in spite of the abuse and neglect she endures.

Mason, Diane Baker.

Last Summer at Barebones. **McArthur & Company, 2001. 618pp. Book Groups** 📖

Dee Graham has never forgiven her sister for making her adolescent life so difficult at Barebones Lake, site of the family cottage, when Teresa was beautiful and Dee was horribly overweight and unloved. Dee is now in her forties, almost anorexic, writing for a gutter tabloid, hiding from society. When Dee happens to encounter her older sister, now herself obese and a stand-up comic, fabricating cruel skits about her younger sister, Dee vows to murder her, in sweet revenge for all the misery she has caused Dee.

> **Second Appeal:** Story
>
> **Subjects:** 1960s • 1970s • Coming of Age • Cottages • Dysfunctional Families • First Novels • Overweight Children • Sisters • Summer • Women Journalists
>
> **Read On:** Wally Lamb's *She's Come Undone* portrays an overweight woman who reflects on her past and the events that have shaped her life from childhood to middle age. A. Manette Ansay's *Sister* also features a young woman working to reconcile her past and present within a dysfunctional family. Told from the perspective of an eleven-year-old child, Kaye Gibbons's *Ellen Foster* is the story of a young girl growing up in a dysfunctional family. David Macfarlane's *Summer Gone* and Sandra Birdsell's *The Chrome Suite* feature pivotal summer events that have a lifelong impact. For a humorous look at a radical change in physical appearance try *Waking Beauty* by Elyse Friedman.

McAdam, Colin.

Some Great Thing. **Raincoast Books, 2004. 408pp. Book Groups** 📖

The sad, broken lives of two very different men, plasterer-turned-developer Jerry McGuinty and bureaucrat Simon Struthers, are alternately revealed as each man yearns to find something that will provide meaning and possibly love in his life. This first novel by McAdam was shortlisted for the Governor General's Literary Award for Fiction.

> **Subjects:** 1970s • Ambition in Men • Fathers and Sons • First Novels • Male–Female Relationships • Men's Lives • Middle-aged Men • Ottawa
>
> **Read On:** Some other novels featuring strong representations of the common man are Mordecai Richler's *Barney's Version* and Austin Clarke's *The Polished Hoe*. Margaret Atwood also explores themes of loss, regret, and yearning in *The Blind Assassin*.

McCormack, Pete.

Understanding Ken. **Douglas & McIntyre, 1998. 242pp.**

A young hockey-obsessed boy attempting to cope with destructive elements in his life—his parent's divorce, abuse, and death—views the desertion of hockey star Ken Dryden from his NHL team as just one more thing in his life that he is not able to understand. This novel was shortlisted for The Stephen Leacock Memorial Award for Humour.

> **Subjects:** Abuse • British Columbia • Children of Divorced Parents • Coming of Age • Dryden, Ken • Dysfunctional Families • Hockey • Young Boys

> **Read On:** McCormack's first novel, *Shelby*, is another coming-of-age story set in British Columbia. Meet another hockey-obsessed boy in Wayne Johnston's *The Divine Ryans*. Peter LaSalle's *Hockey Sur Glace* is a collection of short stories and poems with a hockey theme. Young boys struggling to understand pivotal events in their lives narrate their stories in Nino Ricci's *Lives of the Saints* and Philip Norman's *The Skater's Waltz*.

McGehee, Peter.

Boys Like Us. HarperCollins, 1991. 167pp.

Living in Toronto, Arkansas native Zero MacNoo organizes a support group when he learns his best friend has been diagnosed with AIDS. During this time he tries to work through his latest relationship and heads back home for his mother's second marriage.

> **Subjects:** AIDS • First Novels • Friendship • Gay Men • MacNoo, Zero (Fictional Character) • Toronto • Trilogies

> **Read On:** McGehee continues Zero's story in *Sweetheart*, and his partner Doug Wilson used these characters to write *Labour of Love*, following McGehee's death. The lives of young gay men are chronicled in Shyam Selvadurai's *Funny Boy*, Jane Hamilton's *The Short History of a Prince,* and Derek McCormack's *Dark Rides*. In Charles Foran's *Butterfly Lovers* another man's best friend is stricken with AIDS. A character in one section of Michael Cunningham's *The Hours* has a dear friend helping him cope as he is dying of AIDS. The daughters in Kristen den Hartog's *Water Wings* gather on the eve of their mother's second marriage.

McGill, Robert.

The Mysteries. McClelland & Stewart, 2004. 338pp. Book Groups 📖

Missing for more than two years, the body of local dentist Alice Pederson has recently been found on the local shoreline. The arrival of a young man in town looking for the dead woman sparks a series of reminiscences as the locals, including a tiger who lives on a local game farm, share their perspective on the woman's disappearance and in the process reveal their own secrets.

> **Second Appeal:** Setting

> **Subjects:** Aboriginal Peoples • Land Claims • Missing Persons • Ontario • Small-town Life • Widowers

> **Read On:** The closeness of the small town and the focus on character in this novel suggest Mary Lawson's *Crow Lake* and Cecilia Kennedy's collection of short stories, *The Robbie Burns Revival and Other Stories*. This novel shares both character development and intensity of mystery with Andrew Pyper's *Lost Girls*. A tiger is integral to the storytelling in Yann Martel's *Life of Pi*.

McGoogan, Kenneth.

Visions of Kerouac. **Pottersfield Press, 1993. 268pp.**

Kerouac-obsessed Frankie McCracken, a young man from small-town Quebec, embarks on a road trip through towns from Montreal and Toronto, to Chicago, Boston, New York, and the Haight-Ashbury district of San Francisco, hoping to follow in his hero's footsteps. His trip proves to be a spiritual journey of his own.

Subjects: Bohemianism • Coming of Age • First Novels • Journalists • Kerouac, Jack • Road Novels • San Francisco

Read On: McGoogan revised and re-released this novel as *Kerouac's Ghost* in 1999. His other novels include *Chasing Safiya* and *Calypso Warrior*. He has also written some non-fiction, keeping in the same vein as his fiction, writing about travels of various sorts, as in *Ancient Mariner: The Amazing Adventures of Samuel Hearne, the Sailor Who Walked to the Arctic Ocean.* Jack Kerouac's classic work, *On the Road*, is clearly the inspiration for this novel. Like Kerouac's work, John Espey's *Winter Return* is also an autobiographical road novel. Another man takes an extended road trip and learns much in the process in Roch Carrier's *The Lament of Charlie Longsong*.

McKay, Leo.

🎗 *Twenty-Six.* **McClelland & Stewart, 2003. 388pp. Book Groups** 📖

The impact of a mining disaster in a small Nova Scotia town is revealed through the lives of the men of the Burrows family, father Ennis and brothers Ziv and Arvel. Following the disaster, including the death of Arvel, one of the twenty-six miners who perish, Ziv's shifting reflections on past and present reveal the pain of unexpected death and loss. McKay won the Dartmouth Fiction Award for this novel.

Second Appeal: Setting

Subjects: Family Relationships • Fathers and Sons • First Novels • Mining • Nova Scotia • Small-town Life • Westray Mine Disaster

Read On: McKay has also written a collection of short stories, *Like This*, which won a Dartmouth Fiction Award. Like Alistair MacLeod (*No Great Mischief*) and David Adams Richards (*The Bay of Love and Sorrows* and others), who also set their stories in the Maritimes, McKay reveals the lives of his characters in a multi-layered story. The power of memory is also the device used to reveal the story in David Macfarlane's *Summer Gone.* The impact of a 1958 Nova Scotia mining disaster on the survivors is the subject of the non-fiction work *Last Man Out: The Story of the Springhill Disaster* by Melissa Fay Green.

McWatt, Tessa.

Dragons Cry. **Riverbank Press, 2000. 195pp. Book Groups** 📖

Barbadian-born Simon and his musician wife, Faye, struggle to define themselves within their marriage and their family following the suicide of Simon's older brother, a man who had played a significant role in their lives. McWatt was nominated for the Governor General's Literary Award for Fiction and the Toronto Book Award for *Dragons Cry.*

Second Appeal: Setting

Subjects: Barbadians in Canada • Brothers • Family Relationships • Guyanese-Canadian Authors • Infertility • Musicians • Suicide • Toronto

Read On: McWatt's first novel, *Out of My Skin*, is set against the backdrop of the 1990 Oka crisis in Quebec. Music provides a context for Janice Galloway's *Clara*, in which the marriage between Clara and Robert Schumann poetically unfolds. The family portrayed in Judith Guest's *Ordinary People* is devastated by an older son's death and his younger brother's subsequent response.

Mistry, Rohinton.

A Fine Balance. **McClelland & Stewart, 1995. 748pp. Book Groups** 📖

Two lower-caste tailors, an upper-caste widow, and a student form an unlikely alliance while sharing a cramped apartment during Indira Gandhi's State of Emergency in India in 1975. *A Fine Balance* won the Giller Prize as well as the Commonwealth Writers Prize for Best Book, the *Los Angeles Times* Book Prize for Fiction, and the Winifred Holtby Memorial Prize. It was also shortlisted for the Booker Prize, the International IMPAC Dublin Literary Award for the Novel, and the *Irish Times* International Fiction Award. This novel was also an ALA Notable Book and one of only two Canadian titles selected by Oprah Winfrey for her book club.

Second Appeal: Setting

Subjects: 1970s • Bombay • Family Relationships • Friendship • Gandhi, Indira • India • Political Corruption • Tailors • Violence • Widows

Read On: Besides his major works, Mistry has also written short stories, collected in *Swimming Lessons and Other Stories from Firozsha Baag* and *Tales from Firozsha Baag*. Mistry's epic tales are much like those of Leo Tolstoy (*Anna Karenina* and *War and Peace*) in their scope and vision. The virtuosity of *A Fine Balance* pairs it with Ann-Marie MacDonald's *Fall on Your Knees*. Caste plays an important part in Arundhati Roy's novel *The God of Small Things*. Mistry's harrowing novel has unexpected touches of humour, much like the fiction of Lewis Nordan (*Wolf Whistle* and *The Sharpshooter Blues*, among others).

Mitchell, Gilaine E.

Film Society. **Dundurn Press, 2000. 332pp.**

As seven small-town Ontario women gather to watch and discuss movies, they share the stories of their daily lives, reveal their secrets, and examine the choices that have shaped their past and present.

Second Appeal: Story

Subjects: Alcoholics • Film Clubs • First Novels • Friendship • Marriage • Ontario • Small-town Life • Women • Women's Friendships

Read On: Pictures of life behind closed doors start to emerge in women's discussion groups. Two other novels that explore women's friendships in a discussion-group setting are Mary Alice Monroe's *The Book Club* and Lorna Landvik's *Angry Housewives Eating Bons Bons.* Women share confidences in Joy Fielding's *Grand Avenue,* Fannie Flagg's *Fried Green Tomatoes at the Whistle Stop Cafe,* and Rebecca Wells's *Divine Secrets of the Ya-Ya Sisterhood.* The main character in Elizabeth Hay's *Garbo Laughs* retreats into movies as a means of escape from life.

Mitchell, W. O.

Roses Are Difficult Here. McClelland & Stewart, 1990. 325pp.

A newspaper editor, already questioning the choice he made to move from the east to the Prairies, finds his quiet small-town life upset when a sociologist arrives intent on studying the town's residents.

Second Appeal: Setting

Subjects: 1950s • Alberta • City and Town Life • Humorous Fiction • Newspaper Editors • Small-town Life

Read On: Mitchell's other books include *For Art's Sake, The Black Bonspiel of Willie MacCrimmon, How I Spent My Summer Holidays,* and *Who Has Seen the Wind.* More authors who set their stories in small-town Alberta are W. P. Kinsella (*Box Socials* and others), Gail Anderson-Dargatz (*The Miss Hereford Stories*), and Susan Haley (*Getting Married in Buffalo Jump*). The arrival of a stranger in a small prairie town sets off a series of events that are life-changing for one family in Elizabeth Hay's *A Student of Weather.* In John Grisham's *The Last Juror,* a young newspaper owner/editor experiences tremendous personal growth through his experiences with an elderly woman who served as a juror at a murder trial in a small Southern town.

Mootoo, Shani.

Cereus Blooms at Night. Grove Press, 1998. 249pp. Book Groups 📖

As the gender-bending Nurse Tyler gains the trust of his apparently insane ward Mala, he begins to unravel the tragic secrets of her past. Mootoo's novel was a finalist for the Giller Prize and the Ethel Wilson Fiction Prize, as well as the Chapters/*Books in Canada* First Novel Award and the James Tiptree Jr. Award.

Second Appeal: Setting

Subjects: Caribbean • Child Abuse • Elderly Women • First Novels • Gay Men • Gender Roles • Incest • India • Lesbians • Nurses

Read On: Mootoo's writing style and tone are very similar to Isabel Allende's (*Eva Luna* and others). Characters struggling with gender roles and identity live in Jeanette Winterson's novels *The Passion* and *Written on the Body,* and also in Dinitia Smith's *The Illusionist,* David Ebershoff's *The Danish Girl,* and Rose Tremain's *Sacred Country.* Child abuse and incest are subjects in Georgia Savage's *The House Tibet.*

Moritsugu, Kim.

Old Flames. Porcupine's Quill, 1999. 209pp.

Stay-at-home-mom Beth Robinson looks to make some changes in her life when her new neighbour Rachel's exciting single life rekindles memories of her aspirations for a Broadway dance career.

Subjects: Humorous Fiction • Male–Female Relationships • Middle-aged Women • Women's Friendships

Read On: Moritsugu's first novel, *Looks Perfect,* is also a humorous look at a woman's life and relationships. Marianne Fredriksson's *Two Women* follows the developing friendship between two very different women. When Bridget dies during surgery, her sisters, one a stay-at-home-mom, the other a corporate executive, compete for custody of Bridget's infant child in *The Crossley Baby* by Jacqueline Carey. The young woman in Jennifer Webber's *Defying Gravity* decides to make changes in her life after being abandoned by her fiancé.

Morrissey, Donna.

🎗 *Kit's Law.* Viking, 1999. 383pp. Book Groups 📖

When her feisty grandmother dies, fourteen-year-old Kit Pitman fights to remain with her mentally ill mother in their isolated home on the outer banks of Newfoundland. As the community around her insists that they be separated, Kit will be forced to face secrets better left buried. This novel received the CBA Libris Award: Fiction Book of the Year and the Winifred Holtby Memorial Prize and was shortlisted for the Chapters/*Books in Canada* First Novel Award and the Thomas Head Raddall Atlantic Fiction Award.

Second Appeal: Setting

Subjects: 1950s • Coming of Age • Family Secrets • First Novels • Fishing Villages • Grandmothers • Mental Illness • Mothers and Daughters • Newfoundland and Labrador • Teenage Girls

Read On: Morrissey returns to Newfoundland in her next novel, *Downhill Chance.* More quirky characters struggling in the harsh landscape of Newfoundland appear in Annie Proulx's *The Shipping News.* A young girl faces the challenges of a family in crisis in *Bee Season* by Myla Goldberg. Ann-Marie MacDonald reveals destructive family secrets in *Fall on Your Knees.* Ed Kavanagh shares vivid characters and dialogue with Morrissey in *The Confessions of Nipper Mooney,* another Newfoundland coming-of-age story that chronicles the beauties and horrors of childhood.

Mosionier, Beatrice Culleton.

In the Shadow of Evil. Theytus Books, 2000. 316pp. Book Groups 📖

Children's book author Christine Pelletier's charmed life in the foothills of the Rockies turns tragic with the sudden loss of her husband and child. As she struggles to cope, her childhood memories of a broken home, sibling rivalry, and foster homes begin to surface and to haunt her, forcing her to confront the secrets in her past.

Subjects: Children's Book Authors • Family Relationships • Foster Care • Loss of a Child • Memory • Métis • Redemption • Sisters • Widows

Read On: *In Search of April Raintree* (1983), Mosionier's first novel, is also concerned with Aboriginal children going into foster care and has become an important work in the canon of Aboriginal literature. In Eden Robinson's *Monkey Beach* a young woman faces her spiritual beliefs as she reflects on her relationship with her brother, following a family crisis. The central figure in Jeannette Armstrong's *Whispering in Shadows* is also a creative woman who has used art to survive the memories of her life's events. The young man in Richard Wagamese's *Keeper 'N Me* is another Aboriginal child who has lived much of his childhood in foster homes. Janet Fitch's *White Oleander* very clearly portrays the challenges faced by those in the foster care system.

Payton, Brian.

Hail Mary Corner. **Beach Holme Pub., 2001. 209pp. Book Groups** 📖

In 1982 at a Benedictine seminary on Vancouver Island, Bill MacAvoy was a rebellious student, a leader popular with other boys. Rebellion and leadership, combined with the usual adolescent fun and games, were a potent mixture that ultimately gave way to tragedy. Now years later Bill returns to seek forgiveness for his actions from the person he wronged, but he learns he must find it within himself.

Second Appeal: Language

Subjects: Betrayal • Catholic Schools • Coming of Age • First Novels • Forgiveness • Friendship • Gay Teenagers • Loneliness • Teenage Boys • Vancouver Island

Read On: Bernard MacLaverty's *The Anatomy School* and Michael Carson's *Brothers in Arms* are stories about adolescent boys in Catholic schools. Told from the female perspective, the main character in Priscila Uppal's *The Divine Economy of Salvation* is forced to confront her actions as a teenager while away at boarding school. Other gay teenagers come of age in Edmund White's *A Boy's Own Story*, Ben Neihart's *Hey, Joe,* and Michael Cunningham's *A Home at the End of the World*.

Pollak, Mary Jo.

Summer Burns. **Insomniac Press, 1999. 157pp.**

Joan, a waitress in a summer lake town, grapples with the choices available to a teenager in the 1970s—sex, drugs, and alcohol—and discovers the dark side of life through her relationships with a variety of men.

Second Appeal: Setting

Subjects: 1970s • Coming of Age • Drugs • First Novels • Sexual Awakening • Small-town Life • Summer • Teenagers • Women's Friendships

Read On: The fears experienced by this young woman are also felt by the young girl in Joan Bauer's young adult novel, *Hope Was Here*. Although set a decade earlier, Alice McDermott's *Child of My Heart* chronicles another teenage girl's coming of age in a small-town setting where she slowly discovers her emerging sexuality. Teen experiences during the 1970s unfold against the backdrop of drugs in T. M. McNally's *Almost Home* and Daniel Richler's *Kicking Tomorrow*. Kevin Chong's *Baroque-a-nova* is the story of pivotal events in the life of a young adolescent boy. In Paullina Simons's *Tully*, a dreadful adolescence leads a young woman to make a series of poor choices in her relationships with men.

Preston, Rachel.

Tent of Blue. Goose Lane Editions, 2002. 308pp. Book Groups 📖

The alternating stories of a mother and son mirror one another in their relationships with their mothers (not to mention their absent fathers). As they now look for a way to escape a life of quiet desperation, it is their inner strength that ultimately carries them through.

Second Appeal: Story

Subjects: 1950s • Abusive Relationships • First Novels • Mothers and Sons • Vancouver

Read On: Children with absent fathers appear in Helen DeWitt's *The Last Samurai* and Anne Tyler's *Dinner at the Homesick Restaurant*. The mother in Mary Morris's *A Mother's Love* feels the impact of her past as she struggles to raise her son. The powerful connection between a mother and son is beautifully depicted in Matt Cohen's *Elizabeth and After*. The elderly woman in Dorothy Speak's *The Wife Tree* discovers a depth of untapped inner strength when she finds herself assuming responsibility for her life following her husband's stroke.

Purdy, Al.

A Splinter in the Heart. McClelland & Stewart, 1990. 259pp.

The events of the summer and fall of 1918 change Patrick Cameron forever as the sixteen-year-old experiences first love, betrayal, and death in his small Ontario town.

Second Appeal: Language

Subjects: 1918 • Coming of Age • Explosions • First Novels • Grandfathers • Small-town Life • Teenagers • Trenton Disaster

Read On: This is the first novel by Al Purdy, a poet who has more than thirty collections of poetry to his name and two Governor General's Literary Awards for Poetry (for *The Cariboo Horses* and *The Collected Poems of Al Purdy*). The recounting of another explosion, the Halifax Explosion a year earlier, takes place in Robert MacNeil's *Burden of Desire*. A teenage boy comes of age when faced with dramatic events in John E. Keegan's *Clearwater Summer*. Although a more contemporary story, David Bergen's *The Case of Lena S.* chronicles the angst experienced by another sixteen-year-old teenage boy. Purdy's lyrical descriptions of the small-town residents recall the poetic language of Walt Whitman. Much like the life of the young man here, the lives of the characters in Ian McEwan's *Atonement* are changed forever one pivotal summer.

Pyper, Andrew.

🎗 *Lost Girls.* HarperFlamingoCanada, 1999. 357pp. Book Groups 📖

Toronto criminal lawyer Bartholomew Crane arrives in the down-at-the-heels cottage-country community of Murdoch to defend a half-crazed English teacher accused of murdering two of his students. Crane finds himself drawn into a moral crisis that becomes personal and forces him to confront a dark episode from his own past. Pyper won the Arthur Ellis Award for Best First Novel and was on the shortlist for a Shamus Award for this work.

> **Second Appeal:** Setting
>
> **Subjects:** English Teachers • First Novels • Lawyers • Missing Children • Northern Ontario • Obsession • Repressed Memory • Trials (Murder)
>
> **Read On:** Nancy Lee's *Dead Girls* is a collection of powerful, edgy, disturbing stories that share the theme of missing or murdered young women and a serial killer. Alan Cumyn's *Burridge Unbound* is another uneasy story in which a man must confront his past in order to move forward. The main character in Margaret Atwood's *Alias Grace* also claims to have no memory of the crime for which she was convicted. The community in Wayne Tefs's *Red Rock* is under a similar type of pressure as described here.

Ravel, Edeet.

Ten Thousand Lovers. McArthur & Co., 2003. 283pp. Book Groups 📖

Lily, a middle-aged Canadian professor living in London, recalls time spent in Israel twenty years earlier, just as the Israeli occupation of Palestine was beginning. This was the time of her tragic love affair with Ami, an Israeli army interrogator, a time when she still naively anticipated peace. Ravel's novel was a finalist for the Governor General's Literary Award for Fiction and a *Globe and Mail* Best Book of 2003 and was named one of *Quill & Quire*'s top five Canadian novels of the year.

> **Second Appeal:** Setting
>
> **Subjects:** Arab–Israeli Conflict • First Novels • Interrogators • Israel • Love Stories • Political Fiction • Women Immigrants

> **Read On:** *Doctor Zhivago* by Boris Pasternak and *Gone With the Wind* by Margaret Mitchell weave romance into stories of history and politics. Meyer Levin (*The Settlers* and *The Harvest*) sets his novels in Israel, as do Amy Wilentz (*Martyrs' Crossing*) and Leon Uris (*Exodus*).

Reid, Gayla.

All the Seas of the World. Stoddart, 2001. 303pp.

The friendship between two women, Deirdre and Bernadette, spans three decades, from their rural Australian childhood, to private convent school, and out into the world. This novel was shortlisted for the Ethel Wilson Fiction Prize.

Second Appeal: Story

Subjects: Argentina • Australia • First Novels • Gay Men • Journalists • Male–Female Relationships • New South Wales • Political Fiction • Vietnamese Conflict • Women's Friendships

Read On: Reid won the Ethel Wilson Fiction Prize for her collection of short stories, *To Be There with You,* and she was shortlisted for the same prize for *Closer Apart: The Ardara Variations,* a collection of linked stories. Her most recent collection is *So This Is Love.* She also won the Journey Prize for one short story and the CBC Literary Competition for another. The theme of childhood friendship is one Margaret Atwood has visited in a number of her novels (*Cat's Eye, Lady Oracle,* and *The Robber Bride*). Meg Wolitzer's *Friends for Life* is another novel that follows women who have been friends since childhood. Bryce Courtenay's *Jessica* is an intense story about one young woman, set in rural Australia.

Riche, Edward.

Rare Birds. **Doubleday Canada, 1997. 259pp.**

With both his restaurant and marriage failing, gourmet chef Dave Purcell goes along with his eccentric friend and neighbour Alphonse Murphy's madcap scheme to lure bird-watchers to the area and save the inconveniently located restaurant.

Second Appeal: Language

Subjects: Bird-watchers • First Novels • Humorous Fiction • Restaurants • Restaurateurs

Read On: In his second novel, *The Nine Planets*, Riche remains in Newfoundland to tell the story of the contemporary urban scene in St. John's. The quirky characters found in *Rare Birds* resemble those created by Annie Proulx in *The Shipping News*, Donna Morrissey in *Kit's Law,* and Alistair MacLeod in *No Great Mischief. Rare Birds* also shares the humour and Maritime setting of MacLeod's novel. Timothy Taylor's *Stanley Park* is another novel about a restaurateur who faces the loss of his restaurant. A southern small-town café is the setting of Fanny Flagg's humorous novel *Fried Green Tomatoes at the Whistle Stop Cafe.*

Richler, Daniel.

Kicking Tomorrow. **McClelland & Stewart, 1991. 376pp.**

Eighteen-year-old Robbie Bookbinder is forced to come to terms with his family and confront his anger after he is kicked out by his parents and wanders stoned through downtown Montreal, experiencing life on the streets in the 1970s.

Subjects: 1970s • Adolescence • Coming of Age • First Novels • Montreal • Parent and Teenager • Teenage Rock Musicians • Teenage Romance

Read On: The dark side of Montreal street life is presented in Robert Majzels's *City of Forgetting*. A young girl takes to the streets of Vancouver in Diane Atkinson's *Highways and Dancehalls. Shampoo Planet* by Douglas Coupland and *How Insensitive* by Russell Smith both detail a short period in a young man's life. Teen experiences during the 1970s unfold against the backdrop of drugs in T. M. McNally's *Almost Home.* Kevin Chong's *Baroque-a-nova* is the story of pivotal events in the life of a young adolescent boy.

Richler, Emma.

Sister Crazy. Alfred A. Knopf Canada, 2001. 215pp.

Through a series of disjointed recollections, the middle child of a large family reflects on family events and scenes to weave the stories of her beloved family and what they mean to her.

> **Subjects:** Brothers and Sisters • Childhood • England • Family Relationships • First Novels • Humorous Fiction • Sisters • Young Women

> **Read On:** The intensity of family love in *Sister Crazy* is also expressed in Marianne Langner Zeitlin's *Next of Kin*. For a blend of humour and tenderness in telling a family story read Anne Cameron's *Hardscratch Row*. The young woman in Miriam Toews's *A Complicated Kindness* reflects on her family relationships, and while the analysis is the opposite of the one related here, the two novels share the same wit and humour.

Richler, Mordecai.

♠ *Barney's Version.* Alfred A. Knopf Canada, 1997. 355pp. Book Groups 📖

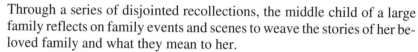

Sixty-seven-year-old Barney, his memory failing, sets down his side of the story following a malicious biographer's threat to unmask him as a wife-beater, a violent drunk, and most probably a murderer. He recounts his Bohemian days in Paris in the 1950s, his circle of famous and infamous acquaintances, his career as a television producer, and his three wildly unsuccessful marriages. This work by Richler received a number of awards: the Giller Prize, The Stephen Leacock Memorial Medal for Humour, the Commonwealth Writers Prize for Best Book in the Caribbean and Canada, and the Hugh MacLennan Prize for Fiction. It was also shortlisted for the Alcuin Society Award for Excellence in Canadian Book Design and the Rogers Writers' Trust Fiction Prize.

> **Second Appeal:** Setting

> **Subjects:** Alzheimer's Disease • Humorous Fiction • Jewish Canadians • Montreal • Paris • Quebec • Satire • Seniors • Television Producers and Directors

> **Read On:** Characters from two of Richler's other books (*The Apprenticeship of Duddy Kravitz* and *Solomon Gursky Was Here*) make an appearance in *Barney's Version*. Tom Drury's *The End of Vandalism* features a man who is his own worst enemy. A grandfather facing Alzheimer's disease wants to set the record straight for his favourite granddaughter and writes her poems, hoping to present himself in a more favourable light, in *Letters for Emily* by Camron Steve Wright. The husband in Tim O'Brien's *In the Lake of the Woods* is also suspected of murdering his wife, and the author presents a number of possible scenarios for the reader to choose from.

Robertson, Ray.

Moody Food. **Doubleday Canada, 2002. 344pp.**

Bill Hansen looks back thirty years to the drug-filled 1960s, when as a University of Toronto dropout he met Thomas Graham, an evasive, draft-eligible American with a large annuity and a vision of making and recording music. He recalls their time in a band as they travelled from Yorkville to California and how it all went wrong.

Second Appeal: Setting

Subjects: 1960s • Bands • Drug Abuse • Musicians • Satire • Toronto • Urban

Read On: Like Mordecai Richler's novel *Choice of Enemies, Moody Food* looks to demystify cultural myths and those who have created them. As does F. Scott Fitzgerald's *The Great Gatsby, Moody Food* begins as a confession, accurately capturing the looks, sounds, tastes, and smells of 1960s Toronto, where the tonics of choice are amphetamines and cocaine. This is Robertson's third novel, and he is every bit as clever, word-drunk, and falling-down funny as Russell Smith (*Noise* and others).

Robinson, Eden.

🎗 *Monkey Beach.* **Alfred A. Knopf Canada, 2000. 384pp. Book Groups** 📖

Weaving stories of her past and present, Lisamarie Hill faces with her parents the possibility that her Olympic-hopeful swimmer brother may have been lost at sea. While the community searches for the missing young man, Lisamarie travels to Monkey Beach, a place of importance for both her and her brother, where she reflects on the past and communes with the spirits of her Haisla culture. *Monkey Beach* was awarded the Ethel Wilson Fiction Prize and shortlisted for the Governor General's Literary Award for Fiction, the Giller Prize, and the Sunburst Award.

Second Appeal: Setting

Subjects: Aboriginal Authors • British Columbia • Brothers and Sisters • Coming of Age • Death of a Sibling • Family Relationships • First Novels • Grandparents • Haisla Nation • Magic Realism

Read On: Robinson is also the author of the short-story collection *Traplines*. The spirit and real worlds combine in Carmen Boullosa's *Leaving Tabasco* and in Nancy Willard's *Things Invisible to See.* Aboriginal author Thomas King also writes with magic realism. His *Green Grass, Running Water* revisits a theme within *Monkey Beach* in telling of Blackfoot Nation members searching to discover the differences between their traditions and their present-day reality. Spiritual journeys are at the heart of the novels by Jeannette C. Armstrong (*Whispering in Shadows*) and Lee Maracle (*Daughters Are Forever*).

Sapergia, Barbara.

Secrets in Water. **Coteau Books, 1999. 404pp. Book Groups** 📖

Leaving behind an ambitious husband and a life that was unravelling in Toronto, Annie Ransome returns to Saskatchewan following her mother's suicide. While dealing with the details of her mother's death and their painful relationship, she discovers her great-grandfather's journal, which reveals an old family secret. This novel was shortlisted for two Saskatchewan Book Awards: the Fiction Award and the Saskatoon Book Award.

Subjects: Death of a Parent • Inheritance and Succession • Mothers and Daughters • Prairies • Suicide • Women

Read On: Sapergia has written another novel, *Foreigners,* as well as a collection of short stories, *South Hill Girls*, which includes "Reading the News," the basis for this novel. To read the stories of women who abandon their husbands hoping for a new beginning try *The Book of Eve* by Constance Beresford-Howe or *Necessary Lies* by Eva Stachniak. Donna Morrissey reveals family secrets in *Kit's Law*.

Sarsfield, Mairuth.

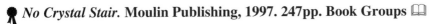

No Crystal Stair. **Moulin Publishing, 1997. 247pp. Book Groups**

Living within the tight-knit black community of the 1940s Little Burgundy district of Montreal, widow Marion Willow works two jobs to support her daughters and struggles to deal with a society that treats them as last-class citizens in the white world. This novel won the National Congress of Black Women Foundation's Literary Award.

Second Appeal: Language

Subjects: 1940s • Black Women • First Novels • Montreal • Quebec • Widows

Read On: The strength possessed by Marion Willow is mirrored in Addy Shadd (in Lori Lansens's *Rush Home Road)* and Morgan Hazzard (in Dorothy Speak's *The Wife Tree)*. Among other authors whose works relate various aspects of the black experience in Canada are Cecil Foster (*Slammin' Tar*), Austin Clarke (*The Question*), and Kenneth Radu (*Flesh and Blood*). The sights and sounds of black urban life are similarly portrayed in Toni Morrison's *Jazz*.

Schoemperlen, Diane.

In the Language of Love: A Novel in 100 Chapters. **HarperCollins Publishers, 1994. 350pp. Book Groups**

Joanna's childhood, with an angry mother and an affair with a married man, complicates her search for happiness; she is eventually rewarded with a satisfying marriage and a wonderful relationship with her son. This debut novel was shortlisted for the Chapters/*Books in Canada* First Novel Award.

Second Appeal: Language

Subjects: Adultery • Coming of Age • Dysfunctional Families • Fathers and Daughters • First Novels • Love Stories • Marriage • Mothers and Sons • Women

Read On: Schoemperlen used 100 stimulus words from the Standard Word Association Test as the framework for this novel. *The Man of My Dreams*, a collection of Schoemperlen's short stories, was nominated for the Governor General's Literary Award for Fiction. Several of

Margaret Atwood's novels share Schoemperlen's themes, particularly *Bodily Harm* and *Life Before Man*. On a quirky note: *Life of Pi* by Yann Martel is also a novel in 100 chapters.

Sedlack, Robert.

The African Safari Papers. Doubleday Canada, 2001. 309pp. Book Groups 📖

Nineteen-year-old Richard Clark graphically records his private thoughts/reflections while in Kenya on safari with his parents. As their increasingly bizarre journey continues, he chronicles, in a drug-induced haze, his mother's descent into madness, his father's drinking, and his family's breakdown in a foreign land. This novel was shortlisted for the Commonwealth Writers Prize for Best First Book in the Caribbean and Canada.

Second Appeal: Language

Subjects: Alcoholics • Canadians in Kenya • Coming of Age • Diaries • Drug Abuse • Dysfunctional Families • First Novels • Kenya • Mothers and Sons • Safaris

Read On: Sedlack followed this novel with *The Horn of the Lamb,* a story that deals with hockey from the perspective of a young man, a one-time hockey phenomenon who now lives with his uncle on the Prairies. Barbara Kingsolver's *The Poisonwood Bible* is a beautifully told story of a family whose fabric quickly unravels over the course of a year in Africa. Young people who use drugs to cloud their stories are found in Mary Jo Pollak's *Summer Burns* and Daniel Richler's *Kicking Tomorrow.*

Selvadurai, Shyam.

Cinnamon Gardens. McClelland & Stewart, 1998. 389pp. Book Groups 📖

In an upper-class suburb of 1920s Ceylon, Annalukshmi, a young teacher destined for an arranged marriage, and her uncle Balendran, a man who must suppress his secret needs, struggle against the conventions of family and society in an attempt to achieve the freedom they desperately desire. This book was shortlisted for the Trillium Book Award.

Second Appeal: Setting

Subjects: 1920s • Class Consciousness • Family • Gay Men • Homosexuality • Sri Lanka • Upper Classes • Young Women

Read On: Women face arranged marriages in Monica Ali's *Brick Lane*, David Bergen's *The Case of Lena S.*, and Amulya Malladi's *The Mango Season*. Michael Ondaatje's *Anil's Ghost* and A. Sivanandan's *When Memory Dies* share the same setting as this novel.

🎗 *Funny Boy.* McClelland & Stewart, 1994. 316pp. Book Groups 📖

As the Sinhalese and Tamil forces clash violently in Sri Lanka in the 1970s and 1980s, a young and sensitive Tamil boy struggles with his emerging homosexuality and the impact it has on both himself and his family. This novel was an ALA Notable Book, won the SmithBooks/*Books in Canada* First Novel Award and the Lambda Literary Award for Gay Men's Fiction, and was shortlisted for the Giller Prize.

Second Appeal: Setting

Subjects: 1970s • 1980s • Coming of Age • Family Relationships • First Novels • Gay Teenagers • Sri Lanka • Tamils • Violence • Young Men

Read On: Other novels set during this time include Rohinton Mistry's *Such a Long Journey* and *A Fine Balance*. Edward Hower's *A Garden of Demons* and Romesh Gunesekera's *Reef* are other coming-of-age stories set in Sri Lanka. For a look at growing up in Sri Lanka in the 1930s, try Karen Roberts's *The Flower Boy.*

Shields, Carol.

Larry's Party. **Random House of Canada, 1997. 339pp. Book Groups**

Larry Weller's relationships with women and his growing interest in designing garden mazes shape his life between 1977 and 1997. Shields won the Orange Prize for *Larry's Party*, which was also shortlisted for the Giller Prize and The Stephen Leacock Memorial Medal for Humour.

Second Appeal: Story

Subjects: Coming of Age • Gardens • Landscape Architects • Male–Female Relationships • Marriage • Men's Lives • Middle-aged Men • Mid-life Crisis • Winnipeg

Read On: Middle-aged men also come of age in Richard Ford's *The Sportswriter* and *Independence Day*. Shields includes among her works such titles as *Happenstance* and *The Stone Diaries,* as well as numerous short-story and poetry collections. The quiet humour of the man here contrasts with Mordecai Richler's main protagonist in *Barney's Version*, who borders on irreverence, satirically telling his life story.

Unless. **Random House of Canada, 2002. 321pp. Book Groups**

Feminist writer Reta Winters, a middle-aged, middle-class wife and mother, finds herself increasingly reflecting on and revisiting her personal and professional past as she struggles to comprehend her daughter's motivation to take to the streets and sit mute, wearing "Goodness" on a sign around her neck. This novel, Shields's last, won the Ethel Wilson Fiction Prize and was nominated for the Man Booker Prize, the Giller Prize, the Governor General's Literary Award for Fiction, the Orange Prize for Fiction, the Commonwealth Writers Prize for Best Book in the Caribbean and Canada, and the CBA Libris Award: Fiction Book of the Year.

Subjects: Family Relationships • Grief • Life-changing Events • Mental Illness • Mothers and Daughters • Rebellion • Teenage Girls • Women Authors

Read On: Middle-aged women reflecting on their lives are the basis for Kate Walbert's *The Gardens of Kyoto* and Anne Tyler's *Back When We Were Grownups*. The characters in the works of Bonnie Burnard (*A Good House*) and Joanna Trollope (*The Best of Friends* and others) are also well crafted. In addition to her many works of fiction chronicling the lives of everyday people, Shields co-edited with Marjorie Anderson the first two collections of women's writings entitled *Dropped Threads: What We Aren't Told.*

Slipperjack, Ruby.

Silent Words. Fifth House Publishing, 1992. 250pp. Book Groups 📖

Danny, an eleven-year-old Aboriginal boy, leaves his abusive home desperate to find his mother. As he makes his way through a series of communities along the Canadian National railway line, he learns about himself and discovers the spirituality of the Aboriginal world that will take him from tragedy to manhood.

Subjects: Aboriginal Authors • Aboriginal Peoples • Coming of Age • Dysfunctional Families • Ojibwa Nation • Physical Abuse • Runaways

Read On: Slipperjack's works include *Honour the Sun* and *Weesquachak and the Lost Ones*. A young boy, naturally filled with wanderlust and unable to withstand his father's abuse, also takes to the road in Jane Urquhart's *The Stone Carvers*. Richard Wagamese's *Keeper 'N Me* is the coming-of-age story of an Aboriginal young man in search of his Ojibwa heritage. In David Macfarlane's *Summer Gone* another young boy takes a journey of self-discovery, and the experiences he has remain with him forever.

Soper-Cook, JoAnne.

Waterborne. Goose Lane Editions, 2002. 175pp. Book Groups 📖

Reclusive, self-mutilating, bulimic author Stella Goulding has been scarred by an abusive childhood; her mother Mim dwells on a life influenced by an unwanted child. Following the death of Stella's father, each shares a life shaped by past and present relationships with her own mother.

Second Appeal: Setting

Subjects: Coming of Age • Identity • Mothers and Daughters • Newfoundland and Labrador • Women

Read On: Soper-Cook's other books include *Opium Lady*, *The Wide World Dreaming,* and *Waking the Messiah*. Women who come to terms with the past appear in Richard Flanagan's *The Sound of One Hand Clapping* and in Pearl Luke's *Burning Ground*, in which Percy Turner's mother had not wanted her either. The writer in Diane Baker Mason's *Last Summer at Barebones* is also shaped by her body image. Soper-Cook weaves elements of Newfoundland's legends into her story in a style that is also part of the novels by Donna Morrissey (*Kit's Law*) and Joan Clark (*Latitudes of Melt*).

Soucy, Gaétan.

The Little Girl Who Was Too Fond of Matches. House of Anansi Press, 2000. 138pp.

Isolated from the outside world until their father's death, two brothers are forced to confront the dark realities of their existence and the family tragedy that was responsible for their sheltered lives. The original French version of this novel was the first Quebec novel ever to be nominated for the Prix Renaudot in France. Translated from the French [*La petite fille qui aimait trop les allumettes*] by Sheila Fischman.

Second Appeal: Language

Subjects: Brothers • Coming of Age • Cruelty • Family Secrets • French Canadian • Guilt • Magic Realism • Translations • Violence

Read On: Soucy revisits the theme of isolation in his novel *Atonement*. The author's third novel, *Vaudeville!*, set in New York in 1929, is also gothic in tone. This gothic sense also emerges in *A Spell of Winter*, Helen Dunmore's novel about siblings living in isolation whose relationship becomes unnatural. Alice Sebold's *The Lovely Bones* is another story told in a child's voice that the reader may expect to be depressing and yet is not.

Spalding, Linda.

The Paper Wife. Alfred A. Knopf Canada, 1994. 238pp.

The lifelong friendship of two young women, Kate and Lily, is tested when Lily, pregnant by Kate's boyfriend Turner, travels to Mexico to have the child and, with Turner, becomes entangled in an illegal child-smuggling ring.

Second Appeal: Language

Subjects: 1960s • Betrayal • Friendship • Mexico • Women's Friendships • Young Women

Read On: Spalding examined obsessive love in her first novel, *Daughters of Captain Cook*. Love, loss, and friendship are explored in Belva Plain's *Looking Back* and Maeve Binchy's *Circle of Friends*. Women's friendship during the 1960s is the subject of Taffy Cannon's *Convictions*, Ruth Harris's *Modern Women,* and Anita Brookner's *The Rules of Engagement*, which also features two women from economically divergent backgrounds. With her daughter Esta Spalding, Linda Spalding co-authored *Mere*, the story of a fugitive mother and daughter who spend their time sailing the Great Lakes.

Speak, Dorothy.

The Wife Tree. Random House of Canada, 2001. 312pp. Book Groups 📖

After a stroke hospitalizes her husband, seventy-five-year-old Morgan Hazzard discovers inner strengths and a long-suppressed zest for life.

Second Appeal: Story

Subjects: Coming of Age • Diaries • Elderly Women • Farm Life • First Novels • Marriage

Read On: Speak is the author of two collections of short stories, *The Counsel of the Moon* and *Object of Your Love*. Other coming-of-age novels featuring elderly women are Pagan Kennedy's *Spinsters*, Stanley Elkin's *Mrs. Ted Bliss,* and Bette Ann Moskowitz's *Leaving Barney*. Morgan Hazzard shares many similarities with the characters created by Carol Shields (*The Stone Diaries* and others) and Joan Clark (*Latitudes of Melt*).

Stiles, John D.

The Insolent Boy. Insomniac Press, 2001. 189pp.

Thirty-eight years of Selwyn Davis's chronicled life include stories of a coddled childhood, a rocky adolescence, a stint as a rock musician on the road, and time spent in Japan before returning to Canada to complete a journey in search of his true self.

Subjects: Coming of Age • First Novels • Japan • Musicians • Nova Scotia • Orphans • Rock Musicians • Small-town Life • Vancouver

Read On: E. L. Doctorow's *Billy Bathgate* is a novel that blends the coming-of-age story with the prodigal son theme. Young musicians take to the road in Dave Margoshes's (*I'm Frankie Sterne*) and Ray Robertson's (*Moody Food*) novels. Feelings of longing and alienation convey the story of three women working and studying in Japan in Dianne Highbridge's *In the Empire of Dreams*.

Strube, Cordelia.

Teaching Pigs to Sing. HarperCollins, 1996. 220pp. Book Groups 📖

Single mother Rita worries constantly that she will not be able to protect her six-year-old son from the evils of their urban world. When her worst fears are realized, she struggles to keep from falling into despair. Strube was nominated for a Governor General's Literary Award for Fiction for *Teaching Pigs to Sing.*

Subjects: Child Abuse • Child Rearing • Mothers and Sons • Single Mothers • Urban Fiction

Read On: Strube writes on the theme of people managing as best they can in today's urban world in *Alex & Zee* and *The Barking Dog*. Strube's ability to convey the mundane events of everyday life with a touch of humour is reminiscent of Carol Shields. Wayne Tefs's Willow Island Trilogy (*Figures on a Wharf, The Canasta Players,* and *Home Free*) explores the lives of families and lovers. In Jacquelyn Mitchard's *The Deep End of the Ocean* every mother's worst nightmare is realized when a child is taken.

Swan, Susan.

The Wives of Bath. Alfred A. Knopf Canada, 1993. 237pp. Book Groups 📖

A young girl's first year at a Toronto boarding school ends disastrously when Mary "Mouse" Bradford and her roommate "Paulie" experiment with their emerging sexuality and identity. Swan was shortlisted for the Trillium Award and the *Guardian* Fiction Award for *Wives of Bath.*

Subjects: 1960s • Boarding Schools • Coming of Age • Girls' Schools • Gothic Fiction • People with Disabilities • Sexual Identity • Sexuality • Teenage Girls • Violence

Read On: Among Swan's other writings are her novels *The Biggest Modern Woman of the World* and *What Casanova Told Me* and a number of books of short stories, such as her collection of cyber tales, *Stupid Boys Are Good to Relax With*. The gothic tone here is echoed in Robert McCammon's coming-of-age story *Boy's Life*. Sexual identity is also explored in Dinitia Smith's *The Illusionist*, Rose Tremain's *Sacred Country,* and Virginia Woolf's *Orlando*.

Taylor, Timothy.

Stanley Park. **Alfred A. Knopf Canada, 2001. 423pp. Book Groups** 📖

Following the loss of his financially strapped restaurant to an unscrupulous competitor, young Vancouver chef Jeremy Papier and his eccentric anthropologist father, currently living in the city's Stanley Park studying the homeless, investigate an unsolved murder as Jeremy plans his culinary revenge. Taylor was shortlisted for the Giller Prize, the Ethel Wilson Fiction Prize, the Rogers Writers' Trust Fiction Prize, and the City of Vancouver Book Award for this title.

> **Second Appeal:** Story
>
> **Subjects:** Anthropologists • Chefs • Cookery • First Novels • Homeless • Murder • Restaurants • Revenge • Satire • Vancouver
>
> **Read On:** Taylor's other work, *Silent Cruise,* is a collection of short stories. Andrew Pyper's first novel, *Lost Girls,* also features a young man who faces the possible ruin of his career against the backdrop of a murder investigation. A failing restaurant is the subject of Edward Riche's *Rare Birds.* Montreal's homeless population are at the centre of Robert Majzel's *City of Forgetting,* and Rosemary Aubert's <u>Ellis Portal Mysteries</u> feature an ex-judge who now leads a basically homeless existence.

Toews, Miriam.

🎗 *A Complicated Kindness.* **Alfred A. Knopf Canada, 2004. 246pp. Book Groups** 📖

It is indeed a complicated kindness that exists in the town of East Village, Manitoba, where sixteen-year-old Mennonite Naomi "Nomi" Nickel experiences life as a misfit. Abandoned by both her mother and her sister, Nomi struggles to find her place within a puritanical religious society at the same time that she agonizes over why half her family disappeared. Toews was awarded the Governor General's Literary Award for Fiction for this novel.

> **Second Appeal:** Setting
>
> **Subjects:** Coming of Age • Fathers and Daughters • Humorous Fiction • Mennonites • Mothers Deserting Their Families • Sisters • Small-town Life • Teenage Girls
>
> **Read On:** Toews is the author of two earlier novels, *Summer of My Amazing Luck* and *A Boy of Good Breeding,* and a work of non-fiction, *Swing Low: A Life.* The feelings of alienation and loneliness experienced by Nomi mirror those at the centre of the classic coming-of-age story *The Catcher in the Rye* by J. D. Salinger. Like the character in Wally Lamb's *She's Come Undone,* the young woman here is forced to confront and deal with tragedy and betrayal within her dysfunctional family. The pain experienced by the teen in this novel is also clearly felt in Stewart O'Nan's *The Night Country.*

Tremblay, Michel.

Chronicles of the Plateau Mont Royal.

This series is a humorous and autobiographical portrait of growing up in working-class Montreal, peopled with eccentrics of all types.

The Fat Woman Next Door Is Pregnant. Talonbooks, 1981.

Thérèse and Pierrette and the Little Hanging Angel. Talonbooks, 1984.

The Duchess and the Commoner. Talonbooks, 1999.

News from Edouard. Talonbooks, 2000.

The First Quarter of the Moon. Talonbooks, 1994.

A Thing of Beauty. Talonbooks, 1998.

This is referred to as the coda to Tremblay's cycle, detailing life in Montreal. In it he depicts his own mother's death and lovingly brings to a close the tales of the people with whom he spent his childhood and adolescence. Translated from the French [*Un objet de beauté*] by Sheila Fischman.

Subjects: Family • French Canadian • Montreal • Quebec • Translations

Read On: Michel Tremblay is an award-winning writer, prolific in his play-writing (*Les belles soeurs* and many others), his translations into French of such titles as Paul Zindel's *The Effects of Gamma Rays on Man-in-the-Moon Marigolds*, his memoirs (*Bambi and Me* and others), and other novels in addition to the series noted here. For other classic depictions of the French working-class family, try Gabrielle Roy's *The Tin Flute* or Roger Lemelin's *The Plouffe Family*. Mordecai Richler's *The Apprenticeship of Duddy Kravitz* is another classic novel portraying a very specific area of Montreal.

Urquhart, Jane.

The Stone Carvers. McClelland & Stewart, 2001. 392pp. Book Groups 📖

This novel tells the story of two monumental feats of architecture: the building of the monument at Vimy Ridge, and the construction of a stone church in the Ontario backwoods. It is intertwined with the story of a brother and sister who will travel from Canada to France to find the peace their lives lack. *The Stone Carvers* was a finalist for the Giller Prize and for the Governor General's Literary Award for Fiction.

Second Appeal: Story

Subjects: Brothers and Sisters • France • Germans in Canada • Rural Life • Stonecutters • Vimy Memorial • War Memorials • Woodcarvers • World War I

Read On: Included among Urquhart's work are the novels *Away* and *The Underpainter*. The redemptive power of art is a theme in Claudia Casper's *The Reconstruction*, which like Genni Gunn's novel *Tracing Iris* also explores love and loss. Like Margaret Atwood (*Alias Grace* and others), Urquhart has crafted a novel featuring strong characters connected to actual Canadian historical events. Read Jack Hodgins's *Broken Ground* for the story of a group of Canadian soldiers who return home after World War I. The horrors of World War I are skilfully depicted by Kevin Major in *No Man's Land*.

★ *The Underpainter.* **McClelland & Stewart, 1997. 340pp. Book Groups** 📖

Seventy-five-year-old Austin Fraser reflects on his life as a painter whose total absorption in his art is responsible for his careless (and cruel) destruction of the lives of his two closest friends. *The Underpainter* won the Governor General's Literary Award for Fiction and was shortlisted for the Rogers Writers' Trust Fiction Prize.

> **Second Appeal:** Language

> **Subjects:** Artists • Elderly Men • Great Lakes Region • Men's Friendships • Men's Lives • New York • Reminiscing in Old Age

> **Read On:** Among other novels, Urquhart has also written *Changing Heaven* and *The Whirlpool*. *What's Bred in the Bone* by Robertson Davies and *My Name Is Asher Lev* by Chaim Potok both offer views of a painter's life. The story of a man who wilfully damages the lives of those who love him is recounted in Merle Miller's *A Gay and Melancholy Sound*.

Vanderhaeghe, Guy.

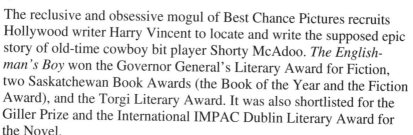

★ *The Englishman's Boy.* **McClelland & Stewart, 1996. 333pp. Book Groups** 📖

The reclusive and obsessive mogul of Best Chance Pictures recruits Hollywood writer Harry Vincent to locate and write the supposed epic story of old-time cowboy bit player Shorty McAdoo. *The Englishman's Boy* won the Governor General's Literary Award for Fiction, two Saskatchewan Book Awards (the Book of the Year and the Fiction Award), and the Torgi Literary Award. It was also shortlisted for the Giller Prize and the International IMPAC Dublin Literary Award for the Novel.

> **Second Appeal:** Language

> **Subjects:** 1920s • 1980s • Aboriginal Peoples • Cowboys • Elderly Men • Motion Picture Industry • Saskatchewan • Western Canada • Western Films

> **Read On:** In addition to collections of short stories, Vanderhaeghe has also written novels with dark, antiheroic characters: *My Present Age* and *Homesick*. Another epic tale of an antihero is Peter Carey's *True History of the Kelly Gang*. Early Hollywood is classically depicted in Nathanael West's *The Day of the Locust*, as well as F. Scott Fitzgerald's *The Last Tycoon*, Peter Lovesey's *Keystone*, and Budd Schulberg's *What Makes Sammy Run* and *The Disenchanted*. Compare the settings of the Canadian West in George Bowering's *Shoot!*, Margaret Craven's *I Heard the Owl Call My Name*, Benedict Freedman's *Mrs. Mike*, and Wallace Stegner's *The Big Rock Candy Mountain*.

★ *The Last Crossing.* **McClelland & Stewart, 2002. 394pp. Book Groups** 📖

The Gaunt brothers, Addington and Charles, led by Jerry Potts, a half-breed guide, embark on an ultimately doomed journey through nineteenth-century Montana and into Saskatchewan with a group of unique Western characters, all facing their own demons, to discover the fate of Simon, the idealistic younger brother who disappeared while in the company of a devious missionary. *The Last Crossing* won the Saskatoon Book Award, the Saskatchewan Book Awards for Fiction and for Book of the Year, and the CBA Libris Award: Fiction Book of the Year, and was a finalist for the Commonwealth Writers' Prize for Best Book in the Caribbean and Canada.

Second Appeal: Setting

Subjects: 1870s • Aboriginal Peoples • American West • Brothers • England • Fathers and Sons • Métis • Missing Persons • Nineteenth Century • Western Canada

Read On: Another nineteenth-century Englishman who finds "adventure" in the Canadian west is portrayed in Thomas Wharton's *Icefields*. The Western setting evoked here is similar to that created by Larry McMurtry (*Lonesome Dove*). McMurtry also recounts stories of the British in the West in several of his novels, including *By Sorrow's River* and *Sin Killer*, the first of the four tales of the Berrybender family.

Wright, Richard B.

Adultery. HarperCollins, 2004. 243pp. Book Groups 📖

While in Europe on business, Daniel Fielding, an editor for a Canadian publishing company, has an affair with a young business associate. When the young woman disappears and is raped and murdered, Fielding is forced to confront the impact of his actions on his own life, his family, and the victim's family in the days leading up to her funeral.

Subjects: Adultery • Family • Guilt • Marriage • Murder • Older Men–Younger Women • Retribution

Read On: Wright is the author of the award-winning novel *Clara Callan* (winner of both the Governor General's Literary Award for Fiction and the Giller Prize), which also explores the impact of a choice made on the lives of its characters. Josephine Hart's *Damage* and Brian Moore's *The Doctor's Wife* are novels that depict the effects of an affair on the lives of those involved. In Joan Barfoot's *Critical Injuries* an act of violence forces both perpetrator and victim to come to terms with the influence of this violence on their lives.

The Age of Longing. HarperCollins, 1995. 242pp. Book Groups 📖

Sixty-year-old Howard Wheeler, the son of a teacher and of a failed hockey player, prepares his mother's home for sale following her death. He begins to reflect on his parents's lives and relationship and the impact their broken dreams had on his life. Wright was on the shortlist for the Giller Prize and the Governor General's Literary Award for Fiction for this title.

Second Appeal: Story

Subjects: Country Life • Family Relationships • Hockey Players • Parent and Child • Small-town Life • Women Teachers

Read On: Wright's other books include *Farthing's Fortunes, Sunset Manor, Final Things, Tourists,* and *The Weekend Man.* Alice Munro's short-story collection *Friend of My Youth* moves between past and present as residents of small towns reflect on their lives. Hugh Garner's *Cabbagetown* describes the challenges young boys faced growing up during the Great Depression in an urban rather than rural setting. Hockey players are also found in Roy MacGregor's *The Last Season* and Bill Gaston's *The Good Body.*

 *Clara Callan.* **HarperFlamingoCanada, 2001. 414p. Book Groups** 📖

The lives of Clara, the elder prim schoolteacher, and her glamorous younger sister Nora, who pursues a career as a radio soap opera star in the late 1930s, are revealed through their correspondence and through Clara's journal entries. This novel received both of Canada's most prestigious literary awards, the Governor General's Literary Award for Fiction and the Giller Prize, as well as the Trillium Book Award and the CBA Libris Award: Fiction Book of the Year.

Second Appeal: Story

Subjects: 1930s • Diaries • Epistolary Novels • New York City • Ontario • Radio Actresses • Sisters • Small-town Life • Women Teachers

Read On: *The Lonely Passion of Judith Hearne* (Brian Moore) also features a lonely woman (a piano teacher) who is taken in by an exploitative man. The stories of sisters whose lives move in different directions are told in *The Agüero Sisters* by Cristina Garcia and *The Anna Papers* by Ellen Gilchrist. To read about another compelling heroine, try *City of Light* by Lauren Belfer.

Yanofsky, Joel.

Jacob's Ladder. **Porcupine's Quill, 1997. 191pp.**

Against the backdrop of the 1995 Quebec Referendum, thirty-something Jacob Glassman, a man who resists change for fear of making a mistake and thus continues to live in his childhood suburban Montreal home long after his parents' deaths, begins to record in a journal the events occurring around him as he passively waits for life to happen to him.

Subjects: Coming of Age • Diaries • Epistolary Novels • First Novels • Humorous Fiction • Montreal • Psychiatry • Quebec • Triangles

Read On: Passive men are also featured in Carol Shields's *Larry's Party* and in Cordelia Strube's *Dr. Kalbfleisch & the Chicken Restaurant.* Marianne Ackerman's *Jump* shares the backdrop of the Quebec Referendum. Jordan Ellenberg's humorous novel *The Grasshopper King* also features a character whose life is left hanging due to indecision.

Zeitlin, Marianne Langner.

Next of Kin. Zephyr Press, 1991. 187pp. Book Groups 📖

Esther Persky's Jewish family, brought together by their grief, struggle to understand her senseless death at the hands of a drunk driver. Her sister Sarah's memories describe the life of the woman who was important to those who loved her most. *Next of Kin* was shortlisted for the Toronto Book Award.

Subjects: Drunk Driving • Family Relationships • Grief • Jewish • Sisters • Violent Deaths

Read On: In Sandra Birdsell's *The Chrome Suite* another sister reflects on memories of her deceased sister. *Brief Candle,* by Martin Boris, also describes the effect of a drunk-driving death on the bereaved family. The main character in Carol Shields's *Unless* experiences the same sense of loss, as a mother who struggles to cope with a daughter "lost" to a life on the streets.

Chapter 4

Language

The exquisite pleasure of a beautifully told story is a joy to be savoured, and for those whose primary pleasure in a novel is language, it is how the author uses language to tell the story that is most important. Language-based novels are often described by readers as poetic; this adjective is very appropriate for some of novels in this chapter. A number of Canadian novelists are also recognized poets who bring their skills for creating poetry to longer works of fiction; included in this group are award-winning poets Anne Michaels (*Fugitive Pieces*), Helen Humphreys (*The Lost Garden* and others), and Theresa Kishkan (*Sisters of Grass*).

Lyrical is another descriptor applied to language-driven novels. The reader experiences a certain pleasure in the rhythm of these novels; this is especially true of Dionne Brand's *At the Full and Change of the Moon*, in which the author creates a haunting story about generations of survivors of the slave trade in the Caribbean. The novels of both Austin Clarke (*The Polished Hoe*) and Rabindranath Maharaj (*The Lagahoo's Apprentice*) are also lyrical; each of these authors creates the voices of the Caribbean and transports the reader into his story.

Language that is best described as gritty can also paint a portrait, realistically capturing or describing a harsher environment, as in Rebecca Godfrey's *The Torn Skirt*. Godfrey is able to situate the reader in the back alleys of Victoria, British Columbia, with a sixteen-year-old runaway.

Another way authors use language to create their stories is to weave mysticism or legends into their work. This is true in the novels of Larissa Lai and Kim Echlin, who capture the reader's imagination through this literary technique, both educating and entertaining.

In this bilingual country, novels are written and recognized in both official languages. The Governor General's Literary Awards each year recognize excellence for novels in French as well as in English. In addition, there is an award given to translators for the best translation into English of a work in French and vice versa. It is the job of skilled translators to capture the essence of the work and make it accessible to the rest of the country and the world.

The titles listed in this chapter share the common element of beautifully rendered words, with the authors speaking to readers to capture their attention and engage them in a journey.

Blais, Marie-Claire.

🎗 *These Festive Nights*. House of Anansi Press, 1997. 293pp. Book Groups 📖

Claude, a judge, and his wife Renata, a lawyer recuperating from lung surgery, are in a small town on the Gulf of Mexico on the eve of the new millennium. Over the course of three days Renata will interact with various relatives, locals, and other visitors to this seemingly idyllic setting and consider the extremes of society as everyone waits for what may be the end of life as they know it. Blais herself won the W. O. Mitchell Prize in 2000 for her body of work, and this novel was awarded a Governor General's Literary Award for Fiction (French), as well as a Translation Prize from the Quebec Writers' Federation. Translated from the French [*Soifs*] by Sheila Fischman.

> **Subjects:** Convalescence • French Canadian • Gulf of Mexico • Millennium • Translations

> **Read On:** Some of the characters in this novel reappear in *Thunder and Light*, the sequel to *These Festive Nights*. Blais is also the author of *The Angel of Solitude*, *Pierre*, and others. Her writing is similar to that of Virginia Woolf, both in style and temperament (*Mrs. Dalloway* and others), where reflections on life are sensitively revealed. Like this work, David Albahari's *Bait* and Thomas Bernhard's *Woodcutters* are written in one long paragraph.

Blaise, Clark.

If I Were Me. Porcupine's Quill, 1997. 112pp.

Middle-aged psycholinguist Gerald Lander, traveling the world on a series of speaking engagements following the success of his bestselling work on language, is distant from his family both emotionally and geographically, ultimately a man in search of himself.

> **Subjects:** Alzheimer's Disease • Middle-aged Men • Psycholinguists • Visions

> **Read On:** Blaise's other work includes *Man and His World*, *Lunar Attractions*, and the non-fiction work, *Time Lord: The Remarkable Canadian Who Missed His Train and Changed the World*, the story of Sir Sandford Fleming, whose determination resulted in the world's adoption of standard time. Another character who reflects on his missed opportunities with family is the narrator of *My Year in the No-Man's-Bay* by Peter Handke. Laird Hunt's *Indiana, Indiana: The Dark and Lovely Portions of the Night* and André Alexis's *Childhood* are powerfully rendered reminiscences of older men on their lives and family relationships.

Bowering, Marilyn.

🎗 *Visible Worlds*. HarperCollinsCanada, 1997. 293pp. Book Groups 📖

The stories and life choices of twin brothers Albrecht and Gerhard, sons of German immigrants, and their childhood friend Nate are revealed following Nate's death during a football game. And what is the connection they all have to a young woman who is trekking across the Polar ice cap of Siberia toward Canada?

Bowering won the Ethel Wilson Fiction Prize for this novel and was shortlisted for the Orange Prize for Fiction.

Second Appeal: Story

Subjects: Brothers • Death • Germans in Canada • Siberia • Twins • Winnipeg

Read On: Like Bowering's other novels, *To All Appearances a Lady* and *Cat's Pilgrimage,* this saga is a complex weaving of story lines. The circus imagery in *Visible Worlds* is also vivid in John Irving's *A Son of the Circus* and Robert Hough's *The Final Confession of Mabel Stark.* The atmospheric imagery of both Prairie and Northern landscapes is echoed in Elizabeth Hay's *A Student of Weather* and Thomas Wharton's *Icefields.* Kevin Major's *No Man's Land* depicts the devastation of war. Jane Urquhart's *The Stone Carvers* also weaves complex stories of love and loss within the context of war.

Brand, Dionne.

At the Full and Change of the Moon. **Alfred A. Knopf Canada, 1999. 302pp. Book Groups** 📖

Generations of survivors of the slave trade in the Caribbean are depicted in this story of Marie Ursule, leader of a secret society of militant slaves, and her descendants.

Second Appeal: Character

Subjects: Caribbean • Historical Fiction • Quests • Slaves • Trinidad and Tobago

Read On: Brand, like Austin Clarke (*The Polished Hoe* and others), chronicles the Caribbean immigrant experience in her other novels *In Another Place, Not Here* and *What We All Long For.* For more of the Caribbean flavour, try *The Mimic Men* by V. S. Naipaul, *Windward Heights* by Maryse Condé and *Flickering Shadows* by Kwadwo Agymah Kamau. Brand's lyrical writing will remind readers of the work of Toni Morrison (*Beloved, Paradise,* and others). Brand is the author of several poetry collections, including *thirsty* and *Earth Magic.*

Bruneau, Carol.

🎗 *Purple for Sky.* **Cormorant Books, 2000. 407pp. Book Groups** 📖

A family quilt creates a connection among three generations of women, each of whom struggles to find and keep her personal identity: middle-aged Lindy, who cares for her ninety-year-old aunt suffering from Alzheimer's; Ruby, who now lives in the past; and Effie, Ruby's mother, who created the quilt as a newly married woman. Bruneau won the Thomas Head Raddall Atlantic Fiction Award and the Dartmouth Book Award for Fiction for this, her debut novel.

Second Appeal: Character

Subjects: Alzheimer's Disease • First Novels • Mothers and Daughters • Nova Scotia • Retail Stores • Women

Read On: Bruneau is the author of two collections of short stories, *After the Angel Mill* and *Depth Rapture.* Both Caryl Phillips's *The Nature of*

Blood and Alison McGhee's *Rainlight* are novels in which the clear, distinct voices of the characters reveal the story. The theme of loss appears in David Helwig's *The Time of Her Life* and Michael Redhill's *Martin Sloane.* A quilt is the thread that connects a group of women in Whitney Otto's *How to Make an American Quilt. Purple for Sky* was published in the United States as *A Purple Thread for Sky: A Novel of Intertwined Lives.*

Bush, Catherine.

The Rules of Engagement. HarperFlamingoCanada, 2000. 300pp. Book Groups 📖

Arcadia Hearne fled Toronto ten years ago after two lovers fought a duel over her. Now a war researcher in London, she is forced by both her sister Lux and her Iranian lover to confront and take responsibility for her actions. This novel was shortlisted for the Toronto Book Award.

Subjects: Canadians in England • Duels • Immigrants and Refugees • Iran • Male–Female Relationships • London • Political Fiction • Toronto • Women Scholars

Read On: Bush is also the author of *Minus Time* and *Claire's Head.* Love affairs set against the violence of the contemporary world are recounted in Marianne Wiggins's *Eveless Eden* and James Buchan's *A Good Place To Die* (U.S. edition entitled *The Persian Bride*). The intelligence of the main character and the tone of the novel bring to mind the novels of Margaret Atwood, especially *Life Before Man* and *Cat's Eye.* Maggie Helwig's *Where She Was Standing* also features a Canadian woman working in London who deals with life, death, and love. The story of a woman who escapes her past by fleeing to England is related in Janice Kulyk Keefer's *Rest Harrow.*

Casper, Claudia.

The Reconstruction. Viking, 1996. 259pp. Book Groups 📖

An assignment to reconstruct the body of Lucy, the prehistoric female primate fossil, is the catalyst sculptor Margaret needs to redeem her life and work after the breakdown of a loveless marriage.

Second Appeal: Character

Subjects: Artists • Depression, Mental • Evolution • First Novels • Fossils • Prehistoric Peoples • Statues • Women Artists • Women Sculptors

Read On: Casper's subtle, direct prose style, reminiscent of Mavis Gallant's work, is evident in her second novel, *The Continuation of Love by Other Means.* William Styron's *Darkness Visible : A Memoir of Madness* is another first-person account of an individual dealing with depression. The redemptive power of art is the theme of Jane Urquhart's *The Stone Carvers.* Carole Corbeil's *In the Wings* explores the connections between art and life.

Chen, Ying.

🎗 *Ingratitude.* Douglas & McIntyre, 1998. 153pp. Book Groups 📖

Twenty-five-year-old suicide victim Yan-Zi explores her oppressive relationship with her mother while examining why she saw suicide as her only option. *Ingratitude,* in its original French, received the Prix Québec-Paris in 1996, and was shortlisted for the Prix Femina and a Governor General's Literary Award for Fiction (French). Translated from the French [*L'ingratitude*] by Carol Volk.

Subjects: Death • Family Relationships • Mothers and Daughters • Parent and Adult Child • Suicide • Suicide Victims' Families • Translations

Read On: Chen is the author of two other novels, *The Memory of Water* and *Chinese Letters*. Much like Alice Sebold in *The Lovely Bones*, Chen uses the voice of a deceased character to relate the impact of death on those left behind. Like Wayson Choy (*The Jade Peony* and *All That Matters*) and Amy Tan (*The Joy Luck Club* and others), Chen clearly articulates Chinese culture and tradition in her novels. The main character in Paullina Simons's *Tully* also makes drastic life choices.

Clark, Eliza.

Bite the Stars. HarperFlamingoCanada, 1999. 223pp. Book Groups 📖

In the week before her son is scheduled to be executed in a Southern prison, single mother Grace reflects on his development from innocent child to juvenile delinquent to convicted felon, and questions how much she may have contributed to his downward spiral despite giving him unconditional love.

Second Appeal: Story

Subjects: Death Row Inmates • Mothers and Sons • Murder • Murderers • Prisoners' Families • Tornadoes

Read On: Clark's *Miss You Like Crazy* is set in the Southern United States as well and deals with the relationship between mothers and their children. Clark has also written *What You Need*. Clark's elegant, fluid language is similar to the language found in Andre Dubus's work (*In the Bedroom* and others). Margaret Laurence's *The Diviners* is another story told in flashbacks. Helen Prejean's *Dead Man Walking* is a powerful non-fiction account of an inmate on death row, and how it is possible to give unconditional love even in the most dreadful situations.

Clarke, Austin.

🎗 *The Polished Hoe.* Thomas Allen, 2002. 462pp. Book Groups 📖

By chronicling her life on a sugar plantation and her relationship with the plantation owner (also the father of her son), Mary hopes to explain how a life of degradation has led her to commit murder. Clarke was a recipient of the 1999 W. O. Mitchell Literary Award. This particular novel was awarded the Giller Prize, the Commonwealth Writers Prize for Best Book, the Torgi Literary Award, and the Trillium Book Award.

Second Appeal: Story

Subjects: 1930s • 1940s • Barbados • Confession • Mistresses • Murder • Plantation Life • Slaves • West Indies • Women Murderers

Read On: The <u>Toronto Trilogy</u> by Clarke (*The Meeting Point, Storm of Fortune, The Bigger Light*) explores the West Indian immigrant's life in

Canada, as do novels by Dionne Brand (*In Another Place, Not Here*) and Makeda Silvera (*The Heart Does Not Bend*). Kate Chopin's *The Awakening* and Patrick Chamoiseau's *Texaco* are other novels that look at Creole culture. Like Margaret Atwood in *Alias Grace*, Clarke slowly and lyrically unravels the details and events behind a murder.

Corey, Deborah Joy.

The Skating Pond. Alfred A. Knopf Canada, 2003. 246pp. Book Groups 📖

Following the disintegration of her already dysfunctional family through her father's abandonment and her mother's death, fifteen-year-old Elizabeth begins a relationship with a much older married man. This obsessive relationship and her unresolved feelings of abandonment consequently shape her life.

Subjects: Abandoned Children • Death of a Parent • Fathers Deserting Their Families • Fishing Villages • Maine • Obsessive Love • Older Men–Younger Women • Teenage Pregnancy

Read On: Corey also focuses on the experiences of a child in *Losing Eddie*. Both Evelyn Lau's *Other Women* and Elizabeth Hay's *A Student of Weather* eloquently share the stories of young women who experience the pain of obsessive love. Death and abandonment leave another young teenage girl alone in Ellen Akins's *Home Movie*.

D'anna, Lynette.

Fool's bells. Insomniac Press, 1999. 150pp.

Naomi, Baby, and Sra, in telling their own stories, describe how sexual abuse has touched and affected their lives.

Second Appeal: Story

Subjects: Abuse • Coming of Age • Crimes Against Women • Trilogies • Women

Read On: D'anna began this coming-of-age trilogy, of which this is the conclusion, with *sing me no more* and *RagTimeBone*. She has also written *Belly Fruit* and *Vixen*. The language D'anna uses to handle a disturbing subject is similar to the language in Pearl Abraham's *The Romance Reader*. Other intensely written novels dealing with sexuality include Robert Olen Butler's *They Whisper* and Kathryn Harrison's *Exposure*. Ann-Marie MacDonald's *Fall on Your Knees*, Doris Grumbach's *The Book of Knowledge,* and Georgia Savage's *The House Tibet* all explore incestuous relationships.

De Vasconcelos, Erika.

My Darling Dead Ones. Alfred A. Knopf Canada, 1997. 195pp. Book Groups 📖

As Fiona recalls the stories of her mother, grandmother, and grand-aunt, she comes to understand the influences these strong women have had in shaping her into the woman she is today.

Second Appeal: Character

Subjects: Family Relationships • First Novels • Immigrants and Refugees • Montreal • Mothers and Daughters • Multi-generational Fiction • Portuguese in Canada • Quebec • Women Immigrants

Read On: De Vasconcelos's novel *Between the Stillness and the Grove* also weaves the stories of three women of the same family. Sylvia López-Medina's *Cantora* is another first novel that explores connections between generations of women; Jill McCorkle's *Tending to Virginia* shares this theme of intergenerational relationships. As in Alice Munro's stories (*Love of a Good Woman, Runaway,* and others), De Vasconcelos's prose powerfully creates the characters and reveals their lives.

Desjardins, Martine.

 *Fairy Ring*. Talonbooks, 2001. 223pp. Book Groups ▦

It is the end of the nineteenth century, and Clara Weiss has just been released from a clinic in New Raven. Still hoping to cure her problems, she has rented a house with her husband in a remote area of Nova Scotia. At the same time, the captain from whom they rented the house is on an expedition to explore the North Pole; while trapped aboard the ship, he records his thoughts of Clara in his diary. *Fairy Ring* won the Governor General's Literary Award for Translation. Translated from the French [*Le cercle de Clara*] by Fred A. Reed and David Homel.

Second Appeal: Character

Subjects: Black Humour • Epistolary Novels • Exploration • French Canadian • Mental Illness • Nineteenth Century • Nova Scotia • Translations

Read On: The woman in D. M. Thomas's *The White Hotel* is Freud's patient, being treated for apparently hysterical pains similar to those experienced by Clara in *Fairy Ring*. *Love Object* by Sally Cooper and *Nine-tenths Unseen* by Kenneth J. Harvey both deal with mental illness. Wayne Johnston's *The Navigator of New York* and Robert Edric's *The Broken Lands* are accounts of journeys of exploration to the North Pole.

 4

Dupré, Louise.

The Milky Way. Simon & Pierre, 2002. 206pp. Book Groups ▦

While in Tunis, architect Anne Martin begins a relationship with an Italian archaeologist twenty years her senior. The stability of this relationship allows her to confront the issues related to her father's abandonment of the family and her aunt's suicide. Dupré's novel was nominated in its original French for Le Prix Littéraire France-Québec Jean-Hamelin, and in English for the Governor General's Literary Award for Translation. Translated from the French [*La voie lactée*] by Liedewy Hawke.

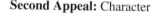

Second Appeal: Character

Subjects: Archaeologists • Fathers and Daughters • Fathers Deserting Their Families • French Canadian • Montreal • Older Men–Younger Women • Translations • Tunisia • Women Architects

Read On: The characters portrayed here are similar to those found in novels by Carol Shields (*Unless* and others). Relationships between younger women and older men appear in Joanna Trollope's *The Men and the Girls* and Anita Shreve's *Fortune's Rocks*. Dupré paints a portrait of landscape that reminds the reader of Jane Urquhart's *The Underpainter*.

Echlin, Kim.

Dagmar's Daughter. Viking, 2001. 211p. Book Groups 📖

This is a mythical tale of three generations of women: Nyssa, who loves music; her mother Dagmar, who has the power to influence the weather; and her grandmother Nora, whose yearning for freedom brought her from Ireland to an island in the Gulf of St. Lawrence.

Second Appeal: Story

Subjects: Family Relationships • Gulf of St. Lawrence • Magic Realism • Mothers and Daughters • Multi-generational Fiction • Women Musicians • Women's Lives

Read On: Echlin's first novel, *Elephant Winter,* also has the theme of mothers and daughters. Annie Proulx's *The Shipping News* is filled with quirky characters. Echlin's richness of language is similar to Gabriel García Márquez's *Love in the Time of Cholera.* The mystical connections among the characters in this novel are also found in Eden Robinson's *Monkey Beach.* Douglas Glover's *Elle,* also set on an island in the Gulf of St. Lawrence, shares the magic realism found in *Dagmar's Daughter.*

Fagan, Cary.

Felix Roth. Stoddart, 1999. 277pp.

Hoping to further his literary ambitions by sharing his written work with his literary idol, Felix abandons his responsibility of chaperoning his brother in New York and sets off instead to find Isaac Bashevis Singer. Unexpectedly, while in the midst of an affair with his boss's wife, he meets and falls in love with Singer's niece.

Second Appeal: Character

Subjects: Authorship • Brothers • Coming of Age • Hasidism • Jewish Families • New York City • Singer, Isaac Bashevis • Young Men

Read On: Other novels by Fagan include *Sleeping Weather* and *The Doctor's House.* Readers looking for other authors who write with an economy of language should try E. L. Doctorow (*City of God*) or Helen Dunmore (*Ice Cream* and others). Naomi Ragen's *The Sacrifice of Tamar* and Tova Mirvis's *The Outside World* also provide a glimpse into the Jewish community in New York.

The Mermaid of Paris. Key Porter Books, 2003. 240pp. Book Groups 📖

Henry Church's ostensibly idyllic life crumbles when his much-adored wife runs off with a visiting Russian strong man. Church, a sometime inventor and puppeteer, abandons his life in a small Southern Ontario town and travels to Paris on an ultimately tragic journey, hoping to find his wife and understand why she abandoned him.

Subjects: Magic Realism • Marriage • Obsessive Love • Ontario • Paris • Puppeteers • Revenge • Small-town Life • Triangles

Read On: Fagan is also the author of *Animals' Waltz* and *The History Lesson.* Fagan's elements of magic realism will remind readers of Chitra Banerjee Divakaruni's work (*Mistress of Spices, Queen of Dreams,* and others). Like Fagan, Isabel Allende examines the sexual relations between men and women in *The Stories of Eva Luna.*

Finley, Robert Stuart Martin.

♠ *The Accidental Indies.* **McGill-Queen's University Press, 2000. 102pp.**

Through diary entries and notes, Christopher Columbus's journey to discover a new route to the Indies unfolds as a fantastical adventure that culminates with the explorer erroneously naming his discovery as his intended target. Finley received a number of awards for this highly creative work: the American Institute of Graphic Arts Design Prize, the Association of American University Presses Book Jacket and Journal Competition, and the Cunard First Book Award, along with a nomination for the Thomas Head Raddall Atlantic Fiction Award.

> **Subjects:** Allegories • Columbus, Christopher • Diaries • Experimental Fiction • Explorers • First Novels • Letters • West Indies

> **Read On:** Jim Crace's *Arcadia*, Anne Michaels's *Fugitive Pieces,* and Michael Ondaatje's *The English Patient* are all written in a similar poetic style. Paula DiPerna's *The Discoveries of Mrs. Christopher Columbus* is another fictional account of the voyages of Christopher Columbus.

Follett, Beth.

Tell It Slant. **Coach House Books, 2001. 153pp. Book Groups** 📖

Montreal photographer Nora Flood struggles to find her own identity within a relationship with an uncommitted, unfaithful lesbian lover; in the process she learns the importance of accepting the right of others to live their own lives while living her own.

> **Second Appeal:** Character

> **Subjects:** Barnes, Djuna • Coming of Age • Experimental Fiction • First Novels • Lesbians • Love Stories • Montreal • Pastiches • Unrequited Love • Women Photographers

> **Read On:** Follett used Djuna Barnes's *Nightwood* as her model to craft this novel. Other novels about lesbian relationships include Emma Donoghue's *Hood* and Jean Swallow's *Leave a Light on for Me.* Follett's prose evokes the sensualist style of Jeanette Winterson (*Gut Symmetries* and others) and Jaimy Gordon (*Bogeywoman*). Jane Urquhart's *Changing Heaven* also features a ghostly literary character (Emily Brontë).

Frenette, Christiane.

♠ *Terra Firma.* **Cormorant Books, 1999. 134pp. Book Groups** 📖

The residents of a small town on the St. Lawrence River attempt to come to terms with the tragic loss of two teenage boys after they set out on the river on a homemade raft and never return. Frenette won the Governor General's Literary Award for Fiction (French). Translated from the French [*Terre firme*] by Sheila Fischman.

> **Second Appeal:** Story

> **Subjects:** First Novels • French Canadian • Missing Persons • Rafts • St. Lawrence River • Teenage Boys • Translations

Read On: Frenette's style of slowly and poetically revealing her story is reminiscent of Helen Humphreys (*The Lost Garden* and *Wild Dogs*). The darkness she is able to craft is also found in Andrew Pyper's *Lost Girls*, another debut novel set in a small town. Russell Banks's *The Sweet Hereafter* and David Bergen's *See the Child* also explore death and grief and how towns and families cope following such an unimaginable tragedy: the loss of children.

The Whole Night Through. Cormorant Books, 2004. 189pp. Book Groups 📖

As a moose lies dying in the yard of her rural Quebec home, Jeanne vividly reflects on her life since university, remembering the people and events that have shaped her life and brought her to this place. Translated from the French [*La nuit entière*] by Sheila Fischman.

Second Appeal: Character

Subjects: Death • Forgiveness • French Canadian • Love Stories • Loss • Obsession • Translations • Women's Friendships

Read On: Frenette's talent for drawing the reader into her protagonist's mind was first affirmed in her novel *Terra Firma,* winner of the Governor General's Literary Award for Fiction (French). Joan Barfoot also proves capable of painstakingly sharing a character's thoughts and feelings in her *Critical Injuries.*

Gaston, Bill.

The Good Body. Cormorant Books, 2000. 271pp. Book Groups 📖

Bobby Bonaduce, a retired hockey player recently diagnosed with multiple sclerosis, enrols at the same university as his son, hoping to find redemption and forgiveness for abandoning his family many years age. Gaston was awarded the inaugural Timothy Findley Prize (2002) for a male writer in mid-career.

Second Appeal: Character

Subjects: Athletes • Fathers and Sons • Fathers Deserting Their Families • Fredericton • Hockey • Multiple Sclerosis Patients • National Hockey League • New Brunswick

Read On: Gaston's short-story collection, *Mount Appetite* (nominated for the Giller Prize), is filled with characters searching for meaning in their lives. The realistic style of language that brings the author's characters alive is reminiscent of the styles of Alistair MacLeod (*No Great Mischief*) and Ken Bruen (*The Hackman Blues* and others). Gaston's ability to capture the emotions of a man who must confront the reality of a career abruptly ended is also reflected in *The Last Season* by Roy MacGregor. Mark Anthony Jarman's *Salvage King, Ya!* is an entertaining look at the life of a hockey player at the end of his career. David Adams Richards's *For Those Who Hunt the Wounded Down* also features a man who returns home seeking redemption.

Gibson, Graeme.

Gentleman Death. McClelland & Stewart, 1993. 256pp. Book Groups 📖

Aging Toronto novelist Robert Fraser is facing a number of life crises, including the recent deaths of his father and brother, an unfinished novel, and the possibility that he has colon cancer.

Second Appeal: Story

Subjects: Aging • Cancer • Death of a Parent • Death of a Sibling • Family Relationships • Mortality • Novelists • Reconciliation • Writers

Read On: Gibson's other novels include *Five Legs*, *Communion,* and *Perpetual Motion*. Gibson's gritty, avant-garde style is echoed in the work of Russell Smith (*Noise, Muriella Pent,* and others), and his way of conveying a serious topic with flashes of humour will remind readers of Jonathan Franzen's *The Corrections*. Martin Amis's *The Information* also features an author in crisis. Other examples of works that feature novels within novels are Margaret Atwood's *The Blind Assassin*, André Brink's *States of Emergency*, and A. S. Byatt's *Babel Tower*.

Gibson, Margaret.

⚑ *Opium Dreams*. McClelland & Stewart, 1999. 248pp. Book Groups 📖

As writer Maggie Glass watches her father slip into memories of the past and the darkness of Alzheimer's, she attempts to make sense of their relationship. Gibson won the Chapters/*Books in Canada* First Novel Award for this work.

Second Appeal: Character

Subjects: Alzheimer's Disease • Family Relationships • Fathers and Daughters • First Novels • Mental Illness • Small-town Life • Women Authors • Writers

Read On: Gibson is the author of a number of short-story collections, the first of which (*The Butterfly Ward*) shared the 1976 City of Toronto Book Award with Margaret Atwood's *Lady Oracle*. Gibson's simple prose style, which describes the ravages of Alzheimer's in *Opium Dreams,* can also be found in Jeffrey Moore's *The Memory Artists*. Sandra Sabatini's collection of short stories, *The One with the News*, similarly portrays the effects of Alzheimer's disease on the patient's daughter. Barbara Kingsolver's *Animal Dreams* features a daughter who returns home to care for herself as well as for an ailing father.

4

Godfrey, Rebecca.

The Torn Skirt. HarperFlamingo, 2001. 202pp.

Abandoned by her father, and with her mother living in a commune, sixteen-year-old Sara leaves home and takes to the back alleys of Victoria during the mid-1980s. She makes friends with another runaway, the elusive Justine, who personifies the adventure and courage Sara is seeking. *The Torn Skirt* was selected as a YALSA Quick Picks for Reluctant Young Adult Readers and was shortlisted for the Ethel Wilson Fiction Prize.

Subjects: Abandoned Children • British Columbia • Coming of Age • First Novels • Parental Deprivation • Runaways • Small-town Life • Teenage Girls • Victoria

Read On: An equally gritty account of life on the streets for teen prostitutes is found in Lee Williams's *After Nirvana*. Another dark novel about teens is Gail Giles's *Shattering Glass*, also selected as a YALSA Quick Pick for Reluctant Young Adult Readers.

Gowan, Lee.

Make Believe Love. Alfred A. Knopf Canada, 2001. 224pp. Book Groups 📖

A small-town Saskatchewan librarian begins an affair with a married journalist, who seeks her help in convincing a local farmer to tell the story of his obsession for a Canadian-born Hollywood starlet. This novel was shortlisted for the Trillium Book Award.

Second Appeal: Setting

Subjects: First Novels • Journalists • Librarians • Male–Female Relationships • Saskatchewan • Small-town Life • Stalkers

Read On: Michael Helm's *The Projectionist*, also set in small-town Saskatchewan, likewise features a protagonist who has trouble in his relationships with women. In Douglas Cooper's *Amnesia*, a librarian is again implicated in a stranger's obsession with another woman, and the main character in David Gilmour's *Sparrow Nights* also finds himself involved in an obsessive relationship. Although *Make Believe Love* does not use magic realism, as do Yann Martel's *Life of Pi* and Douglas Glover's *Elle*, readers are left to decide for themselves which version of the story they will accept.

Gunnars, Kristjana.

Night Train to Nykøbing. Red Deer College Press, 1998. 96pp. Book Groups 📖

After saying goodbye to her lover, a woman boards a night train to Norway and, in an attempt to understand her feelings within an impossible relationship, spends the journey writing letters she doesn't intend to send. This process sends her on a journey of self-discovery.

Subjects: Denmark • Love Affairs • Self-discovery • Separation

Read On: The sparse detail and sentence structure found here parallel those of Francesca Marciano (*Rules of the Wild*) or Jean Rhys (*Quartet*). A sense of longing resonates throughout Elizabeth Hay's *A Student of Weather*. The main character in Richard B. Wright's *Adultery* is forced to confront his participation in an affair and analyze his understanding of his life and himself to move beyond the consequences of his actions.

Hale, Amanda.

Sounding the Blood. Raincoast Books, 2001. 325pp. Book Groups 📖

The spirits of five former inhabitants of a 1915 whaling station on the Queen Charlotte Islands relay their stories to Sophia through dreams and visions when she visits the deserted island station on her own journey of discovery. Hale's novel was shortlisted for the ReLit Award.

Second Appeal: Character

Subjects: 1910s • British Columbia • First Novels • Multiple Points of View • Queen Charlotte Islands • Sea Stories • Whaling

Read On: Barbara Kingsolver's novel *The Poisonwood Bible* tells its story through the voices of alternating characters. Eden Robinson's *Monkey Beach*, also set on the West Coast of Canada, mystically weaves stories of the past. Charles de Lint's eponymous *Onion Girl* also arrives at a point of self-discovery through dreams and visions while in a coma-like state.

Hay, Elizabeth.

Garbo Laughs. **McClelland & Stewart, 2003. 374pp. Book Groups**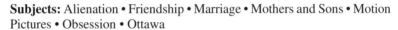

Novelist Harriet Browning has virtually removed herself from everyday life by spending hour upon hour obsessively watching films and writing unsent letters to a legendary film critic. When the city of Ottawa struggles to cope with a January ice storm, Harriet is forced to face the impact her obsession has had on her marriage, family, and friendships. *Garbo Laughs* won the Ottawa Book Award and was shortlisted for the Governor General's Literary Award for Fiction; it was also a *Globe and Mail* Notable Book of the Year, a *Quill & Quire* Top Five Canadian Fiction Book of the Year, and a *Maclean's* Top Ten Book of the Year.

> **Subjects:** Alienation • Friendship • Marriage • Mothers and Sons • Motion Pictures • Obsession • Ottawa

> **Read On:** Hay first introduced to readers her distinct style of weaving the intensity of nature into her novels in *A Student of Weather.* Weather and nature are important characters in much of Canadian literature, particularly in the early years, as seen in the short stories of Sinclair Ross or novels such as Louis Hémon's *Maria Chapdelaine*. Leslie Forbes incorporates the power of weather in India into the events in *Bombay Ice*. Harriet's obsessions and emotional isolation are reminiscent of those exhibited by the female protagonist in Howard Norman's *The Museum Guard*. The unfulfilled longing felt here can also be sensed in *Rules of the Wild* by Francesca Marciano.

A Student of Weather. **McClelland & Stewart, 2000. 368pp. Book Groups**

In 1930s Saskatchewan, the arrival of botanist Maurice Dove at the home of Lucinda and Norma Joyce Hardy is the beginning of an unspoken rivalry between the two sisters as each develops an obsession for Dove that will span several decades, with ultimately tragic results. Hay was the recipient in 2001 of the Marian Engel Award. *A Student of Weather* received the Torgi Literary Award and the CAA Literary Award for Fiction; it was also shortlisted for The Giller Prize, and the Ottawa Book Award.

> **Second Appeal:** Character

> **Subjects:** 1930s • Artists • Coming of Age • First Novels • New York City • Ottawa • Saskatchewan • Sibling Rivalry • Sisters • Unrequited Love

> **Read On:** The harshness of setting is vivid in both contemporary novels such as *The Shipping News* by Annie Proulx and the novels of classic authors such as Thomas Hardy or Charlotte Brontë. Weather also plays a role in Hay's later novel, *Garbo Laughs*. The magic realism created here is also found in Isabel Allende's *The House of the Spirits*. Hay's characters express feelings of longing similar to those conveyed in Jane Urquhart's *The Stone Carvers*.

Heighton, Stephen.

The Shadow Boxer. Alfred A. Knopf Canada, 2000. 384pp. Book Groups 📖

Seeking a writing career, poet-boxer Sevigne Torrins chronicles his early life with an alcoholic father, his journey to Egypt to reconnect with his mother, and his time spent in the Toronto literary scene. He finally returns to his home again, to the remote island family cottage where he faces a crisis of survival and ultimately comes to understand what has shaped him as an artist.

Second Appeal: Setting

Subjects: Boxers • Coming of Age • Family Relationships • Fathers and Sons • First Novels • Poets • Self-discovery • Toronto • Writers

Read On: The urban scene created here by Heighton is similar to those crafted by other young urban authors such as Kevin Chong (*Baroque-a-nova*) and Patricia Seaman (*The Nightingales*). Carol Shields's *Larry's Party* also chronicles a man's life story. Cormac McCarthy's *All the Pretty Horses* features young men on journeys of self-discovery. Heighton's sense of man versus wilderness is similar to Jack London's classic story *To Build a Fire*. The story of a father–son relationship with a boxing element is told in Bruce Graham's *The Parrsboro Boxing Club*. Heighton is the author of a number of poetry collections, including *The Address Book*.

Hollingshead, Greg.

🎗 *The Healer.* HarperPerennialCanada, 1998. 309pp. Book Groups 📖

Despite his scepticism, recently widowed journalist Tim Wakelin will find the redemption he needs to move on when he travels to Northern Ontario to research a proclaimed faith healer, Caroline Troyer, who turns out to be exactly what she claims. *The Healer* received the Georges Bugnet Award for Best Novel as well as the Rogers Writers' Trust Fiction Prize; it was also shortlisted for the Giller Prize.

Second Appeal: Setting

Subjects: Betrayal • Healers • Journalists • Love Stories • Occult • Redemption • Supernatural • Widowers • Women Healers

Read On: Hollingshead won the Governor General's Literary Award for Fiction for his short-story collection, *The Roaring Girl*. The depiction of the landscape is reminiscent of Roberta Rees's portrayal of the Rocky Mountains' Crowsnest Pass in *Beneath the Faceless Mountain*. Hollingshead's intensity here and in his subsequent novel *Bedlam* is also seen in the works of Cormac McCarthy (*All the Pretty Horses* and others). The small Northern Ontario town is darkly captured in Andrew Pyper's *Lost Girls*.

Hood, Hugh.

New Age Series.

This is an epic cycle consisting of twelve novels, begun in 1975, portraying the life of Matthew Goderich, art historian, from his birth in Toronto in 1930 to his death at the family cottage in Southern Ontario in 2012.

🎗 *The Swing in the Garden.* Oberon Press, 1975.

Winner of the Toronto Book Award.

A New Athens. Oberon Press, 1977.

Reservoir Ravine. Oberon Press, 1979.

Shortlisted for the Toronto Book Award.

Black and White Keys. ECW Press, 1982.

The Scenic Art. Stoddart Publishing, 1984.

🎗 *The Motor Boys in Ottawa.* Stoddart Publishing, 1986.

Winner of the Hugh MacLennan Prize for Fiction.

Tony's Book. Stoddart Publishing, 1988.

Property & Value. Stoddart Publishing, 1990.

Be Sure to Close Your Eyes. House of Anansi Press, 1993.

Dead Men's Watches. House of Anansi Press, 1995.

Great Realizations. House of Anansi Press, 1997.

Near Water. House of Anansi Press, 2000.

Eighty-one-year-old art historian Matthew Goderich suffers a stroke as he awaits the return of his long-estranged wife, Edie. Over the course of twenty-four hours, he reflects on his family's journey and metaphorically comes full circle in his own life.

Subjects: Art Historians • Family Chronicles • Ontario

Read On: Like Homer's *The Odyssey*, this is a classic story of a long journey home. A more contemporary telling of a life that will come full circle is John Irving's *The Cider House Rules*. Rory MacLean's *Oatmeal Ark* is another story that portrays the environment (Nova Scotia, in this case) along with the family chronicle.

Humphreys, Helen.

🎗 *Afterimage.* HarperFlamingoCanada, 2000. 247pp. Book Groups 📖

When Annie Phelan arrives to work at Middle Road Farm, a country estate in Victorian England, she soon finds herself at the centre of a love triangle. She becomes the object of affection of her husband-and-wife employers, Isabelle (the photographer) and Eldon (the mapmaker), who then compete for her affections. *Afterimage* won the Rogers Writers' Trust Fiction Prize.

Second Appeal: Character

Subject Headings: Ambition • *Jane Eyre* • Obsessive Love • Pastiches • Photographers' Models • Triangles • Victorian England • Women Photographers

Read On: Readers will find here the imagery that is so evident both in Humphreys's poetry and in her first novel, *Leaving Earth*. The story of Julia Cameron, a Victorian photographer, inspired Humphreys's work, just as the 1996 takeover by the Tupac Amaru of the Japanese Ambassador's home in Lima, Peru, provided the inspiration for Ann Patchett's beautiful *Bel Canto*. *Eva Moves the Furniture* by Margot Livesey is a bittersweet story that reflects the tragedy seen in *Afterimage*. A young woman who takes employment in a remote country house and finds herself becoming deeply involved with her employers appears in Norah Labiner's *Miniatures*.

The Lost Garden. HarperFlamingoCanada, 2002. 183pp. Book Groups 📖

To aid the war effort, horticulturist Gwen Davis leaves London to manage a team of land girls on a country estate simultaneously being used as a billet for Canadian soldiers. More comfortable with plants than people, Gwen finds herself restoring a long-neglected garden, whose message of love ultimately surfaces.

Second Appeal: Character

Subjects: Canadians in England • Friendship • Love Stories • Male–Female Relationships • Unrequited Love • Women Gardeners • Women's Land Army • Woolf, Virginia • World War II

Read On: Humphreys reveals Gwen's transformation in a style that is reminiscent of Carol Shields's in *The Box Garden*. Other stories of love during wartime are *Fugitive Pieces* by Anne Michaels, *Stones from the River* by Ursula Hegi, *The English Patient* by Michael Ondaatje, and *Captain Corelli's Mandolin* by Louis de Bernières. Virginia Woolf also appears in Michael Cunningham's intense love story, *The Hours*.

Ignatieff, Michael.

Scar Tissue. Viking, 1993. 199pp. Book Groups 📖

A professor of philosophy mourns the slow and terrible descent of his mother into senility as a result of Alzheimer's disease and discovers that modern medicine is as powerless as philosophy to help him comprehend what is happening. This novel was shortlisted for the Booker Prize and the Winifred Holtby Memorial Prize.

Second Appeal: Story

Subjects: Alzheimer's Disease • Bereavement • Brothers • Death of a Parent • Mothers and Sons • University Professors

Read On: Ignatieff's other books include *The Russian Album, Asya*, and *Charlie Johnson in the Flames*. In this latter novel, the main protagonist once again embarks on a journey that will demonstrate how powerless he is to change events around him. Beverly Coyle's *In Troubled Waters* includes a character suffering from Alzheimer's disease. *A Time to Dance* by Walter Sullivan shows the effects of Alzheimer's disease from inside the mind of the person suffering from it. Andrew Solomon's *A Stone Boat* also deals with the close relationship between a son and his dying mother. The lack of consolation that philosophy offers in a time of tragedy is also conveyed in Lynne Sharon Schwartz's *Disturbances in the Field*.

Itani, Frances.

🎗 *Deafening*. HarperFlamingoCanada, 2003. 378pp. Book Groups 📖

When illness takes the hearing of Grania at age five, her family initially works to help her deal with the loss; however, it is a school for the deaf that teaches her the skills needed to cope in a silent world. Years later, on the eve of World War I, she meets and marries her husband Jim, only to be separated from him almost immediately when he is sent off to Europe as a stretcher bearer. The horrors of war resonate at home and abroad, ultimately providing an intense connection between husband and wife. *Deafening* has won the Commonwealth Writers Prize for Best Book in the Caribbean and Canada and was chosen as a *Booksense* 76 Selection, an *Atlanta Journal-Constitution* "Best Choices for Gift Giving," and a *Maclean's* Magazine Best Seller. Itani was shortlisted for the CBA Libris Author of the Year and her novel was shortlisted for Fiction Book of the Year.

> **Second Appeal:** Character

> **Subjects:** Coming of Age • Deaf Women • Historical Fiction • Love Stories • Ontario • Sisters • War • World War I

> **Read On:** Other elegant, poetic love stories set against the horrors of war include Michael Ondaatje's *The English Patient* and Louis de Bernières's *Captain Corelli's Mandolin. Birdsong* by Sebastian Faulks, *Regeneration* by Pat Barker, *The Wars* by Timothy Findley, and *No Man's Land* by Kevin Major are haunting novels that similarly capture the essence of World War I.

Keefer, Janice Kulyk.

The Green Library. HarperCollins, 1996. 272pp. Book Groups 📖

A mysterious photograph is the catalyst that sends Eva Chown on a journey of self-discovery to the Ukraine, where she reconnects with her personal and family past. Keefer's novel was shortlisted for the Governor General's Literary Award for Fiction.

> **Second Appeal:** Setting

> **Subjects:** Canadians in Ukraine • Chernobyl • Identity • Immigrants and Refugees • Love Stories • Toronto • Ukraine • Ukrainians in Canada • Women

> **Read On:** Keefer, winner of the Marian Engel Award in 1999, wrote a short-story collection, *Travelling Ladies,* and a subsequent novel, *Thieves,* both of which explore the theme of women who embark on interior journeys. The haunting quality of Keefer's storytelling is reminiscent of Amy Tan's *The Bonesetter's Daughter*, a story in which another daughter learns her family history. Joe Porcelli's *The Photograph* also employs a photograph as the basis for a search for family. The human devastation of the Chernobyl disaster is the subject of Irene Zabytko's *The Sky Unwashed*.

Kishkan, Theresa.

Sisters of Grass. Goose Lane, 2000. 206pp. Book Groups 📖

Anna, a museum curator, vividly imagines the story of a woman photographer who lived in the early years of the twentieth century in British Columbia as she catalogues a box of Margaret Stuart's personal effects for an upcoming exhibit. In doing so she tries to place her own life within the context of the rugged landscape.

> **Second Appeal:** Setting

Subjects: Aboriginal Peoples • Bill Miner Gang • British Columbia • Coming of Age • First Novels • Museum Curators • Women Photographers • Young Women

Read On: Kishkan has written six poetry collections, a book of essays, and a novella. The description of the landscapes here share a vivid sense of place found in Elizabeth Hay's *A Student of Weather*, Annie Proulx's *The Shipping News,* and Wayne Johnston's *The Colony of Unrequited Dreams*. Like Anna, the protagonist in Marian Engel's *Bear* also sets out on a journey of self-discovery as she catalogues the contents of a nineteenth-century library.

Kokis, Sergio.

The Art of Deception. Simon & Pierre, 2002. 349pp.

A loss of artistic integrity and fits of conscience push Willem, former Montreal art student turned master forger, to re-evaluate his work for an international forgery cartel. Translated from the French [*L'art du maquillage*] by W. Donald Wilson.

Subjects: Art Forgeries • Artists • Deception • French Canadian • Montreal • New York City • Obsession • Quebec • Translations

Read On: Kokis's first novel, *Funhouse* (translated from the French by David Homel), won four major literary awards in Quebec: le Grand Prix du livre de Montréal, la Médaille de L'Académie des lettres du Québec, Prix Québec-Paris, and le Prix Desjardins du Salon du Livre de Québec; it too uses the theme of art to tell a coming-of-age story. For another version of the art forger's story, try Judy Lester's *Masterpiece of Deception: An Art Mystery*, Alan Wall's *Bless the Thief,* or Iain Pears's *The Bernini Bust*. The descriptions of personal and artistic obsession, along with the forces that cause a person to realize what has been lost, will remind readers of Peter Carey's *My Life as a Fake*.

Kwa, Lydia.

This Place Called Absence. Turnstone Press, 2000. 218pp. Book Groups 📖

While on a leave of absence following her father's suicide and the breakup with her lesbian lover, Vancouver psychologist Wu Lan begins researching the history of the sex trade in Singapore in the early twentieth century. Through the voices of two prostitutes and her mother she learns of her own family past and discovers an inner resilience that will enable her to move forward in the present. This debut novel was shortlisted for the Amazon.ca/*Books in Canada* First Novel Award and the Lambda Literary Award.

Second Appeal: Character

Subjects: First Novels • Lesbians • Mothers and Daughters • Prostitution • Self-discovery • Singapore • Singaporean-Canadian Authors • Suicide • Vancouver • Women Psychologists

Read On: Singaporean women are featured in Fiona Cheong's *Shadow Theatre* and Shirley Lim's *Joss and Gold*. Kwa creates her characters with the richness of language seen in Amy Tan's *The Bonesetter's Daughter,* another story of a daughter who learns to reconcile her concept of the past to move forward in the

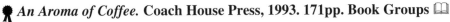

present. Shani Mootoo's *Cereus Blooms at Night* also uses a story-within-a-story structure.

Laferrière, Dany.

🎗 *An Aroma of Coffee.* **Coach House Press, 1993. 171pp. Book Groups** 📖

A ten-year-old boy chronicles the daily events and lives of the residents of a small Haitian town as he spends the summer with his grandmother on her front porch. This work was awarded the Prix Carbet de la Caraïbe. Translated from the French [*L'odeur du café*] by David Homel.

> **Second Appeal:** Character

> **Subjects:** Grandmothers • Haiti • Haitian-Canadian Authors • Rural Life • Translations • Young Boys

> **Read On:** Laferrière's other books in English include *How to Make Love to a Negro, Eroshima, Dining with the Dictator, Why Must a Black Writer Write About Sex?*, and *A Drifting Year*, which also chronicles day-to-day events in the same poetic fragments. Other writers have described boyhood years in the Caribbean, most notably Cecil Foster in his memoir *Island Wings* and Austin Clarke in *The Origin of Waves.*

Lai, Larissa.

When Fox Is a Thousand. **Press Gang Publishers, 1995. 236pp. Book Groups** 📖

Artemis, a young Chinese-Canadian woman who struggles to understand how she fits into her adoptive parents' white world, is haunted by the ancient spirit of a fox. This spirit reveals to her the story of another haunting, in which a T'ang dynasty poet was accused of the murder of a servant. Lai's novel was shortlisted for the Chapters/*Books in Canada* First Novel Award.

> **Second Appeal:** Story

> **Subjects:** Chinese Canadians • Chinese Mythology • Culture Clash • Feminist Fiction • First Novels • Folklore • Foxes • Magic Realism • Mythology

> **Read On:** Lai's novel is based on the old Chinese folktale of the Fox, and in her second novel, *Salt Fish Girl*, the author also moves the characters back and forth through the ages to tell a story of love and politics. Other books based on folktales are Vikram Chandra's *Red Earth and Pouring Rain*, Diana Darling's *The Painted Alphabet*, Timothy Findley's *Not Wanted on the Voyage,* and Kim Echlin's *Dagmar's Daughter.* The feminist threads of this novel are also woven into the work of Alice Walker's *The Color Purple* and Sara Maitland's *Angel Maker,* a short-story collection filled with history, magic, dreams, and the supernatural.

Lau, Evelyn.

Other Women. **Random House of Canada, 1995. 193pp. Book Groups** 📖

Twenty-four-year-old artist Fiona attempts to understand her obsessive, emotional attachment and unrequited passion for an aloof older married man as she recounts the events of the year following their breakup.

Subjects: Adultery • First Novels • Male–Female Relationships • Middle-aged Men • Obsessive Love • Older Men–Younger Women • Young Women

Read On: Lau also focuses on issues of relationships, marriage, loyalty, and emotion in her short-story collection, *Choose Me.* The violence expressed here also appears in novels by Susan Swan (*The Wives of Bath* and others). Both Richard B. Wright (*Adultery*) and Annie Ernaux (*A Simple Passion*) have lyrically captured the passion of an adulterous affair.

Maharaj, Rabindranath.

The Lagahoo's Apprentice. **Alfred A. Knopf Canada. 388pp. Book Groups** 📖

Author Stephen Sagar, commissioned to write the biography of a retired Trinidadian politician, returns to the island home he left sixteen years earlier. At first his homecoming causes him serious culture shock, but in revisiting his past he slowly comes to know himself for the first time.

Second Appeal: Story

Subjects: Canadians in Trinidad • Culture Clash • Immigrants and Refugees • Love Stories • Plantation Life • Self-discovery • Trinidad and Tobago • Trinidadians in Canada • Writers

Read On: Maharaj is the author of the short-story collection *The Interloper* and a debut novel, *Homer in Flight*, which was shortlisted for the Chapters/*Books in Canada* First Novel Award. Other novelists who vividly explore life in the Caribbean are Austin Clarke (*The Polished Hoe* and others) and Dionne Brand (*In Another Place, Not Here* and others). For the tourist's view of life in the Caribbean, try Catherine Jenkins's first novel, *Swimming in the Ocean.*

Majzels, Robert.

City of Forgetting. **Mercury Press, 1997. 168pp. Book Groups** 📖

A group of people play out their lives with unsettling delusions in a homeless persons' camp, against the backdrop of the city of Montreal.

Second Appeal: Character

Subjects: Homeless • Magic Realism • Montreal • Poverty • Quebec

Read On: Majzels's first novel, *Hellman's Scrapbook,* is written in a similar narrative form. Douglas Cooper's *Delirium* is another novel that unfolds against the urban landscape of a Canadian city (Toronto). In *Unless*, Carol Shields describes the impact of a young woman's flight to a life on the streets. Other authors whose works are defined as magic realism are Rudolfo A. Anaya (*Bless Me, Ultima*) and Isabel Allende (*The House of the Spirits* and others).

McCulloch, Ian.

Childforever. **Mercury Press, 1996. 206pp. Book Groups**

Following the death of his father, Will Sawnet discovers not only that he was adopted, but also that he is the son of a Cree woman. Will quits his job and embarks on a road trip in search of his birth mother. This journey, counterpointed by tales of Trickster Coyote, leads him to a Native reservation north of Edmonton, where a crisis of identity and culture clash force him to confront the past.

Second Appeal: Character

Subjects: Aboriginal Peoples • Adoption • Alberta • Cree Nation • First Novels • Journalists • Mothers and Sons • Road Novels

Read On: McCulloch's earlier works include *The Moon of Hunger, The Efficiency of Killers,* and *Parables and Rain.* The blending of humour and lyrical prose is a style also found in Alice Hoffman's *Practical Magic.* Trickster Coyote appears in Thomas King's *Green Grass, Running Water* and Christopher Moore's *Coyote Blue.*

McGillis, Ian.

A Tourist's Guide to Glengarry. **Porcupine's Quill, 2002. 185pp.**

Challenged by a teacher, nine-year-old Neil McDonald records in a journal a single day in his life, a day that should have been like every other day, filled with normal, everyday events. Yet it becomes a pivotal day for the boy as he learns of an impending family move away from his neighbourhood. McGillis was shortlisted for The Stephen Leacock Memorial Medal for Humour, the Hugh MacLennan Prize for Fiction, and the McAuslan First Book Prize (Quebec) for this novel.

Second Appeal: Character

Subjects: 1970s • Alberta • Boys • Community Life • Diaries • Edmonton • First Novels • Glengarry • Humorous Fiction • Life-changing Events

Read On: The life experience of the child in Roddy Doyle's *Paddy Clarke, Ha Ha Ha* is completely opposite to that described here, being closer to the kid-narrated world described in *The Adventures of Huckleberry Finn* by Mark Twain. Filled with down-to-earth prose, this work will remind readers of stories by Garrison Keillor (*Lake Wobegon Days* and others).

McNeil, Jean.

Hunting Down Home. **Phoenix House, 1996. 199pp. Book Groups**

Left by her mother to the care of her grandparents on their harsh Cape Breton farm, seven-year-old Morag becomes a pawn in their increasingly violent relationship.

Second Appeal: Setting

Subjects: Abandoned Children • Cape Breton Island • Coming of Age • Family Relationships • First Novels • Grandparents • Mothers Deserting Their Families • Nova Scotia • Young Women

Read On: Alistair MacLeod's *No Great Mischief* offers another lyrical depiction of grandparents raising children in Cape Breton. This island is the setting for Ann-Marie MacDonald's *Fall on Your Knees* and Lynn Coady's *Saints of Big Harbour*. The despair portrayed here is reminiscent of that felt by David Adams Richards's characters (in *The Bay of Love and Sorrows*).

McNutt, Linda.

Summer Point. Cormorant Books, 1997. 157pp. Book Groups 📖

Working with her boyfriend to close her recently inherited New Brunswick cottage, Sarah recalls the weekend that became a summer spent with extended family. Through her reminiscing, she comes to understand her life and the people in it.

Second Appeal: Setting

Subjects: Coming of Age • Cottages • First Novels • Grandmothers • Grandparents • New Brunswick • Reminiscing • Summer

Read On: A child who spends an idyllic summer with his grandmother is found in Dany Laferrière's *An Aroma of Coffee*. A young girl connecting with her extended family due to a family crisis is the subject of Anita Rau Badami's *The Hero's Walk*. The memories of summer here compare well with those in David Macfarlane's *Summer Gone,* and summer at the cottage is a thread that runs through Diane Baker Mason's *Last Summer at Barebones.*

Michaels, Anne.

🏵 *Fugitive Pieces*. McClelland & Stewart, 1996. 294pp. Book Groups 📖

Despite being rescued and adopted by a kindly Greek geologist during World War II, Jacob Beer forever carries the trauma and grief of witnessing the slaughter of his Polish family. Recognition of the power of this work came from both Canada and beyond; the prizes awarded to this novel include Chapters/*Books in Canada* First Novel Award, Giuseppe Acerbi Literary Award, *Guardian* Fiction Award, Harold U. Ribalow Prize, Jewish Quarterly Prize for Fiction, Lanna Literary Award, Martin & Beatrice Fischer First Novel Award, the Orange Prize for Fiction, the Toronto Book Award, the Trillium Book Award, and the Heritage Toronto Award of Merit. It was also shortlisted for the Giller Prize and the CBA Libris Award for Fiction.

Second Appeal: Character

Subjects: Adoption • Coming of Age • First Novels • Greece • Grief • Holocaust • Ontario • Poland • Refugees • Toronto • World War II

Read On: As evidenced by the number and breadth of the literary awards garnered, *Fugitive Pieces*, a first novel, will resonate with readers on many levels and from many access points. Thus we offer the following suggestions: *Captain Corelli's Mandolin* by Louis de Bernières is also set in Greece during World War II; Marisa Kantor Stark's *Bring Us the Old People* is about a young person whose parents perish during the war; and Andrzej Szczypiorksi's *The Shadow Catcher* is a coming-of-age novel set in Warsaw, Poland, during the rise of Hitler.

Mistry, Rohinton.

🎗 *Family Matters*. McClelland & Stewart, 2002. 487pp. Book Groups 📖

Family relationships are strained in an extended Indian family when an accident forces elderly Nariman Vakeel to move from his stepchildren's care in his spacious, if decaying, apartment into his daughter's cramped home. *Family Matters* received a number of awards: the CAA Literary Award for Fiction, the Kiriyama Pacific Rim Book Prize, and the Torgi Literary Award. An ALA Notable Book, it was also nominated for the International IMPAC Dublin Literary Award for the Novel and the Man Booker Prize, the Commonwealth Writers Prize for Best Book in the Caribbean and Canada, and the James Tait Black Memorial Prize for Fiction.

> **Second Appeal:** Setting
>
> **Subjects:** Apartment Houses • Blended Families • Bombay • Brothers and Sisters • Elderly Men • Friendship • India • Parent and Adult Child • Parkinson's Disease • Reminiscing in Old Age
>
> **Read On:** Mistry's humour in *A Fine Balance* re-emerges here, but the theme of a family in conflict echoes from his first novel, *Such a Long Journey*. The characters in *Brick Lane* by Monica Ali and in *The Namesake* by Jhumpa Lahiri are depicted in a style of language similar to Mistry's.

🎗 *Such a Long Journey*. McClelland & Stewart, 1991. 339pp. Book Groups 📖

Gustad Noble, a devout Parsi who strives to do the right thing for his family and friends, finds himself involved in the political corruption of Indira Gandhi's government, with terrible results. *Such a Long Journey* received the Governor General's Literary Award for Fiction, the Commonwealth Writers Prize for Best Book, and the Chapters/*Books in Canada* First Novel Award; it was also shortlisted for both the Trillium Book Award and the Booker Prize.

> **Second Appeal:** Setting
>
> **Subjects:** Bank Employees • Bombay • Family Relationships • First Novels • Friendship • India • Men's Lives • Zoroastrians
>
> **Read On:** Mistry's blend of humour and tragedy, as well as his playful use of language, are reminiscent of Salman Rushdie's writing, in, for example, *Midnight's Children* and *The Moor's Last Sigh*.

Musgrave, Susan.

***Cargo of Orchids*. Alfred A. Knopf Canada, 2000. 375pp. Book Groups** 📖

A woman on death row, accused of murdering her child by sacrificing the baby for drugs, recounts the events that have brought her to this place in her life as she awaits the results of her final appeal.

> **Second Appeal:** Story

Subjects: Black Humour • Cocaine • Drug Traffic • Filicide • Mothers • Prisons • Women Death Row Inmates • Women Prisoners • Women's Friendships

Read On: Musgrave's earlier titles, *The Charcoal Burners* and *The Dancing Chicken,* share the black humour of this novel. Combining dark humour and poetic language, Pat Conroy (*The Prince of Tides* and others) also draws the reader into the lives of his characters. Writers like Tom Robbins (*Skinny Legs and All* and others) take a satirical look at the conventions of society. In the young adult novel *Monster* by Walter Dean Myers, a teen chronicles his murder trial in a movie-script format.

Niven, Catherine Simmons.

🎗 *A Fine Daughter.* Red Deer Press, 1999. 238pp. Book Groups 📖

Seventeen years ago Fran arrived in Little Cyprus, Alberta, as a pregnant teen-ager. Defying small-town conventions, she kept her daughter, a decision that has set her apart from the town's residents. The unexpected arrival of a migration of monarch butterflies magically signals a possibility for change. *A Fine Daughter* was awarded the Henry Kreisel Award for Best First Book and the Georges Bugnet Award for Best Novel; it was also shortlisted for the Chapters/*Books in Canada* First Novel Award and the City of Calgary W. O. Mitchell Book Award.

Second Appeal: Character

Subjects: First Novels • Illegitimate Children • Mothers and Daughters • Prairies • Role of Women • Small-town Life • Social Outcasts

Read On: The rhythm of Niven's evocative prose is similar to that in Emma Donoghue's work (*Slammerkin* and others). Other novels that feature a daughter's perspective are Natalee Caple's *The Plight of Happy People in an Ordinary World* and Debbie Howlett's linked stories, *We Could Stay Here All Night.*

Ondaatje, Michael.

🎗 *Anil's Ghost.* Alfred A. Knopf Canada, 2000. 311pp. Book Groups 📖

Anil Tissera returns to her home in Sri Lanka on behalf of a human rights organi-zation, to investigate the many murders being committed in the ongoing ethnic, religious, and political violence. *Anil's Ghost* won the 2000 Kiriyama Pacific Rim Book Prize and the *Irish Times* International Fiction Prize, as well as the Giller Prize and the Governor General's Literary Award for Fiction. It was also selected as an ALA Notable Book.

Second Appeal: Setting

Subjects: Brothers • Civil War • Forensics • Human Rights Workers • Massacres • Sri Lanka • Violence • Women Forensic Anthropologists

Read On: Ondaatje himself returns to his home in Sri Lanka (Ceylon) by way of his memoir, *Running in the Family.* He also includes among his writings several poetry collections, as well as *Coming Through Slaughter* and *In the Skin of a Lion,* a CBC Canada Reads winning selection. Another political novel that is nearly as under-stated as Ondaatje's is Lawrence Thornton's *Imagining Argentina.* Other interna-tionally political novels are Patricia Henley's *Hummingbird House* and Barbara Kingsolver's *The Poisonwood Bible.*

🎗 *The English Patient.* **Alfred A. Knopf Canada, 1992. 307pp. Book Groups** 📖

As World War II draws to a close, a young nurse in a bomb-damaged villa near Florence, Italy, devotedly tends a mysterious English patient, a nameless burn victim haunted by his own memories of passion, betrayal, and rescue. *The English Patient* won the Governor General's Literary Award for Fiction, the Commonwealth Writers Prize for Best Book in the Caribbean and Canada, the Trillium Book Award, and the Booker Prize. It was also selected as an ALA Notable Book.

> **Second Appeal:** Character

> **Subjects:** Army • Burn Victims • Italy • Love Stories • Male–Female Relationships • Military Nursing • North Africa • Survival • World War II

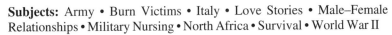

> **Read On:** Ondaatje visits a very different time in the past in his novel *Coming Through Slaughter,* in which he writes of Buddy Bolden, a jazz pioneer in New Orleans. He also has three books of poetry that echo the themes of *The English Patient.* The elegant language that characterizes Ondaatje's novel is also present in Anne Michaels's *Fugitive Pieces* and Jim Crace's *Arcadia.* Penelope Lively's *Moon Tiger* shares the North African setting with Ondaatje's novel, while J. L. Carr's *A Month in the Country* is another novel that describes the effects of war on its survivors.

Redhill, Michael.

🎗 *Martin Sloane.* **Doubleday Canada, 2001. 282pp. Book Groups** 📖

Deserted by her long-time lover, artist Martin Sloane, Jolene reflects on her present and Martin's past in an attempt to move on. Years later, when information about the artist resurfaces, she realizes she must confront the loss again. Redhill's *Martin Sloane* won the Chapters/*Books in Canada* First Novel Award and the Commonwealth Writers Prize for Best First Book in the Caribbean and Canada; it was also shortlisted for the Giller Prize and the Trillium Book Award.

> **Second Appeal:** Character

> **Subjects:** 1980s • Artists • Dublin • First Novels • Ireland • Love Stories • Middle-aged Men • Missing Persons • Older Men–Younger Women • Toronto • Young Women

> **Read On:** As did Alistair MacLeod when writing *No Great Mischief,* Redhill spent almost ten years working on this novel. In Catherine Bush's *The Rules of Engagement* another young woman confronts events from her past. To examine the relationships between older men and younger women in a novel with a similar strength of language, look at Bernard Malamud's *Dubin's Lives.* In a different story, told in a different time and setting, another male author (Sinclair Ross) creates a female narrator struggling in her relationship with her artistic husband, in *As for Me and My House.*

Richards, David Adams.

🏵 *Mercy Among the Children.* **Doubleday Canada, 2000. 371pp. Book Groups** 📖

When his anger almost caused a fatal accident, Sydney Henderson made a pact with God to harm no man; that decision, as well as his failure to defend himself or his family regardless of ongoing persecution, forces his son Lyle to struggle violently in reconciling his feelings about his father's pacifist teachings. In addition to the Giller Prize, this novel was also honoured with the Atlantic Independent Booksellers' Choice Award and the CBA Libris Award: Fiction Book of the Year. It was shortlisted for the Governor General's Literary Award for Fiction, the Trillium Book Award, and the Thomas Head Raddall Atlantic Fiction Award.

Second Appeal: Setting

Subjects: Children • Family • Fathers and Sons • Miramichi River Region • New Brunswick • Religious Fiction • Small-town Life

Read On: Richards has written a trilogy also set in the Miramichi River Region: *Nights Below Station Street*, winner of the Governor General's Award; *Evening Snow Will Bring Such Peace*, winner of the CAA Literary Award for Fiction; and *For Those Who Hunt the Wounded Down*. *The Bay of Love and Sorrows* is a novel that also looks at people who hold back from taking action even when it may be the right thing to do. Another family drama set in the Miramichi and featuring a young man is Larry Lynch's *An Expectation of Home*. Like Alistair MacLeod (*No Great Mischief*), Richards employs a strong narrative voice to evoke both compelling characters and a true sense of place.

Rooke, Leon.

The Fall of Gravity. **Thomas Allen Publishers, 2000. 271pp.**

Wife and mother Joyel Daggle takes to the road, passing through twenty-six states and nine provinces. Followed by drink-sodden husband Raoul and their precocious eleven-year-old daughter Juliette, Daggle encounters a cast of outlandish characters along the way.

Appeal: Language

Subjects: Automobile Travel • Dysfunctional Families • Fathers and Daughters • Humorous Fiction • Missing Persons • Road Novels • Runaway Wives • Surrealistic Fiction • Wyoming

Read On: Leon Rooke, founder of the Eden Mills Writers Festival, was awarded the W. O. Mitchell Prize in 2002 for his output of literary material as well as for mentoring other writers. His *Shakespeare's Dog* won a Governor General's Literary Award for Fiction. The stream-of-consciousness style used here is also found in Marie-Claire Blais's *Deaf to the City*, Carol Bruneau's *Purple for Sky*, and Roddy Doyle's *Paddy Clarke, Ha Ha Ha*.

Schoemperlen, Diane.

Our Lady of the Lost and Found. **HarperFlamingoCanada, 2001. 349pp. Book Groups**

The spiritual journey of a forty-something author begins when she discovers a tired Virgin Mary, an icon in need of rest and relaxation, standing in her living room.

Subjects: Apparitions and Miracles • Magic Realism • Mary, Blessed Virgin • Middle-aged Women • Religious Fiction • Spiritual Journeys • Women Authors • Women's Friendships

Read On: Schoemperlen's other books include *In the Language of Love: A Novel in 100 Chapters* and several short-story collections: *Red Plaid Shirt*, *The Man of My Dreams*, and *Forms of Devotion,* which was awarded the Governor General's Literary Award for Fiction. Gloria Sawai's language in *A Song for Nettie Johnson*, another winner of the Governor General's Literary Award for Fiction, is similar to Schoemperlen's. On a lighter note, Mignon F. Ballard has written some stories with a different celestial visitor, this one in the form of an angel (*An Angel to Die For* and others), and in Joan Brady's *God on a Harley,* another woman embarks on a spiritual journey after an encounter with God in a bar.

Scrimger, Richard.

Mystical Rose. **Doubleday Canada, 2000. 234pp. Book Groups**

In hospital nearing death, Rose Rolyoke struggles to understand her life even as it is ending. Her mind drifting due to the ravages of Alzheimer's disease, she revisits the events of a long life through a one-sided conversation with God.

Second Appeal: Character

Subjects: Alzheimer's Disease • Elderly Women • Memory • Mothers and Daughters • Religious Fiction • Reminiscing in Old Age • Terminally Ill • Women

Read On: Scrimger's first novel, *Crosstown,* also reveals the story of an elderly person in search of redemption. He has also written several novels for younger readers. Other novels that feature reminiscing elderly women are Margaret Laurence's *The Stone Angel,* Carol Shields's *The Stone Diaries,* Dorothy Speak's *The Wife Tree,* and Ethel Wilson's *Swamp Angel.* Keziah Donovan, in Robin McGrath's *Donovan's Station,* is an eighty-four-year-old woman who decides to recapture her life while patiently waiting to die.

Seaman, Patricia.

The Nightingales. **Coach House Books, 2001. 157pp.**

During the summer of 1989 a group of young women in Toronto begin an intense yet ultimately devastating friendship as they desperately search for love.

Subjects: 1980s • Identity • Love Stories • Lust • Ontario • Toronto • Women's Friendships

Read On: *The Nightingales,* like Seaman's wild, sexy, and innovative graphic novel *New Motor Queen City*, portrays the darker side of friendship and desire as they are twisted into ugliness. Anne Dandurand's *The Waiting Room* turns a doctor's waiting room into a lusty experience of the imagination. Although told with the perspective of distance, *Cat's Eye* by Margaret Atwood contains an account of the friendship among a group of young women in Toronto. For a depiction of male friendship, try Lesley Choyce's *The Summer of Apartment X*, which looks at the relationships among four friends from the male perspective.

Shields, Carol.

❧ *The Stone Diaries.* **Random House of Canada, 1993. 361pp. Book Groups** 📖

The long and "ordinary" life of Daisy Stone Goodwill unfolds in bittersweet detail through a collage of narrative, letters, newspaper clippings, and multiple voices. This work by Shields was recognized for excellence both nationally and internationally: it won the Governor General's Literary Award for Fiction, as well as the McNally Robinson Book of the Year and the Torgi Literary Award, the Pulitzer Prize, and the National Book Critics' Circle Award. It was also nominated for the Booker Prize. Carol Shields was presented with the 1990 Marian Engel Award for outstanding work mid-career.

Second Appeal: Character

Subjects: Abandoned Children • Aging • Depression, Mental • Diaries • Family Relationships • Fathers and Daughters • Life-changing Events • Loneliness • Stonecutting • Women's Lives

Read On: Shields is also the author of *Swann, The Box Garden, Various Miracles,* and *Small Ceremonies*, among other works of fiction. Both *Kate Vaiden* and *Roxanne Slade* by Reynolds Price are similarly about the lives of strong women. Alice Munro's *The Progress of Love* details lives of ordinary women in the spare style of Carol Shields.

Smith, Russell.

Muriella Pent. **Doubleday Canada, 2004. 348pp. Book Groups** 📖

In Toronto as part of a cultural exchange, middle-aged Caribbean poet Marcus Royston is the catalyst who brings recently widowed society maven Muriella Pent toward a new level of confidence and understanding of her own sexuality, at the same time fostering her need for self-advancement in the arts community.

Second Appeal: Character

Subjects: Art • Caribbeans in Canada • Middle-aged Women • Satire • Socialites • Toronto • Writers

Read On: Smith's first novel, *How Insensitive*, was shortlisted for the Governor General's Literary Award, and his short-story collection, *Young Men: Stories,* was shortlisted for the Toronto Book Award. The combination of wit and irreverence here is reminiscent of Mordecai Richler's in *Barney's Version*. Smith's portrayal of the writer in this novel is similar to such portrayals found in Martin Amis's *The Information* and John Updike's <u>Henry Bech</u> series (*Bech Is Back* and others). *The Winter Gardeners* by Dennis Denisoff is another urban Toronto novel that explores the themes of art and sexuality in a satirical manner.

Sterns, Kate.

Down There by the Train. Alfred A. Knopf Canada, 2001. 244pp. Book Groups 📖

Newly paroled Levon Hawke takes a wrong turn on his way to a job at his cousin's bakery and finds himself on the doorstep of Obdulia, a woman whose ten years of mourning her mother have her on the verge of committing suicide. This misstep begins a relationship that ultimately helps them both overcome grief.

Second Appeal: Character

Subjects: Death of a Parent • Ex-convicts • Gothic Fiction • Grief • Islands • Magic Realism • Single Women • Stepmothers • Suicide

Read On: Elements of magic realism figure in Stern's first novel, *Thinking About Magritte*. This novel's humour and quirkiness are similar to those in Ben Sherwood's *The Man Who Ate the 747* and Steve Martin's *The Pleasure of My Company*. Magic realism and a love story combine in Jane Urquhart's *Changing Heaven* to tell the story of two people who fall into an affair.

Thomas, H. Nigel.

Behind the Face of Winter. TSAR Publications, 2001. 241pp. Book Groups 📖

After spending his childhood and pre-teen years living with his grandmother on the Caribbean Island of Isabella, Pedro Moore is sent to join his mother, who works as a domestic in Montreal. There he experiences the harsh and often violent life of an immigrant, while struggling to understand his emerging homosexuality.

Second Appeal: Character

Subjects: Black Youth • Coming of Age • Gay Teenagers • Immigrants and Refugees • Montreal • Mothers and Sons • Quebec • Youth

Read On: Thomas's first novel, *Spirits in the Dark,* is also the coming-of-age story of a gay teenager. Another author who writes of the Caribbean/Canadian experience is Austin Clarke (*The Meeting Point, Storm of Fortune, The Bigger Light,* and others). Mairuth Sarsfield's *No Crystal Stair* also features a black mother who works as a domestic in Montreal to support her family. In Edmund White's *A Boy's Own Story,* another gay teen struggles to understand his homosexuality.

Uppal, Priscila.

The Divine Economy of Salvation. **Doubleday Canada, 2002. 408pp. Book Groups** 📖

When Sister Angela receives a package containing evidence from an old crime, she is forced to recall her role in the death of a classmate almost thirty years earlier.

Second Appeal: Story

Subjects: Boarding Schools • First Novels • Guilt • Initiation Rites • Nuns • Ontario • Ottawa • Secret Societies • Teenagers' Friendships • Violence in Adolescence

Read On: Teenage girls connected by violence are found in Susan Swan's *The Wives of Bath*. Like Katherine Govier in *The Truth Teller*, Uppal is able to capture eloquently the relationships among a group of teenage girls at an exclusive girls' school. Heather McGowan's *Schooling* is also set in a boarding school. The Latin teacher in *The Lake of Dead Languages* (Carole Goodman) has also been carrying a secret burden for many years, which returns to haunt her.

Urquhart, Jane.

Changing Heaven. **McClelland & Stewart, 1990. 258pp. Book Groups** 📖

The stories of two women—a present-day Brontë scholar and a turn-of-the-century balloonist who, along with the spirit of Emily Brontë, haunts the English moors where she died—are linked as past and present connect to reveal two stories of obsessive love.

Second Appeal: Character

Subjects: Balloonists • Brontë, Emily • England • Ghost Stories • Magic Realism • Male–Female Relationships • Obsessive Love • Women Scholars

Read On: Other novels that share the otherworldly atmosphere created here are John Banville's *Athena* and Barbara Erskine's *Midnight Is a Lonely Place*. Urquhart's blending of the present and past is reminiscent of A. S. Byatt's *Possession*. Katherine Govier's *Between Men* also looks at obsessive love in a historical setting.

Van Herk, Aritha.

Restlessness. **Red Deer College Press, 1998. 193pp. Book Groups** 📖

Unable to commit suicide, Dorcas hires an assassin, who ironically engages her in a conversation meant to examine her need for this drastic solution.

Second Appeal: Setting

Subjects: Alberta • Calgary • Death • Psychological Fiction • Storytelling • Suicidal Behaviour • Travel • Women

Read On: The macabre atmosphere created here is suggestive of Ian McEwan's *Amsterdam*. Another woman contemplating suicide is the subject of Sarah Dreher's *Solitaire and Brahms*. Elisabeth Harvor's *Excessive Joy Injures the Heart* features a woman who is experiencing intense loneliness. James McManus's *Going to the Sun* examines suicide from a different perspective, as the novel follows a woman coping with the mental anguish of assisting her boyfriend in committing suicide.

Vassanji, M. G.

The In-Between World of Vikram Lall. **Doubleday Canada, 2003. 410pp. Book Groups** 📖

From the vantage point of a life in exile in Canada, Kenyan-born Vikram Lall, the son of Indian parents, reflects on the events of his life, from a childhood of ignorance naïvely unaware of class distinctions and the changing political environment to his adulthood, when he becomes known as "one of Africa's most corrupt men." Vassanji won the Giller Prize for this work, the only author to date to win this prize twice.

Second Appeal: Setting

Subjects: Africa • Culture Clash • Friendship • Historical Fiction • Kenya • Mau Mau Emergency

Read On: Vassanji's *The Book of Secrets,* also set in Kenya, was awarded the inaugural Giller Prize in 1994. Barbara Wood's *Green City in the Sun* is the story of one woman's journey into her family's past in Kenya, told with the same lush detail as in Vassanji's novel. V. S. Naipaul's *A Bend in the River* is the story of a man in Africa caught in the conflict between the modern and the traditional. John Bemrose's *The Island Walkers* is also a portrait of a man who hopes to escape his past but cannot quite leave it behind.

Watson, Sheila.

Deep Hollow Creek. **McClelland & Stewart, 1992. 141pp. Book Groups** 📖

In the 1930s a young teacher comes from the city to teach school in a remote rural district in the interior of British Columbia. There she observes the small-town folk, discovering their inner strength and her place within the community. This second novel of Watson's was nominated for the Governor General's Literary Award for Fiction.

Second Appeal: Character

Subjects: 1930s • British Columbia • Rural Life • Teachers

Read On: Watson's only other work of fiction, *The Double Hook,* was published in 1959. Although it was written in the early 1930s, *Deep Hollow Creek* was not published until 1992. Other novels that share the interior quality found here are J. M. Coetzee's *The Master of Petersburg* and Jane Hamilton's *The Short History of a Prince.* Other novels set in small towns in British Columbia include Jack Hodgins's *Broken Ground* and Ethel Wilson's *Hetty Dorval.*

Woodrow, Marnie.

Spelling Mississippi. **Alfred A. Knopf Canada, 2002. 387pp. Book Groups** 📖

Cleo Savoy seeks out a woman she saw jump into the Mississippi River one evening in New Orleans. As they slowly reveal their stories, Cleo's obsession with this woman becomes personal, and they move toward an intimate relationship. This debut novel was shortlisted for the Amazon.ca/*Books in Canada* first Novel Award.

Second Appeal: Character

Subjects: First Novels • Humorous Fiction • Lesbians • Louisiana • Love Stories • Magic Realism • Mississippi River • New Orleans • Women's Friendships

Read On: Woodrow's first work was a short-story collection, *In the Spice House*. Four female college friends reveal their stories when they reunite on the Mississippi River in Lee Smith's *The Last Girls*. Like Helen Humphreys in *Wild Dogs*, Woodrow poetically creates feelings of love and loss.

Chapter 5

Genre Fiction

Six genres of fiction are covered in this chapter: mystery, science fiction, fantasy, romance, thriller, and horror. The number of subgenres and authors listed is representative of the number of writers active in the genre, as many more Canadians write "mainstream fiction" than genre fiction. The readership for both, however, is wide. The authors and titles included in each section are meant to be a sampling of those either best known or currently writing in this genre. It was not our intent that this chapter (or our other chapters) be all-inclusive. Our aim is to introduce both librarians and readers to the works of Canadian authors who have previously been unknown to them and also to acknowledge that these genre writers are considered part of the Canadian writing scene. The Western genre is not included here, since this is not a genre in which Canadians generally have chosen to tell stories. One notable exception to this is Guy Vanderhaeghe's *The Last Crossing*, a rousing frontier-based novel, which can be found in chapter 3.

As in mainstream fiction, the work of Canadian genre writers is consistently acknowledged as some of the best, with their work winning awards both nationally and internationally. Robert J. Sawyer's *Hominids* won the Hugo Award in 2003, and his novel *The Terminal Experiment* received both the Nebula Award in 1995 and the HOMer Award in 1996. William Gibson's *Neuromancer* was awarded the Hugo, Nebula, and Philip K. Dick Awards in 1984. Candas Jane Dorsey's *Black Wine* won both the Prix Aurora Award and the William F. Crawford Award. Hiromi Goto won the James Tiptree Jr. Award for *The Kappa Child*, while Sean Stewart won the World Fantasy Award for *Galveston*. In addition to being named a *New York Times* Notable Book, *In a Dry Season* by Peter Robinson also won the Anthony Award in 2001, and *Trial of Passion* by William Deverell won both an Arthur Ellis and a Dashiell Hammett Award. Mary Balogh (*More Than a Mistress*) and Jo Beverley (*Emily and the Dark Angel*) have both been recipients of RITA awards.

For each genre and subgenre, we have provided a brief definition and some typical characteristics. These descriptors are not unique to Canadian fiction, but are relevant to the genre as a whole. In order to lead readers through the genres, we have listed a number of genre-specific tools, primarily from the <u>Genreflecting Advisory Series</u>, that will assist the librarian or the reader in gaining a fuller understanding of the genre.

In classifying a work by genre, we have grouped together those that share a number of appeal characteristics. Therefore, as in the earlier chapters, we have included "Read On" suggestions, especially for stand-alone titles. For series titles, we have noted author read-alikes, when appropriate. As in the other chapters, the read-alikes are not confined to Canadian titles only; we offer our suggestions from genre writers at large. These are our suggestions; undoubtedly other advisors will have their own suggestions, rising from their own store of knowledge.

In the preceding chapters we have noted titles that can be the basis of interesting discussions for book groups. When appropriate, we have continued that practice in this chapter, as many of the themes that are discussed in these titles may in fact result in excellent conversations.

Librarians and readers interested in discovering more about Canadian genre fiction are encouraged to explore the Web sites of the various genre associations, SF Canada, CRAN: The Canadian Romance Authors' Network, and the Crime Writers of Canada. Their Web sites, listed in Appendix 1, are excellent sources of further information on the Canadian writers of genre fiction.

Mystery

The character played by Geoffrey Rush in *Shakespeare in Love* constantly responded to the question "Why?" with a shrug of the shoulders and the answer "It's a mystery!" This was no help in the story, but it does illustrate the definition of a mystery as a puzzle, one that has no ready answer. And it is the puzzle that the mystery focuses on, as opposed to the thriller, which focuses on the action and the emotion of the thrill.

In modern mystery writing, however, there is a relatively new phenomenon: the world created by the author in the character series. The series character dates back to the beginnings of crime fiction, with Emile Gaboriau's Monsieur Lecoq, Conan Doyle's Sherlock Holmes, and Agatha Christie's Hercule Poirot. However, the practice has become embedded as a standard element in the genre. Series characters have become the linchpin in the story that makes the reader return, to visit old friends and see how they're doing or see what's new in their lives. The series should be read in order if one wants to keep track of the characters' lives. Initially, the character was the vehicle used to tell the story. Now, for the reader the story is at times the vehicle to develop the character and his or her world. Many of these series characters are amateur sleuths, but many are bona fide detectives—either private or public. But a mystery requires an investigator, so these characters will be one type of investigator or another. However, because of the cross-blending that we refer to so often, you will also find them in the comic subgenre, the cozy, the forensic, the hard-boiled, and the historical. If the characteristics of these subgenres are stronger or more important than the generic amateur detective, private investigator, or police detective, that is where you will find the author's work.

Grant Allen (1848–1899) was Canada's first crime writer, and it was he who developed the motif of the thief-narrator. While Jonathan Gash's Lovejoy in Britain is arguably the best-known in this subgenre, there is no one currently in Canada who comes to mind.

However, that is not to say that crime writing in Canada is not flourishing, even though our pioneer has not been strictly emulated. Canada has an abundance of excellent mystery writers who write in a number of subgenres, some more prolifically than others.

Before going on to the actual annotations, we briefly review the characteristics of the mystery novel as delineated by Joyce Saricks in *The Readers' Advisory Guide to Genre Fiction* (2001, 147). The ingredients that generally constitute a mystery novel are a murder, an investigator with clues to follow and a puzzle to solve, an investigation that usually delves into the life of the victim and those in the victim's life, and a resolution of the puzzle, whether or not justice is served. The frame is often of great interest to the reader, in the form of the location, the profession or hobby of the investigator, or the tone of the story.

Amateur Detective

How many of us read the <u>Nancy Drew Mystery Stories</u> and the <u>Hardy Boys Mystery Stories</u> books as children because we would so love to have had the adventures they had and solved the crimes they did, but would never have had the courage? The same could be said of the adult amateur detectives. They are stronger than we, more inquisitive (nosy?), more clever, more persistent, more courageous, and they certainly encounter more dead bodies than the common reader! It is this situation that truly requires a suspension of disbelief: in some of these small towns, how many murders could actually take place before the citizens started crying foul? The amateur detective subgenre encompasses protagonists with a variety of professions and hobbies, not to mention personality types, and it is this added insight into a perhaps unfamiliar world that increases the appeal for the reader. The nature of this type of mystery is such that the amateur detective is also found quite frequently in the cozy and comic subgenres.

Allin, Lou.

<u>Belle Palmer Mysteries.</u>

Belle Palmer is a realtor, a dog lover, and an environmentalist from Sudbury, Ontario, a city in the northern part of the province.

Northern Winters Are Murder. RendezVous Press, 2000.

In the snowy north, Sudbury realtor Belle Palmer investigates the death of her friend, Jim, in a snowmobile accident. Knowing that he had suspected there were drug traffickers and unscrupulous land-development lobbyists at work, Belle realizes that Jim's death could not have been an accident.

Blackflies Are Murder. RendezVous Press, 2002.

Bush Poodles Are Murder. RendezVous Press, 2003.

Subjects: Environment • Land Developers • Murder • Northern Ontario • Ontario • Palmer, Belle (Fictional Character) • Realtors

Read On: The <u>Melanie Travis Mysteries</u> by Laurien Berenson (*Hot Dog* and others) and Susan Conant's <u>Dog Lover's Mysteries,</u> featuring Holly Winter (*The Wicked Flea* and others), are other cozy mysteries with dog-loving amateur sleuths. The cold north is the setting of Steve Hamilton's <u>Alex McKnight Mysteries,</u> beginning with *A Cold Day in Paradise*.

Amberhill, Bevan.

<u>Jean-Claude Keyes Mysteries.</u>

Jean-Claude Keyes is an actor and writer who has moved to Stratford, Ontario, the home of the Stratford Festival, a repertory theatre festival that places a special emphasis on Shakespeare's plays.

The Bloody Man. Mercury Press, 1993.

Actor-turned-writer Jean-Claude Keyes, in Stratford to finish a biography of a Shakespearean actor and perhaps rekindle an old love affair, investigates the death of a young actor after a performance of *Macbeth*.

The Running Girl. Mercury Press, 1995.

Subjects: Actors and Acting • Keyes, Jean-Claude (Fictional Character) • Murder • Ontario • Shakespeare, William • Stratford • Theatre

Read On: Stanley Hastings is an actor-turned-detective in the <u>Stanley Hastings Mysteries</u> by Parnell Hall (*Actor*). The theatre provides the setting for many mysteries: Lydia Adamson's <u>Alice Nestleton Mysteries</u> (*A Cat in the Wings* and others) and Simon Brett's <u>Charles Paris Mysteries</u> (*Dead Room* and others) are just two examples. The <u>Elizabethan Theatre Series</u> by Edward Marston (*The Bawdy Basket* and others) is set in Shakespeare's time and theatre, while Amberhill's setting is contemporary.

Aubert, Rosemary.

<u>Ellis Portal Mysteries.</u>

Ellis Portal is a former judge, a convicted felon, and a homeless man in Toronto's Don Valley area, trying to get back his respectability as he also tries to help his homeless friends.

Free Reign. Bridge Works, 1997. **Book Groups** 📖

The discovery of a severed hand wearing a ring familiar from his college days sends former Toronto judge Ellis Portal to look for answers; he turns to those in his past with help from the homeless, who are now part of his present. This novel was nominated for the Arthur Ellis Award for Best Novel and the Barry Award for Best First Novel.

🎗 *The Feast of Stephen.* Bridge Works, 1999.

Winner of the Arthur Ellis Award for Best Novel.

The Ferryman Will Be There. Bridge Works, 2001.

Leave Me by Dying. McArthur & Company, 2003.

The Red Mass. McArthur & Company, 2005.

Subjects: Homeless • Judges • Ontario • Portal, Ellis (Fictional Character) • Social Classes • Street Life • Toronto

Read On: George Dawes Green's *The Caveman's Valentine*, Todd Komarnicki's *Free,* and Andrew Vachss's *Choice of Evil* and *Dead and Gone* all feature homeless detectives. Authors who set their mysteries in Toronto include Gavin Scott (*Memory Trace*), Scott MacKay (*Cold Comfort* and others), Ted Wood (*Live Bait*), and Medora Sale (*Pursued by Shadows* and others).

Ballem, John.

Murder As a Fine Art. Dundurn Press, 2002. 261pp.

Aspiring author Laura Janeway launches an investigation into a series of suspicious deaths at the Banff Centre for the Arts; she soon discovers that professional jealousies and affairs lead to several possible suspects.

Subjects: Alberta • Artists • Authors as Detectives • Banff Centre for the Arts

Read On: Alison Gordon's <u>Kate Henry Mysteries</u> (*Safe at Home* and others) also feature a writer pulled into murder investigations. Jealousy plays a role in a murder case in N.J. Lindquist's *Shaded Light: A Manziuk and Ryan Mystery*. Other male authors who feature female sleuths in their novels include James Patterson (*1st To Die* and others), Thomas Perry (*Dance for the Dead* and others), and Alexander McCall Smith, (*The No. 1 Ladies' Detective Agency* and others).

Blair, Michael.

If Looks Could Kill. McClelland & Stewart, 2001. 277pp.

The disappearance of a former girlfriend, shortly after she came to him for help, leads photographer Thomas McCall to investigate. Simultaneously he is attempting to cope with an ineffective assistant, a commitment-seeking girlfriend, and his twelve-year-old daughter, who has recently arrived for her summer visit.

Subjects: British Columbia • Photographers • Vancouver

Read On: Other novels with snappy dialogue that move the story along are among the works of Sarah Andrews (*Mother Nature* and others), Anthony Bourdain (*Gone Bamboo*), and Douglas Preston (*The Cabinet of Curiosities*). Michael Blair has also written another stand-alone mystery, *A Hard Winter Rain*.

Blechta, Rick.

Shooting Straight in the Dark. McClelland & Stewart, 2001. 318pp.

Songwriter-guitarist Kit Mason, still struggling to accept her blindness six years after losing her sight, works with members of her former softball team when they feel the police are not taking the murder of one of their players seriously enough.

Subjects: Blindness • Music Trade • Musicians • Ontario • Toronto • Women Softball Players • Women Songwriters

Read On: Music is an integral element in Blechta's other novels, *Knock on Wood* and *The Lark Ascending*. Other musical mysteries include the <u>Katy Green Series</u> by Hal Glatzer (*Too Dead to Swing* and *A Fugue in Hell's Kitchen*) and *The John Lennon Affair:A Neil Gulliver and Stevie Marriner Novel* by Robert S. Levinson.

Bowen, Gail.

Joanne Kilbourn Series.

Joanne Kilbourn is a professor of political science at the University in Regina, Saskatchewan, and a widow, who sometimes acts as an amateur sleuth.

Deadly Appearances. Douglas & McIntyre, 1990.

Shortlisted for the Smithbooks/*Books in Canada* First Novel Award.

Murder at the Mendel. Douglas & McIntyre, 1991. (Variant title: *Love and Murder).*

The Wandering Soul Murders. Douglas & McIntyre, 1992.

A Colder Kind of Death. McClelland & Stewart, 1994.

Winner of the Arthur Ellis Award for Best Novel.

A Killing Spring. McClelland & Stewart, 1996.

Shortlisted for the Saskatchewan Book Award for Fiction and for the City of Regina Book Award.

Verdict in Blood. McClelland & Stewart, 1998.

When Judge Blackwell, well known for her harsh sentencing, is found murdered in Wascana Park, a slip of paper is discovered in her pocket with the name of a friend visiting Joanne, along with Joanne's phone number. Shortlisted for the Arthur Ellis Award for Best Novel.

Burying Ariel. McClelland & Stewart, 2000.

Shortlisted for the Arthur Ellis Award for Best Novel.

The Glass Coffin. McClelland & Stewart, 2002.

Shortlisted for the City of Regina Book Award.

The Last Good Day. McClelland & Stewart, 2004.

> **Subjects:** Academic Mysteries • Kilbourn, Joanne (Fictional Character) • Murder • Regina • Saskatchewan • Women University Professors

> **Read On:** Other professors-cum-amateur sleuths are J. S. Borthwick's Sarah Deane, Joanne Dobson's Karen Pelletier, and Amanda Cross's Kate Fansler.

Brady, Liz.

Jane Yeats Mysteries.

A jazzy Toronto business writer, Jane Yeats acts as amateur sleuth, often with help from her friends and relatives.

Sudden Blow. Second Story Press, 1998.

With help from an eclectic group of characters including her mother Etta, Toronto business writer Jane Yeats investigates the murder of an unpopular developer at the request of the aunt of the case's most likely suspect, the victim's estranged gay son. This novel won the Arthur Ellis Award for Best First Novel.

Bad Date. Second Story Press, 2001.

See Jane Run. Second Story Press, 2004.

Subjects: Journalists • Ontario • Toronto • Women Sleuths • Yeats, Jane (Fictional Character)

Read On: Brady's sleuth is very similar to Sue Grafton's sleuth Kinsey Millhone ("*A" Is for Alibi* and others). The Stephanie Plum Mysteries by Janet Evanovich is also populated with a varied cast of characters who all attempt to participate in the resolution of the mystery.

Dudley, Karen.

Robyn Devara Mysteries.

Robyn Devara is a biologist and environmental consultant whose work can take her anywhere in the world. Dudley has written a number of natural history titles for children, in a series entitled Untamed World (*Alligators & Crocodiles*, *Bald Eagles*, *Wolves,* and others).

Hoot To Kill. Ravenstone, 1998.

Biologist Robyn Devara, in the logging town of Marten Valley, finds herself battling both loggers and environmentalists when she discovers a murdered man in the woods while surveying for spotted owls. This novel was shortlisted for the Arthur Ellis Award for Best First Novel.

The Red Heron. Ravenstone, 1998.

Macaws of Death. Turnstone Press, 2002.

Subjects: Devara, Robyn (Fictional Character) • Endangered Species • Environmental Consultants • Environmental Mysteries • Women Biologists

Read On: The well-drawn characters portrayed here are also an integral part of the mysteries of L. R. Wright, J. A. Jance, and Jill Churchill. Skye Kathleen Moody also writes environmental mysteries.

Gibson, William.

Pattern Recognition. G. P. Putnam's Sons, 2003. 356pp. Book Groups 📖

Private investigation can take many forms, and in Gibson's non–science fiction novel, it takes the form of market research, performed by a "cool hunter," Cayce Pollard. Cayce is in London, England, on an assignment, and while there she receives a new assignment: find the source of random video footage showing up on the Internet, creating a cult of watchers. This search takes her to a variety of major cities and brings her into personal danger.

Subjects: Business Intelligence • Cyberpunk • England • Internet • London • Market Research • Obsession

Read On: Gibson's novel has a different flavour from most mysteries, particularly with its emphasis on the Internet. Other "cyber-related" stories with a mysterious bent are Bruce Sterling's *Zeitgeist: A Novel of Metamorphosis*, Neil Stephenson's *Cryptonomicon*, and Mark Fabi's *Wyrm*.

Gordon, Alison.

Kate Henry Mysteries.

Kate Henry is a baseball reporter for a local Toronto newspaper. She and her boyfriend, Inspector Andy Munro, often become involved in murder investigations involving various baseball teams.

The Dead Pull Hitter. St. Martin's Press, 1988.

Safe at Home. St. Martin's Press, 1990.

Night Game. St. Martin's Press, 1993.

Striking Out. McClelland & Stewart, 1995.

Prairie Hardball. McClelland & Stewart, 1997.

Toronto baseball reporter Kate Henry and her boyfriend, Inspector Andy Munro, are in Indian Head, Saskatchewan, to see Kate's mother inducted into the Baseball Hall of Fame as a member of the All-American Girls Professional Baseball League. While there they become involved in an investigation into the murder of one of the team's members. Through the investigation Kate comes to know her mother as a young woman.

> **Subjects:** Baseball • Henry, Kate (Fictional Character) • Munro, Andy (Fictional Character) • Murder • Ontario • Police • Toronto • Women Sportswriters

> **Read On:** Readers who enjoy mysteries with a strong female protagonist should try Sue Grafton, Susan Dunlap, or Sara Paretsky. Sarah Gilbert's *A League of Their Own* and Karen Joy Fowler's *The Sweetheart Season* are about the All-American Girls Professional Baseball League, the subject of Gordon's last novel.

Hamilton, Lyn.

Lara McClintoch Mysteries.

Also referred to as the Archaeological Mysteries, these novels feature antique dealer Lara McClintoch, whose collecting takes her to the far corners of the world, where she finds not only rare treasures but rare adventure as well.

The Xibalba Murders. Berkley Prime Crime, 1997. **Book Groups** 📖

Recently divorced, and having lost her share in an antique shop to her ex-husband, Toronto antiquities dealer Lara McClintoch travels to Mexico at the request of a Mexican museum director. There, she finds herself seeking answers to murder and missing Mayan artefacts. This novel was shortlisted for the Arthur Ellis Award for Best First Novel.

The Maltese Goddess. Berkley Prime Crime, 1998.

The Moche Warrior. Berkley Prime Crime, 1999.

The Celtic Riddle. Berkley Prime Crime, 2000.

The African Quest. Berkley Prime Crime, 2001.

The Etruscan Chimera. Berkley Prime Crime, 2002.

The Thai Amulet. Berkley Prime Crime, 2003.

The Magyar Venus. Berkley Prime Crime, 2004.

Shortlisted for the Arthur Ellis Award for Best Novel

The Moai Murders. Berkley Prime Crime, 2005.

> **Subjects:** Antiquities • Archaeology • McClintoch, Lara (Fictional Character) • Murder • Ontario • Toronto • Women Antique Dealers

> **Read On:** The exotic nature of Hamilton's series is paralleled in Elizabeth Peters's Amelia Peabody mysteries. For more mysteries focused on antiquities look at Donna Leon's *Acqua Alta* (set in Venice) and Arthur Phillips's *The Egyptologist* (set in Egypt).

Hayter, Sparkle.

Robin Hudson Mysteries.

Divorced television reporter and reluctant sleuth Robin Hudson, living in Manhattan, is a bit like Bridget Jones, with much adventure and dangerous misadventure thrown in.

 *What's a Girl Gotta Do?* Soho, 1994.

TV reporter Robin Hudson's life is on a downhill slide: her husband has left her for a younger woman, she's been demoted at work, and she's been approached by a blackmailer, who then turns up dead. Naturally she's the prime suspect, so, convinced that she can get herself out of this mess, she embarks on a hilarious quest to find the real murderer. Hayter won the Arthur Ellis Award for Best First Novel for this book.

Nice Girls Finish Last. Viking, 1996.

Revenge of the Cootie Girls. Viking, 1997.

The Last Manly Man. William Morrow, 1998.

The Chelsea Girl Murders. William Morrow, 2000.

Last Girl Standing. Forthcoming in 2005.

> **Subjects:** Hudson, Robin (Fictional Character) • Murder • New York City • Women Journalists

> **Read On:** Wisecracking detectives investigate in the <u>Elvis Cole Mysteries</u> by Robert Crais, the <u>Stephanie Plum Mysteries</u> by Janet Evanovich, and the <u>Spenser</u> novels by Robert Parker. Other journalists who find themselves embroiled in murder include Suzanne North's Phoebe Fairfax (television camerawoman) and Edna Buchanan's Britt Montero (newspaper reporter).

Irving, Karen.

Katy Klein Mysteries.

Katy Klein is a former psychologist, now an astrologer, living in Ottawa with her daughter. She creates astrological charts for a living and seems to have taken up amateur sleuthing as a hobby.

Pluto Rising. Polestar, 1999.

Shortlisted for the Arthur Ellis Award for Best First Novel.

Jupiter's Daughter. Polestar, 2000.

Katy Klein—astrologer, psychologist, single mother, and amateur sleuth—witnesses a death at a cocktail party, the same party at which she meets a handsome but sinister televangelist.

Mars Eclipsed. Polestar, 2001.

> **Subjects:** Astrology • Klein, Katy (Fictional Character) • Ontario • Ottawa • Single Mothers • Women Astrologers • Women Psychologists
>
> **Read On:** For other mysteries featuring astrology, try *Dead on Her Feet* or *Death of a Dustbunny* by Christine Jorgensen, or *Death by Horoscope*, edited by Anne Perry and Martin H. Greenberg. Single mothers become involved in murder investigations in books by Gail Bowen (Joanne Kilbourn) and Jill Churchill (Jane Jeffry).

Kelly, Nora.

Gillian Adams Mysteries.

Gillian is a history professor at a university in Vancouver, British Columbia, but her mother lives in New York, and her lover, a Scotland Yard detective, lives in London, England. No matter where she happens to be, however, she invariably winds up playing the amateur sleuth.

In the Shadow of King's. Collins, 1984.

My Sister's Keeper. HarperCollins, 1992.

Bad Chemistry. HarperCollins, 1993.

Old Wounds. HarperCollins, 1998.

Winner of the Arthur Ellis Award for Best Novel.

Hot Pursuit. Poisoned Pen Press, 2002. **Book Groups** 📖

Professor Gillian Adams recently moved from Vancouver to London to live with her long-time lover, policeman Edward Gisborne. Shortly after her arrival, she rekindles her friendship with Charlotte, her friend from long ago. Their friendship is cut short horribly when Gillian discovers Charlotte dead in her back garden. This novel was shortlisted for the Arthur Ellis Award for Best Novel.

> **Subjects:** Adams, Gillian (Fictional Character) • England • Gisborne, Edward (Fictional Character) • London • Murder • Scotland Yard • University Professors • Women Historians • Women's Friendships
>
> **Read On:** Authors Clare Munnings (*Overnight Float*), Sarah Stewart Taylor (*O'Artful Death*), Lev Raphael (*Death of a Constant Lover*), and Janice MacDonald (*Sticks & Stones*) have all written similar academic mysteries. Veronica Stallwood's mystery series featuring Kate Ivory shares the British (and sometimes even the Oxbridge) setting.

Lester, Judy.

Masterpiece of Deception: An Art Mystery. **Sumach Press, 2001. 181pp. Book Groups** 📖

Fearing that the painting she has been asked to restore may be a fake, art restorer Jerry suggests that her client (a prestigious art dealer) authorize further testing.

His refusal and an attempt on her life send her to Europe to uncover the truth.

> **Subjects:** Art Forgeries • Art Restorers • First Novels • Fraud

> **Read On:** *Landscape of Lies* by Peter Watson is also a fast-paced art thriller in which the mystery within a painting must be uncovered. *The Da Vinci Deception* by Thomas Swan is another novel about art forgery, as is Ross King's *Faking.* For a time-travel mystery involving an art restorer, read James McKean's *Quattrocento.*

MacDonald, Janice.

Randy Craig Mysteries.

Randy Craig starts out as a graduate student and moves up to English instructor at the University of Alberta in Edmonton, where she originally studied. Her third foray finds her not lecturing but working instead for a chat room, surveying for porn and other nefarious behaviour. But no matter her job, her status as amateur sleuth remains strong.

The Next Margaret. Mosaic, 1994.

Sticks & Stones. Ravenstone, 2001.

The Monitor. Ravenstone, 2003.

> **Subjects:** Academic Mysteries Alberta • Craig, Randy (Fictional Character) • Edmonton

> **Read On:** MacDonald's *Sticks & Stones* is similar in theme to Nora Kelly's *My Sister's Keeper* in that they both deal with misogynist behaviour on campus, and her novel, *The Monitor,* can be paired with Linda Hall's *Chat Room.*

Macdonald, Marianne.

Dido Hoare Mysteries.

Antiquarian bookseller and amateur detective Dido Hoare lives in London and often works with her father in solving crimes.

Death's Autograph. Hodder & Stoughton, 1996.

The purchase of a collection of old books becomes the catalyst for a series of events, including two murders, that launch antiquarian bookseller Dido Hoare into an investigation. Her father Barnabas, a retired Oxford English professor, works alongside her to uncover what treasure worth killing for might be hidden in the collection.

Ghost Walk. Hodder & Stoughton, 1998.

Smoke Screen. Hodder & Stoughton, 1999.

Road Kill. Hodder & Stoughton, 2000.

Blood Lies. Hodder & Stoughton, 2001.

Die Once. Hodder & Stoughton, 2002.

> **Subjects:** Antiquarian Booksellers • England • Hoare, Barnabas (Fictional Character) • Hoare, Dido (Fictional Character) • London • Women Booksellers

Read On: Priceless documents are integral to the plot in Medora Sale's *Pursued by Shadows*. John Dunning's <u>Cliff Janeway Mysteries</u> (*Booked to Die* and others) and Carolyn G. Hart's <u>Mysteries</u> (*Death on Demand*, *Death of the Party*, and others) are both mystery series set in the world of books. Like Macdonald's Dido Hoare, Lyn Hamilton's amateur sleuth Lara McClintoch is a single woman, in this case running a collectibles business.

Maffini, Mary Jane.

Camilla MacPhee Mysteries.

Camilla MacPhee is a lawyer whose investigations are always centred around an annual festival in Ottawa, Ontario.

Speak Ill of the Dead. RendezVous Press, 1999.

Ottawa lawyer Camilla MacPhee decides to investigate the murder of a vicious celebrity fashion writer after her best friend Robin becomes the prime suspect. If Camilla succeeds, she will not only liberate her friend, but she will also free herself from cat-sitting Robin's six felines. This novel was shortlisted for the Arthur Ellis Award for Best First Novel.

The Icing on the Corpse. RendezVous Press, 2001.

Little Boy Blues. RendezVous Press, 2002.

The Devil's in the Details. RendezVous Press, 2004.

Subjects: Advocates • Festivals • Lawyers • MacPhee, Camilla (Fictional Character) • Murder • Ontario • Ottawa • Women Lawyers

Read On: Karen Irving's <u>Katy Klein Mysteries</u> (*Pluto Rising* and others) also feature a smart, competent 1990s woman in Ottawa who deals humorously with dangerous (and sometimes stupid) situations. Meet other sassy sleuths in the <u>Southern Sisters Series</u> by Anne George (*Murder Shoots the Bull*) and in the <u>Bubbles Yablonsky Series</u> by Sarah Strohmeyer (*Bubbles Unbound*).

Porter, Anna.

Marsha Hillier Mysteries.

Marsha Hillier is a book editor in New York City, a world that the author herself knows very well.

Hidden Agenda. Irwin, 1985.

Mortal Sins. Irwin, 1987.

The Bookfair Murders. Little, Brown, 1997.

Journalist Judith Hayes and book editor Marsha Hillier are embroiled in murder at the Frankfurt Bookfair. Marsha's leading author, a bestselling romance novelist, leaves the Fair in tears when her literary agent is murdered. When Marsha's friend, a British publisher, is murdered, the German police consider Judith their prime suspect.

Subjects: Authors • Book Trade • Hillier, Marsha (Fictional Character) • Murder • Women Editors

Read On: Anna Porter, also a publisher, has written the biography of a major publisher, Jack McClelland, as well as her own memoir, *The Storyteller: Memory, Se-*

crets, Magic and Lies: A Memoir of Hungary. In addition to Porter's series listed here, Julie Kaewert's *Unsolicited* (and others) and Isaac Asimov's *Murder at the ABA* are also set in the world of publishing.

Quogan, Anthony.

Matthew Prior Mysteries.

Mapleville, Ontario, is the setting for this series of mysteries featuring a British dramatist-in-residence and amateur sleuth.

The Fine Art of Murder. Macmillan, 1988.

The Touch of a Vanished Hand. Macmillan, 1990.

Much Improved by Death. Little, Brown Canada, 1993.

Bodies in Motion. Little, Brown Canada, 1996.

Matthew is commissioned to rewrite Hitchcock's *The Lady Vanishes* for a more contemporary audience; to help him in this endeavour, he is given a trip on the transcontinental train Flying Angel. Little does he expect his trip to turn into its own Hitchcock thriller, with one of the celebrity passengers murdered.

> **Subjects:** Actor-Detectives • Ontario • Prior, Matthew (Fictional Character) • Theatre
>
> **Read On:** Other drama-related mysteries include Simon Brett's <u>Charles Paris Mysteries</u> and Simon Shaw's <u>Philip Fletcher Mysteries</u>. For actor-detectives in Shakespeare's time, there are several series, including Philip Gooden's <u>Shakespearean Murder Mysteries</u>, Edward Marston's <u>Nicholas Bracewell Mysteries,</u> and Simon Hawke's <u>Shakespeare & Smythe Mysteries</u>. Anthony Quogan is the pseudonym for Anthony Stephenson.

Ross, Veronica.

Carolyn Archer Murder Mysteries.

Carolyn is a cookbook author and amateur detective whose sleuthing takes her anywhere in time, from czarist Russia to contemporary central Ontario, where she lives.

Millicent. Mercury Press, 1994.

Millicent Mulvey always claimed that she had entered into a clandestine marriage with Edward, Prince of Wales and future King of England. Following her death, her friend Carolyn Archer, an author and amateur detective, vows to discover the truth.

The Anastasia Connection. Mercury Press, 1996.

The Burden of Grace. Mercury Press, 1997.

Stories and Lies. Mercury Press, 1999.

> **Subjects:** Archer, Carolyn (Fictional Character) • Cookbook Authors • Ontario • Women Authors

Read On: Elliott Roosevelt (*Murder at the Palace* and others) and Max Allan Collins (*Damned in Paradise* and others) also populate their mysteries with real-life characters. Orania Papazoglou's Patience McKenna, in the series by the same name, is an author-detective, and the main protagonist in Lora Roberts's series Liz Sullivan Mysteries is a cookbook author and detective.

Warsh, Sylvia Maultash.

Rebecca Temple Mysteries.

Rebecca Temple is a medical doctor weighed down by guilt because she could not save her own husband from complications of diabetes. She is a young (thirties) Jewish physician living near Kensington Market in Toronto in the late 1970s, and her intrinsic and genuine interest in people often leads her into investigating the crime in their midst. Her investigations take her back in time, thus far to Nazi Germany and the Holocaust and even farther back, to eighteenth-century Poland.

To Die in Spring. Dundurn Press, 2000.

Shortlisted for the Arthur Ellis Award for Best First Novel.

🎗 *Find Me Again.* Dundurn Press, 2003. **Book Groups** 📖

Still mourning her husband's death, and trying to keep in touch with her mother-in-law, a Holocaust survivor, Rebecca meets a charming count from Poland who is writing a historical novel set in the 1740s. When a murder occurs, Rebecca realizes that the solution may be in the count's manuscript. This novel won the Edgar Allan Poe Award for Best Paperback Original and was shortlisted for both the Anthony Award for Best Paperback Original and the Anthony Award for Best Historical Mystery.

> **Subjects:** Jewish Women • Ontario • Temple, Rebecca (Fictional Character) • Toronto • Women Physicians

> **Read On:** Some oddly disparate titles that may yet appeal to readers who like to combine contemporary with earlier history are Lisa See's *Dragon Bones*, Helen Schulman's *The Revisionist,* and Peter Dickinson's *Some Deaths Before Dying.*

Cozy

Agatha Christie and her English villages come to mind when one thinks of the "cozy." This is a mystery that will not upset: the violence takes place off-stage, as it were, and the focus is on the people left behind, their quirks and foibles, and the locale in which they live. The cozy is often humorous, and it often features an amateur sleuth, often an older person.

Benison, C. C.

Her Majesty Investigates.

Jane Bee, originally from Charlottetown, Prince Edward Island, travels to Europe, as many young women do. When she finds her funds depleted, she surprises herself by becoming housemaid to Queen Elizabeth II. Each of these novels, involving both the Queen and Jane Bee, takes place in a different royal palace, as Jane travels with the Queen to various locations.

Death at Buckingham Palace. Bantam Books, 1996.

Buckingham Palace housemaid Jane Bee assists the Queen as she investigates a footman's apparent suicide. This novel won the Arthur Ellis Award for Best First Novel.

Death at Sandringham Palace. Bantam Books, 1996.

Death at Windsor Castle. Bantam Books, 1998.

> **Subjects:** Bee, Jane (Fictional Character) • Elizabeth II, Queen of Great Britain • England • Housemaids • London • Royal Households • Servants
>
> **Read On:** Elizabeth I, the British Queen, investigates murders in Karen Harper's mysteries (*The Poyson Garden, The Tidal Poole* and others). Emily Brightwell's <u>Inspector Witherspoon and Mrs. Jeffries Mysteries</u> also feature an amiable housekeeper, who works along with other members of her staff to solve mysteries. Elements of royalty merge with mystery in Sharyn McCrumb's *The Windsor Knot*, Antonia Fraser's *Your Royal Hostage*, and Jennie Melville's *Windsor Red*. C. C. Benison is the pen name of Winnipeg writer Douglas Whiteway.

Craig, Alisa.

<u>Madoc Rhys Mysteries.</u>

Madoc is an Inspector with the Royal Canadian Mounted Police (RCMP) and is often helped in his investigations by his wife, Janet.

A Pint of Murder. Doubleday, 1980.

Murder Goes Mumming. Doubleday, 1981.

A Dismal Thing to Do. Doubleday, 1986.

Trouble in the Brasses. Avon Books, 1989.

The Wrong Rite. W. Morrow, 1992.

While in Wales for Sir Cardo Rhys's ninetieth birthday, RCMP Detective Inspector Madoc Rhys becomes involved in the investigation of his cousin's murder. Madoc discovers that Mary's death is somehow connected to an old murder case and has links to jewel theft, blackmail, and prostitution.

> **Subjects:** Police • Police Spouses • Rhys, Janet (Fictional Character) • Rhys, Madoc (Fictional Character) • Royal Canadian Mounted Police
>
> **Read On:** Craig is also the author of the <u>Grub-and-Stakers</u> mystery series. Other entertaining whodunits featuring husband-and-wife detective teams include Charlotte Perkins Gilman's *Unpunished* and Carolyn G. Hart's *April Fool Dead.* Craig is the pseudonym of Charlotte MacLeod (*Exit the Milkman* and others).

Wright, Eric.

<u>Lucy Trimble Brenner Mysteries.</u>

Lucy Brenner has a number of occupations on her résumé: she is a part-time librarian who decides to open a bed-and-breakfast operation in

Northern Ontario. But then she inherits a detective agency, and it isn't long before she is a private detective herself.

Death of a Sunday Writer. Foul Play Press, 1996.

Death on the Rocks. St. Martin's Press, 1999.

Toronto P.I. Lucy Brenner learns that the stranger following her client is a British P.I. investigating an inheritance case that may benefit her client. Agreeing to travel to England, she begins to unravel the possible family connections.

> **Subjects:** Brenner, Lucy Trimble (Fictional Character) • Librarians • Ontario • Toronto • Women Private Investigators

> **Read On:** The cozy feel of this mystery is similar to the British cozies of Hazel Holt (*Death of a Dean* and others), Dorothy Cannell (*The Thin Woman* and others), and Ann Granger (*Where Old Bones Lie* and others). Gail Bowen's Joanne Kilbourn, Anne M. Dooley's Elie Meade, and Suzanne North's Phoebe Fairfax are other Canadian female sleuths.

Forensic

The forensic mystery is becoming ever more popular, with writers such as Patricia Cornwell and Kathy Reichs having opened wide the field. Initially this subgenre focused on the medical examiner or pathologist, but the field is broadening to include forensic scientists, psychologists and psychiatrists, and anthropologists and archaeologists, to name but a few. The science of the crime scene or the perpetrator is paramount here, and there is often very explicit detail about subject matter that most readers would not care to lay eyes on. The content of these novels is usually fascinating and an exercise of the intellect, and the tone of the mystery is usually quite serious.

Kelln, Brad.

Michael Wenton Series.

Dr. Wenton is a forensic psychologist in Halifax, Nova Scotia, whose profession brings him into contact with the evil in men's lives. He often works in conjunction with his friend, ex-policeman Tim Dallons.

Lost Sanity. Insomniac Press, 2001. **Book Groups** 📖

Forensic psychologist Dr. Michael Wenton and ex-detective Tim Dallons search for an escaped serial rapist who has the power to render insane his victims and anyone else he comes in contact with.

Method of Madness. Insomniac Press, 2002.

> **Subjects:** Dallons, Tim (Fictional Character) • Evil • Forensic Psychologists • Halifax • Insanity • Nova Scotia • Psychologists • Psychopaths • Wenton, Michael (Fictional Character)

> **Read On:** G.H. Ephron's *Amnesia,* Keith Ablow's *Denial,* and Sarah Lovett's <u>Sylvia Strange Mysteries</u> also feature forensic psychologists. Thomas Harris's *The Silence of the Lambs* is a fast-paced thriller with an especially evil villain.

Malcolm, Murray.

John Smith Mysteries.

John Smith's career as forensic consultant in Regina takes him into various parts of the city and the surrounding countryside as he investigates toxic situations.

Baser Elements. NeWest Press, 1998.

Shortlisted for the City of Regina Book Award.

Nine Dead Dogs. NeWest Press, 2001. **Book Groups**

A series of unexplained dog poisonings sends forensic consultant John Smith into rural Saskatchewan, where he quickly discovers a much deeper motive for the vicious acts than a simple feud between two rivals. This novel was nominated for the Saskatchewan Book Award for Fiction.

> **Subjects:** Forensic Consultants • Poisoning • Regina • Rural Life • Saskatchewan • Smith, John Avery (Fictional Character)

> **Read On:** Forensic detectives use their expertise in the novels of Patricia Cornwell (*The Body Farm* and others), Jeffery Deaver (*The Stone Monkey* and others), and Leonard Goldberg (*Deadly Care* and others). Another mystery set in Saskatchewan and nominated for the Saskatchewan Book Award for Fiction is Anne Dooley's *Plane Death*.

Reichs, Kathy.

Temperance Brennan.

Tempe Brennan is a forensic anthropologist who travels between her home state of North Carolina, working in the Office of the Chief Medical Examiner, and Montreal, Quebec, where she works in the Laboratoire des Sciences Judiciaires et de Médecine Légale. Because she is an anthropologist rather than a pathologist, she usually works with people who have been dead for a while, or with people who are difficult to identify. Her work often requires her to do her own detecting, as she tries to ferret out information that will help her solve her cases.

Déjà Dead. Scribner, 1997. **Book Groups**

Montreal forensic anthropologist Temperance "Tempe" Brennan, a middle-aged North Carolina transplant, struggles to convince the police that the grizzly slayings of several women are the work of a single killer. When she decides to investigate the matter, she puts both her career and her life on the line, becoming a target herself. Reichs won the Arthur Ellis Award for Best First Novel for this work.

Death du Jour. Scribner, 1999.

Deadly Decisions. Scribner, 2000.

Fatal Voyage. Scribner, 2001.

Grave Secrets. Scribner, 2002.

Bare Bones. Scribner, 2003.

Monday Mourning. Scribner, 2004.

> **Subjects:** Brennan, Temperance (Fictional Character) • Forensic Anthropologists • Medical Examiners • Montreal • Murder • North Carolina • Quebec • Women Forensic Anthropologists

> **Read On:** The forensic detail here is also present in Patricia Cornwell's novels (*Postmortem* and others). Sharyn McCrumb's Elizabeth MacPherson (*The PMS Outlaws* and others) and Beverly Connor's Lindsay Chamberlain (*Questionable Remains* and others) represent other female forensic anthropologists. Reichs, like her main protagonist, is a forensic anthropologist.

Zuehlke, Mark.

Elias McCann Mysteries.

Elias McCann is a coroner with no medical experience, living in Tofino, the last stop on the Trans-Canada Highway, and centre for the battle between loggers and environmentalists.

🎗 *Hands Like Clouds.* Dundurn Press, 2000. **Book Groups** 📖

The death of an environmentalist in an ancient rainforest on Clayoquot Sound appears to be suicide, but community coroner Elias McCann is not convinced. When more people start dying, he must discover who from the logging controversy wanted the environmentalist dead. This novel won the Arthur Ellis Award for Best First Novel.

Carry Tiger to Mountain. Dundurn Press, 2002.

Sweep Lotus. Dundurn Press, 2004.

> **Subjects:** British Columbia • Clayoquot Sound Region • Coroners • Environmental Mysteries • McCann, Elias (Fictional Character) • Murder

> **Read On:** Gunnard Landers's *The Violators* and Richard Hoyt's *Whoo?* are other mysteries set within the context of environmental issues. Environmentalists and loggers clash in Lee Wallingford's *Clear-Cut Murder* and in Jerome Doolittle's *Half Nelson*, both set in the West Coast forests of Oregon.

Hard-Boiled

Dashiell Hammett and Raymond Chandler come to mind when one speaks of the hard-boiled mystery: the detectives are tough-talking, usually men, and men more of action than of extensive conversation. Their world is gritty, made up of mean streets, nighttimes, and heartless villains. They too can be heartless at times. "Noir" is another term for this bleak look at man's darker side.

Bolen, Dennis.

Barry Delta Series.

Barry Delta is a parole officer in the gritty section of Vancouver, British Columbia. Often the story develops through the perspective of characters other than Delta himself.

Stupid Crimes. Anvil Press, 1992.

Krekshuns. Random House of Canada, 1997. **Book Groups** 📖

Vancouver parole officer Barry Delta delves into the lives of the parolees he supervises in an attempt to understand how their past has brought them to him.

> **Subjects:** British Columbia • Delta, Barry (Fictional Character) • Parole Officers • Parolees • Vancouver

> **Read On:** Parole officers appear in the <u>Loretta Kovacs and Frank Marvelli</u> stories by Anthony Bruno. The "mean" streets of Vancouver provide the setting for Mark Macdonald's *Flat* as well as the science fiction novels of Luanne Armstrong (*The Bone House*) and Donna McMahon (*Dance of Knives*). The gritty flavour of Bolen's writing is reminiscent of Andrew Vachss.

Redfern, Jon.

🎗 *The Boy Must Die*. ECW Press, 2001. 299pp. **Book Groups** 📖

Vancouver detective Billy Yamamoto's quiet retirement in Southern Alberta ends when a teenage boy's body, bearing the marks of a ritual satanic death, is discovered in the basement of a run-down house, the site of another boy's death several months earlier. Redfern won the Arthur Ellis Award for Best First Novel for this novel.

> **Subjects:** Alberta • Child Abuse • Cults • First Novels • Japanese Canadians • Lethbridge • Murder • Serial Killers

> **Read On:** The graphic descriptions in Redfern's novel echo those in the novels of Kathy Reichs and Karin Slaughter. The crimes in Mignon F. Ballard's *The Widow's Woods*, Michael Slade's *Ripper*, and Abigail Padgett's *Strawgirl* all contain elements of satanic rituals.

Historical

The historical mystery is obviously set in an earlier time period. Its interest comes from the description of the setting and the depiction of the society and its mores. As modern crime solving has become more dependent on technology, these historical mysteries interest readers who want to see how one can solve a crime by sheer persistence and clever thinking, without the help of hardware and mass communication. As with other subgenres, these mysteries could also be placed in other categories (police procedural, humorous, amateur detective), depending on which aspect is strongest. The historical mystery often deals with a real event in history or a real person from that time.

Banks, T. F.

<u>Henry Morton Bow Street Runner Mysteries.</u>

Henry Morton is a constable in the Bow Street Runners, the first organized group of police constables in England, whose main responsibilities were serving writs, detecting crime, and arresting offenders.

The Thief-taker: Memoirs of a Bow Street Runner. Delacorte Press, 2001. **Book Groups** 📖

Henry Morton's investigation into the death of a gentleman in Claridge Square takes him from high society in Regency London to the backstreets and alleys of that same city. This novel was shortlisted for the Arthur Ellis Award for Best First Novel.

The Emperor's Assassin: Memoirs of a Bow Street Runner. Bantam Dell, 2003.

Subjects: Bow Street Runners • England • London • Morton, Henry (Fictional Character) • Murder • Police

Read On: Anne Perry's Charlotte and Thomas Pitt Novels and her William Monk and Hester Latterly Series are both set in nineteenth-century England and also give a clear picture of the society of the times. Caleb Carr's *The Alienist* and *The Angel of Darkness* are mystery novels that delineate the world of nineteenth-century New York City. T. F. Banks is the writing team of Ian Dennis and Sean Russell.

Cooper-Posey, Tracy.

Sherlock Holmes Mysteries.

Cooper-Posey continues where Conan Doyle left off, creating new situations for that most famous detective, Sherlock Holmes.

🎗 ***Chronicles of the Lost Years: A Sherlock Holmes Mystery.*** Ravenstone, 1999.

Winner of the Sherlock Holmes Society Best Pastiche Award.

The Case of the Reluctant Agent: A Sherlock Holmes Mystery. Ravenstone, 2001. **Book Groups** 📖

Reluctantly, Holmes journeys to Constantinople in late 1917 to learn who turned against his brother Mycroft, shooting and leaving him for dead. While there, he encounters a lost love.

Subjects: Holmes, Mycroft (Fictional Character) • Holmes, Sherlock (Fictional Character) • Moriarty, Professor (Fictional Character) • Pastiches • Private Investigators

Read On: Holmes appears as the main protagonist in a number of works by writers such as Laurie R. King (*The Moor* and others), Alan Vanneman (*Sherlock Holmes and the Giant Rat of Sumatra*), and Roger Jaynes (*Sherlock Holmes: A Duel with the Devil*).

Eddenden, A. E.

Inspector Albert Tretheway Mysteries.

Small-town Ontario in the 1940s is the setting in which Police Inspector Albert V. Tretheway and his sister Addie carve out a simple life amid murder and mayhem.

A Good Year for Murder. Academy Chicago Publishers, 1988.

Murder on the Thirteenth. Academy Chicago Publishers, 1992.

It is January 13, 1943, and the town must endure wartime blackouts. But someone or something is not keeping the blackout, as strange lights appear in the marshes. Witchcraft appears to cover a spate of murders in Tretheway's Fort York.

Murder at the Movies. Academy Chicago Publishers, 1996.

Subjects: 1940s • Fort York • Murder • Ontario • Police • Small-town Life • Tretheway, Albert (Fictional Character)

Read On: Eddenden is in good company setting his mystery stories in the 1940s. Other authors who have chosen to set their mysteries earlier in the twentieth century are Stuart Kaminsky (<u>Toby Peters</u> series), Max Allan Collins (<u>Nathan Heller</u> series), and George Baxt (<u>Celebrity Mystery</u> series).

Janes, J. Robert.

<u>Jean-Louis St. Cyr and Hermann Kohler Mysteries.</u>

This is an unusual set of mysteries in the combination of the men working together in wartime France: Jean-Louis St. Cyr is a detective with the Sûreté National, and Hermann Kohler is a detective with the Gestapo.

Mirage. Constable, 1992. (Variant title: *Mayhem*).

Carousel. Constable, 1992.

Kaleidoscope. Constable, 1993.

Salamander. Constable, 1994.

Mannequin. Constable, 1994.

Dollmaker. Constable, 1995.

Stonekiller. Constable, 1995.

Sandman. Constable, 1996.

Gypsy. Constable, 1997.

Madrigal. Gollancz, 1999.

Flykiller. Orion, 2000. **Book Groups** 📖

When the mistresses of four possibly corrupt, high-ranking government officials are murdered, partners Jean-Louis St-Cyr of the Sûreté National and Hermann Kohler of the Gestapo travel to the spa town of Vichy. There they investigate what is either the work of a serial killer or a series of politically motivated killings.

Beekeeper. Orion, 2001.

Subjects: France • German Occupation of France • Gestapo • Kohler, Hermann (Fictional Character) • Police • Saint-Cyr, Jean-Louis (Fictional Character) • Sûreté National • Vichy • World War II

Read On: For a mystery set in Nazi Germany, read Pavel Kohout's *The Widow Killer*. The St. Cyr/Kohler mysteries share a similar pessimistic perspective with Philip Kerr's <u>Bernie Gunther Mysteries</u>, which are set in World War II Berlin.

Jennings, Maureen.

William Murdoch Mysteries.

William Murdoch is the only police detective in the Toronto Police Force at the end of the nineteenth century.

Except the Dying. St. Martin's Press, 1997.

Shortlisted for the Arthur Ellis and Anthony Awards for Best First Novel, and recipient of a Certificate of Commendation from Heritage Toronto.

Under the Dragon's Tail. St. Martin's Press, 1998.

Poor Tom Is Cold. St. Martin's Minotaur, 2001. **Book Groups** 📖

Though Constable Oliver Wicken's death is first deemed a suicide, more evidence is discovered that suggests otherwise. At the same time, his neighbour's wife is committed to the Provincial Lunatic Asylum. Murdoch feels he must find out if there is a connection between the two events.

Let Loose the Dogs. St. Martin's Griffin Press, 2002.

Night's Child. McClelland & Stewart, 2005.

> **Subjects:** Murdoch, William (Fictional Character) • Murder • Nineteenth Century • Ontario • Police • Toronto
>
> **Read On:** For other mysteries set in the nineteenth century, try T. F. Banks's *The Thief-taker: Memoirs of a Bow Street Runner*, the <u>Charlotte and Thomas Pitt Novels</u> by Anne Perry, and the <u>Mary Russell and Sherlock Holmes series</u> by Laurie R. King.

Levine, Allan R.

Sam Klein Mysteries.

Winnipeg, Manitoba, in the early twentieth century is the setting for this historical series featuring Sam Klein, a Jew and a brothel employee who engages in investigations. The subject matter of the series is serious and historical: the Winnipeg General Strike, the Suffragettes, immigrant life in Winnipeg.

🎗 ***The Blood Libel.*** Great Plains, 1997.

Winner of the Margaret McWilliams Medal for Best Historical Fiction; shortlisted for the Chapters/*Books in Canada* First Novel Award and the Arthur Ellis Award for Best First Novel.

Sins of the Suffragette. Great Plains, 2000.

Shortlisted for the Carol Shields Winnipeg Book Award and for the Margaret McWilliams Award for Best Historical Fiction.

The Bolshevik's Revenge. Great Plains, 2001. **Book Groups** 📖

When a prominent capitalist is murdered at the height of the 1919 Winnipeg General Strike, the ruling family compact hires sometime-detective Sam Klein to investigate possible Bolshevik connections. This book was shortlisted for the Margaret McWilliams Award for Best Historical Fiction.

> **Subjects:** Klein, Sam (Fictional Character) • Manitoba • Murder • Private Investigations • Winnipeg

Read On: The mysteries by Faye Kellerman (*False Prophet* and others) also weave family and religious threads into the plot. The Winnipeg General Strike is a major player in *Fox* by Margaret Sweatman and in Stuart James Whitley's *A Reckoning of Angels*. Gillian Linscott's <u>Nell Bray Mysteries</u> feature a detective-suffragette in Great Britain.

Roe, Caroline.

<u>Chronicles of Isaac of Girona.</u>

Fourteenth-century Girona is the setting for this series of mysteries featuring a blind, Jewish physician who has a young Muslim student. Isaac must resolve not only the illnesses of his patients but the mysteries that seem to crop up in his life as well.

Remedy for Treason. Berkley Prime Crime, 1998. **Book Groups** 📖

Physician to the Bishop of Girona, blind Isaac is always accompanied by his daughter Raquel, who acts as his eyes and reports all her observations to him. He is called to the convent to care for the young Isabel (daughter by a first marriage to King Pedro), who is in the convent for protection because she is perceived as competition for the throne. A young nun is murdered, and Isaac is asked to investigate. This novel was shortlisted for the Arthur Ellis Award for Best Novel, the Anthony Award for Best Mystery Novel, and the Barry Award for Best Paperback Original.

Cure for a Charlatan. Berkley Prime Crime, 1999.

🎗 ***An Antidote for Avarice.*** Berkley Prime Crime, 1999.

Winner of the Barry Award for Best Paperback Original and shortlisted for the Anthony Award for Best Mystery Novel.

Solace for a Sinner. Berkley Prime Crime, 2000.

A Potion for a Widow. Berkley Prime Crime, 2001.

A Draught for a Dead Man. Berkley Prime Crime, 2002.

A Poultice for a Healer. Berkley Prime Crime, 2003.

Consolation for an Exile. Berkley Prime Crime, 2004.

 5

> **Subjects:** Blind • Fourteenth Century • Isaac of Girona (Fictional Character) • Jews • Medieval Spain • Physicians • Spain • Teacher–Student Relationships

> **Read On:** Readers of Ellis Peters's <u>Brother Cadfael Series</u>, Peter Tremayne's seventh-century Ireland <u>Sister Fidelma Mysteries,</u> and Mary Reed and Eric Mayer's sixth-century Constantinople series, <u>John the Eunuch,</u> will enjoy these mysteries by Caroline Roe, pseudonym of Medora Sale, a medieval scholar and author of the <u>Inspector John Sanders and Harriet Jeffries Mysteries</u>.

Humorous

Humour is not generally considered a subgenre of mystery, but it is a prevalent characteristic that many readers are attracted to. In these novels, the protagonist is usually fast-talking, participates in witty dialogue, and often gets into comical situations. The titles often border on puns (*One Large Coffin To Go*), and violence and gore are at a minimum.

GoodWeather, Hartley.

DreadfulWater Shows Up. HarperFlamingoCanada, 2002. 233pp.

Cherokee Thumps DreadfulWater, a fine-art photographer and ex-cop, is pulled into a murder investigation when his girlfriend's teenage son becomes the prime suspect in a murder at a resort/casino complex on the reservation next to his small Western town. This novel has also been published under the title *Vapor Trail*.

> **Subjects:** Aboriginal Peoples • Cherokee Nation • DreadfulWater, Thumps (Fictional Character) • Missing Persons • Murder • Photographers • Reservations

> **Read On:** Hartley GoodWeather is the pseudonym for Thomas King, whose novels include *Truth & Bright Water* and *Green Grass, Running Water*. GoodWeather's soft-boiled approach and light humour are also part of the charm of Harry Paul Lonsdale's *Where There's Smoke, There's Murder*, Robert Barnard's mysteries, and Charlotte MacLeod's <u>Peter Shandy</u> series.

Malton, H. Mel.

<u>Polly Deacon Murder Mysteries.</u>

Polly Deacon is a puppet maker living in rural Northern Ontario, having moved there from Toronto after her failed marriage. She is a fast-talking sleuth who will appeal to readers of Karen Kijewski.

Down in the Dumps. RendezVous Press, 1998.

Puppet maker Polly Deacon has returned home to rural Northern Ontario from Toronto to live a rustic existence (no indoor plumbing) following a failed marriage. This "back-to-the-land" life is thrown into turmoil when she discovers the body of her best friend's abusive husband. Determined to keep her friend from being convicted of the murder, her quest for answers has the fast-talking Polly digging into the darker side of her small town.

Cue the Dead Guy. RendezVous Press, 1999.

Dead Cow in Aisle Three. RendezVous Press, 2001.

One Large Coffin To Go. RendezVous Press, 2003.

> **Subjects:** Cedar Falls • Country Life • Deacon, Polly (Fictional Character) • Murder • Northern Ontario • Ontario • Puppet Makers • Small-town Life • Women's Friendships

> **Read On:** For more humorous mysteries with a small-town setting, read the <u>Arly Hanks Mysteries</u> by Joan Hess or the <u>Lucy Stone Mysteries</u> by Leslie Meier.

North, Suzanne.

<u>Phoebe Fairfax Mysteries.</u>

Phoebe is an Alberta television camera operator and reluctant amateur sleuth who maintains her sense of humour even in the midst of dire circumstance.

Healthy, Wealthy and Dead. NeWest Press, 1994.

Shortlisted for the Arthur Ellis Award for Best First Novel.

Seeing Is Deceiving. McClelland & Stewart, 1996.

Bones To Pick. McClelland & Stewart, 2002.

Phoebe Fairfax becomes involved in the murder investigation of a scientist who claimed to have discovered a new hominoid species. Not only was he murdered, but the fossils proving his theory have also disappeared.

> **Subjects:** Alberta • Fairfax, Phoebe (Fictional Character) • Murder • Television Camera Operators

> **Read On:** Bold female sleuths investigate mysteries by Jan Burke, Medora Sale, and Marcia Muller. Other witty, humorous authors are Susan Conant (*Gone to the Dogs* and others) and Karen Kijewski (*Katwalk* and others).

Phillips, Edward.

Geoffry Chadwick Mysteries.

Geoffry is a gay lawyer in Montreal whose life has not been all that smooth up to now, and who deals with his various crises in unusual ways.

Sunday's Child. McClelland & Stewart, 1981.

 Buried on Sunday. McClelland & Stewart, 1986.

Winner of the Arthur Ellis Award for Best Novel.

Sunday Best. Seal Books, 1990.

Working on Sunday. Riverbank Press, 1998.

Geoffry Chadwick, a sixty-year-old gay lawyer coping with the decline of an aged parent, the recent loss of his beloved partner, Patrick, and his surprising fascination with a recently widowed woman, starts receiving murder threats just as the frenzy of the Christmas season begins.

A Voyage on Sunday. Riverbank Press, 2004.

> **Subjects:** Chadwick, Geoffry (Fictional Character) • Gay Men • Lawyers • Montreal • Quebec

> **Read On:** Phillips is also the author of *The Landlady's Niece, No Early Birds,* and others. Phillips blends mystery and satirical comedy of manners in a style that resembles Carol Shields's *Swann.* Other authors who write comedy-of-manners novels are Kingsley Amis (*The Old Devils* and others) and Penelope Fitzgerald (*The Gate of Angels* and others).

 5

Police Procedural

The police procedural is often of great interest to the reader for the insights it provides into a world the general public rarely sees, or hopes to rarely see. The investigation is delineated step-by-step, sometimes almost to the point of drudgery, and it is made quite clear what the life of a police detective can often be like. Many authors focus on multi-faceted teams who work together to solve crimes, rather than on a single detective. The reader often witnesses political issues within the department, sees what teamwork can be like (either positive or negative), and takes vicarious rides with the siren wailing. In the case of series detectives, the reader is usually privy to the private life of the detective, often a lonely and sometimes "world- weary" life, all of which can affect the nature of the job in the police department and the concomitant behaviour of the police detective.

Blunt, Giles.

John Cardinal series.

Set in the fictional town of Algonquin Bay, Ontario (based on the real city of North Bay), this series features a detective who is plagued by his history and disturbed by his wife's manic depression. But he is a dedicated policeman and will pursue the investigation despite the roadblocks in his way.

🎗 *Forty Words for Sorrow.* Random House of Canada, 2000. **Book Groups** 📖

Detective John Cardinal persists in looking for four teenagers who have gone missing, continuing long after his department has considered the case futile. When the body of one of the teenagers surfaces, Cardinal knows he is involved in something deadly and horrifying. Blunt won the Crime Writers' Association Silver Macallan Award for this novel, which was also shortlisted for the Arthur Ellis Award for Best Novel.

🎗 *The Delicate Storm.* Random House of Canada, 2003.

Winner of the Arthur Ellis Award for Best Novel, and shortlisted for the Dashiell Hammett Award, the Macavity Award, and the Anthony Award for Best Novel.

Blackfly Season. Random House of Canada, 2005.

> **Subjects:** Algonquin Bay (Imaginary Place) • Cardinal, John (Fictional Character) • Chippewa Nation • Mental Illness • Northern Ontario • Ontario • Police

> **Read On:** Lydia LaPlante's *Cold Shoulder* features another persistent detective who is also out of favour with the department. The depth of characterization in this series brings to mind other series in which the character of the detective is as central to the writing as the mystery itself, series by writers such as Ruth Rendell (Inspector Wexford), Peter Robinson (Alan Banks), Colin Dexter (Inspector Morse), and Deborah Crombie (Duncan Kincaid).

Brady, John.

Matt Minogue Mysteries.

Matt Minogue is a member of the Garda in Dublin, Ireland, a man of complexity who must at times deal with the conflict between his job and his political beliefs.

🎗 *A Stone of the Heart.* Collins, 1988.

Winner of the Arthur Ellis Award for Best First Novel.

Unholy Ground. Collins, 1989.

Kaddish in Dublin. HarperCollins, 1990.

Shortlisted for the Arthur Ellis Award for Best Novel.

All Souls. HarperCollins, 1993.

Shortlisted for the Arthur Ellis Award for Best Novel.

The Good Life. HarperCollins, 1994.

Shortlisted for the Arthur Ellis Award for Best Novel.

A Carra King. McArthur & Company, 2001.

Wonderland. McArthur & Company, 2002. **Book Groups** 📖

The economic boom in Ireland has created havoc for the Garda in Dublin. As Matt Minogue wrestles with the suicide of a woman he is investigating for fraud, two Albanian men are murdered, and a teenager lies dead of an overdose.

> **Subjects:** Dublin • Garda Murder Squad • Ireland • Minogue, Matt (Fictional Character)

> **Read On:** Bartholomew Gill's series also features a Dublin policeman, Peter McGarr, while Jim Lusby writes a series with Police Inspector Carl McCadden, in Waterford; Eugene McEldowney takes us to Northern Ireland with his policeman, Cecil Megarry.

Brooke, John.

Aliette Nouvelle Mysteries.

Alsace, France, is the home of Aliette Nouvelle, single woman and inspector in the Police Judiciaire in her town.

The Voice of Aliette Nouvelle. Nuage Editions, 1999.

All Pure Souls. Signature Editions, 2001. **Book Groups** 📖

French Inspector Aliette Nouvelle has been told to sign off on what is thought to be an open-and-shut case: the murder of a Marilyn Monroe look-alike prostitute. After all, the evidence has already been assembled and the prime suspect is in jail. But Nouvelle is convinced that it is not quite this simple, and when her investigation leads her to a sisterly cult, she soon discovers that all is not as it first appeared. This novel was shortlisted for the Hugh MacLennan Fiction Award.

> **Subjects:** Alsace • France • Murder • Nouvelle, Aliette (Fictional Character) • Police • Women Inspectors

> **Read On:** France is the setting for Norman Bogner's mysteries, *To Die in Provence* and *The Deadliest Art*. Robert Daley's *Nowhere to Run* features a French Inspector.

Farrow, John.

Emile Cinq-Mars Series.

Emile Cinq-Mars is a sergeant-detective in the Montreal Urban Community Police, an introspective man who prefers to work on his own. Farrow uses very current topics as catalysts for his plots, such as motorcycle gangs and pharmaceuticals for AIDS. He also invokes a strong sense of place in Montreal and its environs.

City of Ice. HarperCollins, 1999.

Ice Lake. HarperCollins, 2001. **Book Groups** 📖

Emile Cinq-Mars and his partner, Bill Mathers, are lured to an ice-fishing spot, where they discover a corpse in an ice hole. Their investigation eventually connects this murder to a deadly competition among pharmaceutical companies to find a cure for AIDS.

> **Subjects:** Cinq-Mars, Emile (Fictional Character) • Mathers, Bill (Fictional Character) • Montreal • Montreal Urban Community Police • Quebec

> **Read On:** Montreal also features in a series of mysteries by Kathy Reichs (*Déjà Dead, Death du Jour,* for example). The policeman who investigates on his own terms, as does Cinq-Mars, is personified in such characters as Robert Wilson's Zé Coelho (*A Small Death in Lisbon*) and John Harvey's Charlie Resnick (*Last Rites*). John Farrow is the pseudonym for Trevor Ferguson.

Furlong, Nicola.

A Hemorrhaging of Souls. Salal Press, 1998. 288pp. Book Groups 📖

Following the second death of a child at a Vancouver Island girl's academy, child psychologist Dr. Tempest Ivory and Constable Patrick Painter realize that they are not investigating a child's suicide, but rather murder. The deeper they dig into the past the more they realize how this case may become personal for Tempest.

> **Subjects:** British Columbia • Child Psychologists • Girls' Schools • Murder • Police • Vancouver Island

> **Read On:** Furlong is the author of *Teed Off!,* a mystery set on a golf course. She has also contributed several volumes to the Church Choir Mystery series (*The Angel's Secret, The Nervous Nephew, No Safe Arbor, Plots and Pans,* and others). Alex Delaware, a fictional child psychologist, is the main protagonist in the novels by Jonathan Kellerman (*Bad Love, Self-defense, The Web,* and others). Other fictional psychologists involved in mysteries are Michael Stone (written by Anna Salter), Anne Menlo (written by Maxine O'Callaghan), and Alan Gregory (written by Stephen White).

Gough, Laurence.

Willows and Parker Mysteries.

Jack Willows and Claire Parker are partners in the Vancouver Police Department. As the series progresses, their partnership at work evolves into a personal partnership as well.

🎗 *The Goldfish Bowl.* Gollancz, 1987.

Winner of the Arthur Ellis Award for Best First Novel.

Death on a No. 8 Hook. Gollancz, 1988. (Variant title: *Silent Knives*).

🎗 *Hot Shots.* Gollancz, 1989.

Winner of the Arthur Ellis Award for Best Novel.

Serious Crimes. Viking, 1990.

Shortlisted for the Arthur Ellis Award for Best Novel.

Read On: Other series that combine a depth of characterization with a police procedural include John Brady's <u>Matt Minogue Mysteries</u> (*A Carra King* and others), Ian Rankin's <u>John Rebus</u> (*Resurrection Men* and others), Bartholomew Gill's <u>Peter McGarr</u> (*The Death of an Irish Sinner* and others), and Peter Robinson's <u>Alan Banks</u> (*Aftermath* and others).

Hill, John Spencer.

<u>Detective Carlo Arbati Mysteries.</u>

A poet and a detective, Inspector Carlo Arbati lives in Florence, Italy, working for the Florentine Questura. These novels combine Italian culture with human malice.

The Last Castrato. St. Martin's Press, 1995. **Book Groups** 📖

Cordelia Sinclair, in Florence, Italy, to conduct research into early Italian opera, happens to meet Inspector Carlo Arbati, a detective and lyric poet. He is investigating a series of murders in which the victims have had their vocal cords severed. Cordelia becomes involved when her research leads her to the body of the next victim. This novel won the Arthur Ellis Award for Best First Novel, as well as the Critics' Choice Award in the *San Francisco Review of Books*.

Ghirlandaio's Daughter. Constable, 1996; McClelland & Stewart, 1997.

Subjects: Arbati, Carlo (Fictional Character) • Florence • Italy • Poet-Detectives • Police

Read On: P. D. James's Adam Dalgliesh is also a poet-detective. Other mysteries set in Italy include Donna Leon's *Death at La Fenice* (and others), Andrea Camilleri's *The Shape of Water* (and others), and Michael Dibdin's *Ratking* (and others).

Lindquist, N. J.

Shaded Light: A Manziuk and Ryan Mystery. St. Kitts Press, 2000. 337pp.

A variety of motives for murder emerge as new partners Detectives Paul Manziuk and Jacqui Ryan set aside their personal differences and question the guests at a weekend house party. A second murder has them looking for connections between the two as they follow a twisted trail to the identity of the killer.

Subjects: 1990s • Blackmail • Homicide Detectives • Murder • Ontario • Serial Murders • Toronto

Read On: Lindquist combines the elements of the modern police procedural with the traditional twists, turns, and red herrings reminiscent of Agatha Christie. The English country house is a favourite setting for many mysteries: both Ellen Hart's *Vital Lies* and Peter Dickinson's *Some Deaths Before Dying* unravel in this venue.

MacKay, Scott.

<u>Barry Gilbert Mysteries.</u>

Barry Gilbert is partnered with Joe Lombardo in the Toronto Police Force, where they work as detectives in the Homicide Division

Cold Comfort. Carroll & Graf Publishers, 1998. **Book Groups** 📖

Despite a declining police budget and departmental pressure to quickly wrap up their investigation into the murder of a prominent politician's stepdaughter, Toronto detective Barry Gilbert and his partner Joe Lombardo strike out on their own. Ignoring the most obvious suspect and a potential frame-up, they set out to unravel the victim's complicated family connections and a history of abuse. This novel was shortlisted for the Arthur Ellis Award for Best Novel.

Fall Guy. St. Martin's Press, 2001.

Old Scores. St. Martin's Minotaur, 2003.

> **Subjects:** Gilbert, Barry (Fictional Character) • Lombardo, Joe (Fictional Character) • Metropolitan Toronto Police Force • Murder • Ontario • Toronto

> **Read On:** Crossing genres, MacKay has also written a World War II thriller (*A Friend in Barcelona*) as well as a number of science fiction novels (*The Meek, Outpost,* and others). Rhys Bowen's <u>Constable Evans</u> mysteries (*Evans to Betsy* and others) and John Harvey's <u>Charlie Resnick</u> mysteries (*Easy Meat* and others) are police procedurals with strong characters and setting. Police working in an urban setting appear in Ed McBain's <u>87th Precinct Mysteries</u> (*Downtown* and others) and Dan Mahoney's <u>NYPD</u> novels (*Detective First Grade* and others).

Miller, Stephen.

The Woman in the Yard. **Picador, 1999. 294pp. Book Groups** 📖

When two black women are murdered in Wilmington, North Carolina, in 1954, only Acting Sheriff Q. P. "Kewpie" Waldeau seems concerned. When a white woman is subsequently murdered, racial tensions explode.

> **Subjects:** 1950s • First Novels • Murder • North Carolina • Race Relations • Racism • Serial Killers • Sheriffs • Wilmington

> **Read On:** John Grisham's *A Time to Kill* details events in a small Southern town when a black man kills the two white men who raped his daughter. In Terry Kay's *The Runaway* a small-town sheriff faces racism and injustice while investigating a murder. The tension in Miller's novel is also felt in the novels of Harlan Coben (*Tell No One* and others) and Ridley Pearson (*The Art of Deception* and others).

Mofina, Rick.

<u>Tom Reed and Walt Sydowski Novels.</u>

San Francisco is the home of Tom Reed, crime reporter, and Walt Sydowski, homicide inspector for the San Francisco Police Department.

If Angels Fall. Pinnacle Books, 2000. **Book Groups** 📖

Haunted by the voices of his three drowned children, Edward Keller believes that if he can re-create the tragedy they will return to him. As children begin to disappear in San Francisco, reporter Tom Reed and

Detective Walt Sydowski, both plagued by their own demons, work frantically to connect enough clues to solve the case before more children die.

Cold Fear. Pinnacle Books, 2001.

🎗 *Blood of Others.* Pinnacle Books, 2002.

Winner of the Arthur Ellis Award for Best Novel.

No Way Back. Pinnacle Books, 2003.

Be Mine. Pinnacle Books, 2004.

> **Subjects:** California • Murder • Police • Reed, Tom (Fictional Character) • Reporters • San Francisco • Sydowski, Walt (Fictional Character)

> **Read On:** Crime reporters are often found in mystery fiction, some partnering with the police and some in adversarial positions against them. Britt Montero (Edna Buchanan) often works with the police in Miami, but Jack McMorrow (Gerry Boyle) might find himself facing a hostile police force. And Irene Kelly (Jan Burke) is a crime reporter married to a policeman.

Preston, Alison.

Frank Foote Mysteries.

Police Inspector Frank Foote is a family man living in Winnipeg, Manitoba, specifically Norwood Flats, where he is often called upon to help others who have been involved in, or have stumbled upon, serious crimes.

The Rain Barrel Baby. Signature Editions, 2000.

The Geranium Girls. Signature Editions, 2002.

Winnipeg letter-carrier Beryl Kyte discovers a body in the woods, the first in a series of killings. As she follows the newspaper reports, Beryl begins to see a pattern. When she herself becomes the target of petty crimes she fears she may be the killer's next victim.

Cherry Bites. Signature Editions, 2004.

> **Subjects:** Foote, Frank (Fictional Character) • Manitoba • Murder • Police • Winnipeg

> **Read On:** James Patterson's *1st To Die* and *2nd Chance*, and Cathy Vasas-Brown's *Every Wickedness,* are thrillers in which the violence and actions of the killer are not graphically depicted. Like Giles Blunt's *Forty Words for Sorrow*, this mystery is set in a small town, a place where people traditionally feel safe.

Reynolds, John Lawrence.

Joe McGuire Mysteries.

Joe McGuire is a Boston homicide detective who marches to his own drum. McGuire is rather world-weary and tries often to retire, but he finds that retired life never really suits him.

🎗 *The Man Who Murdered God.* Viking, 1989.

Winner of the Arthur Ellis Award for Best First Novel.

And Leave Her Lay Dying. Viking, 1990.

Whisper Death. Viking, 1991.

 Gypsy Sins. HarperCollins, 1993.

Winner of the Arthur Ellis Award for Best Novel.

Solitary Dancer. HarperCollins, 1994.

Haunted Hearts. McClelland & Stewart, 2003. **Book Groups**

Retired and not particularly liking it, Joe McGuire tries unsuccessfully to be hired back part-time by the Boston Police Department; once again he has disobeyed orders and taken matters into his own hands, thus ruining his chance to be rehired. When he finds a job as in-house investigator for a law firm, his work takes him back full circle to the Boston Police Department, as he himself becomes a suspect in the murder of one of the lawyers in his firm.

> **Subjects:** Boston • Massachusetts • McGuire, Joe (Fictional Character) • Murder

> **Read On:** The "world-weary detective" might be called a subgenre unto itself, and such a character was an integral part of Dashiell Hammett's writing, as evidenced by a fairly recent collection of his short stories, *Nightmare Town*. Other such detectives are Aurelio Zen (Michael Dibdin), Inspector Anders (Marshall Browne), and Mario Balzic (K. C. Constantine).

Robinson, Peter.

Inspector Alan Banks Series.

Alan Banks left the Metropolitan London Police Force early in his career to move to the small town of Eastvale in Yorkshire. As Detective Chief Inspector, however, he still encounters the troubled human spirit, acting out in criminal ways.

Gallows View. Viking, 1987.

Shortlisted for the Arthur Ellis Award for Best First Novel and the John Creasey Award for Best First Crime Novel.

A Dedicated Man. Viking, 1988.

Shortlisted for the Arthur Ellis Award for Best Novel.

A Necessary End. Viking, 1989.

The Hanging Valley. Viking, 1989.

Shortlisted for the Arthur Ellis Award for Best Novel.

 *Past Reason Hated.* Viking, 1991.

Winner of the Arthur Ellis Award for Best Novel and the Torgi Literary Award.

Wednesday's Child. Viking, 1992.

Shortlisted for the Arthur Ellis Award for Best Novel and the Edgar Allan Poe Award.

Final Account. Viking, 1994. (Variant title: *Dry Bones That Dream*).

🎗 *Innocent Graves.* Viking, 1996.

Winner of the Arthur Ellis Award for Best Novel and shortlisted for the Dashiell Hammett Award for Best Literary Crime Novel.

Dead Right. Viking, 1997. (Variant title: *Blood at the Root*).

Shortlisted for the Arthur Ellis Award for Best Novel.

🎗 *In a Dry Season.* Viking, 1999. **Book Groups** 📖

Alan Banks's nemesis, Chief Constable Jimmy Riddle, gives Banks what he thinks is a dead-end job, investigating the discovery of a long-dead human skeleton. Banks, however, finds an extinct city, and its mysteries come into view during a long dry season. This novel won the Anthony Award for Best Mystery, the Barry Award, the Grand Prix de Littérature Policière (France), and the Martin Beck Award (Sweden); it was shortlisted for the Arthur Ellis Award for Best Novel.

🎗 *Cold Is the Grave.* Viking, 2000.

Winner of the Arthur Ellis Award for Best Novel, and shortlisted for the *Los Angeles Time* Book Award.

Aftermath. McClelland & Stewart, 2001.

Shortlisted for the Arthur Ellis Award for Best Novel.

The Summer That Never Was. McClelland & Stewart, 2003. (Variant title: *Close to Home*).

Shortlisted for the Arthur Ellis Award for Best Novel and the Anthony Award for Best Mystery Novel.

Playing with Fire. McClelland & Stewart, 2004.

Strange Affair. McClelland & Stewart, 2005.

> **Subjects:** Banks, Alan (Fictional Character) • England • Murder Investigation • Police • Yorkshire

> **Read On:** For the British mystery atmosphere and likeable police detectives, also try Deborah Crombie's Duncan Kincaid and Gemma James Mysteries or Elizabeth George's Thomas Lynley Mysteries. Robinson's fiction has also been compared to that of P. D. James and Ruth Rendell. Robinson was awarded the Crime Writers' Association Dagger in the Library Award in 2002, a prize given for the body of work.

Rotenberg, David.

Zhong Fong Mysteries.

Zhong Fong starts out as head of Shanghai's Special Investigation Unit, but his career there is as shaky as his marriage to his actress wife.

The Shanghai Murders: Of Love and Ivory. St. Martin's Press, 1998.

A *Library Journal* Best Mystery selection.

The Lake Ching Murders: A Mystery of Fire and Ice. McArthur, 2001.
Book Groups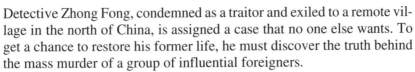

Detective Zhong Fong, condemned as a traitor and exiled to a remote village in the north of China, is assigned a case that no one else wants. To get a chance to restore his former life, he must discover the truth behind the mass murder of a group of influential foreigners.

The Hua Shan Hospital Murders. McArthur, 2003.

Shortlisted for the Arthur Ellis Award for Best Novel.

The Hamlet Murders. McArthur, 2004.

> **Subjects:** China • Fong, Zhong (Fictional Character) • Murder • Police Investigations • Shanghai

> **Read On:** Xiaolong Qiu's *Death of a Red Heroine*, Tom Brady's *The Master of Rain,* and Lisa See's *Flower Net* all involve murder investigations in China.

Sale, Medora.

Inspector John Sanders and Harriet Jeffries Mysteries.

> John Sanders is a police inspector with the Metropolitan Toronto Police Force, and Harriet Jeffries is an architectural photographer who becomes involved with him, both professionally and personally.

🎗 ***Murder on the Run.*** Penguin Books Canada, 1986.

Winner of the Arthur Ellis Award for Best First Novel.

Murder in Focus. Viking, 1989.

Murder in a Good Cause. Viking, 1990.

Sleep of the Innocent. Viking, 1991.

Pursued by Shadows. Maxwell Macmillan Canada, 1992.

Shortlisted for the Arthur Ellis Award for Best Novel.

Short Cut to Santa Fe. Maxwell Macmillan Canada, 1994.

As they begin a vacation in New Mexico, Harriet and John encounter two children at the airport who just missed their bus. Jeffries and Sanders offer to follow the twins' bus, not knowing it has been hijacked. They end up as unwitting hostages in kidnappings and murder.

> **Subjects:** Jeffries, Harriet (Fictional Character) • Ontario • Police Inspectors • Sanders, John (Fictional Character) • Toronto • Women Photographers

> **Read On:** Sale also writes as Caroline Roe, in a different time and setting. Other photographer-detectives appear in *Click* by Dan Whipple, the <u>Andy Derain Series</u> by Rex Dancer, and the <u>Tony Lowell Mysteries</u> by E. C. Ayres.

Smith, Frank.

Detective Chief Inspector Neil Paget Mysteries.

Tenacious Detective Chief Inspector Neil Paget is a dour widower living in Shropshire, England. He and his sergeant, young John Tregalles, make a good team in ferreting out the information they need to solve their cases.

Fatal Flaw. St. Martin's Press, 1996.

Stone Dead. St. Martin's Press, 1998. **Book Groups** 📖

The investigation into the murder of a man found at the bottom of a village well initially appears to be an open-and-shut case. As they realize they are being mis-directed by lies at every step, the police begin to look for the truth through village gossip.

Candles for the Dead. St. Martin's Press, 1999.

Thread of Evidence. St. Martin's Minotaur, 2001.

Acts of Vengeance. St. Martin's Minotaur, 2003.

Subjects: England • English Villages • Murder • Paget, Neil (Fictional Character) • Police • Shropshire • Tregalles, John (Fictional Character) • Village Life

Read On: Catherine Aird (*After Effects* and others), W. J. Burley (*Wycliffe and the Cycle of Death* and others), and John Harvey (*In a True Light* and others) also write British police procedurals. Village gossip is an integral part of the detection in Clare Curzon's *Cat's Cradle* and Jill Paton Walsh's *A Presumption of Death*.

Wright, Eric.

Inspector Charlie Salter Mysteries.

Charlie Salter is a police inspector with the Toronto Police Force. Like many po-lice detectives, he is dour, somewhat puritanical, his own person, and often in trouble with his supervisors.

🎗 *The Night the Gods Smiled.* Collins, 1983.

Winner of the Arthur Ellis Award for Best Novel, the John Creasey Award for Best First Crime Novel, and the Toronto Book Award.

Smoke Detector. Collins, 1984.

🎗 *Death in the Old Country.* Collins, 1985.

Winner of the Arthur Ellis Award for Best Novel.

A Single Death. Collins, 1986. (Variant title: *The Man Who Changed His Name*).

A Body Surrounded by Water. Collins, 1987.

A Question of Murder. Collins, 1988.

A Sensitive Case. Doubleday, 1990.

Final Cut. Doubleday, 1991.

When petty acts of sabotage on the set lead to murder, Charlie Salter's latest as-signment as an advisor on a low-budget thriller filming in Toronto becomes a hunt for a killer.

A Fine Italian Hand. Doubleday, 1992.

Death by Degrees. Doubleday, 1993.

The Last Hand. Dundurn Group, 2001.

> **Subjects:** Murder • Ontario • Salter, Charlie (Fictional Character) • Toronto • Toronto Police Force

> **Read On:** Wright is the author of a number of other mystery series, featuring such characters as Mel Pickett, a retired Toronto policeman; Joe Barley, a part-time college English teacher; and Lucy Trimble Brenner, a part-time librarian and bed-and-breakfast owner who inherited a private investigation agency. Other authors who set their mysteries in Toronto include Rosemary Aubert (*The Ferryman Will Be There* and others), Scott MacKay (*Fall Guy* and others), James W. Nichol (*Midnight Cab*), and Sylvia Maultash Warsh (*To Die in Spring*).

Mel Pickett Mysteries.

Mel Pickett, now retired, had appeared in a Charlie Salter mystery, *A Sensitive Case*. He heads to Larch River in Northern Ontario to enjoy his retirement, but life and crime will not leave him in peace.

Buried in Stone. Scribner, 1995; Doubleday, Canada, 1996.

Death of a Hired Man. Thomas Dunne Books, 2001.

Now that he has remarried and does not always need the cabin he built in Larch River, Mel rents it out to someone else, who winds up murdered.

> **Subjects:** Ex-police Officers • Northern Ontario • Ontario • Pickett, Mel (Fictional Character) • Retirees • Small-town Life

> **Read On:** It is often difficult for a police officer to retire, as evidenced in *Shadow Men* by Jonathon King, *House of Guilt* by Robert Rosenberg, and *Mexican Hat* by Michael McGarrity.

Wright, L. R.

Karl Alberg Mysteries.

Staff Sergeant Karl Alberg of the Royal Canadian Mounted Police (RCMP) lives and works in Gibsons, British Columbia, on the Sunshine Coast. But life is not always sunny there, and Alberg is often required to look into the nastier bits that people leave behind. On the bright side, however, is his relationship with the town librarian, Cassandra Mitchell.

The Suspect. Doubleday Canada, 1985.

Winner of the Edgar Allan Poe Award for Best Novel.

Sleep While I Sing. Doubleday Canada, 1986.

A Chill Rain in January. Macmillan of Canada, 1990.

Winner of the Arthur Ellis Award for Best Novel.

Fall from Grace. Viking, 1991.

Shortlisted for the Arthur Ellis Award for Best Novel.

Prized Possessions. Doubleday, 1993.

Shortlisted for the Arthur Ellis Award for Best Novel.

A Touch of Panic. Doubleday, 1994.

Shortlisted for the Arthur Ellis Award for Best Novel.

🎗 *Mother Love.* Doubleday, 1995. **Book Groups** 📖

Maria Buscombe mysteriously disappeared seven years ago. She returns home suddenly and is then murdered, leaving RCMP Inspector Karl Alberg to uncover the reasons behind her disappearance. Wright won the CAA Literary Award for Fiction for this as well as the Arthur Ellis Award for Best Novel.

Strangers Among Us. Doubleday, 1996.

Acts of Murder. Doubleday, 1997.

Shortlisted for the Dashiell Hammett Award for Best Literary Crime Novel.

> **Subjects:** Alberg, Karl (Fictional Character) • British Columbia • Librarians • Mitchell, Cassandra (Fictional Character) • Murder • Police Chiefs • Royal Canadian Mounted Police • Village Life

> **Read On:** In addition to her mystery fiction, Wright also wrote mainstream fiction (*Love in the Temperate Zone, Among Friends,* and others). L. R. Wright died in February 2001, and in the spring of 2001, the Crime Writers of Canada posthumously honoured her with the Derrick Murdoch Award for Lifetime Achievement and Outstanding Contribution to Crime Fiction. Her rich, fully drawn characters resemble those in the writings of Ruth Rendell (*Adam and Eve and Pinch Me* and others), P. D. James (*A Certain Justice* and others), and Laurie R. King (*With Child* and others).

Edwina Henderson Mysteries.

Wright retired her RCMP-officer-and-librarian team and replaced Karl Alberg with Eddie (Edwina) Henderson. While Karl and Cassandra have gone off to retire, Edwina is hard at work trying to fit in as the new boss and trying not to have her personal life interfere too much.

Kidnap. Doubleday, 2000.

Shortlisted for the Arthur Ellis Award for Best Novel.

Menace. Doubleday, 2001.

Eddie Henderson is trying to sort out her new staff and her new position as head of the RCMP detachment, when she is faced with two seemingly unrelated incidents; neither seems terribly serious, but when she puts them together and adds some more information, she finds she is facing a situation of stalking by a psychopath.

> **Subjects:** British Columbia • Henderson, Edwina (Fictional Character) • Murder • Police Chiefs • Royal Canadian Mounted Police • Village Life

> **Read On:** Another title that includes a female RCMP officer is *Appetite for Murder* by Dolors Toole. Toole's novel, however, is set at the other end of the country, in Newfoundland. Women police chiefs figure in Charlene Weir's <u>Susan Wren Mysteries</u>, Stuart Woods's <u>Holly Barker Series</u>, and Patricia Cornwell's <u>Judy Hammer Series.</u>

Young, Scott.

Matthew Kitologitak Mysteries.

"Matteesie" Kitologitak is a mid-fifties Inuit RCMP officer living in an environment that can be as hostile as the criminals he is chasing.

Murder in a Cold Climate. Macmillan Canada, 1988.

The Shaman's Knife. Macmillan Canada, 1993.

The investigation of a double murder becomes personal for Inuit Mountie Matteesie Kitologitak when he learns that his ninety-year-old mother has been injured by the fleeing murderer. The prime suspect is a much-admired old shaman from a tiny Northwest Territories village.

Subjects: Inuit • Kitologitak, Matthew "Matteesie" (Fictional Character) • Murder • Northwest Territories • Royal Canadian Mounted Police

Read On: Other mysteries with an Arctic setting include those located in Alaska by Sue Henry (*Murder on the Iditarod Trail* and others) and Dana Stabenow (*Fire and Ice* and others). Young's portrait of the Arctic landscape resembles Tony Hillerman's depiction of the desert environment (*The First Eagle* and others).

Private Investigator

The private investigator (P.I.), or private eye, is not bound by the restrictions of the police detective. There are no higher-ups to answer to (except the paying client) and no political situation driving the investigation. However, there may be a social or political issue that convinces the investigator to take on the case. The private investigator is usually a loner and has to be more resourceful than a police detective because of the lack of access to such resources as a crime lab. In this subgenre the reader also sees the step-by-step process required to solve the mystery.

The P.I. is often a former police officer who was not able to work within the confines or strictures of a formal institution and who then went out on his own, or it might be someone who retired early and then found it impossible to remain retired. It would seem that the former police detectives are primarily male, whereas the women went into private investigation without having begun as police officers.

Beasley, David R.

New York Library Mysteries.

The New York Public Library provides the backdrop in this mystery series as its security guard, Rudyard Mack, and his girlfriend, Vine Arbuthnott, president of the Library Union, become involved in investigations of crimes committed at the library.

The Jenny. Davus Publishing, 1994.

Security guard Rudyard Mack investigates an international stamp cartel and double murder following the theft of rare stamps from the New York Public Library's Miller Stamp Collection.

The Grand Conspiracy. Davus Publishing, 1997.

Subjects: Libraries • Mack, Rudyard (Fictional Character) • Murder • New York City • New York Public Library • Vine, Arbuthnott (Fictional Character)

Read On: Allen Kurzweil's complex literary mysteries feature the New York Public Library and librarian Alexander Short (*A Case of Curiosities* and *The Grand Complication*). The fast pace of Beasley's mysteries keeps up with Dan Brown's *Angels & Demons*, another behind-the-scenes thriller that looks at an institution, in this case the Vatican.

Douglas, Lauren Wright.

Caitlin Reece Mysteries.

Caitlin Reece is a gay private investigator living on Vancouver Island, whose main focus is crimes against women, children, and animals.

The Always Anonymous Beast. Naiad Press, 1987.

🎗 *Ninth Life.* Naiad Press, 1990.

Winner of the LAMBDA Award for Best Lesbian Mystery.

The Daughters of Artemis. Naiad Press, 1991.

A Tiger's Heart. Naiad Press, 1992.

Goblin Market. Naiad Press, 1993.

A Rage of Maidens. Naiad Press, 1994.

Clive Cluhaine has hired Vancouver Island P.I. Caitlin Reece to protect his daughter Andy from the man she helped convict of sexually assaulting her sister, a man who vowed to take revenge upon his release from prison.

Subjects: British Columbia • Crimes Against Women • Lesbians • Reece, Caitlin (Fictional Character) • Vancouver Island • Women Detectives

Read On: The Lauren Laurano Mysteries by Sandra Scoppettone also feature a lesbian P.I., as do the Helen Keremos Mysteries by Eve Zaremba. A woman seeks to help the victims of crime, especially women and children, in the Jane Whitefield Novels by Thomas Perry. Douglas has also written a mystery series featuring Allison O'Neil.

Engel, Howard.

Benny Cooperman Series.

Living in the fictional town of Grantham, Ontario (modeled on the city of St. Catharines), Benny Cooperman makes his living as a private investigator. In addition to this series, Engel is the author of some stand-alone titles, *Murder in Montparnasse* and *Mr. Doyle & Dr. Bell: A Victorian Mystery*.

The Suicide Murders. Clarke, Irwin, 1980.

Ransom Game. Clarke, Irwin, 1981.

Murder on Location. Clarke, Irwin, 1982.

🎗 *Murder Sees the Light.* Clarke, Irwin, 1984.

Winner of the Arthur Ellis Award for Best Novel.

A City Called July. Viking, 1986.

A Victim Must Be Found. Viking, 1988.

Dead and Buried. Viking, 1990.

There Was an Old Woman. Viking, 1992.

Getting Away with Murder. Viking, 1995.

The Cooperman Variations. Penguin, 2001.

Following the murder of a colleague staying at her home, TV executive Vanessa Moss hires P.I. Benny Cooperman to act as her bodyguard. As Benny investigates, he begins to suspect there is a connection between Vanessa's fears and the death of a famous cellist.

> **Subjects:** Cooperman, Benny (Fictional Character) • Grantham, Ontario (Imaginary Place) • Jewish Men • Ontario
>
> **Read On:** Other mystery series that share Engel's charming style are Christine Green's <u>Kate Kinsella</u> (*Deadly Partners*), Michael Allegretto's <u>Jake Lomax</u> (*Grave Doubt*), and Ralph McInerny's <u>Andrew Broom</u> (*Cause and Effect*). Another appealing Canadian detective is Eric Wright's Charlie Salter (*The Night the Gods Smiled* and others). Wright and Engel co-wrote *My Brother's Keeper*, featuring each of their series protagonists, Charlie Salter and Benny Cooperman.

Hall, Linda.

Teri Blake-Addison Mystery Series.

Teri Blake is a Christian private investigator in Maine.

🎗 *Steal Away.* Multnomah Publishers, 2003.

Teri is asked to find out what really happened to the minister's wife when she went missing in a sailing mishap. As usual, Teri finds out more than she is asked to. This novel has won the Beacon Award for Best Inspirational Novel, the Winter Rose Award for Best Inspirational Novel, the Award of Excellence from the Colorado Romance Writers for Inspirational Fiction, and the Word Guild Award for Best Mystery in Canada.

Chat Room. Multnomah Publishers, 2003.

> **Subjects:** Blake-Addison, Teri (Fictional Character) • Christian Fiction • Maine • Murder Investigation • Women Detectives

> **Read On:** Linda Hall has written a number of mystery series, most notably those set on the coast of Maine, plus the series featuring Sergeant Sheppard of the Royal Canadian Mounted Police (*April Operation, November Veil*, and *August Gamble*). Some other Christian mystery series are Terri Blackstock's <u>Newpointe 911</u>, Tim Downs's <u>Bug Man Novels</u>, Athol Dickson's <u>Garr Reed Mysteries,</u> and Audrey Stallsmith's <u>Thyme Will Tell Mysteries</u>.

Spring, Michelle.

Laura Principal Mysteries.

A Cambridge private investigator working with her personal partner, Sonny, Laura Principal prefers to take on cases that involve social justice issues: violent children, student prostitutes, migrant workers. She moves easily between the academic world of Cambridge and the town side of it, depending on the needs of the case.

Every Breath You Take. Pocket Books, 1994.

Shortlisted for the Arthur Ellis Award for Best First Novel and the Anthony Award for Best First Mystery Novel.

Running for Shelter. Pocket Books, 1996.

Standing in the Shadows. Ballantine Books, 1998.

Shortlisted for the Arthur Ellis Award for Best Novel.

Nights in White Satin. Ballantine Books, 1999.

🏅 ***In the Midnight Hour.*** Ballantine Books, 2001. **Book Groups** 📖

There is a new young busker in town, eerily resembling the four-year-old Liam, who went missing twelve years ago. Laura is asked by the missing boy's parents to determine, without confronting the young musician, if he is in fact their missing son. This novel won the Arthur Ellis Award for Best Novel.

> **Subjects:** Cambridge • England • Principal, Laura (Fictional Character) • Women Private Investigators
>
> **Read On:** Nora Kelly's Gillian Adams, a former student at Cambridge, returns there in *In the Shadow of King's,* and P. D. James's Cordelia Grey finds herself investigating a case there in *An Unsuitable Job for a Woman.* Dorsey Fiske (*Academic Murder* and others) and Jill Paton Walsh (*The Wyndham Case*) have also set their mysteries in Cambridge, England.

Wright, Eric.

Joe Barley Mysteries.

Joe Barley is a permanent part-time sessional instructor of English literature at a community college in Toronto. On the side he is occasionally employed by a security company as a "watcher." It is in this capacity that he finds himself involved in investigations, which he has to field along with his own personal problems.

🏅 ***The Kidnapping of Rosie Dawn.*** J. Daniel and Co., 2000.

Joe's cleaning lady approaches him one day to say that another woman for whom she cleans, known only to her as Rosie Dawn, has gone missing, and she would like Joe to find her. This novel won the Barry Award and was shortlisted for the Edgar Allan Poe Award, the Arthur Ellis Award for Best Novel, and the Anthony Award for Best Mystery Novel.

The Hemingway Caper. Dundurn Group, 2003.

> **Subjects:** Barley, Joe (Fictional Character) • English Teachers • Ontario • Toronto
>
> **Read On:** Other sleuths, perhaps more amateurish than Joe Barley, who are also teachers are Amanda Pepper (Gillian Roberts), Sarah Deane (J. S. Borthwick), and Tom Mason and Scott Carpenter (Mark Richard Zubro).

Zaremba, Eve.

Helen Keremos Mysteries.

Helen is a middle-aged lesbian private detective living in Vancouver. She's tough, she gets around, and she has her own strong opinions about life, but she's there for her friends, even when it endangers her life.

A Reason to Kill. Paperjacks, 1978.

Work for a Million. Amanita, 1986.

Beyond Hope. Amanita, 1987.

Uneasy Lies. Second Story Press, 1990.

The Butterfly Effect. Second Story Press, 1994.

White Noise. Second Story Press, 1997.

Lesbian P.I. Helen Keremos foils an attempt to kidnap her former client Sonny after he calls, warning that he is in trouble but does not know why. Subsequently she gets pulled into the middle of a crime involving both theft and murder as she looks for the truth.

> **Subjects:** British Columbia • Keremos, Helen (Fictional Character) • Lesbians • Vancouver • Women Private Investigators

> **Read On:** Lauren Wright Douglas's lesbian P.I. Caitlin Reece also works out of British Columbia (*A Tiger's Heart* and others). Other lesbian private investigators are protagonists in series by Katherine Forrest (Kate Delafield in *Murder at the Nightwood Bar* and others) and Val McDermid (Kate Brannigan in *Star Struck* and others).

Science Fiction

Science fiction is the genre in which the author asks the reader to consider the question "What if . . . ?" and then goes on to explore the possibilities of taking a situation or event and looking at it in a different way through science and technology. This genre has also been referred to as "speculative fiction"; Judith Merril, one of Canada's most respected SF authors, describes speculative fiction by saying that it "makes use of the traditional 'scientific method' to examine some postulated approximation of reality" (Merril 1995). Once authors formulate a concept, they then go on to create a world in which their proposed changes can exist, a world that the reader is willing to enter and believe in. Regardless of which term is used, these are stories that are meant to foster a sense of wonder in the reader.

In *Genreflecting: A Guide to Reading Interests in Genre Fiction*, Diana Tixier Herald describes this genre as follows: "Science fiction novels are those that deal with scientific topics, space travel, aliens, and recognizably Earth-variant worlds or life-forms that have not been touched by magic" (2000, 269). Some characteristics seem to be relevant throughout the genre:

1. Science fiction explores ideas based on scientific principles and technology to evoke a sense of wonder.

2. The plot and events, although not yet reality, need to be believable, as the reader is asked to accept that what is being described is possible and a potential precursor to life in the future.

3. Through the storyline the author may be commenting on issues of concern facing society at the moment, but they are placed in the context of the future or another world.

4. The storyline is generally most important; however, the characters (which may be either aliens or other life forms) are often developed and enhanced over the course of a series.

5. Setting is also an important appeal, as authors create "future worlds," dystopias, parallel worlds, etc.

6. Authors do not usually contradict known scientific facts, but they may adapt and develop their own scientific theories.

When working with readers, advisors may want to consider that although often closely aligned with the fantasy genre, science fiction also shares many characteristics with the mystery genre, featuring puzzle-solving, futuristic detectives who seek to right a wrong or find justice; in other words, classic tales of good versus evil. In addition, readers may be interested in exploring authors and titles not only in this genre but also in the adventure thriller genre as well, a subgenre in which the stories are often filled with fast-paced action and protagonists who take matters into their own hands, but always for the right reasons.

To explore this genre more fully, librarians and readers are directed to *Strictly Science Fiction: A Guide to Reading Interests* by Diana Tixier Herald and Bonnie Kunzel (2002). In this work the authors outline the history of the genre, the subgenres, awards, resources, and more; for more specifically Canadian content, the Web site *Made in Canada* (http://www.geocities.com/canadian_sf/index.html) is an excellent source of information about Canadians involved in science fiction. This site has over 350 pages of information on Canadian authors, actors, filmmakers, magazines, and Web sites, as well as short fiction, essays, and convention lists.

Action/Adventure

One of the largest subgenres of science fiction, these adventurous, highly accessible stories are filled with fast-paced action. Here readers find classic battles of good versus evil in which the hero triumphs. Many of the novels in this category relate to popular science fiction–based television and movie series, such as *Star Trek* and *Star Wars*, and this subgenre is often the first one young readers experience; in addition, a number of titles listed here feature young protagonists with whom young readers may relate. Readers of other adventure authors and genres, especially military-based thrillers (Matthew Reilly's *Scarecrow* and others) or action thrillers (Clive Cussler's *Valhalla Rising* and others), may successfully be introduced to this category.

Czerneda, Julie.

The Trade Pact Universe.

In the future, a number of species have aligned themselves, forming a trade pact; this alliance governs trade, commerce, and more. Sira, a member of the telepathic

Clan, and Jason Morgan, the human who will become her life partner, battle prejudice that would keep them apart, while working for stability within the universe.

A Thousand Words for Stranger. DAW Books, 1997.

Sira, a member of the Clan—a people with powerful mental powers who chose not to join the alliance—finds herself on the run with human trader Jason Morgan, following an attack and an attempted kidnapping. This situation is further complicated when Sira's memory of her extraordinary powers becomes blocked, and she no longer knows whom to trust.

Ties of Power. DAW Books, 1999.

To Trade the Stars. DAW Books, 2002.

> **Subjects:** Human–Alien Encounters • Morgan, Jason (Fictional Character) • Sira (Fictional Character) • Telepathy
>
> **Read On:** Czerneda's balance of science and character development can be found in Alexander Jablokov's *Carve the Sky*, Linda Nagata's *The Bohr Maker,* and Catherine Asaro's *Primary Inversion*.

Gardner, James Alan.

League of Peoples.

In this series of linked novels all set in the same universe, society's flawed members are the designated explorers.

Expendable. Eos, 1997.

Festina Ramos, born with a facial birthmark, is a member of the Explorers Corp, an elite group assigned to land on hostile planets and make contact with alien cultures. Festina and her partner Yarrun ultimately realize their current mission is meant to be their last when they are assigned to escort a banished admiral to a planet from which a number of the team members have never returned.

Vigilant. Avon Books, 1999.

Hunted. Eos, 2000.

Ascending. Eos, 2001.

Trapped. Eos, 2002.

> **Subjects:** Explorers • Human–Alien Encounters • Oar (Fictional Character) • Ramos, Festina (Fictional Character) • Space Opera
>
> **Read On:** Like Julie Czerneda's <u>The Trade Pact Universe</u>, several of the titles in this series feature strong female protagonists.

Huff, Tanya.

Valor's Choice. DAW Books, 2000. 409pp.

A platoon of marines, commanded by Staff Sergeant Torin Kerr, is assigned to escort a diplomatic delegation to a meeting with a newly discovered aggressive species, the lizard-like Silviss. What begins as a purely ceremonial duty very quickly becomes a war when the transport carrying the delegation crashes, and a battle for survival begins against a group of Silviss adolescent males.

> **Subjects:** Human–Alien Encounters • Kerr, Torin (Fictional Character) • Life on Other Planets • Military Fiction • Space Opera • Space Warfare

> **Read On:** Huff continues this story in *The Better Part of Valor*. Huff's short-story collection *What Ho, Magic!* includes pieces from all her writing genres—fantasy, science fiction, and horror. S. M. Stirling's *On the Oceans of Eternity* uses the same historical battle as Huff. For other examples of combat science fiction, try Jerry Pournelle's series (<u>Falkenberg's Legions</u> or <u>CoDominium</u>) or David Drake's <u>Hammer's Slammers.</u>

Lowachee, Karin.

Burndive. Warner Books, 2003. 417pp.

Handsome and eligible, Ryan Azarcon is a troubled young man, haunted by nightmares and fractured family relationships. When Ryan's father, a starship captain, brokers a controversial truce in the current interstellar wars to go after the "real" enemy, Ryan becomes the target of assassins and is forced to examine where he is in his life, a step that will lead him toward maturity and an understanding of the conflicts in his life. *Burndive* is considered to be a sequel to *Warchild* (see next entry).

> **Subjects:** Coming of Age • Interstellar War • Space Warfare • War

> **Read On:** Set in the same universe as Lowachee's earlier novel, *Warchild*, this work can be read as a stand-alone title, although the main protagonist from that novel does make an appearance in this story. Other authors who also create well-drawn characters and complex worlds include Karl Schroeder (*Ventus*) and Orson Scott Card (<u>Enders Series</u>).

♠ *Warchild.* Warner Books, 2002. 451pp.

Young Jos is orphaned and enslaved at the age of eight, after pirates slaughter his parents; he escapes but finds himself in the hands of the Strits, Earth's alien enemies, who train him to be a spy. Although taught to wage war, his ultimate battle is to secure his own destiny. This novel won the Warner Aspect First Novel Contest, was shortlisted for both a Prix Aurora Award and a Philip K. Dick Award, was on the Locus Recommended Reading list, and was listed as Science Fiction *Chronicle*'s "One of the Year's Best SF Novels."

> **Subjects:** Captivity • Coming of Age • First Novels • Guyanese-Canadian Authors • Interstellar War • Orphans • Space Warfare • Survival • War

> **Read On:** Lowachee's coming-of-age story shares a style with Orson Scott Card's *Ender's Game*. To meet another orphan who comes of age during an interstellar conflict, read Karl Schroeder's *Permanence*.

MacKay, Scott.

Outpost. Tor Books, 1998. 349pp.

Seventeen-year-old Felicitas is imprisoned for a crime she cannot remember committing in a rapidly decaying prison controlled by machines. She plans an escape to the unknown world on the outside, and once there she begins to recover her memory. She discovers that in order to resolve present-day conflicts, she must look for answers in sixteenth-century Italy.

Subjects: Alternative Histories • Life on Other Planets • Mind Control • Penal Colonies • Prisoners • Space Warfare • Time Travel

Read On: MacKay's other science fiction titles are *The Meek* and *Orbis*. Apart from science fiction, he has also written mysteries and a World War II thriller. Humans imprisoned in penal colonies are also a subject in Anne McCaffrey's *Freedom's Choice*, which features interspecies interactions. For more science fiction titles that blend elements of science fiction, adventure, and mystery, read Jerry Jay Carroll's *Inhuman Beings* and Timothy Zahn's *A Coming of Age*.

Munroe, Jim.

Flyboy Action Figure Comes with Gasmask. HarperFlamingoCanada, 1998. 248pp.

Shy university student Ryan can turn himself into a fly, and waitress Cassandra can make things disappear—they are made for each other. Together, in the guise of their alter egos of Flyboy and Ms. Place, they set out to correct injustices by battling forces of perceived evil (such as the tobacco companies Ryan blames for his mother's cancer).

Subjects: First Novels • Generation X • Humorous Fiction • Male–Female Relationships • Social Justice • Superheroes • Tobacco Industry • Toronto • Transformations (Magic) • University Students

Read On: Munroe's quirky storytelling is further revealed in subsequent novels, *Angry Young Spaceman*, *An Opening Act of Unspeakable Evil*, and *Everyone in Silico*. Another normal human takes on the guise of a superhero in Michael Bishop's *Count Geiger's Blues*. While Munroe's book is not a graphic novel, it shares a similar level of storytelling with graphic novels like Peter David's *Spider-Man 2* and Dan Clowes's *Ghost World*. Munroe's novel was included as one of the titles on the *Booklist* Editors' Choice Award for Adult Fiction for Young Adults.

Reeves-Stevens, Judith, and Garfield Reeves-Stevens.

Star Trek: Deep Space Nine: Millennium.

At a time when a truce currently exists between the forces of Cardassia and Bajor, Captain Benjamin Sisko, a man of science and a Starfleet officer, leads the crew of Deep Space Nine as they deal with the transients that come to inhabit the station. This series is co-authored by Garfield Reeves-Stevens.

The Fall of Terok Nor. Pocket Books, 2000.

The murder of a smuggler on the space station is the catalyst that will lead Jake Sisko on a search for a trio of lost orbs that reportedly are the key to a wormhole, a secret that has the potential to destroy the Federation.

The War of the Prophets. Pocket Books, 2000.

Inferno. Pocket Books, 2000.

> **Subjects:** Space Stations

> **Read On:** While best known for their *Star Trek* books, this writing team has also authored the series <u>Chronicles of Galen Sword</u> (*Shifter* and *Nightfeeder*) as well as *Icefire* and its sequel *Quicksilver*, which are less science fiction and more technothriller. Garfield Reeves-Stevens has written a number of solo works, including *Children of the Shroud*, *Nighteyes,* and *Dark Matter.*

Sawyer, Robert J.

♥ *Golden Fleece.* Tor Books, 1999. 252pp.

Aaron Rossman, refusing to believe that his ex-wife's death is the result of suicide, will not rest until he uncovers the individual responsible for her death. As he searches for answers on his colony ship *Argo*, headed for a distant world, he comes to fear that his own life may also be in danger when he discovers that the ship's artificially intelligent computer JASON is responsible for his-ex-wife's death. This novel, the author's first, originally published in 1990, won the Prix Aurora Award in 1992 and was reissued in 1999.

> **Subjects:** Artificial Intelligence • Colonization • First Novels • Space Travel

> **Read On:** The intelligent computer in this novel will remind readers of HAL, the computer in Arthur C. Clarke's *2001: A Space Odyssey.*

♥ *Starplex.* Ace Books, 1996. 289pp.

For twenty-some years, interstellar exploration has taken man through artificial wormholes and brought him into contact with non-human intelligent races, with little thought for how or who created these portals. Responsible for establishing first contact, the starship *Starplex* must confront this very issue when a vessel arrives through a newly created portal. This novel won the Prix Aurora Award.

> **Subjects:** First Contact • Interstellar Travel • Space Opera

> **Read On:** In this work, as in several others, such as his <u>Quintaglio Ascension</u> (*Far-Seer*, *Fossil Hunter,* and *Foreigner*), Sawyer has created a wonderful cast of aliens. Other adventurous novels of space exploration include Ben Bova's *Mars* and *Return to Mars*, C. J. Cherryh's *Finity's End,* and Arthur C. Clarke's classic *2001: A Space Odyssey.*

Schroeder, Karl.

♥ *Permanence.* Tor Books, 2002. 447pp.

The discovery of an alien starship showers fame and fortune on young Rue Cassels, igniting political intrigue and intergalactic warfare. This coming-of-age novel set in a classic space adventure raises interesting social, philosophical, and religious questions about interstellar travel. This novel won the Prix Aurora Award.

> **Subjects:** Interstellar Travel • Nanotechnology • Space Flight • Space Ships • Young Women

> **Read On:** In the same hard science fiction tradition, read Greg Egan (*Diaspora*), Ken MacLeod (*The Star Fraction*), and Gregory Benford (*COSM*). For strictly mili-

tary science fiction, read the <u>Honor Harrington Series</u> (*Changer of Worlds* and others) by David Weber, or the military exploits of Esmay Suiza (*Against the Odds*) by Elizabeth Moon.

Shatner, William.

<u>Quest for Tomorrow.</u>

In the far distant future, a group of young spacefarers, the Stone Cowboys, are led by young, charismatic leader Jim Endicott, whose DNA has been encoded to bring minds together to work like a human computer. Through the series, the group finds themselves facing the dangers and adventures of the empire. To provide scientific accuracy, the author includes a bibliography in each volume of this series.

Delta Search. HarperPrism, 1997.

Learning of his whereabouts, government agents target sixteen-year-old Jim Endicott for murder in an attempt to destroy the secret embedded in his DNA.

In Alien Hands. HarperPrism, 1997.

Step into Chaos. HarperPrism, 1999.

Beyond the Stars. HarperPrism, 2000.

Shadow Planet. Eos, 2002.

> **Subjects:** Artificial Intelligence • Cyberthrillers • DNA • Futurism • Space Flight

> **Read On:** The young protagonists in this series will remind readers of the work of Robert Heinlein (*Rocket Ship Galileo* and others).

Stirling, S. M.

The Ship Avenged. Baen, 1997. 364pp.

Belazair, the leader of the Kolnar, is looking for revenge following a defeat in battle many years earlier. He hires Joat, a young commercial ship owner, to carry a highly infectious disease designed to destroy the brain functions of the enemy society.

> **Subjects:** Aliens (Non-humanoid) • Artificial Intelligence • Biological Warfare • Space Opera • Space Warfare

> **Read On:** This novel is a sequel to *The City Who Fought*, which was co-authored with Anne McCaffrey; it is number seven in McCaffrey's <u>Brain/Brawn Series</u>. Other space operas that include artificial intelligence as part of the world are John Clute's *Appleseed* and Dan Simmons's *Ilium*.

Watts, Peter.

<u>Rifter Series.</u>

In the twenty-first century, the world is facing overcrowding, and natural resources are dwindling. In an effort to confront these crises, ocean-based power plants have been established on deep-sea rift zones.

The "rifters," cyborg creatures who inhabit this undersea world, time and again come into conflict with their land-based "masters."

Starfish. Tor Books, 1999.

Surgically modified societal misfits able to "breathe" water deep in the Pacific Ocean staff an underwater, geothermal energy power plant. Initially, the workers thrived in their isolated world, but it now appears that there is a threat coming from the sea bottom. *Starfish* was an Aurora Award finalist, a *New York Times* Notable Book of the Year, and a Locus "recommended first novel."

Maelstrom. Tor Books, 2001.

Behemoth: B-Max. Tor Books, 2004.

Behemoth: Seppuku. Tor Books, 2004.

> **Subjects:** Clarke, Lenie (Fictional Character) • Deep-sea Ecology • Future • Marine Life • Oceanographic Research Stations • Twenty-first Century • Underwater Exploration

> **Read On:** The final volume in this trilogy was published as two volumes: *Behemoth: B-Max* and *Behemoth: Seppuku.* Watts's setting and the technology he creates have a similar feel to those found in Arthur C. Clarke's *The Deep Range*; his environment is equally as harsh and isolated as that found in Joel Champetier's *The Dragon's Eye.*

Wilson, Robert Charles.

🎗 *The Chronoliths.* Tor Books, 2001. 301pp. Book Groups 📖

Mysterious pillars called "Chronoliths" begin appearing in twenty-first-century Southeast Asia, bearing plaques commemorating military conquests years in the future. Scott Warden, an out-of-work American software developer, and Sue Chopra, a physicist, attempt to discover the meaning of these arrivals and Scott's connection to them. This title was awarded the John W. Campbell Memorial Award for Best Science Fiction Novel of the Year; was nominated for the Hugo, Nebula, and Sunburst Awards; and was a *New York Times* Notable Book.

> **Subjects:** Time Travel • Twenty-first Century • Unexplained Phenomena

> **Read On:** This adventure combines elements of futuristic time travel and solid science that have much in common with Robert J. Sawyer's *Hominids.* Readers looking for a blend of adventure and time-travel elements should try Connie Willis's *Doomsday Book* or Jack Finney's *Time and Again.*

🎗 *Darwinia.* Tor Books, 1998. 320pp. Book Groups 📖

In March 1912, the "Miracle" occurs, and Europe is replaced, covered by an alien wilderness of unknown life forms and vegetation called Darwinia. Photographer Guilford Law travels in 1920 into the wild interior of Darwinia as part of a U.S. scientific expedition looking for answers to an event that has caused both religious and scientific confusion. This work received the Prix Aurora Award.

> **Subjects:** Alternative Histories • Apocalypse • Europe • Good vs. Evil • Twentieth Century

Read On: Other works by this author include *Memory Wire, Gypsies, The Divide, A Bridge of Years, The Harvest,* and *Mysterium.* In this Prix Aurora Award-winning title, the author takes an alternate look at the history of the early twentieth century. Other novels that also look at the world experience in this way include Philip K. Dick's *The Man in the High Castle,* Harry Turtledove's The Great War series (*American Front, Walk in Hell,* and *Breakthroughs*), and William Gibson and Bruce Sterling's *The Difference Engine.*

Aliens/First Contact

Man has long searched for confirmation that "he" is not alone in the universe. In the novels in this subgenre, authors tell stories that confirm that other life forms exist and describe what happens when these cultures finally meet. In some cases, the existence of humankind is threatened, and in others very different species must work together if either has any hope of survival; these are stories in which the authors may in fact be making a statement on the political situations that relate to their own community and world.

Czerneda, Julie.

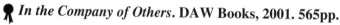

In the Company of Others. DAW Books, 2001. 565pp.

Biologist Gail Smith, determined to eradicate the Quill, a deadly life form contaminating planets humans have created for colonization, searches for a man legend says has survived contact with the menace. Her search leads her to Aaron, who suffers from a rare condition that causes him to experience severe physical pain if he has any type of close human contact. Gail comes to suspect the condition is the result of a network of fine gold lines just under his skin, possibly embedded by the Quill shortly after his birth. This work was shortlisted for the Philip K. Dick Award, was the winner of the Prix Aurora Award, and was a *Romantic Times* Reviewers' Choice Award winner, an award that was also presented to two novels by Catherine Asaro (*The Radiant Seas* and *Ascendant Sun*).

Subjects: Human–Alien Encounters • Love Stories

Read On: Czerneda's The Trade Pact Universe trilogy (*A Thousand Words for Stranger, Ties of Power,* and *To Trade the Stars*) and Web Shifters (*Beholder's Eye, Changing Vision,* and *Hidden in Sight*) also feature well-developed alien characters.

 5

Survival. DAW Books, 2004. 401pp.

Biologist Mackenzie "Mac" Connor's research into the annual Rocky Mountain salmon run is interrupted by the appearance of Brymn, a Dhryn archaeologist and the first of his race to visit Earth. Brymn is in need of the assistance of a biologist to help him with his research into the Chasm, a region of space left lifeless by unknown forces. Initially reluctant to help him, Mac is forced to join forces with the alien when his base is attacked by another alien force, the Ro.

Subjects: Alien Invasions • Biologists • Human–Alien Encounters • Life on Other Planets

Read On: This is the first in a new trilogy (<u>Species Imperative</u>) in which the author blends mystery, suspense, and science fiction. Other novels with two settings, Earth and an alien planet, include Louise Marley's *The Child Goddess* and Catherine Asaro's *Catch the Lightning*.

Sinclair, Alison.

Cavalcade. Millennium, 1998. 299pp.

Aliens have extended an invitation to earthlings to join them on an interstellar journey; all that is required is to rendezvous at an appointed location. Among the many who decide for their own reasons to make the journey are a NASA scientist, his rebellious and pregnant teenage niece, a research pathologist who is hoping the aliens will lead her to a cure for her family's genetic illness, and a young criminal on the run. Transported to the ship, they quickly discover that this voyage of discovery may in fact turn into a journey of survival. Their stories are revealed in alternating chapters, as each struggles with the challenges of building a new life and forging the new relationships necessary for survival. *Cavalcade* was nominated for the Arthur C. Clarke Award.

Subjects: Colonization • First Contact • Survival

Read On: This is Sinclair's third science fiction novel after *Legacies* and *Blueheart*; she has also co-authored *Throne Prince* with Lynda Williams. *A Paradigm of Earth* by Candas Jane Dorsey is another novel in which the question of human relationships and behaviour is explored in connection with aliens and first contact. A scientist in Robert J. Sawyer's *Frameshift* makes decisions based on the fact that he is living in the shadow of a degenerative disease.

Wilson, Robert Charles.

♟ *Blind Lake*. Tor Books, 2003. 399pp. Book Groups 📖

Scientists at Blind Lake, a federal research facility, observe the daily lives of a species of aliens on a distant planet. When the facility is unexpectedly put into lockdown and any outside contact is blocked by the military, lead scientist Nerissa Iverson and a recently arrived journalist, Chris Carmody, begin to investigate. They come to believe the inconceivable: perhaps the aliens aren't as unaware of the human observers as originally thought. This work was recognized with two awards: it was listed as a *New York Times* Notable Book of the Year, and it won a Prix Aurora Award. It was also nominated for a Hugo Award and a Sunburst Award.

Subjects: Alien Contact

Read On: Wilson's other novels include *Darwinia*, *Mysterium*, and *Second Fire*. Robert J. Sawyer has explored human–alien contact in several of his novels, including *Calculating God*, *Factoring Humanity*, and *Illegal Alien*. Wilson's well-developed characters will appeal to readers of the work of Connie Willis (*The Doomsday Book*, *Bellwether*, and others).

Cyberpunk

The classic cyberpunk title *Do Androids Dream of Electric Sheep?* by Philip K. Dick is considered by many to have launched this subgenre; science fiction writer William Gibson's debut novel *Neuromancer* is another pivotal title. These novels are an extension of hard science fiction as they integrate technology and pop culture, and in these stories the protagonist is often a marginalized member of society who refuses to be integrated into "the system," which is usually the enemy. In this clash, there is an attempt to turn the system's technological tools to the protagonist's own ends.

Gibson, William.

Bridge Trilogy.

The stories of a group of recurring characters in the post-millennial period are told with a high level of detail, as they utilize cybertechnology to face the challenges of the new age.

🎗 *Virtual Light.* Bantam Books, 1993.

In 2005, bicycle courier Chevette Washington and ex-cop Berry Rydell join forces against a corrupt security firm after they discover that the sunglasses Chevette impulsively stole are programmed with industrial secrets and enable the wearer to see virtual images. This title won the Prix Aurora Award.

Idoru. Putnam, 1996.

All Tomorrow's Parties. Putnam, 1999.

> **Subjects:** High Technology • Technological Advances • Twenty-first Century • Virtual Reality

> **Read On:** Gibson's early cyberpunk novel, *Neuromancer* (1984), received the Hugo, the Nebula, and the Philip K. Dick Awards, a rare achievement. *Count Zero* and *Mona Lisa Overdrive* are among Gibson's other cyberpunk novels. Another "classic" cyberpunk novel is John Shirley's *City Come A-Walkin'*, which shares a similar near-future setting.

5

McMahon, Donna.

Dance of Knives. Tor Books, 2001. 416pp.

Twenty-first-century Vancouver is a violently divided city, controlled by gangs and rival tongs. Klale, a Fisher Guild member, has turned her back on her past after her father's death and has moved into the city to look for a new life. She finds herself caught up in a struggle to rescue Blade, a gang enforcer more automaton than human being.

> **Subjects:** British Columbia • Cyberpunk • Dystopias • First Novels • Gangs • Twenty-first century • Vancouver

> **Read On:** Gangs battle in *Bloodtide* by Melvin Burgess and the YA novel *Nevernever* by Will Shetterly. Kim Stanley Robinson's Orange County Trilogy (also known as The Three Californias Trilogy: *The Wild Shore,*

The Gold Coast, and *Pacific Edge*) looks at a broken society, the future, and the impact of technology on both the society and the future.

Dystopias/Parallel Worlds

Dystopian novels explore societal decay, presenting an image of the potential future of our society, suggesting that unless changes in direction are made, society should prepare for the worst. These stories are presented as cautionary tales against possible doom. The tone of these novels is usually dark and often depressing, and many, such as Margaret Atwood's *The Handmaid's Tale* and *Oryx and Crake*, are capable of creating a deep sense of dread in the reader.

Parallel world novels are those in which the characters discover, through a variety of means, that a parallel world or other dimension exists alongside their own. These worlds will often hold a commodity of value that must be protected or individuals whose skills are needed if some challenge is to be overcome. These novels present an alternate way to examine reality and may, depending on the story lines, come the closest to blending science fiction and fantasy. Life in the other world does not have to conform to realistic standards and may thus contain "fantastical" elements, while the resolution may involve some type of quest. Readers of this subgenre may want to consider the titles in the alternate and parallel worlds section in the fantasy section of this chapter as well.

Armstrong, Luanne.

The Bone House. New Star Books, 2002. 277pp. Book Groups 📖

Fleeing a now-ravaged Vancouver, Lia joins a commune in the interior of British Columbia. Together the members struggle to survive and keep their land out of the hands of corporations.

> **Subjects:** British Columbia • Communal Living • Survival • Vancouver • Young Women

> **Read On:** Armstrong's depiction of Vancouver is reminiscent of the city Paul Auster portrays in *In the Country of Last Things*. Survival is a recurring theme in Mike Tanner's *Acting the Giddy Goat*. A family flees the city following environmental and social collapse in Knut Faldbakken's dystopian novel *Twilight Country*. While not science fiction, the harshness of the Vancouver landscape comes forth in Mark Macdonald's *Flat*. Other titles by Armstrong are *The Colour of Water* and *Bordering*.

Atwood, Margaret.

Oryx and Crake. McClelland & Stewart, 2003. 378pp. Book Groups 📖

In the near future, Jimmy, now known as Snowman, is very much alone, with little more than his recollections of the world as he once knew it. With Earth now virtually a wasteland, lacking even time, Jimmy revisits his life and the ultimately apocalyptic events that led to the end of civilization. While doing so he considers the role his best friend, "Crake," and a young woman named Oryx played in the destruction. This novel was nominated for the Governor General's Literary Award for Fiction, the Man Booker Prize, and the Orange Prize for Fiction.

Subjects: Biotechnology • Ecological Disaster • Environmental Degradation • Futurism • Genetic Engineering • Men's Friendships • New York • Triangles

Read On: This is Atwood's eleventh novel, and of all the titles in her body of work, *The Handmaid's Tale* most closely reflects the themes and feel of this novel set in the near future. T. Coraghessan Boyle's *A Friend of the Earth* is another novel in which the main character reflects back on how the environment of the near future came to its current state.

Doctorow, Cory.

🕮 *Down and Out in the Magic Kingdom*. **Tom Doherty Associates, 2003. 208pp.**

In the twenty-second century, 100-year-old Jules, currently inhabiting the body of a forty-year-old, has secured his ultimate dream job: he runs the Haunted Mansion ride at Disney World. When he awakens in a cloned body, he realizes he has been murdered and sets out to uncover what he believes is a plot by a rival group to take control of the park. This novel won the Locus Award for Best First Novel.

Subjects: Clones and Cloning • Disney World, Florida • Dystopias • Satire • Twenty-second Century

Read On: Doctorow also weaves suspense into his second novel set in the near future, *Eastern Standard Tribe.* Like William Gibson in *Neuromancer,* Doctorow places his flawed characters in situations that reveal the imperfections of the society he creates. Other novels that combine science fiction and satire are Ben Bova's *Cyberbooks* and Bruce Wagner's *The Chrysanthemum Palace.*

Donovan, Rita.

The Plague Saint. **Tesseract Books, 1997. 155pp.**

Hiding from the ruling theological group in a plague-ridden twenty-first-century Canada, Lily Dalriada, a woman whose child was illicitly conceived by actual intercourse, takes refuge with a virtual-sex-scenarios creator to avoid becoming the church's next saint. While in hiding she discovers a door that will lead her into the medieval and Renaissance periods.

Subjects: Florence • Italy • Plague • Time Travel • Twenty-first Century • Virtual Reality • Women Saints

Read On: Donovan won awards for *Daisy Circus* and *Landed.* Women's control over procreation in the future is a theme in *The Handmaid's Tale* by Margaret Atwood and *The Misconceiver* by Lucy Ferriss. Ann Benson's *The Plague Tales* is another novel that blends past and future in a plague environment.

Hopkinson, Nalo.

Midnight Robber. Warner Books, 2000. 329pp. Book Groups 📖

Tan-Tan calls upon the skills and characteristics of the Robber Queen, a character from her childhood imaginary games, as she attempts to adapt to life on a harsh prison planet.

> **Subjects:** Adultery • Fathers and Daughters • Incest • Magic • Murder • Mythology • Space Colonies

> **Read On:** Hopkinson is also the creator of the highly imagined world in *Brown Girl in the Ring,* recipient of the Locus Award for Best First Novel and the first book to win the Warner Aspect First Novel Contest. Readers of *A Clockwork Orange* by Anthony Burgess will enjoy the Caribbean-inspired dialect of *Midnight Robber.* Pauline Melville's *The Ventriloquist's Tale* also combines myth with language to create her story, set in Guyana.

Ryman, Geoff.

Air. St. Martin's Griffin, 2002. 400pp. Book Groups 📖

In 2020, Kizuldah, Karzistan, is a small rice-farming village relatively untouched by international culture, and with limited access to current information technologies. In short, it remains much as it has been for centuries. However, this is all about to change because Air, a UN-sponsored new technology designed to turn the mind into a super receiver, is about to be launched. Dressmaker Mae Chung is the local fashion expert, and through her visits to larger neighbouring towns, she has become regarded as a somewhat informal leader. During the course of the test, Mae takes on the memories of her elderly neighbour, who dies during the test, and armed with knowledge of past, present, and future, she struggles to carry on as her community descends deeper into turmoil.

> **Subjects:** Communication • Dystopias • Memory • Technological Innovations

> **Read On:** In this novel Ryman revisits themes discussed in two of his earlier novels. In *The Unconquered Country* he looks at colonialism, and in *The Child Garden* he chronicles the story of a supposedly outcast woman who is perceived to be powerless, and who ultimately rises to the challenges she faces. Like Margaret Atwood's *The Handmaid's Tale* and *Oryx and Crake,* this novel of speculative fiction is a cautionary tale warning the reader to look at where the world is going.

Sawyer, Robert J.

Neanderthal Parallax.

In this trilogy, Sawyer explores the religious experience as a function of brain chemistry, in a fascinating and challenging way, through the development of a relationship between a Neanderthal and a human physicist who come from parallel worlds.

🎗 *Hominids*. Tor Books, 2002.

During a quantum-computing experiment, Ponter Boddit, a Neanderthal, crosses over from a parallel Earth to our world. Ponter, a quantum scientist, struggles to understand the human society so different from his own, while working with his human colleagues to find a way for him to return to his own world. This work received the Hugo Award.

Humans. Tor Books, 2003.

Ponter Boddit brings Mary Vaughan back to his very different world in this sequel to *Hominids*. Neanderthal society has developed in distinctly more ecologically sound ways than human society and has found ways to ensure its citizens a crime-free life in a safe environment. Mary and Ponter's relationship develops further in this instalment, which highlights Mary's experiences as the outsider in an unfamiliar culture.

Hybrids. Tor Books, 2003.

Neanderthals and humans have been in contact with each other for some time now, long enough that tension begins to rise within each society. Will humans, who have been polluting and overpopulating their planet, decide to try to stake out a claim on the Neanderthal's unblemished world? Ponter and Mary's relationship continues, with a child on the way. How will the child be raised, and will it be instructed in religion—or can it be?

> **Subjects:** Alternative Histories • Eco-fiction • Neanderthals • Parallel Universes • Physicists • Toronto
>
> **Read On:** Sawyer's exploration of other worlds and societies will appeal to readers of *The Clan of the Cave Bear* by Jean Auel or *Darwin's Radio* by Greg Bear. This trilogy will also appeal to those who look for character-driven novels, such as the stories written by Nora Roberts, in which readers connect to the romantic lives of the characters.

Wilson, Robert Charles.

🏵 *Mysterium.* Bantam Books, 1994. Book Groups 📖

> When the governing "Proctors" discover the knowledge needed to build an atomic bomb, and a small community becomes the first designated test site, a small group of townspeople decide they must work against the controlling government before it is too late. This novel received the Philip K. Dick Award.
>
> **Subjects:** Dystopias • Michigan • Unidentified Flying Objects
>
> **Read On:** Wilson creates a world with a structured government and restricted freedoms that is reminiscent of two classic speculative novels, *1984* by George Orwell and *Brave New World* by Aldous Huxley.

Wright, Ronald.

🏵 *A Scientific Romance.* **New York, Picador, 1998. 352pp. Book Groups** 📖

> English archaeologist David Lambert travels in a time machine to a future Britain in AD 2500 and discovers a world that is at once familiar and completely alien and dangerous. This novel received the David Higham

Prize for Fiction, and *The New York Times* included it on its Notable Books list in 1998.

> **Subjects** England • London • Post-apocalyptic • Time Machines • Twenty-fifth Century
>
> **Read On:** Wright has used the classic time-travel novel, H. G. Wells's *The Time Machine*, as a jumping off point for his novel. He then goes on to craft a literary work rich in scientific Victoriana. The post-apocalyptic imagery found here is similar to Nevil Shute's *On the Beach.* Wright combines history, adventure, romance, and mystery in his second novel, *Henderson's Spear*, the story of a young woman who journeys to the South Seas and is imprisoned in a Tahitian jail; while there she works through her past and the past of a long-deceased relative.

Genreblending: Science Fiction and Mystery

Science fiction author Robert J. Sawyer once remarked that the two genres that have the most in common are science fiction and mystery, and that therefore the blending of the two is a natural. He went on to say, "Both prize the intellectual process of puzzle solving, and both require stories to be plausible and hinge on the way things really do work. In well-written science fiction, you don't explain the background of the story; rather, you drop subtle clues throughout the text, letting the reader piece together the nature of reality in the world you're portraying; the science-fiction reader is a natural detective—the genre demands it" (Sawyer 1997). In the stories found here, a futuristic detective, whether cop, P.I., or someone attempting to right a wrong, seeks justice.

Gotlieb, Phyllis.

Flesh and Gold. Tor Books, 1998. 286pp.

> Shortly after agreeing to handle a case for a senior judge on the mining planet Fthel V, Skerow, a gill-breathing lizard-woman judge, must deal with the fact that this senior judge has been implicated in both the trial and a subsequent murder. At the same time she happens to see an amphibious human enslaved and on display to promote a local brothel. Initially not suspecting a connection between these two events, she is quickly on the trail of the murderers somewhere within the sex-trade and snuff-film world.

> **Subjects:** Aliens • Interstellar Relations • Judges • Murder

> **Read On:** Many of the characters in this novel reappear in *Violent Stars* and *Mindworlds*, set in the same GalFed universe; included among Gotlieb's other works of science fiction are *The Kingdom of the Cats* and *Heart of Red Iron*. Like other writers in this subgenre, Gotlieb combines elements of hardboiled mystery and science fiction in a style reminiscent of Philip K. Dick (*Do Androids Dream of Electric Sheep?* and others). English Canada's first juried award for science fiction, The Sunburst Award for Canadian Literature of the Fantastic, is named for Gotlieb's first novel, *Sunburst*. In 1982 she received Canada's Prix Aurora Award for best novel for *A Judgment of Dragons* and for her lifetime contribution to Canadian science fiction and fantasy.

Green, Terence M.

Blue Limbo. Tor Books, 1997. 253pp.

In the near future, scientists have developed the Blue Limbo, a process that brings back the dead, even if only for a short time. Following a series of events such as the murder of his partner and several other murder attempts including one against himself, recently fired Toronto cop Mitch Helwig takes matters into his own hands. Helwig convinces doctors to give his murdered partner the Blue Limbo treatment and sets out to gain justice through whatever means it takes.

Subjects: Crime • Police • Toronto • Twenty-first Century

Read On: More mystery than science fiction, this novel will be enjoyed by readers looking for a protagonist who takes to the "mean" streets, such as in an early work by Philip K. Dick, *Do Androids Dream of Electric Sheep?* or K. W. Jeter's works (*Noir* and others).

Sawyer, Robert J.

Flashforward. Tor Books, 1999. 319pp.

A group of physicists conducting research into the nature of an elusive nuclear particle are suddenly propelled, very briefly, twenty-one years into the future, where they glimpse their own destiny. Upon "awakening" from this experience, in which the whole world has participated, thus causing worldwide havoc, they are faced with the challenge of righting what has gone so horribly wrong in their lives, to ensure that they have a future. This novel received the Prix Aurora Award

Subjects: Physicists • Time Travel

Read On: In both *Frameshift* and *Illegal Alien*, Sawyer blends mystery and science fiction into a compelling tale. Many authors set their stories in the near future, including Greg Bear (*Darwin's Radio*), Michael Flynn (*Firestar*), and Nancy Kress (*Maximum Light*). Another novel that has scientists in a race against time is *Timeline* by Michael Crichton, which blends historical detail and time travel into a fast-paced story.

The Terminal Experiment. HarperPrism, 1995. 333pp.

Dr. Peter Hobson, while conducting research into the human brain and theories of immortality, creates three clones of himself. When these AI experiments escape the bounds of Hobson's system, and one begins to kill, Hobson must decide how to deal with these copies of himself. This novel won the Nebula Award and the HOMer Award.

Subjects: Artificial Intelligence • Clones and Cloning • Immortality • Scientific Experiments

Read On: Other authors who blend science fiction and mystery include Terence M. Green (*Blue Limbo*) and J. D. Robb (In Death books). The main character in Connie Willis's *Passage* is also involved in research into near-death experiences. Greg Egan's *Permutation City* also explores immortality and artificial intelligence. This novel originally appeared in instalments in the science fiction magazine *Analog*, entitled "Hobson's Choice."

Shatner, William.

Tek Series.

In this fast-paced series set in the twenty-second century in a high-tech world of robots and androids, hard-boiled P.I. Jake Cardigan is an ex-cop and ex-con based in Los Angeles who wages a war against those drug lords who manufacture and distribute the designer drug "Tek," the world's deadliest drug.

TekWar. Putnam, 1989.

TekLords. Putnam, 1991.

TekLab. Putnam, 1991.

Tek Vengeance. Putnam, 1993.

Tek Secret. G. P. Putnam's Sons, 1993.

Tek Power. G.P. Putnam's Sons, 1994.

Tek Money. G. P. Putnam's Sons, 1995.

Tek Kill. G. P. Putnam's Sons, 1996.

Tek Net. G. P. Putnam's Sons, 1997.

The kidnapping of his partner Sid's ex-wife pits Jake and Sid against the TekLords, who will do anything to stop the distribution of a new form of the drug Tek. This new form can be transmitted through computer networks and would render obsolete their original product.

Subjects: Androids • Drug Traffic • Los Angeles • Robots • Twenty-second Century

Read On: For a classic novel set in the twenty-second century, try Arthur C. Clarke's *The Fountains of Paradise*. Other series set in this same century are Babylon 5 by Greg Keyes and the Emortals Series by Brian Stableford, in which biotechnology is at the centre of the plot development.

Stewart, Sean.

♣ *Passion Play.* Beach Holme Publishing, 1992. 231pp.

Diane Fletcher is a recognized "Shaper": she has the ability to see and feel the emotions of others. As a freelance detective she works with the police to solve crimes and see the perpetrators brought in for televised justice. Following the death of one of the country's leading actors, she is brought into the investigation and soon finds herself somewhere between justice and vengeance. This novel, a blend of science fiction and mystery, was recognized with awards in both categories, a Prix Aurora Award and an Arthur Ellis Award for Best First Novel.

Subjects: Actors and Acting • Women Mediums

Read On: In Raphael Carter's *The Fortunate Fall*, another futuristic mystery, the thoughts and feelings of the female protagonist are open to millions of people through virtual reality technology implanted in her brain. The female protagonist in J. D. Robb's In Death books also experiences similar questions of conscience as she investigates crime.

Fantasy

Among those who really know the genre of fantasy fiction, there is an ongoing debate as to its definition. For the general populace who would like to know just a little something about the genre, however, let us quote Diana Tixier Herald, author of *Fluent in Fantasy: A Guide to Reading Interests*: "Fantasy is the stuff of myth, of flights of fancy, folklore, fairy tales, magic, and heroes" (1999, 3). There are some characteristics that seem to be relevant throughout the genre:

1. The story/world created follows its own rules of order and is not bound by scientific or natural laws. This world often provides the greatest appeal for the reader.

2. The rules of order are created by the author, thus making the author responsible for the logic and consistency found therein.

3. Usually the changing force is magic or some other supernatural element.

4. The author often (but not always) creates an entire new world with its own geography, population, and rules of order. J. R. R. Tolkien (Middle Earth) and C. S. Lewis (Narnia) are early and noted exemplars of this.

5. These worlds are often populated with mythical beasts and creatures such as dragons, fairies, and elves.

The difficulty in classifying subgenres of fantasy is that there is a lot of cross-blending with science fiction, horror, and even mainstream fiction in the form of magic realism or alternative history. And within the subgenres themselves, there is much mixing of types. Because we have a relatively small sample here, we have created larger groupings of subgenres and combined novels that include characteristics of similar subgenres.

Sword and Sorcery

This subgenre is perhaps the best known, or most expected, in fantasy fiction. It includes such elements as the invented world, a quest, magical creatures, good versus evil, a large cast of characters including wizards and sorcerers, and often a setting resembling the medieval world. There is often one hero, often a young one, pitted against many. For our purposes, we have included in this subgenre the fairy tale, the high/epic fantasy, and the heroic.

Baird, Alison.

The Dragon Throne.

This adult work by an established young adult fantasy writer combines mythology, the quest, and mythical beasts along with the epic battle between good and evil.

The Stone of the Stars. Aspect/Warner Books, 2004.

Four young people gather together in search of the Stone of the Star, trying to reach it before the Prince of Darkness finds it. They are also involved in the search for the long-prophesied Tryna Lia, the woman who will use the Stone of the Star to defend her people against this same Prince of Darkness.

The Empire of the Stars. Aspect/Warner Books, 2004.

The Archons of the Stars. Aspect/Warner Books, 2005.

> **Subjects:** Dragons • Magic • Mythic Beasts • Prophecies • Quests • Trilogies

> **Read On:** This trilogy falls firmly in the tradition of Marion Zimmer Bradley (the <u>Avalon</u> Series) and Stephen Lawhead (<u>The Pendragon Cycle</u>).

Bakker, R. Scott.

The Prince of Nothing.

An epic fantasy, this as yet unfinished trilogy centres on the world of Eärwa, about twenty years before the Second Apocalypse. It explores the origins of religious violence, using as its model the Wars of the Crusades; the Holy War in this trilogy becomes a character as clearly delineated as the four main protagonists.

The Darkness That Comes Before. Penguin Canada, 2003. **Book Groups** 📖

Two millennia following the Apocalypse, the world of Eärwa is roiling with rumours about the reappearance of the No-God Mog, whose heretical sect had captured the Holy City of the Inrithi church. Pitted against him are Anasûrimbor Kellhus, a descendant of ancient kings, and Drusus Achamian, sorcerer and spy. This title was on the lists of SF Site's Reader's Choice Best SF and Fantasy Books of 2003; Best of 2003: Locus Recommended Reading; and Editor's Pick: Amazon.ca Best of 2003.

The Warrior-Prophet. Penguin Canada, 2004.

> **Subjects:** Apocalypse • Crusades • Good vs. Evil • Magic • Power Struggles • Sorcerers • Trilogies • Warriors

> **Read On:** The completeness of Bakker's world of Eärwa has been compared to Tolkien's (<u>The Lord of the Rings</u>) and Frank Herbert's (<u>Dune</u>). The fine detail in the series is much like that of Greg Keyes in *The Briar King*.

Bradley, Rebecca.

Gil Trilogy.

Tig is the central character in all three volumes of this trilogy, as he grows from a young man, through an arranged marriage, to being the father of a grown son. Throughout the trilogy, Tig has a significant involvement with the Lady in Gil, a statue with legendary powers.

Lady in Gil. V. Gollancz, 1996.

Tig's older brother Arkolef should have gone on the quest for the Lady in Gil, but when he broke his leg putting his armour on backwards, Tig was the natural choice, however unsuited he himself felt for the task. He must return to the land (the Island of Gil) from which his royal family had been exiled in order to find the magical statue of the Lady in Gil.

Scion's Lady. V. Gollancz, 1997.

Lady Pain. V. Gollancz, 1998.

> **Subjects:** Exile • Kingdoms • Prophecies • Quests • Trilogies

> **Read On:** Bradley's writing has been described as a cross between Terry Pratchett and Glen Cook.

Duncan, Dave.

A Handful of Men.

This series is the sequel to an earlier series, <u>A Man of His Word.</u> The loophole left in the previous series meant that evil would prevail if the monarchs Rap and Inos did not embark on yet another adventure to wield their particular magic and save their kingdoms.

The Cutting Edge. Ballantine, 1992.

Shortlisted for a Locus Award.

Upland Outlaws. Ballantine, 1993.

The Stricken Field. Ballantine, 1993.

The Living God. Ballantine, 1994.

> **Subjects:** Dwarfs • Elves • Magic • Wizards

> **Read On:** Other series of this genre are R. A. Salvatore's <u>The Crimson Shadow</u>, Dennis McKiernan's <u>Hèl's Crucible Duology,</u> and, of course, J. R. R. Tolkien's <u>The Lord of the Rings</u>.

Tales of the King's Blades.

The King's Blades are students sent to Ironhall for rebellious behaviour who are then trained to become the world's best swordsmen. They are riveted in their loyalty to the king by the piercing of their own hearts with a magical sword. Each book in this series can stand on its own, but the series as a whole presents the larger picture.

The Gilded Chain. Avon, 1998.

Shortlisted for a Locus award.

Lord of the Fire Lands. AvonEos, 1999.

Sky of Swords. AvonEos, 2000.

> **Subjects:** Courtiers • Imaginary Kingdoms • Knights • Loyalty • Swordsmen

> **Read On:** Other schools for preparing students in these arcane arts include the most famous one of all, J. K. Rowling's Hogwarts School of Witchcraft in her <u>Harry Potter</u> series; lesser-known schools create the setting for E. Rose Sabin's *A School for Sorcery* and Caroline Stevermer's <u>A College of Magics</u>.

Chronicles of the King's Blades.

A continuation of the series <u>Tales of the King's Blades</u>, this series involves three of Ironhall's best Blades. Young Beaumont proves his mettle at the outset but ultimately returns to the king in shame and disgrace, bested for the moment by the tyrant Czar Igor.

Paragon Lost. Eos, 2002.

Impossible Odds. Eos, 2003.

The Jaguar Knights. Eos, 2004.

> **Subjects:** Bodyguards • Imaginary Kingdoms • Knights • Magic • Quests • Swordsmen
>
> **Read On:** Perhaps the best-known swordsmen are Dumas's three Musketeers, whose story Steven Brust re-creates in a parallel world in the series <u>The Viscount of Adrilankha.</u> Other swordfighter stories include Michael Moorcock's *The Fortress of the Pearl* and Ellen Kushner's *Swordspoint.*

Erikson, Steven.

A Tale of the Malazan Book of the Fallen.

A complete world, Malazan is an intercontinental empire, constantly embroiled in war in order to maintain its sovereignty. Warrior-mages, gods, and imperial troops battle with and against each other for all the reasons battles are fought around the world. This epic fantasy series is projected to comprise ten volumes.

Gardens of the Moon. Bantam, 1999.

Military engineers Sergeant Whiskeyjack and his Bridgeburners, and Tattersall, the field-grade mage, are all ready to go home from wars already fought when their empress, Laseen, commands yet another battle, this time against the Free City of Darujhistan. She is trying to expand her empire and has found resistance in an alliance between Moon's Spawn (a free-floating fortress) and the free cities.

Deadhouse Gates. Bantam, 2000.

Memories of Ice. Bantam, 2001.

House of Chains. Bantam, 2002.

Midnight Tides. Bantam, 2004.

> **Subjects:** Imaginary Wars and Battles • Loyalty • Magicians • Malazan (Imaginary Place) • Warriors
>
> **Read On:** Another military fantasy in the vein of Erikson's series is Glen Cook's <u>The Chronicles of the Black Company</u> series. But Erikson's world is more than a battleground, and he has also been favourably compared to George R. R. Martin (<u>A Song of Ice and Fire</u> series) and Robert Jordan (<u>The Wheel of Time</u> series).

Greenwood, Ed.

Band of Four.

A tetralogy written by the creator of the <u>Forgotten Realms®</u>, this quest-based fantasy series focuses on the world of Aglirta and the Band of Four, given the task of restoring the king to the throne and keeping him there. The Band consists of the warrior Hawkril, the thief Craer, the healer Sarasper, and the sorceress Lady Embra Silvertree. There is a fifth novel, *The Silent House* (Tor Books, 2004), which is the beginning of a new series entitled <u>A Chronicle of Aglirta</u>. This novel goes beyond the <u>Band of Four</u> to explore the land of Aglirta on a larger scale.

The Kingless Land. Tor Books, 2000.

As warring barons fight to gain control of Aglirta, two outlawed soldiers join forces with the daughter of a rival baron and a reclusive healer to seek out the legendary worldstones; these stones have the power to awaken the sleeping King of Aglirta and restore order to the land.

The Vacant Throne. Tor Books, 2001.

A Dragon's Ascension. Tor Books, 2002.

The Dragon's Doom. Tor Books, 2003.

> **Subjects:** Aglirta (Imaginary Place) • Imaginary Kingdoms • Magic • Quests • Rulers • Sorcery • Warriors

> **Read On:** This quest-based fantasy series will appeal to readers of Tolkien's <u>The Lord of the Rings</u> series. Greenwood shares a similar style of storytelling with Dave Duncan and Steven Brust.

Huff, Tanya.

Quarters Series.

The Quarters, or Kigh, are the four elements—air, water, fire, earth—that exist within us, and the bards in this series are often able to sing or call these elements forth. Some can call only one or two, but others can call all four, and this they do if one or more has left someone's body, or if the bards need special help with other difficulties. And difficulties abound for those in the Empire of Shkoder.

Sing the Four Quarters. DAW, 1994.

Fifth Quarter. DAW, 1995.

Shortlisted for the Sapphire Award.

No Quarter. DAW, 1996.

Shortlisted for the Prix Aurora Award.

The Quartered Sea. DAW, 1999.

 Shortlisted for the Gaylactic Spectrum Award.

 5

> **Subjects:** Bards • Imaginary Kingdoms • Magic • Power Struggles • Quests • Survival

> **Read On:** For different takes on the bardic fantasy, try Anne Bishop (*Shadows and Light*), Patricia McKillip (*Song for the Basilisk*), or Kristine Kathryn Rusch (*The White Mists of Power*).

Jones, Dennis.

The House of the Pandragore.

Billed as a trilogy, this sword-and-sorcery series provides thus far two novels that could each stand alone, were a reader to pick up just one. The unifying character in both books is Theatana, an evil sorceress with designs on the throne. She is willing to perform maleficent deeds regardless of the relationship she has with her potential victims.

The Stone and the Maiden. HarperCollinsCanada, 1999.

As the evil Tathars start their invasion, Mandine Dascaris begins a quest to search for a little-known artefact, the Signata, which may be the key to saving her people from the destruction of the evil sorcerer Erkai the Chain, leader of the Tathars.

The Mask and the Sorceress. HarperCollinsCanada, 2001.

Subjects: Barbarians • Magic • Quests • Sorcerers • Talismans

Read On: Other authors of the sword-and-sorcery genre include Juliet Marillier, Robert Jordan, Mercedes Lackey, Tanith Lee, Patricia McKillip, and Anne McCaffrey.

Kay, Guy Gavriel.

♣ *Tigana*. Penguin Books, 1990. 673pp. Book Groups 📖

While the sorcerer Brandin is fighting for control of one province in the Peninsula of the Palm, he sends his beloved son Stevan to Tigana, to fight for control of that province. When Stevan is killed, Brandin vows revenge and places a curse on the province, saying that no one not born there will ever hear its name. Total subjugation and oppression of the province is now his vengeful goal. Kay won the Prix Aurora Award for this, his first stand-alone novel, which was also shortlisted for the World Fantasy, the Locus, and the Mythopoeic Awards.

Subjects: Good vs. Evil • Revenge • Sorcery • War

Read On: Revenge is at the heart of many battle-filled stories and can involve individuals or entire countries, sparked by personal harm done, as in Brandin's loss of his son, or harm done on a more political level. Just a few stories inspired by a need for revenge are Harry Turtledove's <u>Darkness</u> series, Raymond Feist's <u>Conclave of Shadows</u> series, and Robin Hobb's <u>The Farseer</u> trilogy.

Marston, Ann.

The Rune Blade Trilogy.

Three generations of a royal family take charge of the Kingmaker's Sword, a magical blade that will help them defend against the wicked sorcerers.

Kingmaker's Sword. HarperCollinsCanada, 1996.

Raised as a slave, a young Tyran prince escapes his captors, carrying with him a sword taken from a bounty hunter. He joins forces with a man who is in fact his uncle, who adopts him and names him Kian. A beautiful warrior from Skai hires them to locate the lost grandson of the king of a rival kingdom. This mysterious woman understands the power of the sword and the role it will play in Kian's destiny. This novel was shortlisted for the HOMer Award

The Western King. HarperCollinsCanada, 1996.

♣ *Broken Blade*. Harper CollinsCanada, 1997.

Winner of the HOMer Award.

Subjects: Celts • Sword and Sorcery • Trilogies

Read On: Marston's mix of sword-and-sorcery fantasy with humour will appeal to readers of Katherine Kurtz's <u>The Heirs of Saint Camber</u> series or Jennifer

Roberson's <u>The Sword-Dancer Saga</u>. Romance and fantasy are blended in R. Garcia y Robertson's Robyn Stafford novels.

Patton, Fiona.

Tales of the Branion Realm.

The power of the Living Flame inhabits the incumbent ruler of Branion, but it is only as good as the vessel that carries it, and if the incumbent ruler fails in the battle of good versus evil, the Flame will go the way of the ruler.

The Stone Prince. Daw, 1997.

In the first book of the <u>Tales of the Branion Realm</u> series, Patton creates a world of gender equality and sexual freedom. In this first volume, Crown Prince Demnor must take control of his birthright power while overcoming the traitors who plot to overthrow the Heathlands.

The Painter Knight. DAW, 1998.

The Granite Shield. DAW, 1999.

The Golden Sword. DAW, 2001.

> **Subjects:** Branion (Imaginary Place) • Gender Equality • Gender Freedom • Identity

> **Read On:** The political intrigues central to Patton's plots are writ large in any number of fantasy writings. To name a few: *The Golden Key* by Melanie Rawn, Jennifer Roberson, and Kate Elliott; *Kushiel's Dart* by Jacqueline Carey; and *Illusion* by Paula Volsky.

Russell, Sean.

The Swans' War.

Set in medieval times, this high fantasy pits two families against each other, dividing the kingdom in their attempts to win the throne of that kingdom for their children.

The One Kingdom. EOS, 2001.

Three young men from a vale north of Ayr travel down the river Wynnd looking for a little adventure. They find it in the feud between the Renné and the Wills families, fighting for supremacy over the Kingdom of Ayr.

The Isle of Battle. EOS, 2002.

The Shadow Roads. EOS, 2004.

> **Subjects:** Ayr Kingdom (Imaginary Place) • Family Feuds • Inheritance and Succession • Political Intrigue • Sorcery • Trilogies

> **Read On:** The kingdom and its successors are also at stake in Joanne Bertin's *The Last Dragonlord*, C. J. Cherryh's *Fortress of Dragons* and in Greg Keyes's series, <u>The Kingdoms of Thorn and Bone</u>.

Sagara, Michelle.

Book of the Sundered.

This tetralogy pits the very basic Light against the Dark, and for much of the series, it looks as though Dark will surely win out.

Into the Dark Lands. Del Rey, 1991.

Children of the Blood. Del Rey, 1992.

Lady of Mercy. Del Rey, 1993.

Chains of Darkness, Chains of Light. Del Rey, 1994.

Subjects: Enchantment • Good vs. Evil • Magic • Memory • Warriors

Read On: Tanya Huff's *Gate of Darkness, Circle of Light,* and *The Fire's Stone*; Jane Yolen's <u>The Great Alta Saga</u> (*Sister Light, Sister Dark*; *White Jenna*; and *The One-Armed Queen*); and Oliver Johnson's <u>The Lightbringer Trilogy</u> (*The Forging of the Shadows*, *The Nations of the Night*, and *The Last Star at Dawn*) all treat the theme of the Light battling to overcome the Darkness. Michelle Sagara also writes as Michelle West.

Stewart, Sean.

🎖 *Nobody's Son*. Maxwell Macmillan, 1993. 233pp. Book Groups 📖

Nobody's son is Shielder's Mark, a commoner who breaks the spell of the Red Keep, winning for himself the right to have granted whatever wish he desires. And what he desires is to win the king's youngest daughter, Gail. But this does not mean the typical end of the fairy tale: life becomes complicated, particularly at court, and particularly in marriage to an independent woman he barely knows. Stewart won the Prix Aurora Award for this novel, and was shortlisted for the Phantastik award, a German prize awarded to Best Foreign Novel.

Subjects: Coming of Age • Courts • Kings • Magic • Spells

Read On: It is not unusual for fantasy novels to have young adolescents as their heroes. Other such stories in which young people save the day (or the kingdom) include *The Knight* by Gene Wolfe, *A Song for Arbonne* by Guy Gavriel Kay, and *The Chosen*, the first in <u>The Stone Dance of the Chameleon</u> series by Ricardo Pinto.

Tower, S. D.

The Assassins of Tamurin. HarperCollinsCanada, 2003. 464pp. Book Groups 📖

Befriended by the Despotana of Tamurin, a woman who later proves to be a deadly sorceress, the orphan Lale has been trained as an assassin and sent to eliminate Terem Rathai, ruler of Bethiya. Makina, the Despotana, wants him assassinated to avenge the death of her own son, but Lale has fallen in love with Terem and must find a way to circumvent the orders given her by Makina.

Subjects: Assassins • Imaginary Kingdoms • Orphans • Revenge • Spies

Read On: Life does not always follow a logical path for the assassins in some fantasies, where the would-be assassin falls in love with the intended target or otherwise has a change of heart. Judith Tarr's *Alamut* and Robin Hobb's *Assassin's Quest* are two such novels. Orphans are not unusual in fantasy fiction, as they can be credible pawns. Orphans are major characters in *Across the Nightingale Floor* (volume 1 in the <u>Tales of the Otori</u>) by Lian Hearn, *Daughter of Exile* by Isabel Glass, and *Lens of the World* by R. A. MacAvoy (the first volume in <u>The Lens of the World Trilogy</u>).

West, Michelle.

The Sun Sword.

This series loosely follows on an earlier duology by West, <u>The Sacred Hunt</u>, with characters from that first series appearing here. In this series, there are two major kingdoms, the Dominion of Annagar and the Essalieyan Empire, each culturally different from the other. In the early part of the series story, the two kingdoms fight between themselves, but as the larger story progresses, they begin more and more to join forces against a greater evil.

The Broken Crown. DAW, 1997.

The Uncrowned King. DAW, 1998.

The Shining Court. DAW, 1999.

Sea of Sorrows. DAW, 2001.

The Riven Shield. DAW, 2003.

The Sun Sword. DAW, 2004.

> **Subjects:** Alliances • Dominion of Annagar (Imaginary Place) • Essalieyan Empire (Imaginary Place) • Good vs. Evil • Magic • World Domination

> **Read On:** Other broad series that focus on alliances and power struggles are Robert Jordan's <u>The Wheel of Time</u> and George R. R. Martin's <u>A Song of Ice and Fire</u>. The strong women in the patriarchal society of West's kingdoms are also at the heart of Sasha Miller's *Ladylord*. Michelle West also writes as Michelle Sagara.

Alternate and Parallel Worlds

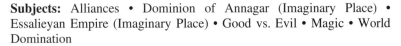

These novels are set in a world that is partially familiar to the reader, usually in a historical context. The story could be in a historical setting with magical elements or mythical creatures, or the tale might be about changing the course of history through a supernatural or magical element.

Duncan, Dave.

The Great Game.

Created in a world parallel to that of World War I, this series concerns a battle between Edward Exeter and Death, Edward having been long prophesied as the Liberator of Nextdoor from Death.

Past Imperative. W. Morrow, 1995.

Present Tense. Avon, 1996.

Future Indefinite. Avon, 1997.

> **Subjects:** Gods and Goddesses • Parallel Universes • Prophecies • Trilogies • World War I

> **Read On:** The other major author who has written about a universe parallel to World War I is Harry Turtledove, in his <u>The Great War</u> series. Dave Duncan also writes science fiction, including *Hero!* and *Strings.*

Jakober, Marie.

The Black Chalice. **Edge Science Fiction and Fantasy Pub., 2000. 460pp. Book Groups** 📖

Elderly monk Paul von Ardiun, charged by the pope to record the history of a civil war thirty years earlier, is put under a spell that forces him to record only the truth. The result is a journey through his youth as he confronts the self-deception and self-serving accounts of the past, including the conflict of Karelian, Count of Lys, with German noblemen over who would rule as the Holy Roman Emperor. *The Black Chalice* was shortlisted for the Sunburst Award.

> **Subjects:** Crusades • Germany • Middle Ages • Obsession • Occult • Paganism • Quests • Twelfth Century • Witchcraft

> **Read On:** Other books by Jakober include another fantasy (*High Kamilan*) and a work of historical fiction (*Only Call Us Faithful: A Novel of the Union Underground*). Fans of medieval fantasy might enjoy authors such as Katherine Kurtz (<u>The Chronicles of Deryni</u>) or Judith Tarr (<u>The Hound and the Falcon Trilogy</u>). Marion Zimmer Bradley's novel *The Mists of Avalon* also explores the conflict between pagan and Christian ways.

Kay, Guy Gavriel.

The Last Light of the Sun. **Viking, 2004. 501pp. Book Groups** 📖

Billed by Penguin as Book One in the <u>Northland Series</u>, this historical fantasy is set in the England of King Alfred the Great; it also involves the Vikings (Erlings) and the Welsh (Cyngael), with the Cyngael and the Anglcyn joining forces to fend off the invading Erlings. But somehow a renegade group of Erlings joins the Islanders to defend against their own people. Alongside these temporal battles are more spiritual ones, between the new religion of Jad and the age-old half-world of the faeries. Guy Kay has won the International Goliardos Prize for his contributions to the literature of the fantastic.

> **Subjects:** Celts • Fairies • Invasion • Ninth Century • Saxons • Vikings

> **Read On:** Alternative histories abound, some in the fantasy field and some not, and they cover the range of historical events. Sagas dealing with the Anglo-Saxon period often tell of the Arthurian legend, but there are others, such as Kay's beginning series here, Harry Harrison's <u>Hammer and the Cross</u> trilogy (*The Hammer and the Cross*, *One King's Way*, and *King and Emperor*), and Susan Squires's *Danelaw,* that skirt the Arthurian tale while staying in the relevant time period. Diana L. Paxson straddles the border with a different take on Arthur, in her series <u>The Hallowed Isle</u>.

The Sarantine Mosaic.

Inspired by sixth-century Byzantium, this duology celebrates the glory of art as it centres on the creation of a monumental mosaic commissioned by the emperor. Of course there are political intrigues, interpersonal wrangling, and power struggles throughout, all set within a parallel world created by the author. Apart from the honours accorded the individual titles, the omnibus combining this diptych was also shortlisted for the Mythopoeic Award.

Sailing to Sarantium. HarperPrism, 1998.

Mosaic artist Crispin, embittered by the death of his family, agrees to journey to Sarantium to fulfill an imperial commission to create a mosaic for a newly constructed cathedral. He finds himself immersed in the intrigues of the emperor's court as he tries to conceal the fact that he carries a secret message from the young queen of his home province to the emperor, a message he has been charged to deliver in person. This novel was shortlisted for the World Fantasy, the Prix Aurora and the Locus Awards.

Lord of Emperors. Viking, 2000.

Shortlisted for the Sunburst, World Fantasy, and Locus Awards.

> **Subjects:** Byzantine Empire • Hagia Sophia Church • Justinian I • Mosaicists • Political Intrigue • Sixth Century

> **Read On:** The intricate complexity in Kay's work is integral in two series by Dorothy Dunnett (The Lymond Chronicles and The House of Niccolò).

Russell, Sean.

The Initiate Brother Duology.

In this two-part series, Russell creates an alternate universe in Asia (specifically Japan), strongly influenced by *The Tale of Genji*. Brother Shuyun, a young Botahist monk endowed with mystical powers, finds himself responsible for saving his empire, and his religious order, from complete annihilation.

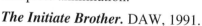

The Initiate Brother. DAW, 1991.

Shortlisted for the Locus Award for Best First Novel.

Gatherer of Clouds. DAW, 1992.

> **Subjects:** Japan • Magic • Martial Arts • Monks • Mysticism

> **Read On:** Richard La Plante's *Tegne* also tells the tale of a monk, but this monk teaches another the Zen martial arts to enable him to carry out his responsibilities. Other fantasies set in Japan are *Genpei* by Kara Dalkey, *Cloud of Sparrows* by Takashi Matsuoka, and both *The Fox Women* and *Fudoki* by Kij Johnson.

Moontide and Magic Rise.

Farrland is another parallel universe, but this time it is one caught in the battle between magic and science. The main protagonist is Tristam Flattery, a naturalist who, despite his best efforts, cannot rid himself of his magical powers, powers he inherited from his great uncle, the last of the great mages. Tristam must combine his magical powers with his scientist's knowledge to help his king.

World Without End. DAW, 1995.

Shortlisted for a Locus Award.

Sea Without a Shore. DAW, 1996.

Shortlisted for a Locus Award.

> **Subjects:** Botany • Flattery, Tristam (Fictional Character) • Magic • Naturalists • Psychic Ability • Quests • Voyages

> **Read On:** Robert Jordan's *A Crown of Swords* involves weather as its natural phenomenon at stake, and in Greg Keyes's <u>The Age of Unreason</u> tetratology, science is turned on its axis as Newton discovers alchemy instead of the laws of nature.

Contemporary

This subgenre is similar to the alternate or parallel worlds, except that it is usually set in the world as we know it today. We have combined here the urban fantasy (often gritty reality), magic realism, the use of celebrity characters, and time travel. In these novels, the setting is contemporary, often a familiar city such as Vancouver or Houston, and the world turns as we know it, but magic exists as a normal part of the world. In many cases, the magic world begins to take over the natural world.

Blais, Philippe.

Leonardo's Flight. **Gates & Bridges, 2000. 342pp.**

A group of college students who have uncovered a plan to sabotage a new jet-fighter project receive guidance and support from a most unlikely source, a time-traveling Leonardo da Vinci.

> **Subjects:** Computers • da Vinci, Leonardo • Time Travel

> **Read On:** Connie Willis's *To Say Nothing of the Dog* shares the element of time travel with Blais's novel. Thrillers with a da Vinci connection include Thomas Swan's *The Da Vinci Deception*, Dan Brown's *The Da Vinci Code,* and Cameron West's *The Medici Dagger.*

de Lint, Charles.

🏴 ***The Little Country.*** **W. Morrow, 1991. 636pp. Book Groups** 📖

A fantasy novel for those who do not normally read fantasy, this story takes place in Cornwall, in the little village of Mousehole. It concerns a young musician, a piper, who finds a single-edition book hidden among her grandfather's effects. The book differs for each person who reads it, but Janey Little is the one who becomes haunted by the music within, and by the mysterious and strange events that take place after its discovery. Selected as a New York Public Library Best Book for the Teen Age in 1992, this stand-alone work also won a HOMer Award.

> **Subjects:** Celtic Folklore • Cornwall • England • Family • Good vs. Evil • Magic • Quests • Villages

Read On: De Lint is said to be a master in contemporary fantasy, but there are others in the field as well, notably Neil Gaiman (*American Gods, Neverwhere,* and others) and Terry Brooks (*A Knight of the Word*). There are newer authors such as Emma Bull (*War for the Oaks*) and Elfie Leddy (*On Silver Wings: A Mystic Tale from Celtic Lore*) on the scene as well.

The Newford Chronicles.

This series is united by its locale, the fictional city of Newford, and combines novels with collections of short stories to make up the whole. Characterized as urban fantasy, the series is broad in scope, making use of both the spirit world and the Internet in the storytelling.

From a Whisper to a Scream. Orb Books, 1992.

Originally published under the pseudonym Samuel M. Key.

Dreams Underfoot. Tor Books, 1993.

Short stories.

Memory and Dream. Tor Books, 1994.

The Ivory and the Horn. Tor Books, 1995.

Short stories.

Trader. Tor Books, 1997.

Someplace To Be Flying. Tor Books, 1998.

Moonlight and Vines. Tor Books, 1999.

Short stories.

The Newford Stories. SF Book Club, 1999.

An omnibus of short stories and novels.

Forests of the Heart. Tor Books, 2000.

The Onion Girl. Tor Books, 2001. **Book Groups** 📖

While recovering in the hospital following a car accident, Jill dwells in a coma-like state, half in and half out of the unpredictable landscape of dreamtime or spirit world. There, with the guidance of Celtic and North American Aboriginal mythological figures, she gradually develops the strength to explore the truths and half-truths of a bitter family secret long buried in her psyche.

5

Tapping the Dream Tree. Tor Books, 2002.

Short stories.

Spirits in the Wires. Tor Books, 2003.

The Blue Girl. Viking, 2004.

> **Subjects:** Celtic Folklore • City and Town Life • Magic Realism • Mythology • Newford (Imaginary Place) • Young Women
>
> **Read On:** Neil Gaiman's *American Gods* exists in a similar cultural background where money, obsession, and power form the novel's moral prem-

ise. Robert J. Sawyer's morally and intellectually challenging *Calculating God* argues about the existence of God versus evolutionary science.

Dorsey, Candas Jane.

🎗 *Black Wine*. Tor Books, 1997. 285pp. Book Groups 📖

Through a complex, non-sequential narrative involving three to four plotlines, Dorsey explores the themes of love and freedom and the societal issues women face. Encompassing five generations of women in an indeterminate future, the central story weaves back and forth between the rigid life of a young woman bound in slavery and that of a fugitive trying to escape an oppressive family. This powerful telling requires multiple readings to appreciate fully the complexities of both Dorsey's themes and her challenging narrative. Dorsey won the Prix Aurora Award, the Crawford Award, and the James Tiptree Jr. Award for this novel.

> **Subjects:** Female Relationships • First Novels • Freedom • Gender Roles • Identity • Women in Society

> **Read On:** Various feminist speculative writers come to mind: first and foremost the renowned Ursula K. Le Guin of <u>Earthsea</u> fame, followed by Joanna Russ (*The Female Man*), Suzy McKee Charnas (*Motherlines*), Marion Zimmer Bradley (*The Shattered Chain*), C. J. Cherryh (*Gate of Ivrel*), and Sheri S. Tepper (*Raising the Stone*), to mention only a few.

Goto, Hiromi.

🎗 *The Kappa Child*. Red Deer Press, 2001. 278pp. Book Groups 📖

A Kappa is a Japanese mythological trickster figure, which Goto combines with contemporary mythology in the form of aliens, who abduct the narrator's mother, providing her with her only means of escape from an abusive husband. The narrator herself is transformed by the Kappa, but not before we share the hardships experienced by her, her three sisters, and their mother, largely at the hands of their father. Goto won the James Tiptree Jr. Award for this novel and was shortlisted for both the Sunburst and the Gaylactic Spectrum awards.

> **Subjects:** Alberta • Dysfunctional Families • Farm Life • Japanese Canadians • Mythological Creatures • Prairies • Sisters

> **Read On:** Despite its mythological character and magic realism, *The Kappa Child* shares descriptions and worlds created by other mainstream authors, specifically Joy Kogawa's rural setting in *Obasan* and Julie Shigekuni's multi-generational world in *A Bridge Between Us*. The mixing of myth and legend into the storytelling is similar to that in Lan Cao's *Monkey Bridge*. Goto is the author of the award-winning *Chorus of Mushrooms*.

Hopkinson, Nalo.

🎗 *The Salt Roads*. Warner, 2003. 394pp. Book Groups 📖

Hopkinson leaves her science fiction worlds to create a world of magic realism, a fantasy wherein a goddess is created by the mournful cries of three women burying a stillborn child. This goddess then inhabits and helps three other women from different times and places, all suffering from their respective roles in life: Mer is a healer and a slave in colonial Haiti; Jeanne is the lover of poet Charles

Baudelaire; Meritet is a Nubian prostitute who travels to Egypt, where she reforms herself to the point that she becomes known as Saint Mary of Egypt. Hopkinson won the Gaylactic Spectrum Award for this novel and was shortlisted for a Nebula award.

Subjects: Egypt • Fourth Century • France • Goddesses • Haiti • Magic Realism • Nineteenth Century • Spirit Possession • Time Travel

Read On: Although it also uses Caribbean mythology, Hopkinson's *Midnight Robber* is more appropriately classed as science fiction, as is her *Brown Girl in the Ring*, winner of the Locus First Novel Award. Hopkinson's writing style, lesbian themes, and Caribbean setting bring to mind the works of Dionne Brand (*In Another Place, Not Here*). The reader who enjoys Hopkinson's use of spirit possession of real people might want to try Bonnie Marson's *Sleeping with Schubert*.

Huff, Tanya.

The Keeper's Chronicles.

Because it is possible to poke holes in the walls separating the real world from the magical world, thereby letting in evil creatures, it is necessary to have keepers of these potential gaps. Claire is just such a keeper, and she and her talking cat Austin are relegated to the Elysian Fields Guest House. In this series Claire's life and her gatekeeping job are sometimes complicated, sometimes helped by the presence of a lascivious ghost, her younger sister Diana, and the good-looking caretaker Dean.

Summon the Keeper. DAW Books, 1998.

The Second Summoning. DAW Books, 2001.

Long Hot Summoning. DAW Books, 2003.

Subjects: Good vs. Evil • Hansen, Claire (Fictional Character) • Magic • Portals

Read On: Other comedic fantasy writers are Robert Asprin (<u>Myth</u> series), Esther Friesner (<u>Majyk</u> series), and Mark E. Rogers (<u>Samurai Cat</u> series).

Major, Kevin.

Gaffer: A Novel of Newfoundland. **Doubleday Canada, 1997. 202pp. Book Groups** 📖

Tormented by the death of his father on an offshore oil rig and drawn to the sea, teenager Gaffer discovers he can transform himself into an amphibious creature, at home both on land and in the sea. His additional ability to travel backward and forward in time allows him to confront disasters and events throughout Newfoundland and Labrador's rocky history—its past, present, and future.

Subjects: Black Humour • Fathers and Sons • Newfoundland and Labrador • Satire • Shapeshifters • Teenage Boys • Time Travel

Read On: Fantasy writer C. J. Cherryh's <u>Morgaine</u> series (*Gate of Ivrel, Well of Shiuan, Fires of Azeroth,* and *Exile's Gate*) recounts journeys back and forth through time. Confederate leader Robert E. Lee relates the events of the Civil War through the dreams of a young woman in Connie Willis's time-travel book, *Lincoln's Dreams*; her novel *Doomsday Book* has a similar dark feeling. The language used in *Gaffer* to recount island legend and lore is also seen in Kim Echlin's *Dagmar's Daughter*.

Meynard, Yves.

The Book of Knights. Tor Books, 1998. 222pp. Book Groups 📖

A young boy resolves to become a knight after escaping his own oppressive reality through the pages of *The Book of Knights*. This resolution takes him to a sage for training, and from there it sends him on a journey to test the abilities that will lead him to manhood. This novel was shortlisted for the Locus and the Mythopoeic Awards.

Subjects: Books • Coming of Age • Knights • Step-parents

Read On: J. K. Rowling's <u>Harry Potter</u> series relates a young boy's journey as he learns the art of wizardry and looks for answers about his past. Katherine Kurtz's <u>The Chronicles of the Deryni</u> series details a knight's coming of age, while other young men's stories appear in Eve Forward's *Animist* and Robin Hobb's *Assassin's Apprentice*.

Stewart, Sean.

🎗 *Galveston*. Ace Books, 2000. 454pp. Book Groups 📖

Mardi Gras in Galveston, Texas in 2004 unleashes a magic that freezes half the island in that time frame: the party-goers must party at Mardi Gras endlessly. The other half, the "real half," suffer from deprivation and a loss of the normal necessities of life. This urban fantasy is peopled by such characters as Momus, the king of carnival and god of magic; Jane Gardner, ex-lawyer, trying to keep the real city from completely dying through the agency of Odessa, a witch; and Sloane, Jane's daughter, who is able to travel between the two parts of the city but must grow up substantially in order to save the community after her mother's death. This novel won the World Fantasy and the Sunburst Awards and was shortlisted for a Locus Award.

Subjects: Carnival • Galveston • Magic • Mardi Gras • Survival • Texas

Read On: Other urban fantasies include Will Shetterly's *Elsewhere,* which describes a world straddling a malignant magical world and the real city; Marc Scott Zicree's <u>Magic Time,</u> in which magic floods another island; and Tim Powers's *Last Call*, which also shares poker playing with *Galveston*.

Mockingbird. Ace Books, 1998. 278pp. Book Groups 📖

This novel is an unusual direction for Stewart, as it is set in modern-day Houston. The setting is an alternate universe only in the magic realism Stewart brings to play. This magic takes the shape of the Riders—six spirits who occasionally inhabited Toni's mother's mind and body until her death. Toni hoped she and her sister would be free of their influence now, but Elena (Toni's mother) had other plans. Toni is given the Mockingbird cocktail to drink, thus unknowingly becoming hostess herself to these six Riders. Stewart was shortlisted for several awards for this: World Fantasy, James Tiptree Jr., Locus, and Nebula.

Subjects: Houston • Magic • Magic Realism • Mothers and Daughters • Sisters • Spirits • Texas • Voodoo

Read On: Not everyone wants to be a magician or sorcerer, as evidenced in stories by Dawn Cook (*First Truth*), S. L. Farrell (*Holder of Lightning*, the first in <u>The Cloudmages</u> series), and Juilene Osborne-McKnight (*Bright Sword of Ireland*).

Wharton, Thomas.

❦ *Salamander*. McClelland & Stewart, 2001. 372pp. Book Groups 📖

For Nicholas Flood, printer extraordinaire of highly creative books, the salamander is his symbol of creativity. And creativity is demanded of him when a Slovakian count hires him to add to his own eclectic collection of books by devising an "infinite" book, his own version of the neverending story, one with no beginning and no ending. This commission takes Flood on a fantastic quest, complicated by the multi-faceted outcome of a love affair with the count's daughter, to various parts of the world. This novel of magic realism won the Georges Bugnet Award for Best Novel and was shortlisted for the Sunburst Award, the Governor General's Literary Award for Fiction, and the Rogers Writers' Trust Prize for Fiction.

Subjects: Books and Reading • Europe • Fathers and Daughters • Inventors • Magic Realism • Obsession • Printers • Quests

Read On: There are several directions in which one could go to find books similar in theme to *Salamander*. To choose but one—the book itself as the plot catalyst—try Jeffrey Moore's *Prisoner in a Red-Rose Chain*, Charles de Lint's *The Little Country*, Yves Meynard's *The Book of Knights,* and Jasper Fforde's <u>Thursday Next</u> series.

Two titles remain in the fantasy genre, each a noteworthy exemplar of a specific subgenre, and for this reason we have kept them separate.

Humorous Fantasy

The humorous or comic fantasy is often a parody of the fantasy genre, with the writer exaggerating the characteristics. At other times, the fantasy is simply a light-hearted or humorous story set in a fantasy world. The title cited below combines the humorous genre (as a parody) with science fantasy, a subgenre wherein elements of science fiction blend with the elements of the fantasy.

Hughes, Matthew.

<u>Archonate.</u>

This satirical series, in the tradition of Jack Vance or Jonathan Swift, could also be classed as science fantasy, as it melds the components of fantasy (dwarfs, quests, fantastic new worlds) with those of science fiction (far future, spaceships, aliens), but the first two volumes are more fantasy than science.

Fools Errant. Maxwell Macmillan Canada, 1994.

Filidor Vesh, heir to the Archon of Old Earth, is commissioned to deliver a package to his uncle, the current Archon. While journeying across the planet with a mysterious dwarf, he finds himself facing many challenges in the new lands he encounters.

Fool Me Twice. Warner Aspect, 2001.

Black Brillion. Tor Books, 2004.

> **Subjects:** Adventure • Dwarfs • Quests • Vesh, Filidor (Fictional Character) • Voyages

> **Read On:** Another writer of science fantasy is David Gemmell, author of <u>A Drenai Saga Adventure</u> series, especially in his latest in the series, *The Swords of Night and Day*. Some other well-known humorous fantasy writers are Tom Holt, Terry Pratchett, Robert Asprin, and Christopher Moore. You may also want to have a look at *The Mammoth Book of Comic Fantasy*, edited by Mike Ashley.

Arthurian Fantasy

King Arthur, Merlin, the Sword Excalibur, the Knights of the Round Table are extremely popular in the fantasy world, and in Canada, Jack Whyte is the *éminence grise* of this subgenre. His deep and long-standing interest in history and in the story of Arthur is played out in his <u>A Dream of Eagles</u> series.

Whyte, Jack.
<u>A Dream of Eagles.</u>

> Jack Whyte's dual interests in the history of Roman Britain and in the story of King Arthur have combined to create a vast series filling in all the detail of the Arthurian legend and what went before to set the stage for this legendary king. This series is also known as <u>The Camulod Chronicles.</u>

The Skystone. Viking, 1992.

In the early fifth century as many Roman citizens were leaving Britain for Rome, two British-born Romans, Publius Varrus and Caius Britannicus, decide to stay; together they build the foundation for the future Court of King Arthur and the Knights of the Round Table.

The Singing Sword. Viking, 1993.

The Eagles' Brood. Viking, 1994.

The Saxon Shore. Viking, 1995.

The Sorcerer: The Fort at River's Bend. Viking, 1997. (Book One of the Fifth Volume).

The Sorcerer: Metamorphosis. Viking, 1997. (Book Two of the Fifth Volume).

> **Subjects:** Ancient Britain • Arthur, King • Britons • Dark Ages • Excalibur (Sword) • Merlin

> **Read On:** Gillian Bradshaw's *Imperial Purple* and Mary Stewart's <u>Arthurian Saga</u> are also set in the fifth century. T.H. White's *The Once and Future King* is the classic telling of the legend of King Arthur.

Romance

"And they lived happily ever after." This is the contract between the writers of romance fiction and the reader. Regardless of what may happen along the rocky road of love, the reader knows that in the end the two main characters in the story will come together.

Kristin Ramsdell, in *Romance Fiction: A Guide to the Genre,* defines the romance as "a love story in which the central focus is on the development and satisfactory resolution of the love relationship between two main characters, written in such a way as to provide the reader with some degree of vicarious emotional participation in the courtship process" (1999, 5).

Like all genres of fiction, there are many subgenres of romance fiction, which are defined by setting and plot, but all these stories share two basic elements: the all-important central love story and the optimistic or happy ending. The readers of romance fiction, of which there are many (according to the Romance Writers of America, in 2002 there were 51.1 million readers in America) are not that different from readers of other genres. They are involved and committed to this genre and often become completely connected to the character they come to know through the pages of a novel.

Other general characteristics of the genre include the following:

1. Both lovers share their point of view regarding the relationship with the reader.

2. The relationships usually go through several stages: there is initial reluctance or hesitation to get involved, then the attraction increases, and finally comes love.

3. The relationship is often subjected to outside conflicts from either another person or a potentially insurmountable problem.

4. Generally, the female protagonist is a strong, intelligent woman.

Regency Romance

Regency romances are initially defined by their time period: these stories are set during the Regency period in England, which lasted from 1811 to 1820. In 1811 when King George III was deemed too ill to continue to rule, his eldest son, the Prince of Wales and future George IV, was declared Regent. Most often, these are stories about the English aristocracy, set in the various locations they frequented at the time, whether London or the countryside or on the continent. Some of the characteristics of this subgenre that draw readers may include fast-paced reads that blend humour with light, lively storytelling; elements of a mystery or some type of challenge, relating to the time period, that must be overcome; gentle descriptions of sexual relations, if any; the presence of extended family members who may be involved in the progress and development of the relationship; the reappearance of these family members in other series titles; and the ultimate goal of discovering one's lifelong mate.

Balogh, Mary.

Bedwyn Series.

Balogh introduced the Bedwyn family in *A Summer to Remember* (see below). In this series filled with well-drawn characters, she chronicles the journey each of these siblings takes to find true love and happiness.

Slightly Married. Dell, 2003.

Slightly Wicked. Dell, 2003.

Slightly Scandalous. Dell, 2003.

Slightly Tempted. Dell, 2004.

Slightly Sinful. Dell, 2004.

Slightly Dangerous. Dell, 2004.

Wulfric Bedwyn, Duke of Bewcastle, has long been considered cold, unapproachable, and definitely not in the market for a wife; then at a country house party he meets the widowed Christine Derrick and finds himself enchanted with her unconventional behaviour.

> **Subjects:** England • Male–Female Relationships • Nobility

> **Read On:** This family-based series following the romantic encounters of the Bedwyn family will appeal to readers of Stephanie Laurens's <u>Cynster</u> series (*The Perfect Lover* and others).

🎗 *More Than a Mistress*. Delacorte Press, 2000. 343pp.

The Duke of Tresham decides that Jane Ingleby, who was working as a milliner's assistant when she came upon two men about to engage in a duel, must pay for the interference that ended with his being shot in the leg. As Jane spends the next three weeks nursing him, and standing up to him, Tresham finds her appealing; when it becomes clear that Jane is in danger the duke comes to her rescue. Balogh received the RITA Award for Best Historical for this novel.

> **Subjects:** Duels • Dukes • England • Nineteenth Century • Nobility

> **Read On:** Readers of Balogh's Regencies will also enjoy the novels of Jo Beverley, Mary Jo Putney, and Amanda Quick.

Signet Regency Romances.

These Regency period romances from Signet all feature unconventional, determined heroines who are often a bit older than the usual Regency heroine. These are women who may have been married before or who have had other relationships and experiences.

A Promise of Spring. Signet, 1990.

Sir Perry Lampman proposes marriage to the sister of his best friend in an attempt to save her from financial ruin following her brother's death, despite the fact that she is ten years his senior and has a questionable past.

A Certain Magic. Signet, 1991.

The friendship between Alice and Piers is tested to its limits when he seeks her help as he plans to marry a much younger woman.

Christmas Beau. Signet, 1991.

A seduction for the purposes of revenge doesn't follow the Marquess of Denbigh's plan at a country house party at the height of the Christmas season.

A Counterfeit Betrothal. Signet, 1992.

In an attempt to bring her parents back together after many years of separation, Sophia enters into a less-than-suitable engagement, hoping her parents will make her future happiness their joint priority.

A Christmas Bride. Signet, 1997.

Promising his father he will find a wife by Christmas, Edgar Downes heads to London. However, instead of the young woman he expected to find, he becomes enamoured of the widowed Lady Helena Stapleton, a woman who will need to confront her past in order to find love.

The Temporary Wife. Signet, 1997.

Charity Duncan agrees to pose as the new wife of the Marquess of Staunton as a way to support her siblings. When she is presented to his family, they both begin to realize that each is different from what they had originally thought, and an undeniable attraction begins.

The Last Waltz. Signet, 1998.

Now widowed, Christina is forced to confront her husband's cousin, the new earl, the man she had once jilted.

Subjects: Betrothal • England • Male–Female Relationships • Nobility

Read On: These spirited, feisty heroines share similar qualities with the women found in romances by Amanda Quick. Many libraries will have these titles in their collections, although most are out of print, but the author's Web site (http://www.marybalogh.com) indicates that some of her earlier works may be re-issued. Readers of the novels of Carola Dunn and Marion Chesney will enjoy these titles.

A Summer to Remember. **Delacorte Press, 2002. 313pp.**

The scandalous Kit Butler, Viscount Ravensburg, is courting Lauren Edgeworth on the basis of a wager. When Lauren learns of the wager, she agrees to act as his fiancée for the summer, if Kit will give her a summer of adventure and then fulfill her goal to remain independent and unmarried.

Subjects: England • Nobility • Viscounts • Wagers

Read On: Lauren Edgeworth also appears in Balogh's *One Night for Love*. Other Regencies featuring strong-willed, independent female characters include those by Jane Feather, Mary Jo Putney, and Stephanie Laurens.

Beverley, Jo.

Company of Rogues.

This series is also set in the Regency period, and while the books have the added element of intense issues such as rape and abuse, these issues are tempered with humour and sensual romance.

An Arranged Marriage. Zebra, 1991, 1999.

Seeing no other options available to her after she is raped, an act planned by her brother, Eleanor agrees to a hastily arranged marriage to Nicholas Delaney. Understanding that this is an arranged marriage, Eleanor accepts that her new husband has a mistress, but she recognizes her growing attraction for him. However, Nicholas is involved in this affair only in an attempt to unmask a spy, and though he must continue the relationship for the good of his country, he cannot deny his growing love for Eleanor. This novel was a RITA Finalist.

An Unwilling Bride. Zebra, 1992, 2000.

Winner of the RITA Award for Best Regency and the Golden Leaf Award for Best Historical.

Christmas Angel. Zebra, 1992, 2001.

Forbidden. Zebra, 1994, 2003.

Dangerous Joy. Zebra, 1995, 2004.

The Dragon's Bride. Signet, 2001.

Finalist for the RITA Award.

Skylark. Signet, 2004.

Subjects: England • Male–Female Relationships • Nineteenth Century

Read On: The novels of Bertrice Small (*The O'Malley Saga* and others) are highly sensual romantic novels, containing graphic sexual descriptions. Readers of this series will enjoy the work of Amanda Quick and Carla Kelly, as well as Mary Jo Putney's Silk Trilogy. The publisher has recently reissued certain titles in this series; therefore the dates listed reflect the original date plus this new availability. Several other novels by Beverley are set in the same world as the Company of Rogues: *The Devil's Heiress*, *Hazard*, and *St. Raven*.

Emily and the Dark Angel. **Walker and Company, 1991. 201pp.**

Emily's quiet and peaceful life is thrown into turmoil when she becomes involved with Piers Verderan, a handsome and charming man, alternately known as the Dark Angel, a title earned due to a dark and dangerous reputation. This novel was recognized with the RITA Award for Best Regency and the *Romantic Times* Award for Best Regency Rake.

Subjects: Fathers and Daughters • Male–Female Relationships

Read On: This title is loosely linked to three of Beverley's novels: *Lord Wraybourne's Betrothed*, *The Stanforth Secrets,* and *The Stolen Bride*. This traditional Regency romance resembles the historical romances of Elizabeth Lowell, as well as the stories told by Patricia Veryan and Mary Jo Putney. Jo Beverley is best known for her Regency romances: her work has received multiple awards, and she is a member of the Romance Writers of America Hall of Fame. She has also written a number of period romances as well. Libraries interested in adding some of this author's titles to their collections should visit the author's Web site (http://www.jobeverley.com) for a listing of the recent reissues of titles that had previously been out of print. Beverley's other award-winning titles include *An Unwilling Bride* and *Deirdre and Don Juan*.

Period Romance

Readers looking to experience another time as they watch two people find love are drawn to period (or historical) romances; however, it is always understood that romance is still the primary appeal, being more important than the history. These novels often contain a wealth of well-researched and accurate historical detail. Advisors working with readers looking for novels in this subgenre should note that some titles in this genre might contain elements of both violence and rougher sexual encounters than other romances. Furthermore, in order to depict more closely the time period, accepted social practices will not match today's experience, nor will the heroes have the attitudes of the more enlightened modern hero.

Balogh, Mary.

Heartless. **Berkley, 1995. 389pp.**

Lucas Kendrick, Duke of Harndon, recently back in England after a ten-year absence, decides a wife will ease his transition into his new role as head of his family. He marries Lady Anna Marlowe after only a week's acquaintance. Each of them has been hurt in the past, but together they will find the future each desires.

Subjects: Georgian England • Intrigue • London

Read On: Readers of this Georgian period novel will enjoy Catherine Coulter's *Devil's Daughter* and Christina Dodd's *Priceless*.

Longing. **Topaz, 1994. 377pp.**

Newly arrived in Wales to oversee his recently inherited mines, the Marquess of Craille finds himself becoming involved with the illegitimate daughter of a wealthy English landowner when he hires her as a governess. As their attraction grows, so too does the unrest in the mines.

Subjects: Mining • Nineteenth Century • Victorian Era • Wales

Read On: Balogh's storytelling in this novel is similar to the style of Amanda Quick and Jo Beverley.

Tangled. **Topaz, 1994. 384pp.**

In this Victorian romance, a marriage of convenience with her deceased husband's best friend will ultimately become true love when Lady

Rebecca Cardwell finally realizes the husband she idealized wasn't the man she thought he was.

> **Subjects:** Crimean War • England • Nineteenth Century • Victorian Era

> **Read On:** Other romantic stories about love that develops after a marriage of convenience are Stephanie Laurens's *A Convenient Marriage* and Heather Cullman's *Scandal*.

Truly. Berkley, 1996. 343pp.

Estranged childhood friends Geraint and Marged discover love when, unbeknownst to each other, they don disguises and participate in a campaign against Welsh toll roads in the 1840s.

> **Subjects:** Nineteenth Century • Wales • Welsh Riots

> **Read On:** Other Balogh titles with a Welsh connection include *Daring Masquerade, One Night for Love,* and *Silent Melody.*

Beverley, Jo.

Dark Champion. NAL, 2003. 392pp.

This fast-paced, passionate romance takes place in the early 1100s. This title was the winner of the Golden Leaf Award for Best Historical.

> **Subjects:** Castles • Europe • Knights • Medieval

> **Read On:** Beverley featured another character from this novel in the medieval romance *Lord of Midnight.* Beverley's historical romances will appeal to readers of Rexanne Becnel (*My Gallant Enemy* and others), Catherine Coulter (*Earth Song* and others), Claire Delacroix (The Bride Quest series), and Julie Garwood (*The Prize, The Secret,* and others).

Lord of My Heart. NAL, 2002. 384pp.

This title, the author's first historical romance (1992) and now back in print, is set in 1068, the period just following the Norman Conquest.

> **Subjects:** Medieval

> **Read On:** Readers who enjoy the more graphic style of storytelling here may enjoy Margaret Moore's *The Welshman's Way* or Patricia Ryan's *Heaven's Fire.*

Malloren Chronicles.

This fast-paced, sensual series is filled with details of life in eighteenth-century Georgian England. Each title in the series focuses on the exploits and love affairs of the Malloren siblings and their soon-to-be life partners.

My Lady Notorious. Avon, 1993; Signet, 2002.

Her reputation already destroyed, Chastity Ware disguises herself as a highwayman to steal a coach and help her sister escape an abusive relationship. Her scheme brings her into the coach of Cyn Malloren, recently returned from the war. Recognizing that the highwayman is no man, he decides to assist in the plan as a bit of an adventure, and in the process ends up rescuing Chastity from both her father and being shunned by society. This title was listed as one of the top 100

Historicals of all time by *Affaire de Coeur* and also received a RITA and a Golden Leaf Award as Best Historical.

🎗 *Tempting Fortune.* Zebra, 1995, 2002.

Romantic Times Reviewers' Choice Award.

Something Wicked. Topaz, 1997, 2005.

🎗 *Secrets of the Night.* Topaz, 1999, 2003.

Romantic Times Reviewers' Choice Award.

🎗 *Devilish.* Signet, 2000.

Winner of a RITA Award for Best Long Historical Romance and named one of *Romantic Times*'s Best Romances of the Past 20 Years.

Winter Fire. Signet, 2003.

A Most Unsuitable Man. Signet, 2005.

> **Subjects:** Clans • Eighteenth Century • Georgian England • Nobility • Yorkshire

> **Read On:** Readers looking for other period romance series featuring recurring characters will enjoy Mary Balogh's Bedwyn Series or Susan Carroll's *The Bride Finder* and *Midnight Bride*. Several of Nora Roberts's contemporary romance trilogies and series, including Chesapeake Bay, Concannon Sisters, and the Three Sisters Trilogy, also feature recurring characters.

Delacroix, Claire.

The Bride Quest.

This series of medieval romances is characterized by spirited women, reluctant to be drawn into marriage, and the men who are attracted to them and who must work to win their hearts.

The Princess. Dell, 1998.

The Damsel. Dell, 1999.

The Heiress. Dell, 1999.

The Countess. Dell, 2000.

The Beauty. Dell, 2001.

The Temptress. Dell, 2001.

> **Subjects:** Male–Female Relationships • Medieval

> **Read On:** These stories share both setting and levels of sensuality with titles such as *Joining* by Johanna Lindsey and *The Border Hostage* and *The Marriage Prize* by Virginia Henley. Delacroix has also written a number of series for Harlequin Historicals (The Sayerne Trilogy, The Unicorn Trilogy, The Moorish Books, and The Rose series). The writer known as Claire Delacroix also writes as Claire Cross.

Rogues of Ravensmuir.

From their keep, Ravensmuir, on the east coast of Scotland, the Lammergeier clan has long trafficked in religious relics and other less-than-legal enterprises. Each book in this series tells the story of three men of this clan and the women who rule their hearts. The writer known as Claire Delacroix also writes as Claire Cross.

The Rogue. Warner Books, 2002.

Rather than live a life based on a lie, newly married Ysabella leaves her husband, Merlyn Lammergeier, determined to make her own way despite the cost. Five years later she finds herself back in the keep, now heir to her husband's home and fortune. Learning that Merlyn is not really dead, she works with him to discover who was behind the plot to murder the Laird of Ravensmuir, while both struggle to protect their hearts and deeply held secrets.

The Scoundrel. Warner Books, 2003.

The Warrior. Warner Books, 2004.

> **Subjects:** Male–Female Relationships • Scotland

> **Read On:** Delacroix's storytelling style is similar to both Johanna Lindsey's and Jude Deveraux's.

MacLean, Julianne.

American Heiress.

This series features sexy, romantic stories whose heroines are American sisters in late-Victorian London looking for husbands among the nobility.

To Marry the Duke. Avon, 2003.

American Sophia and her mother are in London for the season to find a husband with a title. As the Duke of Wentworth needs a rich wife, each seems to fill the needs of the other perfectly, but then the sparks start to fly.

An Affair Most Wicked. Avon, 2004.

Like her sister Sophia, American Clara Wilson finds herself in London looking for an aristocratic husband. Problems begin to develop when she finds herself with a growing attraction to the Marquess of Rawdon, a scandal-ridden rake.

My Own Private Hero. Avon, 2004.

Adele, the youngest and most sensible of the Wilson sisters, had agreed to marry the first eligible nobleman who asked for her hand, but she reconsiders this decision when the cousin of her betrothed rescues her following a kidnapping, and the attraction is undeniable.

> **Subjects:** England • Male–Female Relationships • Marriage • Nineteenth Century • Sisters • Victorian Era

> **Read On:** Karyn Monk's *The Wedding Escape* features an American heiress in England who ultimately finds true love.

Monk, Karyn.

The Orphans Series.

A group of street urchins and young children are rescued from the horrors of the nineteenth-century Scottish prison system by a beautiful young woman, herself a social outcast. Together they form their own family unit, grow up, and find the love they each deserve.

The Prisoner. Bantam Books, 2001.

While on her latest mission to rescue a young boy from the horrors of prison, Genevieve MacPhail meets Haydon Kent, Marquess of Redmond, imprisoned for a murder he claims was an act of self-defence. He escapes and seeks refuge with Genevieve, and as they work together to prove his innocence, they discover a growing passion for each other.

The Wedding Escape. Bantam Books, 2003.

My Favorite Thief. Bantam Books, 2004.

Every Whispered Word. Bantam Books, 2005.

> **Subjects:** England • Nineteenth Century • Orphans • Prisoners • Scotland

> **Read On:** Monk has written a number of historical romances, including *Surrender to a Stranger, The Rebel and the Redcoat, Once a Warrior, The Witch and the Warrior,* and *The Rose and the Warrior.* These period romances that blend historical detail with passion will appeal to readers of Julie Garwood and Jude Devereaux.

Moore, Margaret.

Warrior Series.

This is a fast-paced historical romance series filled with well-developed characters. In these stories, the heroes are not of noble birth, but rather men who are forced by circumstance to make a name for themselves in order to secure their own future and happiness. The women are strong-willed and determined and will not give themselves over to marriage without first determining if it is right for them.

A Warrior's Heart. Harlequin, 1992.

A Warrior's Quest. Harlequin, 1993.

A Warrior's Way. Harlequin, 1994.

Knowing it is time for his daughter to be married, Liliana's father successfully arranges for her to meet and then marry Welshman Hu Morgan. Hu is then faced with the challenge of convincing his new bride that he is the one for her.

The Welshman's Way. Harlequin, 1995.

The Norman's Heart. Harlequin, 1996.

The Baron's Quest. Harlequin, 1996.

A Warrior's Bride. Harlequin, 1998.

A Warrior's Honor. Harlequin, 1998.

A Warrior's Passion. Harlequin, 1998.

The Welshman's Bride. Harlequin, 1999.

A Warrior's Kiss. Harlequin, 2000.

The Overlord's Bride. Harlequin, 2001.

A Warrior's Lady. Harlequin, 2001.

In the King's Service. Harlequin, 2003.

> **Subjects:** Knights • Male–Female Relationships • Medieval

> **Read On:** Moore has written other historical romances, including *Bride of Lochbarr* and *The Maiden and Her Knight.* Similar medieval romances featuring conflict between the main protagonists are Jo Beverley's *Lord of My Heart,* Catherine Coulter's *Fire Song,* Virginia Henley's *The Border Hostage,* and Lynsay Sands's *The Chase.*

Contemporary Romance

Simply defined, contemporary romances take place during the time period in which they are written, reflecting the times and social customs of the period. There is a trend in today's novels to portray heroines who have both a personal and a professional life, reflecting the dual role filled by many women today. The women in contemporary romances, unlike those found in novels from several decades ago, are women of experience and often powerful in their own right; the relationships that they become involved in are usually not their first intimate experience, thus reflecting contemporary values and reality.

Careless, Anna.

Where the Fishermen Sing. Creative Bound, 1992. 198pp.

> Tom and Laurie have crossed paths a number of times, just not at the right time. When they meet again after many years, Laurie hopes this time it will last.

> **Subjects:** First Novels • Fishing • Nova Scotia • Older Couples • Quebec

> **Read On:** Careless's second novel, *An Unfortunate Likeness,* is set in the same small Nova Scotia town. Christian fiction authors Neva Coyle (*Sharon's Hope* and others) and Tracie Peterson (*A Slender Thread* and others) combine romance with the inner struggles of people seeking love. Careless's setting in this romance and others will appeal to readers of Nora Roberts's <u>Chesapeake Bay</u> series (*Sea Swept, Rising Tides, Inner Harbor,* and *Chesapeake Blue*).

Cross, Claire.

Double Trouble. Berkley, 2005. 341pp.

> Maralys is called upon by her nephews to help when their mother, her twin sister Marcia, abandons the boys and their father, James. Maralys had never liked James, but in helping out the abandoned family, she finds James is capable of positive change and is actually quite an attractive man.

> **Subjects:** Divorce • Sisters • Twins

Read On: Cross's work encompasses a number of contemporary romances, to which she adds elements of humour, and some historicals, including several novels in the time-travel series <u>Time Passages</u>. In both *Double Take* by Brenda Joyce and *A Tangled Web* by Judith Michael, a twin sister steps into her sister's life in a time of need. The writer known as Claire Cross also writes as Claire Delacroix.

Third Time Lucky. Berkley, 2005. 341pp.

After a fifteen-year absence, Nick turns up at Phillipa's door looking for help when he suspects he is being framed for the supposed murder of his missing grandmother.

> **Subjects:** Humorous Fiction • Murder

> **Read On:** Romance novelist Cathie Linz (*Too Stubborn to Marry* and others) is known for her humorous romances that include elements of suspense. The writer known as Claire Cross also writes as Claire Delacroix.

Grant, Vanessa.

Think About Love. Zebra, 2001. 256pp.

Businesswoman Samantha Jones and her boss agree to a marriage to help her adopt her orphaned infant niece. However, their relationship changes significantly when he finds he wants more.

> **Subjects:** Motherhood • Technology Industry

> **Read On:** Grant's other novels include *Seeing Stars*, *The Colors of Love*, and *If You Loved Me*. Other titles in the <u>Zebra Bouquet Romance</u> series are Marcia Evanick's *Jeremiah's Return*, Sara Howard's *Fantasy Man,* and Lisa Plumley's *Her Best Man*.

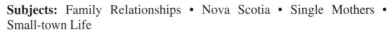

Haley, Susan.

Maggie's Family. Gaspereau Press, 2002. 281pp.

With her marriage in shambles, Maggie Ribbinski moves back to her small Nova Scotia town with her two teenage daughters; there she rekindles a relationship with her high school sweetheart. This man brings into her life a number of people who will redefine her definition of family.

> **Subjects:** Family Relationships • Nova Scotia • Single Mothers • Small-town Life

> **Read On:** Haley's other novels, *Getting Married in Buffalo Jump* and *The Complaints Department,* also touch on the relationship between husbands and wives. An older woman finds love and a new life in Barbara Taylor Bradford's *Love in Another Town. Friend of My Youth* by Alice Munro looks at women's relationships in a collection of stories set in small-town Ontario.

Perrin, Kayla.

The Sisters of Theta Phi Kappa. **St. Martin's, 2001. 352pp.**

The lives of four highly successful sorority sisters are about to be shattered when one of them begins to receive letters threatening to expose a long-buried secret, known only to them, or so they thought.

Subjects: African-American Women • Secrets • University Graduates • Women's Friendships

Read On: This romantic suspense novel featuring a woman in peril is similar to the work of Sandra Brown and Karen Robards. In Perrin's next sorority novel, *The Delta Sisters,* a story of three generations of women in one family is told, along with the consequences of keeping secrets that may lead to deadly results. Perrin has also written a number of other contemporary romances, including *Tell Me You Love Me* and *In a Heartbeat.*

Paranormal/Time-Travel Romance

In these stories, one of the lovers travels through time to find true love, either from the past into the present or from the present into the past. Once the lover arrives, how he or she confronts the challenge of adapting to an unknown time period is an integral element of the story. If the move is back in time, these novels often contain a wealth of rich detail of the time period and may be enjoyed not only for the time-travel element but also for the historical detail. Readers who enjoy this genre of romance are willing to accept the concept of time travel and may be willing to read science fiction novels that contain elements of both time travel and romance, such as Connie Willis's *To Say Nothing of the Dog.*

There are several characteristics of this subgenre that appeal to the reader: the notion that love can reach across time and space; the presence of both romance and history, in which the historical details may be limited, but the reader is still provided with information on the time period and some social history (living conditions, food, clothing, and child rearing); the way the characters respond to both setting and society with elements of humour as they either adapt or attempt to bring their new situation into line with their own ideas; and the variety within the genre, including ghost stories, past lives, reincarnation, or spirits and other worldly beings.

Cross, Claire.

The Last Highlander. **Berkley, 1998. 339pp.**

Past and present come together in the 1980s when an American woman touring Scotland encounters a man who claims that she has summoned him from the fourteenth century.

Subjects: Fourteenth Century • Scotland • Witches

Read On: *The Last Highlander* is another title in the publisher's series Time Passages. A sixteenth-century knight comes forward in time in Jude Deveraux's *A Knight in Shining Armor.* The writer known as Claire Cross also writes as Claire Delacroix.

The Moonstone. **Berkley, 1999. 336pp.**

A talisman transports a woman accused of witchcraft to twentieth-century Canada, where she encounters a man who is the image of someone from her past.

> **Subjects:** British Columbia • England • Time Travel • Witches

> **Read On:** This title is in the <u>Time Passages</u> publisher's series; other titles in this series include *An Echo in Time* by Sherry Lewis and *Yesterday's Flame* by Elizabeth Hallam. The writer known as Claire Cross also writes as Claire Delacroix.

Freiman, Kate.

Lady Moonlight. **Jove Books, 2000. 352pp.**

In 1899 in County Sligo, Ireland, Aisling Ahearn, about to be sold into marriage by her father, flees into the night and becomes trapped by a leprechaun's curse. Now living in the faerie realm and only visible to humans on nights of the full moon, she must find true love in the next 100 years or spend eternity with the leprechauns.

> **Subjects:** Arranged Marriages • Fairy World • Ireland • Magic

> **Read On:** *Irish Moonlight* picks up the story of Aisling and her fiancé, Conlon O'Hara, on the eve of their wedding and introduces two of their friends, Erin and Phelan, who, despite their better judgment, find themselves attracted to each other. The situation is complicated because Erin believes Conlon may be marrying for the wrong reasons and wants to save him from a possible gold digger. Although the sequel doesn't contain the same blending of romance and fantasy, it continues the story with a similar use of romance and humour. Other romances featuring a similar paranormal element include Christine Feehan's *Dark Challenge* and Antoinette Stockenberg's *Time After Time*. Finding your one true love is the basis of Susan Carroll's *The Bride Finder*.

Kearsley, Susanna.

🎗 *Mariana*. **Seal Books, 1998. 352pp.**

As the new owner of a sixteenth-century English farmhouse, Julia begins a new life in the quiet countryside. Soon she is repeatedly drawn back in time to the seventeenth century, living the life of another woman, Mariana. While there she confronts the horrors of the time, including the plague. She is also faced with the growing realization that she may have met her eternal soul mate. Kearsley won England's Catherine Cookson Fiction Prize for this novel.

> **Subjects:** England • Historical Romance • Past Lives • Seventeenth Century • Time Travel

> **Read On:** This title, originally published in 1993, was reissued in 1998. Kearsley is the author of a number of other Gothic-style novels, including *The Shadowy Horses*, *Named of the Dragon,* and *The Splendour Falls*. Similar to Kearsley in atmosphere is Barbara Erskine (*Lady of Hay, House of Echoes,* and others). To find other works blending history and time

travel, try Diana Gabaldon's <u>Outlander</u> series (*Drums of Autumn* and others) and *A Knight in Shining Armor* by Jude Deveraux.

Sands, Lynsay.

Argeneau Series.

In this humour-filled and sensuous series, the Argeneau family, all vampires, ultimately discover the life partners who are destined to bring a real zest for living into their lives.

Love Bites. Love Spell, 2004.

A prequel to *Single White Vampire*, this novel features Lucern Argeneau's brother Etienne and the events that lead to his marriage to Dr. Rachel Garrett.

Single White Vampire. Love Spell, 2003.

Reclusive romance writer and vampire Lucern Argeneau, whose family has been a source of inspiration for his romance novels, gives in to the harassment of his new editor and agrees to do some publicity for his books. Believing he will only be doing a few signings and interviews, he is shocked to find himself at the *Romantic Times* convention. As he attempts to cope with being out in the light and away from his usual food source, he also finds himself in danger of losing his heart!

Tall, Dark & Hungry. Love Spell, 2004.

> **Subjects:** Male–Female Relationships • Vampires

> **Read On:** Sands has a number of historical romances to her credit, including *The Deed*, *Always,* and *The Key*; her sense of humour is evident in her romantic comedy novel *The Loving Daylights*. Katie MacAlister is another author who combines vampires and romance in a compellingly sensual way.

Veighey, Cicely.

The Grass Beyond the Door. Frontenac House, 1999. 197pp.

Lucy Lightfoot has long been fascinated by Sir Edward Estur, a fourteenth-century crusader; unfortunately they are separated by approximately 500 years. One evening during a violent storm, Lucy is seen going into the church that contains a carved effigy of Estur and is never seen again. Transported back in time, Lucy meets the man of her obsession, but she finds herself drawn to another man as well. It will be more than thirty years before the mystery of her disappearance is revealed, through a newly discovered fourteenth-century manuscript.

> **Subjects:** Crusades • Fourteenth Century • Legends • Obsession

> **Read On:** Traveling through time to find romance is a popular theme. Veighey's story is rich in historical details and will be enjoyed by readers of R. Garcia y Robertson's <u>War of the Roses</u> series or Diana Gabaldon's <u>Outlander</u> series.

Christian/Inspirational Romance

Stories categorized as Christian or inspirational exist in all categories of fiction. These are stories in which the main characters are often faced with a crisis of faith. In the romance genre this crisis will often be the result of an attraction to a non-believer. Christian publishers Tyndale House and Bethany House publish the works of well-known romance novelists Janette Oke, Beverly Lewis, Catherine Palmer, and others. Some of the appeals of these novels, also referred to as gentle reads, is that the characters do not engage in sexual activity outside of wedlock or with members of the same sex, and the authors do not include profanity in the work. The examples here tell the stories of individuals who find their faith tested as they work through the challenges faced by building a life in a new land; the historical settings of these novels are reflected in the values of the time.

Glover, Ruth.

Saskatchewan Saga.

This series, filled with romance, humour, and history along with a strong Christian message, chronicles the adventures of settlers whose paths lead to Bliss, Saskatchewan, in the late 1800s.

A Place Called Bliss. Revell, 2001.

The lives of two couples who leave Scotland for a chance at a new life in Canada are permanently connected by a tragedy that occurs on the voyage.

With Love from Bliss. Revell, 2001.

Journey to Bliss. Revell, 2001.

Seasons of Bliss. Revell, 2002.

Bittersweet Bliss. Revell, 2003.

Back Roads to Bliss. Revell, 2003.

> **Subjects:** Frontier and Pioneer Life • Saskatchewan • Scots in Canada • Women Immigrants
>
> **Read On:** Glover's The Wildrose Series is another gentle series about frontier life in Saskatchewan. Her style of storytelling is similar to that of Janette Oke in *The Meeting Place* and others. Alan Morris (Guardians of the North series) also set his stories about faith on the Canadian Prairies, while Gilbert Morris sets his Christian historical romances in the United States (The Spirit of Appalachia series and others).

Oke, Janette.

A Prairie Legacy.

This heart-warming series begins twenty years after the close of the Love Comes Softly series, focusing on the lives of the grandchildren of Marty and Clark Davis as they grow into their own spiritual maturity.

The Tender Years. Bethany, 1997.

Teenager Virginia, already struggling with the rules and strictures of her devout small-town family, finds herself caught up in a situation that quickly spirals out of her control when an independent, strong-willed new girl arrives in town from the big city and brings with her ideas and values that go against those of Virginia's family. It is Virginia's experience with a tragedy that ultimately reconnects her with her faith.

A Searching Heart. Bethany House, 1999.

A Quiet Strength. Bethany House, 1999.

Like Gold Refined. Bethany House, 2000.

> **Subjects:** Coming of Age • Country Life • Prairie Life
>
> **Read On:** A prolific writer of inspirational fiction, Oke has been credited with founding the genre of evangelical fiction with her 1980s series Love Comes Softly.

Canadian West.

This series chronicles the love and lives of a young woman from the East and a rowdy cowboy from the Prairies. They face the challenges of creating a life together amid the harsh conditions that existed on the Canadian Prairies in the late nineteenth century. Four of the titles in this saga were originally released in the 1980s.

When Calls the Heart. Bethany House, 1983, 2005.

When Comes the Spring. Bethany House, 1985, 2005.

When Breaks the Dawn. Bethany House, 1986, 2005.

When Hope Springs New. Bethany House, 1986, 2005.

Beyond the Gathering Storm. Bethany House, 2000.

Siblings Christine and Henry, seeking lives beyond their adoptive home, discover love. Christine's relationship is violent, but through her Christian faith she is ultimately able to move on.

When Tomorrow Comes. Bethany House, 2001.

> **Subjects:** Frontier and Pioneer Life • Prairie Life • Royal Canadian Mounted Police • The West (Canada)
>
> **Read On:** Oke is the author of several series, including the ongoing A Prairie Legacy series; she has also co-written a series called Song of Acadia with T. Davis Bunn. Other authors whose style of inspirational romance resembles Oke's include Barbara Jean Hicks (*Coming Home*), Deborah Raney (*A Vow to Cherish*), Lance Wubbels (*The Bridge over Flatwillow Creek*), Judith Pella, B. J. Hoff, Catherine Marshall, and Lori Wick.

Song of Acadia.

Oke collaborated with T. Davis Bunn on this series, set in eighteenth-century Acadia, the area now known as Nova Scotia. The story begun here then continues in the Heirs of Acadia series.

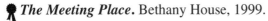*The Meeting Place.* Bethany House, 1999.

Amid the conflict between the French and English, a chance encounter between two young women from opposing sides of the conflict leads to a friendship in which each shares her struggle to reconcile faith and hope for a family during turbulent times. This title received the Christy Award.

The Sacred Shore. Bethany House, 2000.

The Birthright. Bethany House, 2001.

The Distant Beacon. Bethany House, 2002.

The Beloved Land. Bethany House, 2002.

> **Subjects:** Acadia • Eighteenth Century • Friendship

> **Read On:** Readers of the perennially popular Oke will also enjoy the works of Tracie Peterson (*The Hope Within* and others), Marian Wells (*The Wedding Album*), and Lauraine Snelling (*Daughter of Twin Oaks* and others).

Women of the West.

In this series Oke presents the stories of strong women with traditional values who rely on their faith as they try to make a difference.

The Calling of Emily Evans. Bethany House, 1990.

Ignoring her self-doubts, Emily Evans accepts God's calling and takes on the challenge of ministering in a small pioneer community; here she meets and falls in love with a man who has experienced a loss of faith. It is seeing Emily's determination and intensity of faith that ultimately leads him back to God.

Julia's Last Hope. Bethany House, 1990.

Roses for Mama. Bethany House, 1991.

A Woman Named Damaris. Bethany House, 1991.

They Called Her Mrs. Doc. Bethany House, 1992.

The Measure of a Heart. Bethany House, 1992.

A Bride for Donnigan. Bethany House, 1993.

 5

Heart of the Wilderness. Bethany House, 1993.

Too Long a Stranger. Bethany House, 1994.

The Bluebird and the Sparrow. Bethany House, 1995.

A Gown of Spanish Lace. Bethany House, 1995.

Drums of Change. Bethany House, 1996.

> **Subjects:** Frontier and Pioneer Life • Women's Lives

> **Read On:** Tracie Peterson's <u>Heirs of Montana</u> is another series that tells the stories of pioneering women.

Thriller

Thriller, action, adventure, suspense, and mystery are all terms bandied about by different people to mean different things, and sometimes the same thing. Often in a library how one defines these terms dictates where the work will be shelved: if it has a corpse and a question about whodunit, it goes in mystery; if not, it goes in general fiction. But this is not by any means a standard. Any number of fiction titles that may have a corpse and a question of whodunit do not properly belong in a "mystery" collection. These are often grouped under the broad heading of thriller.

We are using the term thriller to include the action/adventure novel, the suspense novel, and a myriad of other subgenres. These books are characterized by the following:

1. The how of the chase is more important than who is being chased.

2. There is a heightened emotional impact, engendering fear, anticipation, excitement, a sense of danger—in short, a thrill.

3. The plot is usually fast-paced, with unexpected turns.

4. There is a lot of action, which often includes daring feats and narrow escapes.

As with other genres, there is much cross-blending among the thriller novels and between thriller and mystery. This results in the categorization being somewhat subjective, thus engendering endless debate as to whether or not such-and-such a title/author should be included in a thriller section or a mystery section.

The subgenres of the thriller include action/adventure, conspiracy, espionage/spy, legal, medical, military/war, political, psychological, romantic suspense, and technological (or technothriller). In Canadian fiction, the thriller is not so widely represented as are other genres, so we do not have the list broken down into all of these subgenres.

Action/Adventure

This subgenre almost needs no definition, as the name seems self-explanatory. These are the novels that leave the reader particularly breathless, in which the characterization is not very deep and the feats are the most daring, and disbelief must often be suspended.

Hyde, Anthony.

Formosa Straits. **Viking, 1995. 251pp.**

> A Chinese American, Nick Lamp, is in Taiwan on business. While there he stumbles on the dead body of a gangster leader, who was an old friend of Nick's family. Nick becomes implicated in the gangster's death and travels through Taiwan and then on to mainland China in an effort to regain his own safety.
>
> **Subjects:** Americans in China • China • Gangsters • Murder • Taiwan
>
> **Read On:** For another action-packed thriller set in China and Taiwan, try Philip Shelby's *By Dawn's Early Light;* this time the business person is a woman. *The Hell Screens* by Alvin Lu and *Dragon Teeth* by E. Howard Hunt are other thrillers involving Taiwan and China.

Hyde, Christopher.

Black Dragon. **Morrow, 1992. 272pp.**

Organized crime has penetrated the highest echelons of the American government, and retired Colonel Phillip Dane is brought back to do damage control. Chinese crime syndicates, opium, and a murdered presidential advisor all mix together to spell Black Dragon, a criminal network.

Subjects: Assassins • Conspiracies • Hong Kong • Organized Crime • Secret Societies

Read On: You will recognize popular thriller writers in these authors who delve into the conspiratorial world of Chinese triads, drugs, and government infiltration, with titles such as *Hong Kong* (Stephen Coonts), *China White* (Peter Maas), and *Riding the Snake* (Stephen J. Cannell).

Pyper, Andrew.

The Trade Mission. **HarperFlamingoCanada, 2002. 292pp. Book Groups** 📖

Two bright dot-com entrepreneurs on the edge of the millennium go on a trade mission to Brazil to sell their new software, Hypothesys, a virtual "morality machine" that will advise the user on the best moral decision to make given the user's answers to specific questions combined with the latest polling information on the topic. But the two young businessmen and their entourage make an unwise decision by deciding to take an eco-tour through the Amazon River Valley, where they are kidnapped by extortionists.

Subjects: Amazon River Region • Brazil • Canadians in Brazil • Computer Software • Entrepreneurs • Jungles • Kidnapping • Survival • Torture

Read On: Computers and the millennium combined with a trip into the Amazon jungle might make R. J. Pineiro's Thriller, *01-01-00: The Novel of the Millennium* seem like a clone of *The Trade Mission*, but in fact it is a distinct thriller on its own. Other necessary and thrilling trips into the jungle occur in William Christie's *Mercy Mission* and James Rollins's *Amazonia.*

Stroud, Carsten.

🎗 *Lizardskin.* **Bantam Books, 1992. 374p.**

Beau McAllister is a Montana Highway Patrolman, once widowed, once divorced, whose private life does not give him respite, even while he is in the midst of trying to determine why there was a shootout between Joe Bell (truck stop owner) and several Native Americans. McAllister must keep these two factions from killing each other while he is trying to get to the bottom of the mystery. Stroud won the Arthur Ellis Award for Best Novel for this title.

Subjects: Conspiracies • Dakota Indians • Montana • Police Investigations • Political Activists

Read On: Stroud also won the Arthur Ellis Award for Best First Novel and was nominated for the Smithbooks/*Books in Canada* award for his thriller *Sniper's Moon*. Stroud has been compared to Raymond Chandler in his portrayal of the detective persona, but the sheer excitement and complexity of characterization in his books are comparable to John Sandford's <u>Prey</u> novels, particularly *Shadow Prey*, or Robert Tanenbaum's <u>Butch Karp and Marlene Ciampi</u> series.

Trower, Peter.

<u>Terry Belshaw Trilogy.</u>

The title character in this trilogy is a logger in the British Columbia woods. It is backbreaking work, but not without its adventures and misadventures, as Belshaw discovers as he becomes embroiled in affairs, rivalries, and murder in the woods and in Vancouver's gritty tenderloin, all taking place in 1950s British Columbia.

Grogan's Cafe: A Novel of the Woods. Harbour Publishing, 1993.

Dead Man's Ticket: A Novel of the Streets and the Woods. Harbour Publishing, 1996.

The Judas Hills: A Novel of the B. C. Woods. Harbour Publishing, 2000.

Shortlisted for the Ethel Wilson Fiction Prize.

Subjects: 1950s • Belshaw, Terry (Fictional Character) • British Columbia • Loggers • Lumber Camps • Trilogies

Read On: Peter Trower, a lumberman himself, is better known for his books of poetry, the latest one (*Haunted Hills and Hanging Valleys* published in 2004) a compilation of some of his work from 1969 onward. Among other fiction writers who have chronicled British Columbia's interior history are Martin A. Grainger in *Woodsmen of the West* and George Godwin in *The Eternal Forest.*

Ward, Gregory.

Kondor. Little, Brown Canada, 1997. 400pp. Book Groups 📖

The Kondor is a new minivan produced by a German automobile company, Dorner. The release and success of the Kondor are integral to the continued health of the manufacturer, but a murder and a secret film (dating back to wartime Germany) appear to be on the verge of shutting down the company and its employees. The designer of the car, his father, the driving force behind the company, and an agent of the German Federal Criminal Police all become involved in the unravelling of this conspiracy to tell trade secrets.

Subjects: Automobile Industry • Cleveland • Germany • Trade Secrets

Read On: Nazi-era Germany and its hidden secrets provide rich fodder for thriller writers, enabling them to use a variety of frames to hold the essential theme. Some of these novels are *Thunder Point* (Jack Higgins), *The Confessor* (Daniel Silva), and *The Last Prophecy* (Jon Land).

Legal Thriller

John Grisham is likely the best-known writer of the legal thriller. The protagonist of this subgenre is usually a lawyer who generally does the investigating and will take the case to trial, or not. Some legal thrillers focus on the investigation, while others are centred primarily in the courtroom. These thrillers tend to be more intellectually satisfying, as the thrill is in the cleverness of the lawyer's defence (or offence if it's a Crown or District Attorney).

Deverell, William.

Slander. McClelland & Stewart, 1999. 409pp.

Elizabeth Finnegan is a young lawyer shocked by the lenient sentence given by a judge to a convicted rapist. A few days later, she has cause to take the same judge to court on a long-standing rape charge.

Subjects: British Columbia • Date Rape • Judges • Seattle • Trials • Women Lawyers

Read On: Date rape is the subject of Alan Dershowitz's novel, *The Advocate's Devil*. Jeffrey Ashford has also written a number of mysteries involving this subject, including *A Web of Circumstances*. Tom Wolfe wrote *A Man in Full*, a novel merging the subjects of acquaintance rape and political corruption.

🎗 *Trial of Passion.* McClelland & Stewart, 1997. 390pp.

Arthur Beauchamp, first encountered in *The Dance of Shiva*, has been called back to the courtroom from his semi-retirement on the Gulf Island of Garibaldi. The acting Dean of Law at the University of British Columbia has been accused of rape by one of his female students, and Beauchamp's former colleagues need him there to help. Deverell won the Arthur Ellis Award for Best Novel and the Dashiell Hammett Award for Best Literary Crime Novel for this novel.

Subjects: Beauchamp, Arthur (Fictional Character) • British Columbia • Gender Politics • Rape • Sex Role • Trials • University Professors • Vancouver

Read On: The writing in this novel has been compared to the sophisticated writing of Scott Turow's *Presumed Innocent*. A good legal thriller often has a twist, as does *Trial of Passion*; others of interest are Mark Stern's *Inadmissible* and Jay Brandon's *Fade the Heat*. Deverell is the creator of the television series *Street Legal*.

Giroux, E. X.

<u>Robert Forsythe Mysteries.</u>

A London barrister and criminologist, Robert Forsythe investigates many of his own cases.

A Death for Adonis. St. Martin's Press, 1984.

A Death for a Dancer. St. Martin's Press, 1985.

A Death for a Darling. St. Martin's Press, 1985.

A Death for a Doctor. St. Martin's Press, 1986.

A Death for a Dilettante. St. Martin's Press, 1987.

A Death for a Dietician. St. Martin's Press, 1988.

A Death for a Dreamer. St. Martin's Press, 1989.

A Death for a Double. St. Martin's Press, 1990.

A Death for a Dancing Doll. St. Martin's Press, 1991.

A Death for a Dodo. St. Martin's Press, 1993.

London barrister and criminologist Robert Forsythe, convalescing in a luxury nursing home following knee surgery, befriends a group of guests and patients. When one of them is murdered along with a nurse, a connection to unsolved murders in the past emerges.

> **Subjects:** Barristers • Criminologists • England • Forsythe, Robert (Fictional Character) • Lawyers • London • Murder • Sanderson, Abigail "Sandy" (Fictional Character) • Secretaries

> **Read On:** To encounter British lawyers who find themselves in threatening situations outside the courtroom, meet M. R. D. Meek's Lennox Kemp, Michael Underwood's Rose Epton, and Sara Woods's Anthony Maitland. E. X. Giroux is the pseudonym of Doris Shannon.

Melnitzer, Julius.

Dirty White Collar. ECW Press, 2002. 254pp. Book Groups 📖

While in prison, lawyer Jerome Wyndham forges a connection with a Colombian drug lord, based on their love for their own children. Upon release from prison, they begin a journey together to resolve their personal situations.

> **Subjects:** Caribbean • Drugs • Fathers and Daughters • First Novels • Lawyers • Murder • Ontario • Toronto

> **Read On:** Sheldon Siegel's *Criminal Intent*, John Grisham's *The Firm* and Phillip Margolin's *The Associate* are all examples of fast-paced legal thrillers. Dennis Lehane's *Mystic River* is a thriller in which a father searches for answers to explain his daughter's death. Like the lawyer in his book, Melnitzer also spent time in prison for "white collar crime" and recounted his time there in the non-fiction work *Maximum, Medium, Minimum: A Journey Through Canadian Prisons*.

Medical Thriller

The prototype of the medical thriller can be found in Robin Cook's novels, in which the setting is often a hospital, the protagonist is a medical person, and/or the plot revolves around a number of possible choices: biological disaster with the potential unleashing of a new strain of virus; a discontented or sick doctor who seeks revenge by insidiously killing patients; an individual in the hospital (doctor, nurse, technician) fighting against a monolithic organization such as an HMO, a pharmaceutical company, or a hospital. These of course are not all the possibilities, but they are quite common in the genre. The fear for readers is that this could easily happen to them.

Clement, Peter.

Dr. Earl Garnet Medical Thrillers.

Earl Garnet is the chief of the emergency room at St. Paul's Hospital in Buffalo, New York, and his wife is an obstetrician. In the course of the series, he is often the main suspect in suspicious deaths, which requires his investigating these deaths in order to clear his own name. Clement has tackled a variety of topics in this series, from biological contamination and the death of an abused woman to HMOs and SARS.

Lethal Practice. Ballantine, 1998.

Death Rounds. Ballantine, 1999.

The Procedure. Ballantine, 2001.

Mortal Remains. Ballantine, 2003.

The Inquisitor. Ballantine, 2004.

Subjects: Buffalo • Emergency Physicians • Garnet, Earl (Fictional Character) • Hospitals • New York

Read On: The medical thriller genre includes exciting stand-alone titles such as Gregg Andrew Hurwitz's *Do No Harm* and David Farris's *Lie Still*, but it also lends itself well to the series, as we see in Peter Clement's series, as well as in Jerry Labriola's <u>Dr. David Brooks Medical Mysteries</u> and Neil McMahon's <u>Carroll Monks Mysteries</u>.

Sullivan & Steele Medical Thrillers.

Dr. Kathleen Sullivan is a geneticist and the lover of Dr. Richard Steele, an emergency room physician. Their professions take them into the greedy and dangerous world of those who want to re-engineer the world through genetic modification, human experimentation, and more.

Mutant. Ballantine Books, 2001.

Critical Condition. Ballantine Books, 2002.

Geneticist Kathleen Sullivan, paralysed by a brain hemorrhage, relies on her partner Dr. Richard Steele for protection when two corrupt physicians, attempting to further their stem cell research, use her as a human guinea pig.

5

Subjects: Conspiracies • Emergency Physicians • Manhattan • Medical Ethics • New York • Physicians • Steele, Richard (Fictional Character) • Sullivan, Kathleen (Fictional Character)

Read On: Clement's style of storytelling resembles other medical thriller writers, including Robin Cook, Michael Palmer, and Leonard Goldberg. F. Paul Wilson's *The Select* uses a similar setting in a fast-paced thriller in which a woman finds herself in peril in a hospital environment.

Hyde, Anthony

Double Helix. Viking, 1999. 322pp.

Deborah Graham, a Toronto stockbroker, begins a torrid love affair with a man she meets while holidaying in Venice. When a client is murdered, she discovers a link between her lover and the stock in a drug company that the victim wanted to buy. When the police drop the murder investigation, Deborah joins forces with a female doctor to uncover the truth behind the murder and an unscrupulous drug company's gender-selective birth control drug.

> **Subjects:** Biotechnology • Birth Control • Brazil • Canadians in Brazil • Conspiracies • Human Reproductive Technology • Missing Persons • Murder • Sex Determination • Women Stockbrokers

> **Read On:** Hyde's other thrillers include *China Lake* and *The Red Fox. Final Venture* by Michael Ridpath is a thriller that combines investments with biotechnology. Leonard S.Goldberg (*Deadly Exposure* and others) and Tess Gerritsen (*Bloodstream*) also write in the medical thriller genre.

Oppel, Kenneth.

The Devil's Cure. HarperCollinsCanada, 2000. 363pp. Book Groups 📖

The devil's cure is the blood of a killer on death row, whose blood has been found capable of killing cancer cells. Because of his strong religious beliefs, which had caused him to kill several doctors, David Haines does not want to give his blood to Laura Donaldson, the doctor who has been doing cancer research. When she visits him in prison, he effects an escape, leading Laura and FBI agent Kevin Sheldrake to Seattle in pursuit of him. They need to catch him before he can kill his only son to prevent the boy's blood from being exploited.

> **Subjects:** Cancer Research • Cults • Death Row Inmates • Escaped Convicts • FBI Agents • Medical Ethics • Murderers • Women Physicians

> **Read On:** Oppel is the author of the popular children's series Silverwing and the award-winning children's fantasy *Airborn*. This is his first foray into adult fiction writing, and he joins such thriller writers as Phillip Margolin, Ridley Pearson, and T. Jefferson Parker. For edge-of-the-seat stories about escaped convicts, try Patricia Cornwell's *Point of Origin*, Robert W. Walker's *Pure Instinct*, Alan Dunn's *Payback*, or Gregg Andrew Hurwitz's *The Tower*.

Military/War

Novels in this subgenre might be set in a war zone, or they may simply deal with military weapons and/or preparation for war. They often tell one version of a real battle, peopled with real characters, but they may also try for an alternate version of a war-related situation, without becoming fantastic. The military/war thriller may also be classified at times as a technothriller, if the setting is current-day or even a bit into the future. We have combined both types here. Often this subgenre lends itself to series.

Reeves-Stevens, Judith, and Garfield Reeves-Stevens.

Mitch Webber and Cory Rey.

Mitch Webber is a U.S. Navy captain, and Cory Rey, Mitch's former lover, is an oceanographer. Their combined talents take them to such varying places as Antarctica and the International Space Station, the latter to prevent the sabotage of the Space Shuttle *Constitution* (*Freefall*).

Icefire. Pocket Books, 1998.

Navy SEAL Captain Mitch Webber and oceanographer Cory Rey are in a race against time to stop the destruction of most of the Pacific Rim after a group of insurgent Chinese military officers release a devastating displacement wave.

Freefall. Pocket Books, 2005.

Subjects: Disasters • International Intrigue • Nuclear Weapons • Rey, Cory (Fictional Character) • Technothrillers • Terrorism • Webber, Mitch (Fictional Character)

Read On: The technological language used in these novels is also intrinsic to the technothrillers by Tom Clancy (*The Hunt for Red October* and others), Clive Cussler (*Trojan Odyssey* and others), and Stephen Coonts (*Flight of the Intruder* and others).

Rohmer, Richard.

Caged Eagle. **Killick Press, 2002. 245pp.**

In a penitentiary in 2001, Garth Peters reflects back on his life as a fighter pilot in World War II, in which he earned the Distinguished Flying Cross (as did the author, also a fighter pilot). Although highly skilled in aviation, Peters is less skilled in his personal relations, and toward the end of the war, he applies the nastier parts of his personality to acquire a major business that he ruthlessly leads into the billion-dollar category. We do not learn until the very end of the novel why he is writing his story from prison.

Subjects: Air Pilots • Businessmen • Reminiscing in Old Age • Royal Canadian Air Force • Veterans • World War II

Read On: Another veteran sits reminiscing about his days as a pilot in World War II in *The Two-Headed Eagle* by John Biggins. *Squadron* is a novel about a bomber pilot written by a Canadian, Spencer Dunmore, and *A Real Good War* (Sam Halpert) is yet another novel featuring a bomber pilot.

Slater, Ian.

MacArthur Must Die. **D. I. Fine, Inc, 1994. 296pp.**

In 1942 the Japanese, who hold control in the Pacific Rim, plan an assassination plot against General Douglas MacArthur, convinced that this event would destroy the morale of the Allies and turn the tide of World War II.

Subjects: Assassination Plots • MacArthur, Douglas • War in the Pacific • World War II

Read On: Slater was an Australian Joint Intelligence Bureau defence officer before moving to Vancouver, and he has written more than twenty military thrillers, including the WWIII series. Leaders from all sides in the Second World War are the targets of assassination attempts in Glenn Meade's *The Sands of Sakhara*, Maynard Allington's *The Grey Wolf,* and Benjamin King's *The Loki Project.*

USA vs. Militia.

This is civil war in a not-so-future world, with the U.S. government enlisting General Douglas Freeman, commander of the American Forces in World War III, to combat the various militia groups in the United States who are willing to use cutting-edge military technology to maintain their freedom, their values, and their property.

Showdown. Fawcett, 1997.

Battle Front. Fawcett, 1998.

Manhunt. Fawcett, 1999.

Force 10. Ballantine Books, 2000.

Knockout. Ballantine Books, 2001.

Subjects: Civil War • Militia Movements • Paramilitary Forces • War Stories

Read On: In S. Wise Bauer's *The Revolt*, a militia group does succeed in breaking Virginia and North Carolina away from the United States. Mack Bolan, in Don Pendleton's *Rebels and Hostiles,* goes undercover to discover a plot to begin a second American Revolution, and in Jack Williamson's *The Silicon Dagger*, a group of militia in Kentucky are planning to declare independence from the American government.

Smith, Taylor.

Deadly Grace. Mira Books, 2001. 477pp.

FBI agent Alex Cruz considers Jillian Meade the prime suspect in the deaths of her mother and two former World War II resistance workers. With Jillian in a psychiatric hospital suffering from shock, Alex has only her journals to lead him to the truth.

Subjects: Cruz, Alex (Fictional Character) • FBI Agents • Holocaust Survivors • Mothers and Daughters • Murder • Nazis • Resistance Movement • World War II

Read On: Thrillers penned by Catherine Coulter (*Hemlock Bay*), Francine Mathews (*The Cutout*), and Gayle Lynds (*Masquerade*) evince an atmosphere reminiscent of Smith's thrillers. Barbara Fradkin's *Once upon a Time* is a mystery in which a grown child learns of a parent's role in the Holocaust.

Political

The political thriller is very popular with writers and readers alike. It may deal directly with politics, focusing on an American president, a senator, a member of Parliament, or a prime minister, or it may involve itself with a political situation in a country or city. The situation could be global or local, and it may involve a conspiracy, but it usually deals with power of some sort. We have included here various samples of the political thriller, broadly defined.

Fraser, John.

Stolen China. **McClelland & Stewart, 1996. 251pp.**

Jamie Halpert is a correspondent for a major Toronto newspaper, just finishing a stint in China. Before he leaves, however, he is invited to a remote village, an invitation that seems to spark a number of sinister events, the primary one being the murder of his friend Gordon. Jamie returns to Toronto but cannot forget the events of that fateful time.

> **Subjects:** Canadians in China • China • Foreign Correspondents • Interracial Marriage • Murder • Ontario • Toronto

> **Read On:** Novels about foreign correspondents usually combine excitement and suspense with exotic travel. A few such novels to try are *Blood Cries* by John Weisman, *Cover Story* by Robert Cullen, or *Unholy Trinity* by Paul Adam.

Hyde, Christopher.

The Second Assassin. **New American Library, 2002. 392pp.**

In 1939, a group of powerful men, hoping to ensure a victory for Germany by keeping the United States from entering the war, hire an assassin to kill the King and Queen of England while the royals are on U.S. soil.

> **Subjects:** Assassination Plots • Assassins • Conspiracies • International Politics • World War II

> **Read On:** Hyde's other thrillers include *A Gathering of Saints, Wisdom of the Bones, The House of Special Purpose,* and *Hard Target*, another novel about an assassination attempt, also published as *White Lies*. Ian Slater also writes about an assassination attempt during the war in *MacArthur Must Die*. For other thrillers set in Europe during World War II try Jack Higgins (*The Eagle Has Landed* and others) and Robert Harris (*Fatherland, Enigma*). Tom Clancy's *Patriot Games* also includes an assassination plot involving members of the royal family.

  5

Moore, Brian.

Lies of Silence. **Lester & Orpen Dennys, 1990. 194pp. Book Groups** 📖

Michael Dillon struggles with a series of ongoing moral decisions that begin when IRA terrorists break into his home, hold his wife hostage, and force him to participate in a bombing—all on the same night he had planned to leave his wife for another woman. He continues to wrestle with his conscience as he decides on the right course of action once the terrorists have been caught.

> **Subjects:** Affairs • Belfast • Irish Republican Army • Northern Ireland • Terrorism

> **Read On:** Moore has an eclectic list of books to his credit. Some of his other thrillers are *The Statement*, *No Other Life*, and *The Color of Blood*.

The violence in Ireland is a subject in John McGahern's *Amongst Women*, James Hynes's *The Wild Colonial Boy*, and Paul Watkins's *The Promise of Light*.

Platz, Jonathon.

Work of Idle Hands. Great Plains Publications, 2002. 256pp. Book Groups 📖

In a South American country in the 1970s, Amnesty International Worker Peter Quinfell cracks from all the inhuman abuse, repression, and corruption he has witnessed during his sojourn in South America. He takes the law into his own hands and begins to assassinate all those whom he deems to have been guilty of crimes against humanity. A burned-out Royal Canadian Mounted Police officer becomes his hunter. This debut novel was shortlisted for the Arthur Ellis Award for Best First Novel and for the Eileen McTavish Sykes Award for Best First Book.

> **Subjects:** 1970s • Amnesty International • Argentina • Assassins • First Novels • Good vs. Evil • Justice • Political Persecution • Royal Canadian Mounted Police

> **Read On:** Writing about political persecution can take a variety of forms. In Tom LeClair's *Well-Founded Fear*, the protagonist works for the Office of the UN High Commissioner for Refugees; she also tries to take things into her own hands, with disastrous results. *The Angel of Darkness* is a translation of an original work by Ernest Sabato; he has placed himself in the middle of his novel about the battle between good and evil in Argentina in the 1970s. And J. M. Coetzee has written an allegory about torture and persecution in *Waiting for the Barbarians*. *They Forged the Signature of God* (Viriato Sención) is an award-winning novel of church-state oppression in the Dominican Republic.

Stroud, Carsten.

Cobraville. Simon &Schuster, 2004. 415pp.

Stroud keeps up with current affairs and political activity in this novel as he pits a covert CIA cadre against al Qaeda and other terrorist forces in the Philippines. Also inadvertently involved is the CIA mission leader's estranged father, a Democratic senator and member of the Senate Select Committee on Intelligence. It becomes his self-appointed task to learn the identity of the group responsible for the betrayal of his son's unit.

> **Subjects:** Central Intelligence Agency • Conspiracies • Covert Operations • Intelligence Officers • Mindanao Island • Philippines • Terrorism

> **Read On:** As the political landscape changes across the globe, so too must the focus of political thriller writers, if they are interested in telling a current and relevant tale. John Weisman's *SOAR*, Stephen Coonts's *Liberty*, and Vince Flynn's *Memorial Day* all reflect today's political intelligence situation.

Taylor, Patrick.

Pray for Us Sinners. Insomniac Press, 2000. 305pp.

Lieutenant Marcus Richardson, a British army explosives expert, agrees to take on one final assignment: the infiltration of the Provisional IRA. In doing so, he finds himself in the middle of the "Troubles" in Belfast in 1974.

Subjects: Belfast • British in Northern Ireland • First Novels • Northern Ireland • Political Violence • Soldiers • Undercover Operations

Read On: Taylor's short-story collection, *Only Wounded: Ulster Stories,* also examines the conflict in Northern Ireland. Gerald Seymour's *Field of Blood* is another thriller set in Northern Ireland, as is Daniel Silva's *The Marching Season,* although in the later period of the 1990s. Silva's Gabriel Allon novels (*The Kill Artist* and others) tell the story of a man reluctantly drawn into performing just one more mission for his government. Brian Moore's *Lies of Silence* explores the daily violence of Northern Ireland's conflict and its effects on the people who love their country.

Waddell, Ian.

A Thirst to Die For. NeWest Press, 2002. 253pp. Book Groups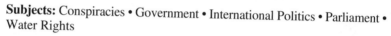

A long-time member of Parliament, Ian Waddell has turned his hand to fiction to tell the story of a conspiracy to sell Canada's water to the United States. His protagonist is also a member of Parliament, a young half-Native from British Columbia who finds himself fighting the very government he has promised to serve.

Subjects: Conspiracies • Government • International Politics • Parliament • Water Rights

Read On: A preeminent thriller writer, Clive Cussler has also tackled the subject of water rights in *Blue Gold.* Another Canadian writer, Varda Burstyn, treats the subject of water supply in Quebec in her novel *Water Inc. Blue Gold* is also the title of a non-fiction work on the question of selling water, in Maude Barlow's work, *Blue Gold: The Battle Against Corporate Theft of the World's Water.*

Psychological

The psychological thriller is different from the other thrillers in that characterization is much more important, and the fast-paced action is not usually so present as in some of the other subgenres. This thriller often has a sexual nature to it—psychosexual thrillers—and the antagonist is either a serial killer or a serial rapist. Much of the tension in the plot comes from trying to determine how the criminal thinks, where he (more often than she) will strike next. Often the protagonist is a potential victim, thus heightening the suspense and tension. This type of thriller is generally the most intellectually oriented.

Appignanesi, Lisa.

The Dead of Winter. McArthur, 1999. 356pp.

Following the Montreal massacre of fourteen women students, actress Madeleine Blais fears that someone is determined to kill her, too.

Subjects: Actresses • Assassins • Crimes Against Women • École Polytechnique Montreal • Lépine, Marc • Montreal • Montreal Massacre • Murder • Quebec

Read On: Heidi Rathjen's *December 6: From the Montreal Massacre to Gun Control* touches on the circumstances and the aftermath of the massacre.

The Montreal Massacre, edited by Louise Malette, Marie Chalouh, and Marlene Wildeman, is a collection of essays, poems, and letters to the editor, describing the impact of this tragedy on other women. The protagonist of Cathy Vasas-Brown's *Every Wickedness* also fears that she is the next victim of a serial killer.

Fielding, Joy.

Whispers and Lies. Doubleday Canada, 2002. 307pp.

Middle-aged nurse Terry Painter worries about her personal safety and well-being as the young woman to whom she rents her guesthouse gradually works her way into Terry's life.

Subjects: Florida • Landlord and Tenant • Middle-aged Women • Nurses • Single Women • Women's Friendships

Read On: Fielding has written many other psychological thrillers, including *The First Time*, *Lost,* and *Puppet*; the psychological-suspense style in her plot-twisting novels resembles that of Patricia Highsmith (*The Talented Mr. Ripley* and others) and Patricia Carlon (*The Souvenir* and others). To read more novels with surprise endings, try *Exclusive* by Sandra Brown, *Not a Penny More, Not a Penny Less* by Jeffrey Archer, and *High Crimes* by Joseph Finder.

Forbes, Leslie.

Bombay Ice. Farrar, Straus & Giroux, 1998. 417pp. Book Groups 📖

After receiving a cryptic letter from her sister, journalist Rosalind Bengal returns home to Bombay, where she confronts her past while investigating a series of murders that may involve her sister's husband.

Subjects: Bombay • British In India • England • First Novels • India • Motion Picture Producers and Directors • Murder • Sisters • Women Journalists

Read On: Forbes is also the author of *Flesh, Blood and Bone*, an intense thriller that takes a woman on a journey following a murder. Iain Pears's *An Instance of the Fingerpost* also falls in the category of literary thriller. The H.R.F. Keating mysteries featuring Ganesh Ghote are set in contemporary India. The young woman in Catherine Bush's *The Rules of Engagement* must also resolve her past before she can move on with her life.

Gray, John MacLachlan.

A Gift for the Little Master. Random House of Canada, 2000. 345pp. Book Groups 📖

Set in a West Coast city, this novel by Vancouver writer John Gray is peopled by a variety of characters: Delores, a night-owl cable TV reporter; Eli, a bike courier; and Turner, a vigilante policeman, hot on the trail of a serial killer. Their stories become interrelated in this gritty portrayal of life at night in an urban environment.

Subjects: Bicycle Messengers • City and Town Life • Serial Killers • Vigilantes • Women Television Journalists

Read On: John MacLachlan Gray, former columnist for *Maclean's, The Vancouver Sun,* and *The Globe and Mail,* is also the author of the renowned play *Billy Bishop Goes to War*. Apart from his non-fiction writing, he has also written two novels in what may become a series featuring an investigative journalist in Victorian London: *The Fiend in Human* and *The White Stone Day*. His writing style has been compared to Graham Greene and Evelyn Waugh, but the gritty nature of his serial killer story can be compared to Bob Leuci's *Double Edge* or Soledad Santiago's *Nightside*.

Hall, Linda.

Sadie's Song. **Multnomah Press, 2001. 301pp. Book Groups** 📖

In a small New England town a child has disappeared, and Sadie Thornton, who has hidden her husband's abuse from her pastor and church, fears his violence may have turned in another direction.

> **Subjects:** Christian Fiction • Maine • Marriage • Missing Children • Wife Abuse

> **Read On:** Hall's other novels set in Maine include *Island of Refuge*, *Margaret's Peace,* and *Steal Away*. Christian novels take on the difficult topic of wife abuse and family violence in *Sharon's Hope* by Neva Coyle, *The Touch* by Patricia Hickman, and *Serenity Bay* by Bette Nordberg. The terror of child abduction is portrayed in Tami Hoag's *Night Sins* and *Guilty as Sin*.

Hunter, Catherine.

The Dead of Midnight. **Ravenstone, 2001. 360pp. Book Groups** 📖

Imagine being a member of a book club, reading and discussing your way through a series (the <u>Midnight Mystery Series</u>), and then finding that life is beginning to resemble art too much, as each member of the book club falls victim to murder, in much the same way as each murder is described in the series.

> **Subjects:** Book Clubs • Manitoba • Serial Murders • Winnipeg

> **Read On:** Book club members enjoy reading books about book discussion groups, in the hopes of learning new titles and finding out how closely the book group in the novel resembles their own book group. The field is starting to broaden in this area, with such titles as *Angry Housewives Eating Bons Bons* (Lorna Landvik), *The Jane Austen Book Club* (Karen Joy Fowler), *He Had It Coming* (Camika Spencer), and *The Book Club* (Mary Alice Munroe).

Nichol, James.

🎗 *Midnight Cab.* **Alfred A. Knopf, 2002. 337pp. Book Groups** 📖

Nineteen-year-old Walker Devereaux receives help in uncovering buried family secrets from a dispatcher at the cab company where he works. As he looks for answers to why a mother he barely remembers would abandon him at age three, he finds himself in danger from a psychopath. Nichol won the Arthur Ellis Award for Best First Novel for this debut work.

Subjects: Abandoned Children • Family Relationships • First Novels • Identity • Mothers and Sons • Ontario • Taxicab Drivers • Teenage Boys • Toronto

Read On: This fast-paced thriller set in Toronto will appeal to fans of David Lindsey (*An Absence of Light*), Michael Connelly (*Void Moon*), and Lisa Gardner (*The Next Accident*).

Slade, Michael.

Special X.

This series has been growing and changing since its inception; in fact the series name was not originally part of it. Michael Slade has always "been" different writers, with Jay Clarke at its core. The series crosses a number of genres, primarily thriller, mystery, and horror, with the occasional science fiction added in, but the thrill is paramount, so we have included it here. Special X is an elite task force of the Royal Canadian Mounted Police, headquartered in Vancouver, British Columbia, and its sole purpose is to track serial killers, which it often does in conjunction with other police departments.

Headhunter. Thomas Allen, 1984.

Ghoul. Beach Tree Books, 1987.

Cutthroat. Signet, 1992.

Ripper. Signet, 1994.

Evil Eye. Viking, 1996.

Primal Scream. Viking, 1998.

Burnt Bones. Viking, 1999.

Hangman. Viking, 2000.

RCMP Inspector Zinc Chandler teams with Maddy Thorne of the Seattle PD to track down a cross-border serial killer playing a savagely gruesome game of hangman with his victims.

Death's Door. Viking, 2001.

Bed of Nails. Penguin, 2003.

Subjects: British Columbia • Chandler, Zinc (Fictional Character) • Craven, Nick (Fictional Character) • de Clerq, Robert (Fictional Character) • Murder • Police • Royal Canadian Mounted Police • Serial Killers • Vancouver

Read On: Each novel highlights different members of its group, much as Lisa Scottoline does in her Philadelphia Legal Thriller series featuring Benny Rosato's law firm. William Bayer (*Mirror Maze* and others) and Andrew Vachss (*Safe House* and others) also write gritty psychological thrillers.

Soles, Caro.

The Tangled Boy. Baskerville Books, 2002. 249pp. Book Groups 📖

Teenager Cory Williams is struggling to understand his emerging homosexuality. His life becomes increasingly complex as he deals with friends who persecute him, the murder of a man with whom he had had a brief encounter, and a blackmailer.

Subjects: Blackmail • Coming of Age • Coming Out • Gay Teenagers • Murder • Sexual Identity • Sexual Orientation • Witnesses

Read On: Soles is the author of the science fiction novel *The Abulon Dance*, as well as several short-story collections. In Dennis Cooper's *My Loose Thread* another teenage boy struggles with his emerging sexual identity, while Timothy Murphy's *Getting Off Clean* adds the dimension of racial tension to the issue of coming out.

Vasas-Brown, Cathy.

Every Wickedness. **Doubleday Canada, 2001. 293pp.**

In San Francisco a serial killer known as the Spiderman is stalking and killing women. When interior designer Beth Wells, whose roommate was one of the killer's victims, starts receiving threatening notes, she and police lieutenant Jim Kearns begin to fear that she may be the Spiderman's next target.

Subjects: California • First Novels • Interior Designers • Police • San Francisco • Serial Killers

Read On: The serial killer novel has almost become a genre of its own. Some authors who write in this genre are Mary Higgins Clark (*You Belong to Me* and others), John Katzenbach (*State of Mind* and others), John Lutz (*The Night Caller*), and Stuart Woods (*Worst Fears Realized*). Robert Graysmith's *Zodiac Unmasked: The Identity of America's Most Elusive Serial Killer Revealed* is the true story of a serial killer who was responsible for more than thirty murders in California. Vasas-Brown has followed this thriller with another, *Some Reason in Madness,* about a rapist who returns to plague the woman responsible for his imprisonment.

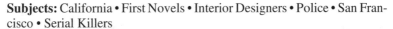

Horror

The horror genre can be described as the stuff of nightmares, stories in which the worst wasn't imagined and yet it happens. Classics of this genre, Mary Shelley's *Frankenstein* (1818) and Bram Stoker's *Dracula* (1897), have become legendary and are now read and enjoyed by a wide variety of readers. A number of authors have been and continue to be solid storytellers in this genre; the most prominent and widely read of these authors are Stephen King, Dean Koontz, and Anne Rice.

Webster's Collegiate Dictionary gives the primary definition of horror as "a painful and intense fear, dread, or dismay." From this definition, we conclude that one of the primary appeals of this genre is that, like the romance genre, it elicits strong emotional responses from the reader. However, unlike romance or even mystery, the reader is never sure how the story will end. As the story unfolds, with both the reader and the protagonist learning or experiencing events at the same time, the author takes the reader through a series of highs and lows, building a sense of dread, and then bringing in a twist to jolt the reader when least expected; the unexpected is expected! This is done with the intention of allowing readers to face their fears within the safe confines of their own space. While there are certainly elements of horror in almost every genre, including science fiction, romance, thrillers, and mystery/suspense, we feel that the titles listed here fit the definition of the genre as articulated by Anthony Fonseca and June Pulliam: A horror text is one that "contains a monster, whether it be supernatural, human, or a metaphor for . . . psychological torment" (2003, 3).

Advisors looking for additional read-alikes for each subgenre listed here are referred to Fonseca and Pulliam's *Hooked on Horror: A Guide to Reading Interests in Horror Fiction*; this tool covers print (monographs and short stories) as well as films in this genre. Librarians and readers looking for an introduction to the work of Canadian authors writing in this genre are referred to the <u>Northern Frights</u> series (volumes 1–5) and *Wild Things Live There: The Best of Northern Frights,* all edited by Don Hutchison. Finally, advisors working with readers are reminded that some titles in this genre might include graphically described sex and violence, and this should be a point of discussion in the readers' advisory interview. Joyce Saricks, in *The Readers' Advisory Guide to Genre Fiction* (2001), describes the specifics of this interaction for each genre, and advisors are referred to this tool for further information.

The titles in this genre share a number of common characteristics:

1. Ordinary situations and events take unexpected, even improbable turns that may involve supernatural or demonic powers.

2. The characters in many of the novels are people whom readers identify with; this heightens the terror because readers feel the events could happen to them.

3. These novels explore the darker side of the human psyche.

4. The atmosphere in these novels is often dark, foreboding, or menacing as the author works to elicit an immediate strong, emotional response from the reader.

Dark Fantasy

In this subgenre, authors write stories that are characterized by their dark or bleak view of the world being created. The emphasis here is on atmosphere, and to enhance the dark tone, the storytelling is often done through short sentences with sparse, terse dialogue. Often these stories will incorporate elements of both magic and adventure as the characters face off in a conflict of good versus evil, with the horror being increased because the reader is prepared to believe that this could happen.

Bassingthwaite, Don.

If Whispers Call. Wizards of the Coast, 2000. 299pp.

Following a visit to an unconsecrated cemetery, a young couple become the target of a spirit. The pregnant young woman falls into an unexplained coma, and the spirit, who seems to have plans for their unborn child, pursues her husband. A team of phantasmic experts from a clandestine agency begin to investigate, in an attempt to understand how this spirit is able to defy the normal rules of the spirit world as it shifts from the cemetery to the hospital.

Subjects: Chicago • Coma Patients • Ghosts • Hospitals • Mind Control

Read On: Bassingthwaite has written a number of dark fantasy titles, including *Such Pain* and *Pomegranates Full and Fine*; he has also collaborated on a number of titles in the <u>Forgotten Realms®</u> series (*The Yellow Silk* and, with Dave Gross, *Mistress of the Night*). *If Whispers Call* is the second book in the <u>Dark Matter</u> series; the rest are Gary A. Braunbeck's *In Hollow Houses* (Bk. 1), G. W. Tirpa's *In Fluid Silence* (Bk. 3), Monte Cook's *Of Aged Angels* (Bk. 4), and Bassingthwaite's *By Dust Consumed* (Bk. 5). This ghostly premise with much of its action in a hospital setting will appeal to readers of F. Paul Wilson's *The Select* and Connie Willis's *Passage*.

de Lint, Charles.

Mulengro. Tom Doherty, 2003. 400pp.

The perpetrator of a series of killings in the city's Gypsy community eludes the police. Someone is killing off those who have made a life beyond the circle of the local Romany community. As the police search for a human suspect, there are those in the Romany community who know better, realizing they are up against a darker, ghostly force they have named Mulengro.

Subjects: Good vs. Evil • Gypsies • Ottawa • Outcasts

Read On: This title was originally published in 1985 and recently re-issued. The blending of evil and magic found in this dark fantasy will appeal to readers of Stephen King's <u>The Dark Tower</u> series. Other authors who also write in this genre include Terry Brooks (*Running with the Demon* and others) and Tim Powers (*Last Call* and others). De Lint's *Moonheart*, part of <u>The Newford Chronicles</u>, which include *Forests of the Heart, The Onion Girl*, and *Spirits in the Wires,* among others, is the work that established him within the urban fantasy genre, stories set on contemporary city streets.

Key, Samuel M.

From a Whisper to a Scream. Tom Doherty, 2003. 320pp.

Two years ago Newford police officer Thomas Morningstar killed and saw buried a child killer. Now someone is killing again, and the killer's style bears a striking resemblance to that of the long-dead killer. Morningstar, a Native American seeking to better himself outside the confines of the traditional ways, begins to work with a photographer, looking for a runaway who appears in the crime scene photos. As they search for the young woman, Morningstar comes to believe that he is on the trail of a spirit, and he must turn back again to his traditional beliefs if he is to triumph in his ultimate encounter with evil.

Subjects: Child Abuse • Good vs. Evil • Magic • Newford (Fictional Place)

Read On: Samuel M. Key is the pseudonym of Charles de Lint. De Lint wrote three dark, urban fantasies under the Key pseudonym; the other titles, *Angel of Darkness* and *I'll Be Watching You*, have recently been reprinted, along with *From a Whisper to a Scream*. In these works de Lint explores a variety of social issues such as child and wife abuse. This is de Lint's first full-length novel set in his city of Newford, although in this case he explores the darker side of the city known as The Tombs. This blending of magic, mystery, and horror is also found in the dark urban crime novels of Andrew Vachss's <u>Burke</u> series (*Only Child* and others).

Tirpa, G. W.

In Fluid Silence. Wizards of the Coast, 2003. 288pp.

Following the disappearance of their partner, two covert agents from a special paranormal agency find themselves chasing a charismatic Nazi leader as they attempt to unravel a plot designed to create the ultimate master race.

Subjects: Conspiracies • Magic • Nazis

Read On: This novel is part of the <u>Dark Matter</u> series that includes Gary A. Braunbeck's *In Hollow Houses* (Bk. 1), Monte Cook's *Of Aged Angels* (Bk. 4), and Don Bassingthwaite's *If Whispers Call* and *By Dust Consumed* (Bks. 2 and 5). Nazis are integral to the sense of horror created in Graham Masterton's *The Burning* and James Herbert's *The Spear*.

Ghosts and Haunted Houses

The stories in this category focus on "haunting" by either a spirit or a place. In ghost stories, spirits are not limited to or connected to a place and are attempting to connect with a human to bring a warning from beyond the grave. In the haunted house novel, the horror is psychological and based on some past guilt that is being transferred to the individual now within its walls.

Kearsley, Susanna.

The Shadowy Horses. McClelland & Stewart, 1997. 370pp.

Verity leaves her job at the British Museum to join a dig in Scotland—at what she soon learns is believed to be the site of the Legio IX Hispana, a lost Roman legion. While there she meets a young boy with "the sight" and a very handsome but aloof fellow archaeologist.

Subjects: Antiquities • Archaeology • Ghost Stories • Scotland • Supernatural • Women Archaeologists

Read On: The Gothic feeling conveyed here is also found in the novels of Barbara Erskine (*Midnight Is a Lonely Place* and others) and Barbara Michaels (*Stitches in Time* and others). Other women archaeologists can be found in different mystery series by such authors as Beverly Connor (<u>Lindsay Chamberlain</u> series) and Sharyn McCrumb (<u>Elizabeth MacPherson</u> series). Lyn Hamilton's archaeological mysteries feature an antiques dealer (Lara McClintoch). Kearsley won England's Catherine Cookson Fiction Prize for her romance novel, *Mariana*. She is also the author of the romantic mystery *The Splendour Falls*. Kearsley's novels will appeal to readers of Jayne Ann Krentz (*Light in Shadow* and others) and Amanda Quick (*Wicked Widow* and others).

Moloney, Susie.

The Dwelling. Random House of Canada, 2003. 408pp.

Real estate agent Glenn Darnley finds herself repeatedly selling a charming Victorian home as a series of occupants tragically meet its ghosts.

Subjects: Ghosts • Haunted Houses • Realtors

Read On: Moloney created psychological horror in her earlier novels, *Bastion Falls* and *A Dry Spell*. To visit more haunted houses, read *The Haunting of Hill House* by Shirley Jackson and *A Winter Haunting* by Dan Simmons. The intensity of atmosphere created here will appeal to readers of Stephen King (*The Shining*, *The Dead Zone*, and others) and Stephen King's collaborations with Peter Straub (*The Talisman*, *Black House*, and others).

Pullinger, Kate.

Weird Sister. McArthur & Co, 1999. 308pp.

A beautiful American tourist, Agnes Samuel, appears in the ancient English village of Warboys, charming members of the Throckmorton family in order to ruin them in retribution for a witch-hanging 300 years earlier.

Subjects: England • Gothic Fiction • Occult • Retribution • Witchcraft • Witches

Read On: The best-known Gothic novel of the twentieth century is Daphne du Maurier's *Rebecca*. The pull of the English countryside in *Weird Sister* also appears in Nicola Thorne's *Repossession*. Andrew Halfnight, like Pullinger's Agnes Samuel, has the same fatal effect on people he gets close to in Eric McCormack's *First Blast of the Trumpet Against the Monstrous Regiment of Women*.

Stewart, Sean.

Perfect Circle. Small Beer Press, 2004. 248pp.

William "Dead" Kennedy's ability to see and connect with ghosts is usually more trouble than it's worth, but after losing his job, his cousin's offer of a thousand dollars to get rid of the ghost haunting his garage is just the thing he needs. As he works to exorcise the murdered girl, "DK," also haunted by his long-deceased uncle, begins to realize he has been something of a floating spirit in the lives of those he loves.

Subjects: Death • Fathers and Daughters • Ghosts • Haunting • Revenge • Texas

Read On: Stewart is the winner of the Arthur Ellis Award for Best First Novel (*Passion Play*), the Prix Aurora Award (*Passion Play* and *Nobody's Son*), and the World Fantasy Award (*Galveston*); two of his novels (*Mockingbird* and *Resurrection Man*) were placed on the *New York Times* Notable Books lists. Dean Koontz's *Odd Thomas*, another similarly told horror novel with elements of humour, also has a main character with the ability to see ghosts.

Psychological Horror

The works in this subgenre are written to generate terror in the mind of the protagonist and the reader. There are rarely external elements to generate the fear; rather, it is in the *perception* of danger. Readers of both thrillers and adventure novels may be drawn to these novels.

Italiano, Marcy.

Pain Machine. Cosmos Books, 2003. 180pp.

Outwardly, sixty-year-old Dr. Veronica Laka seems harmless enough, but the punishment inflicted on her as a child by her father has had a far-reaching impact. Now, with her partner Dr. Mark Ivy, she has developed the pain machine. As they begin the testing phase of a device that is capable of transferring pain from one person to another, the pain and horror from Veronica's past will directly influence her participation.

> **Subjects:** Child Abuse • First Novels • Pain • Psychological Horror

> **Read On:** Like F. Paul Wilson's *The Select*, this novel is fast paced, and the terror is heightened by the reader's imagination. Another author whose novels are also fast-paced psychological horror tales is Andrew Klavan (*The Animal Hour* and others). *Pain Machine* was shortlisted for a Bram Stoker Award for First Novel.

Moloney, Susie.

A Dry Spell. Doubleday Canada, 1997. 385pp.

A four-year drought in Goodlands, North Dakota, has devastated life in the small town, in ways more than just the foreclosure of many family farms. With the drought has come a force that has pitted the townspeople against each other. When a self-proclaimed rainmaker arrives in town, many wonder if he can bring them much-needed salvation, or if the worst is yet to come.

> **Subjects:** Drought • Good vs. Evil • Natural Disasters • North Dakota • Small-town Life

> **Read On:** Moloney's spine-tingling tale of good versus evil is similar in tone to Charles Grant's *Symphony*. Small-town terror is created in Richard Bachman's *The Regulators*.

Vampires/Werewolves/Witches

The works in this subgenre are populated with creatures, often human, who have supernatural or shape-shifting abilities; because they do resemble humans, readers often are able to identify with them and do not see them as something to fear. These novels are often highly erotic or sensual, which can be an important appeal element for the reader. There may be some crossover reading in this subgenre by readers of paranormal romances.

Armstrong, Kelley.

Women of the Otherworld.

In this series, which begins with the story of the only female werewolf in the world, the author moves on to tell the story of a young apprentice witch. One of the strengths of this series is the way the author incorporates the supernatural into the real world.

Bitten. Random House of Canada, 2001.

Elena, the only female werewolf in the world, is attempting to remain in human society, despite the call of her pack. Elena finds herself caught in a classic struggle between her wolf nature and the love of two men, one human and the other werewolf.

Stolen. Seal Books, 2003.

Dismissing the warning that a group of humans has been kidnapping supernaturals, female werewolf Elena finds herself locked in a cell, separated from her pack. With no other option but to find a way to destroy the ring of kidnappers, she must first determine whom among the other kidnapped supernaturals she can trust. *Stolen* was awarded the *Romantic Times* Reviewers' Choice Award Best Contemporary Paranormal Romance.

Dime Store Magic. Random House of Canada, 2004.

Industrial Magic. Seal Books, 2004.

Haunted. Seal Books, 2005.

> **Subjects:** Toronto • Triangles • Werewolves • Witches

> **Read On:** A female werewolf is featured in Alice Borchardt's work (*The Silver Wolf, Night of the Wolf, and The Wolf King*), and werewolves are central to the series by Susan Krinard (*Touch of the Wolf, Once a Wolf,* and *Secret of the Wolf*) and <u>The Devoncroix Chronicles</u> series by Donna Boyd (*The Passion* and *The Promise*). Enthusiasts of this genre should try paranormal romance novelist Laurell K. Hamilton's <u>Anita Blake, Vampire Hunter</u> series. The sexuality found in *Bitten* compares to that in Anne Rice's *Interview with the Vampire*.

Baker, Nancy.

The Night Inside: A Vampire Thriller. Viking, 1993. 312pp.

Ardeth Alexander, recently kidnapped and held hostage as a vampire's food source, realizes her only option is to forge an alliance with him. Becoming a vampire herself, she seeks revenge with him against those who had held them captive.

> **Subjects:** Erotic Fiction • First Novels • Hostages • Toronto • Vampires

> **Read On:** The 1995 edition of this title was published as *Kiss of the Vampire*. Baker wrote a sequel to *The Night Inside, Blood and Chrysanthemums* (1994). Another Baker novel, *A Terrible Beauty,* is a retelling of the fairytale *Beauty and the Beast*. Kelley Armstrong's *Stolen* reverses Baker's plot, recounting the kidnapping of the vampires. Nick Knight, vampire-detective, also lives in Toronto in Anne Hathaway-Nayne's series (*Forever Knight: These Our Revels* and others).

Girón, Sèphera.

Borrowed Flesh. Dorchester, 2004. 340pp.

Vanessa, a Tarot-card-reading witch, has learned the secret of immortality, knowledge that comes with a price: she must sacrifice young virgins for their flesh in order to maintain a "youthful" appearance. Following the death of her latest victim, Vanessa's life takes a number of twists, and when men start disappearing and the best friend of her last victim starts searching for her, she begins to suspect that there may be forces working against her.

Subjects: Erotic Fiction • Immortality • Occult • Witches

Read On: In *Eternal Sunset*, Girón tells the story of how Vanessa gained her immortality; she is also the author of a number of other horror novels including, *The Birds and the Bees* and *House of Pain*. Other authors who have written erotic horror fiction include Richard Laymon and Poppy Z. Brite.

Huff, Tanya.

Blood Series.

Victory (Vicki) Nelson, a Toronto ex-policewoman turned private investigator, and her friend, romance author Henry Fitzroy, who is the illegitimate son of Henry VIII as well as a vampire, work together to solve crimes of the paranormal kind. The alternate title for this series is <u>Vicki Nelson, Investigator</u>.

Blood Price. Daw Books, 1991.

Nelson and Fitzroy investigate a series of murders being committed by a 450-year-old vampire in Toronto.

Blood Trail. Daw Books, 1992.

A family of werewolves hires Nelson and Fitzroy to uncover the individual responsible for the shooting of family members.

Blood Lines. Daw Books, 1992.

Blood Pact. Daw Books, 1993.

Blood Debt. Daw Books, 1997.

Subjects: Fitzroy, Henry (Fictional Character) • Nelson, Vicki (Fictional character) • Toronto • Vampires

Read On: This series will appeal to readers of Laurell K. Hamilton's <u>Anita Blake, Vampire Hunter</u> series; other novels that blend fantasy, horror, and mystery are in Hamilton's <u>Meredith Gentry</u> series and the <u>Three Sisters Trilogy</u> by Nora Roberts.

Kilpatrick, Nancy.

Eternal City. Five Star, 2003. 290pp.

Widowed Claire Mowatt inherits a summer cottage north of Toronto from her aunt. Seeing this inheritance as a windfall that will secure her son David's future, she is thrilled to receive an immediate offer to purchase the property from a local land developer. Surprised to discover a polluted lake and the locals in a land dispute with the developer, Claire is drawn to discover what is actually going on in the nearby Nirvana, The Eternal City development, a decision that will prove that the promises of finding perfection are not what they seem.

Subjects: Environmental Pollution • Good vs. Evil • Land Developers • Vampires

Read On: In this novel, Kilpatrick, working with co-author Michael Kilpatrick, blends horror and mystery; other authors who tell similar genre-blended tales include Tim Waggoner (*Necropolis*) and Chet Williamson (*Second Chance*).

Power of the Blood.

The stories, lives, and loves of contemporary vampires are explored as they seek to forge relationships and protect their existence.

Child of the Night. Raven Books/Robinson, 1996, 2003.

Carol has recently recovered her memory of bearing a child by wealthy vampire André many years ago. Now she must travel to Quebec to search for the son she had been forced to abandon.

Near Death. Pocket Books, 1994, 2004.

Reborn. Pumpkin Books, 1998.

Bloodlover. Baskerville Books, 2000.

A power struggle ensues between Julien and Jeanette, both strong-willed and determined individuals, in 1960s London.

> **Subjects:** Erotic Fiction • Male–Female Relationships • Vampire Clans

> **Read On:** Kilpatrick also writes as Amarantha Knight (<u>Darker Passions</u>). Authors Poppy Z. Brite, Laurell K. Hamilton, and Anne Rice share Kilpatrick's darkly erotic style of writing.

Spence, Fara.

That Hurt Thing. HAWK Publishing, 2002. 215pp.

Through the pages of a book purchased at a used bookstore, Nick O'Brien conjures up a beautiful genie. With the promise of three wishes ahead of him, his excited anticipation gradually dissipates as his life becomes a living nightmare and he realizes that the beautifully seductive genie is nothing but pure evil.

> **Subjects:** Evil • First Novels • Magic • Murder

> **Read On:** Poppy Z. Brite's *Lost Souls*, Richard Laymon's *Friday Night in Beast House,* and Douglas Preston's *Reliquary* also blend together horror, magic, and sensuality.

van Belkom, Edo.

Blood Road. Kensington Publishing, 2004. 352pp.

Looking to escape an abusive relationship, waitress Amanda takes to the road, hitchhiking with no clear destination in mind. Ultimately realizing how ill prepared she is, she decides to return home, a decision that lands her in the truck of a serial killer vampire who has discovered an endless supply of victims along the highway.

> **Subjects:** Hitchhiking • Ontario • Serial Killers • Vampires

> **Read On:** This prolific author has many titles to his credit, including *Teeth, Scream Queen, Wolf Pack,* and the Bram Stoker Award–winning short story "Rat Food," which he co-authored with David Nickle. The fast-paced storytelling found here, in which the vampire is anything but a traditional romantic figure, is similar in style to Richard Laymon (*Bite* and others) and Simon Clark (*Blood Crazy* and others).

Zinger, Steve.

Ray McMickle & the Kentucky Vampire Clan. AuthorHouse, 2004. 216pp.

Roy Stanich wanders into the small Kentucky town of Lebanon Junction and soon realizes that things here are not what they first appear to be. As he meets the town's cast of unusual characters, he encounters the evil-incarnate Ray McMickle, the leader of a group of vampires, who is intent on capturing his soul.

Subjects: Gothic Fiction • Kentucky • Small-town Horror • Vampires

Read On: Zinger's second novel, *The Sab,* is another vampire tale with a similar level of Gothic tone to it. To read other fast-paced Gothic horror novels, try *Shadows Bend: A Novel of the Fantastic and Unspeakable* by David Barbour or *Fiends* by John Farris.

Appendix 1

Resources and Web Sites

Resources

The development of Canadian literature and its importance to the greater literary community has been discussed in a number of works. The following titles will prove useful to anyone interested in gaining a fuller understanding of Canadian literature, as well as those interested in developing a collection of Canadian literature.

Atwood, Margaret. *Survival: A Thematic Guide to Canadian Literature*. McClelland & Stewart, 2004.

The Cambridge Companion to Canadian Literature. Edited by Eva-Marie Kröller. Cambridge University Press, 2004.

Encyclopedia of Literature in Canada. Edited by W. H. New. University of Toronto Press, 2002.

Moritz, A. F. *The Oxford Illustrated Literary Guide to Canada*. Oxford University Press, 1987.

New, W. H. *A History of Canadian Literature*. McGill-Queen's University Press, c2003.

The Oxford Book of Stories by Canadian Women in English. Edited by Rosemary Sullivan. Oxford University Press, 1999.

The Oxford Companion to Canadian Literature. Edited by Eugene Benson and William Toye. Oxford University Press, 1997.

Thacker, Robert. *English-Canadian Literature*. Michigan State University Press, 1996.

Vancouver Public Library. *Great Canadian Books of the Century*. Douglas & McIntyre, 1999.

Web Sites

Information related to Canadian authors, their work, and awards is readily available on the Internet. The following are some sites that provide up-to-date information for those seeking to learn more.

Library and Archives Canada

http://www.collectionscanada.ca.

The official Web site of Library and Archives Canada, this site is maintained by the government of Canada. It includes full bibliographic records for books published in Canada, with entries arranged by Dewey number. The titles listed in the Forthcoming section, however, are arranged by release date.

Author/Title Information

Amazon.ca

http://www.amazon.ca

This is the Canadian version of the online bookseller Amazon.com.

Canadian Authors Association

http://www.canauthors.org/index.html

This national association works to support the development of the Canadian writing community; the site provides links to a variety of writing resources including awards, publishers, bookstores, journals, and Canadian newspapers and magazines.

Canadian Literature Archive Author List

http://www.umanitoba.ca/canlit/authorlist/index.shtml

This site, hosted by the University of Manitoba, provides access to the home pages of some Canadian authors.

Canadian Romance Authors' Network (CRAN)

http://www.canadianromanceauthors.com/

This collective of published romance authors works to promote romance fiction to readers, booksellers, librarians, and the media. The site contains information on authors, current releases, lists of novels set in Canada, and works in French, awards, and more.

chapters.indigo.ca

http://www.chapters.indigo.ca

This is the Web site of a Canadian online bookseller.

Crime Fiction Canada

http://www.brocku.ca/crimefictioncanada/

This site, the work of two professors at Brock University, is a continually developing bibliographic tool related to Canadian crime/mystery/detective narratives in a variety of media, including print, film, and television. In addition to the extensive bibliographies the site also includes links to related sites from around the world.

Crime Writers of Canada

http://www.crimewriterscanada.com/

CWC states as its mission, "to promote Canadian crime writing and to raise the profile of Canadian crime writers from coast to coast." The site includes information on awards, member biographies, and links to author Web sites.

Index of Native American Book Resources on the Internet

http://www.hanksville.org/NAresources/indices/NAbooks.html

Self-described as a "Virtual Library [for] American Indians," this site provides information resources to the Native American community, which comprises both the United States and Canada.

Made in Canada • The Homepage for Canadian Science Fiction

http://www.geocities.com/Canadian_sf/

This site contains a wealth of information related to Canadians who are involved in the science fiction genre; included are links to Web sites of authors, actors, and filmmakers related to this genre, as well as convention information.

SF Canada

http://www.sfcanada.ca/

This is the Web site of an association of Canadian writers and other professionals working in the fields of science fiction, fantasy, horror, and speculative fiction; resources on this site include articles, news, awards information, member lists, and Web sites.

The Writers' Union of Canada

http://www.writersunion.ca

The Writers' Union is a national organization of professional writers of books for the general public. The site includes author biographies, bibliographies, and links to author Web sites.

Provincial Writers' Associations

Across the country there are associations, federations, unions, and guilds whose goal is to promote and foster the work of their members.

Federation of BC Writers

http://bcwriters.com/

"The Federation advocates policies that enhance the literary arts in BC and strives to raise the visibility of writers and gain public recognition of the contribution that writers offer to BC's and Canada's cultural identity." Included on the site are links to awards, writing groups and associations, publishers, libraries, and writer resources.

Manitoba Writers' Guild Inc.

http://www.mbwriter.mb.ca

The stated primary goal of this guild is to promote and advance the art of writing, in all its forms, in the province of Manitoba; the site contains literary links, awards, and information on writers' contests and events.

Newfoundland and Labrador Arts Council (NLAC)

http://www.nlac.nf.ca/

The association works to foster the development of the arts in the province through the administration of programs, services, and grants.

The P.E.I. Writers' Guild

http://www.peiwriters.ca

The P.E.I. Writer's Guild is an association of those interested in promoting the interests of Island writers. Information is provided on programs and events, and there are links to information about writers and writing in Canada.

Saskatchewan Writers Guild (SWG)

http://www.skwriter.com/

The mission of the guild is to foster and improve the status of the writers of Saskatchewan. Links are provided to events and literary competitions, and there are writers' links.

Saskatchewan Writes

http://www.lights.com/saskwrites

Created by the Saskatchewan Writers Guild with input from educators and librarians, the site contains information related to Saskatchewan writers, including biographies and bibliographies.

Union des écrivaines et des écrivains québécois (UNEQ) [in French only]

http://www.uneq.qc.ca

This union's mission is to promote and foster the work of writers in the province of Quebec. The Web site contains information on authors, their work, and literary prizes, as well as a calendar of literary events.

The Writers' Federation of New Brunswick

http://www.umce.ca/wfnb/

Established in 1982, this federation has more than 200 members and works to promote and encourage the recognition of the writers of New Brunswick; it also sponsors an annual literary competition. Links are provided to Canadian periodicals and publishers, as well as to member Web sites.

Writers' Federation of Nova Scotia (WFNS)

http://www.writers.ns.ca

This federation fosters and promotes the development of writers in the province of Nova Scotia both regionally and nationally. The site offers author and publisher information, events listings, periodical and writer resources, and more.

Writers Guild of Alberta (WGA)

http://www.writersguild.ab.ca

The mission of this provincial organization, which represents both professional and emerging writers, is to support and encourage the writers of Alberta. The site provides links to awards, literary festivals, member pages, and more.

Review Sources

Books in Canada: The Canadian Review of Books

http://www.booksincanada.com

Self-described as "the definitive source for reviews of Canadian books, by outstanding Canadian authors," this reviewing journal is also available online.

Canadian Literature Reviews

http://www.canlit.ca/reviews

This Web site contains selected reviews from *Canadian Literature: A Quarterly of Criticism and Review* that explore and celebrate the best of Canadian authors and their writing.

January Magazine

http://www.januarymagazine.com

This is an excellent site for reviews and other book-related articles and author interviews, offering a number of electronic newsletters that can assist in collection development.

Quill & Quire Reviews

http://www.quillandquire.com/reviews/

This Web site provides access to reviews from the trade journal of Canada's book trade from 1996 onwards. This journal is self-described as "Canada's Magazine of Book News and Reviews."

Appendix 2

Literary Awards

The work of Canadian authors has been recognized internationally, nationally, regionally, and locally. For the awards listed here, Canadian writers have either won or been shortlisted.

General Sites

Canadian Awards and Literary Prizes

http://www.mala.bc.ca/~soules/english/awards.htm

This is the online version of a work of the same title by R. G. Siemens, published by the University of Toronto Press. It lists not only the awards, but the winners as well.

La Bibliothèque Nationale du Québec

Prix littéraires du Québec

http://www.bnquebec.ca/portal/ressources_en_ligne/index_repertoires/prix_litteraires/i-r_prix_litt.htm#

This French site provides an index to more than 100 literary award winners in Quebec. French.

Specific Awards

ALA Stonewall Book Award

http://www.ala.org/ala/glbtrt/stonewall/stonewallbook.htm

This award has been around in various incarnations since 1971, often taking its name from the name change of the committee administering the award. It has gone from the Gay Book Award through several name changes to its current names for two awards: the Stonewall Book Award: Barbara Gittings Literature Award for Fiction, and the Stonewall Book Award: Israel Fishman Award for

Non-Fiction. Its purpose is to honour "exceptional merit relating to the gay/lesbian/bisexual/transgendered experience."

Alberta Book Awards

http://www.writersguild.ab.ca/programs/alberta_book_awards.asp

These awards are presented annually by Alberta Community Development, the Writers Guild of Alberta, and the Book Publishers of Alberta Association and are open to all Alberta authors who have published a book during the previous calendar year. Also included in the Alberta Book Awards, but not sponsored by the Writers Guild of Alberta, are the City of Calgary W. O. Mitchell Book Prize, the City of Edmonton Book Prize, and the Grant MacEwan Author's Award. There are separate entries for each of these awards listed below. The awards for works of fiction are:

Georges Bugnet Award for Novel. This is awarded for the best published novel by an author who has been a resident of Alberta for twelve of the previous eighteen months.

Henry Kreisel Award for Best First Book. This is awarded for the best first book written by a resident of Alberta. (This award has been discontinued. The last award granted in this category was in 2003.)

The Amazon.ca/*Books in Canada* First Novel Award

http://www.amazon.com/

Awarded since 1977, The Amazon.ca/*Books in Canada* First Novel Award is given annually to the best first novel in English published the previous year by a citizen or resident of Canada. Its name has changed with its funding; it began as the *Books in Canada* First Novel Award, which changed to the Smithbooks/*Books in Canada* First Novel Award when Smithbooks took over its management. When Chapters bought out Smithbooks, the award became the Chapters/*Books in Canada* First Novel Award. In 1999 Chapters ended its affiliation, and now it is the Amazon.ca/*Books in Canada* First Novel Award.

Anthony Award for Best Mystery Novel

http://www.bouchercon.net

The Anthony Awards are named after former *New York Times* mystery critic Anthony Boucher; they are presented each year during the Bouchercon World Mystery Convention, also named after Anthony Boucher. The award categories for novels include Best Novel, Best First Novel, Best Paperback Original, and Best Historical Mystery. The Web site changes each year with the new Bouchercon Convention.

Arthur C. Clarke Award

http://www.appomattox.demon.co.uk/acca/

This award is given for the best British science fiction novel from the previous year. Eligibility for this award is extended to Canadians.

Arthur Ellis Awards

http://www.crimewriterscanada.com/files/awards.html

The Arthur Ellis Awards, often called "The Canadian Edgars," are named after the pseudonym used by Canada's last official hangman. The awards have been presented annually since 1983 by Canada's national association of mystery-fiction writers, The Crime Writers of Canada, for works in the crime genre. The two most relevant categories here are Best Crime Novel and Best First Crime Novel. To be eligible for this award, titles must have been published for the first time in the previous year by authors living in Canada, regardless of their nationality, or by Canadian writers who reside outside of Canada. Sleuth of Baker Street (bookstore) and Harlequin Enterprises are long-time supporters of these awards.

Atlantic Independent Booksellers' Choice Award. *See* Atlantic Writing Awards

Atlantic Writing Awards

http://www.writers.ns.ca

The **Atlantic Independent Booksellers' Choice Award** honours popular books, with roots in the Atlantic region. Both bookstores and readers select the winner of this award.

The **Best Atlantic Published Book** award (new in 2004), is sponsored by Manitoba printers Friesen and Hignell's Printing and administered by the Atlantic Publishers Marketing Association; it recognizes the book that best represents Atlantic Canada to the reader.

The **Dartmouth Fiction Award** was established in 1988 to honour Nova Scotian fiction and non-fiction by Canadian authors.

The **Margaret and John Savage First Book Award** was established in 2003 to recognize the best first book of fiction or non-fiction written by a first-time book-published author in Atlantic Canada. (It was formerly the Cunard First Book Award.)

The **Thomas Head Raddall Atlantic Fiction Award** debuted in 1991, honouring the best book of fiction written by an Atlantic Canadian in the previous calendar year.

Aurora Awards. *See* Prix Aurora Awards

Author of the Year. *See* CBA Libris Awards

The Barry Awards

http://www.deadlypleasures.com/Barry.htm

These awards are granted by the staff of *Deadly Pleasures* magazine and recognize excellence in crime fiction in the categories of Best Novel, Best First Novel, Best British Novel, and Best Paperback Original.

BC Book Prizes

http://www.bcbookprizes.ca/

Established in 1985, these awards acknowledge achievements of British Columbia writers and publishers. The prizes for fiction are:

The **Ethel Wilson Fiction Prize** is an award given to the author of the best work of fiction, who is a B.C./Yukon resident or has lived in B.C. or the Yukon for three of the past five years.

The **Bill Duthie Bookseller's Choice** is presented to the originating publisher, based in B.C. or the Yukon, and author of the best book, based on public appeal and content.

Bennington Gate Book Award. *See* The Newfoundland and Labrador Book Awards

The Betty Trask Prize and Awards

http://www.societyofauthors.net/index.php4

Established in 1984 by the late Betty Trask to honour first novels in English, this award is presented to a Commonwealth citizen under the age of thirty-five, whose work must be "of a romantic or traditional nature." It is administered by The Society of Authors.

Bill Duthie Bookseller's Choice. *See* BC Book Prizes

Book of the Year. *See* Saskatchewan Book Awards

Booker Prize. *See* Man Booker Prize

Books in Canada First Novel Award. *See* Amazon.ca/*Books in Canada* First Novel Award

Booksellers' Choice Award. *See* Atlantic Writing Awards

The Bram Stoker Awards

http://www.horror.org/stokers.htm

Established in 1987, these awards acknowledge "superior achievement" in the horror genre.

Brenda MacDonald Riches First Book Award. *See* Saskatchewan Book Awards

CAA Literary Awards

http://www.canauthors.org/awards/awards.html

In 1975 the Canadian Authors Association reinstated its awards for literary achievement, a program originally begun in 1937 with the creation of the Governor General's Medals for literature. Authors give these awards to authors.

Calgary, City of, W. O. Mitchell Book Prize. *See* **City of Calgary W. O. Mitchell Book Prize**

The Canada-Japan Literary Award

http://www.canadacouncil.ca/prizes/canada_japan_literary/

Sponsored by the Canada Council for the Arts, this award recognizes literary excellence by Canadian writers who are writing on Japan, a Japanese theme, or themes that promote mutual understanding between Japan and Canada, or by Canadian translators of such books from Japanese into English or French.

Canadian Authors Association Literary Awards. *See* **CAA Literary Awards**

Canadian Booksellers Association Libris Awards. *See* **CBA Libris Awards**

Canadian Jewish Book Awards

http://www.kofflercentre.com/jewish_book_awards.shtml

Established in 1989 and awarded biannually, these awards honour writing on subjects of Jewish interest in a number of categories including fiction. The funding comes from various sectors of the community, but Martin and Beatrice Fischer have endowed the Martin & Beatrice Fischer Prize for Fiction, which has been dedicated variously to Fiction and to First Novels.

Carol Shields Winnipeg Book Award. *See* **Manitoba Writing Awards**

CBA Libris Awards

http://www.cbabook.org/awards/default.asp

These awards of the Canadian Booksellers Association are nominated and voted on by members of the Canadian bookselling community and honour outstanding achievement in Canada's bookselling industry.

Author of the Year is presented to the Canadian author of an outstanding literary work that contributes to Canadian culture.

Fiction Book of the Year is presented to a Canadian work of fiction published that had an outstanding impact on the Canadian bookselling industry, created wide media attention, brought people into bookstores, and had strong sales.

Chapters/*Books in Canada* First Novel Award. *See* **Amazon.ca/*Books in Canada* First Novel Award**

City of Calgary W. O. Mitchell Book Prize

http://www.calgary.ca/

Named after the celebrated Canadian author, this prize was established by the City of Calgary to acknowledge outstanding literature emerging from Calgary.

City of Edmonton Book Prize

http://www.writersguild.ab.ca/programs/alberta_book_awards.asp

Established in 1995, this prize requires that nominees must focus on some aspect of the City of Edmonton: history, geography, current affairs, its art, or its people.

City of Regina Book Award. *See* **Saskatchewan Book Awards**

City of Vancouver Book Award

http://www.city.vancouver.bc.ca/commsvcs/oca/Awards

Established in 1989, this is awarded annually to the author of the best book from any genre that demonstrates excellence and contributes to the appreciation and understanding of Vancouver's history, unique character, or achievements.

Commonwealth Writers Prize

http://www.commonwealthwriters.com/

This award was established in 1987 to encourage, reward, and promote new Commonwealth fiction titles. The shortlisted titles come from the winners of four regions of the Commonwealth: Africa, the Caribbean and Canada, Eurasia (which includes the United Kingdom), and Southeast Asia and the South Pacific. In each region a Best Book and a Best First Book are chosen.

Crawford Award. *See* **William F. Crawford IAFA Fantasy Award**

The Crime Writers' Association

http://www.thecwa.co.uk/

This British association awards a number of prizes for crime writing, both fiction and non-fiction. Those that are thus far relevant to Canadian writers are listed below:

The **John Creasey Memorial Award for Best First Crime Novel** is awarded by the Crime Writers' Association to an author who has not yet published a full-length work of fiction.

Macallan Dagger Awards: The Gold Dagger is given to the best crime novel of the year, and the Silver Dagger to the runner-up.

Cunard First Book Award. *See* **Atlantic Writing Awards**

The Dagger Awards. *See* **The Crime Writers' Association, Macallan Dagger Awards**

Dartmouth Fiction Award. *See* **Atlantic Writing Awards**

The Dashiell Hammett Awards

http://www.crimewritersna.org/

Established in 1992, these awards are presented by the North American Branch of the International Association of Crime Writers, for a work of literary excellence (fiction or non-fiction) in the field of crime writing, by an American or Canadian author.

The Edgar Allan Poe Awards

http://www.mysterywriters.org/

These awards, often referred to as The Edgars, are named after Edgar Allan Poe and are awarded to authors of distinguished work in various categories of the mystery and crime-writing genre, particularly Best Mystery Novel, Best First Novel, and Best Paperback Original.

Edmonton, City of Book Prize. *See* City of Edmonton Book Prize

Eileen McTavish Sykes Award for Best First Book. *See* Manitoba Writing Awards

The Endeavour Award

http://www.osfci.org/endeavour/

A collaboration between writers and fans of science fiction and fantasy, this award is given for a distinguished science fiction or fantasy book written by a Pacific Northwest author(s) and published in the previous year.

Ethel Wilson Fiction Prize. *See* BC Book Prizes

F. G. Bressani Prize

This award is sponsored by the Italian Cultural Centre in Vancouver, British Columbia.

The Ferro-Grumley Awards

http://www.publishingtriangle.org/awards.asp

Established in 1990, these awards recognize excellence and experiment in literary fiction. Two awards are granted, one for a male writer, one for a female writer. This award is administered by The Publishing Triangle, the association of lesbians and gay men in publishing.

Fiction Award. *See* Saskatchewan Book Awards

Fiction Book of the Year. *See* CBA Libris Awards

Gaylactic Spectrum Awards

http://www.spectrumawards.org/

Known as the Spectrum Awards, the full name is the Gaylactic Spectrum Awards. These awards were established in 1998 to honour works in speculative fiction—science fiction, fantasy, and horror—which include positive explorations of gay, lesbian, bisexual, or transgender characters, themes, or issues.

Georges Bugnet Award for Novel. *See* **Alberta Book Awards**

The Giller Prize

http://www.thegillerprize.ca

Founded in 1994 by Jack Rabinovitch as a tribute to his wife, Doris Giller, this annual prize is presented to the best English language Canadian novel or short-story collection.

Governor General's Literary Awards/Prix Littéraires du Gouverneur Général

http://www.canadacouncil.ca/prizes/ggla/default.asp

Considered to be Canada's preeminent national literary awards, these awards were inaugurated by Governor General Lord Tweedsmuir (John Buchan, author of *The Thirty-nine Steps*) for books published in 1936. This award, now administered by the Canada Council, presents awards in seven categories each in French and English (Fiction, Literary Nonfiction, Poetry, Drama, Children's Literature [text], Children's Literature [illustration], and Translation) to works by Canadian authors published in Canada or abroad.

Grant MacEwan Author's Award

http://www.cd.gov.ab.ca/

This annual award was established by the Alberta government and is presented to an Alberta author whose book best reflects Alberta and/or Dr. MacEwan's interests.

***Guardian* First Book Award**

http://books.guardian.co.uk/

Launched in 1999, this award replaces the *Guardian* Fiction Prize. It recognizes new writing regardless of genre (including fiction, poetry, biography, memoirs, history, politics, science, and current affairs). An interesting aspect of this award is the involvement of reading groups.

Harold U. Ribalow Prize

http://www.hadassah.org/

Administered by *Hadassah Magazine,* this award is for Jewish fiction, either novels or short story collections, published in English. (To find information on this prize on the Web site, go to New, Media & Publications, then Periodicals, then Ribalow Prize.)

Henry Kreisel Award for Best First Book. *See* **Alberta Book Awards**

Heritage Toronto Awards

http://www.heritagetoronto.org/home.show

These awards are granted in a wide variety of fields, all directed towards recognizing those who have excelled in raising awareness of Toronto's archaeological, built, cultural, and natural history. The award is no longer given to works of fiction.

HOMer Awards

http://www.locusmag.com/SFAwards/Db/Homer.html

The Science Fiction and Fantasy Literature Forum on the CompuServe Information Service founded these awards in 1991. The members of the Forum nominate and vote on their choice of Best in Novel, Novella, Novelette, Short Story, and Dramatic Presentation.

Hugh MacLennan Prize for Fiction. *See* **Quebec Writers' Federation Awards**

IAFA Fantasy Award. *See* **William F. Crawford IAFA Fantasy Awards**

IMPAC Award. *See* **International IMPAC Dublin Literary Award for the Novel**

International Fiction Prize. *See* **The *Irish Times* Literature Prizes**

International IMPAC Dublin Literary Award for the Novel

http://www.impacdublinaward.ie/

Established in 1995 as a joint venture between the Municipal Government of Dublin City and the IMPAC Company, this award is given to a novel chosen from titles nominated by libraries around the world.

The *Irish Times* Literature Prizes

http://www.readireland.ie/links/it.html

Among the various prizes awarded by the *Irish Times* is the International Fiction Prize, given to the author of a work of fiction written in English and published in Ireland, the United Kingdom, or the United States.

The James Tait Black Memorial Prize for Fiction

http://www.englit.ed.ac.uk/jtbinf.htm

This prize has been awarded since 1919 to a work of fiction written in English and first published or co-published in the United Kingdom, regardless of the author's nationality.

The James Tiptree Jr. Award

http://www.tiptree.org/

Created in 1991, this award is presented to the author whose work of science fiction or fantasy expands or explores the understanding of gender.

John Creasey Memorial Award for Best First Crime Novel. *See* **Crime Writers' Association**

The John Glassco Translation Prize

http://www.attlc-ltac.org/glasscoe.htm

Established in 1982, this award is presented to a Canadian citizen or landed immigrant for a literary translation of a work into French or English.

Kiriyama Pacific Rim Book Prize

www.kiriyamaprize.org/

Established in 1996, this award is presented annually to books that promote understanding and cooperation among the peoples and nations of the Pacific Rim. Since 1999, awards have been given to both fiction and non-fiction.

Lambda Literary Awards

http://www.lambdalit.org/lammy.html

Established in 1998, these awards, presented in twenty categories, recognize and honour the best in lesbian, gay, bisexual, and transgender literature.

Lannan Literary Awards

http://www.lannan.org/lf/lit/awards-and-fellowships/

Established in 1989, these awards honour both established and emerging writers whose work is deemed to be of exceptional quality.

Libris Awards. *See* CBA Libris Awards

The Locus Awards

http://www.locusmag.com/SFAwards/Db/Locus.html

Established in 1971, these awards are presented to the winners of the annual readers' poll taken by *Locus: The Magazine of theScience Fiction & Fantasy Field*. Categories include novel (Science Fiction, Fantasy/Horror, and First Novel), short fiction, anthology, collection, non-fiction, art book, publisher, magazine, and artist.

Macallan Dagger Awards. *See* Crime Writers' Association

Man Booker Prize for Fiction

http://www.themanbookerprize.com

Established in 1968 and referred to as the Booker Prize until 2002, this prize honours the very best of contemporary fiction written by a citizen of the Commonwealth or Republic of Ireland. Prior to 2002, the prize was sponsored by Booker-McConnell plc and administered by the National Book Council. The prize is currently sponsored by Man Group plc and administered by The Booker Prize Foundation.

Manitoba Writing and Publishing Awards

http://www.mbwriter.mb.ca/mwapa/mwapa.html

The **Carol Shields Winnipeg Book Award** is an annual prize established in 1999, which honours books that evoke the special character of, and contribute to the appreciation and understanding of, Winnipeg. All genres are eligible.

The **Eileen McTavish Sykes Award for Best First Book** is awarded annually to a Manitoba author whose first professionally published book is deemed the best, regardless of category.

The **McNally Robinson Book of the Year Award** is awarded to the best adult English language book by a Manitoba writer.

The **Margaret Laurence Award for Fiction** is awarded to the best adult fiction written in English by a Manitoba writer.

The **Mary Scorer Award** is given for the best book published by a Manitoba publisher and written by a Manitoba author for the trade, bookstore, educational, academic, or scholarly markets.

Le Prix littéraire Rue-Deschambault is named after a novel written by Gabrielle Roy, Manitoba's preeminent French writer, and is presented biannually to the best book in French by a Manitoba writer.

Margaret and John Savage First Book Award. *See* Atlantic Writing Awards

Margaret Laurence Award for Fiction. *See* Manitoba Writing Awards

Margaret McWilliams Award

http://www.mhs.mb.ca/info/awards/mcwilliams.shtml

Established in 1955 by then Lieutenant-Governor Roland F. McWilliams, this award is to encourage the study and interpretation of the history of Manitoba, in a number of categories including fiction.

The Marian Engel Award. *See* The Writers' Trust of Canada Awards

Martin & Beatrice Fischer Prize for Fiction. *See* Canadian Jewish Book Awards

The Mary Scorer Award for Best Book by a Manitoba Publisher. *See* Manitoba Writing Awards

Matt Cohen Prize. *See* The Writers' Trust of Canada Awards

McAuslan First Book Prize. *See* Quebec Writers' Federation Awards

The McNally Robinson Book of the Year Award. *See* Manitoba Writing Awards

Miles Franklin Literary Award

http://www.permanentgroup.com.au/awards/Miles_Franklin.htm

This is an Australian prize, awarded to a novel that is of "the highest literary merit and which must present Australian life in any of its phases."

The Mythopoeic Fantasy Award for Adult Literature

http://www.mythsoc.org/awards.html

Established in 1971, this award is presented to the fantasy novel, multi-volume, or single-author story collection for adults that best exemplifies "the spirit of the Inklings."

National Book Critics Circle Awards

http://www.bookcritics.org

Established in 1974, these awards are presented annually to honour the year's best books in five categories, including fiction; in 1997 non-Americans whose work was published in the United States became eligible for these awards.

Nebula Awards. *See* SFWA Nebula Awards

The Newfoundland and Labrador Book Awards

http://www.writersalliance.nf.ca/awards.html

Administered by the Writers' Alliance of Newfoundland and Labrador, these awards are presented biannually for books written by residents of Newfoundland and Labrador. Non-fiction and poetry alternate with fiction and children's literature/young adult. Originally the fiction prize was sponsored by NewTel, but this sponsorship was taken over by the Bennington Gate Bookstore. The winner must be a resident of Newfoundland and Labrador.

NewTel Book Award. *See* The Newfoundland and Labrador Book Awards

Orange Prize for Fiction

http://www.orangeprize.co.uk/

Established in 1995, this award honours a work of fiction written in English by a woman and published in the United Kingdom.

Ottawa Book Award

http://ottawa.ca/city_services/culture/arts/arts_book_en.shtml

Established in 1986, the award in alternate years recognizes fiction and non-fiction works of excellence written by authors residing in Ottawa. (It was formerly known as the Ottawa-Carleton Book Award.)

Ottawa-Carleton Book Award. *See* Ottawa Book Award

Philip K. Dick Award

http://www.philipkdick.com/links_pkdaward.html

Established in 1983 and presented annually, this award honours science fiction published in paperback original form in the United States.

Prix Aurora Awards

http://www.sentex.net/~dmullin/aurora/

Established in 1980, awards are annually presented for the best Canadian science fiction and fantasy by the Canadian Science Fiction and Fantasy Association.

Prix France-Québec. *See* **Prix Littéraire Philippe-Rossillon/Association France-Québec**

Prix Goncourt

http://www.academie-goncourt.fr/

This is a prize awarded to the best new work in French literature and is sponsored by l'Académie Goncourt in Paris.

Prix Littéraire France-Québec Jean-Hamelin

http://www2.biblinat.gouv.qc.ca/prixlitt/fiches/4688.htm

This French prize is sponsored by l'Association des écrivains de langue française (ADELF) and given to a Quebec writer, with support from the Quebec Consul General in Paris. (It is not to be confused with the Prix Littéraire Philippe-Rossillon/Association France-Québec, also commonly known as the Prix France-Québec.)

Prix Littéraire Philippe-Rossillon/Association France-Québec

http://www2.biblinat.gouv.qc.ca/prixlitt/fiches/4211.htm

This prize was a celebration of the thirtieth anniversary of l'Association France-Québec and was named in honour of a founding member of the association, a defender of Quebec and its causes. It is often confused with Le Prix France-Québec Jean-Hamelin.

Le Prix littéraire Rue-Deschambault. *See* **Manitoba Writing Awards**

The Pulitzer Prizes

http://www.pulitzer.org/

Established in 1917, these awards are presented for works of excellence. The Book Award category acknowledges distinguished fiction by an American author, preferably dealing with American life.

QSPELL Awards. *See* **Quebec Writers' Federation Awards**

Quebec Writers' Federation Awards

http://www.qwf.org/

Established in 1988, these awards (originally named the QSPELL Awards) honour excellence in the categories of fiction, non-fiction, poetry, translation, and first book written in English by a resident of Quebec.

The **Hugh MacLennan Prize for Fiction** was initially called the QSPELL Fiction Prize, but the name was changed in 1991.

The **McAuslan First Book Prize** was established in 2002 and can be awarded to either fiction or non-fiction.

The **Translation Prize** alternates each year between translations into English and translations into French.

Regina, City of, Book Award. *See* Saskatchewan Book Awards

ReLit Awards

http://relitawards.com/

Founded by author Kenneth J. Harvey, this award was established in 2000 to acknowledge works published by independent Canadian publishers.

Ribalow Prize. *See* Harold U. Ribalow Prize

RITA Awards

http://www.rwanational.org/

Previously named the Golden Medallion from 1982 to 1989, these awards are presented to outstanding works of romance fiction in a variety of categories by the Romance Writers of America.

The Rogers Writers' Trust Fiction Prize. *See* The Writers' Trust of Canada Awards

The Royal Society of Literature Ondaatje Prize. *See* The Winifred Holtby Memorial Prize

Saskatchewan Book Awards

http://www.bookawards.sk.ca

Established jointly in 1993 by the Saskatchewan Writers Guild, Saskatchewan Publishers Group, and Saskatchewan Library Association, these awards include the following fiction prizes:

The **Book of the Year** award is presented to a Saskatchewan author for the best book, regardless of category (children's, drama, fiction, non-fiction, and poetry).

The **City of Regina Book Award** is presented to a Regina writer for the best book in a number of categories, including fiction.

The **Fiction Award** is presented to a Saskatchewan author for the best book of fiction (novel, short fiction).

The **First Book (Brenda MacDonald Riches Award)** considers books from the following categories: children's, drama, fiction, non-fiction, and poetry.

The **Saskatoon Book Award** is presented to a Saskatoon writer for the best book in several genres, including fiction.

Saskatoon Book Award. *See* **Saskatchewan Book Awards**

Seiun Award

http://www.nippon2007.org/eng/oversea/e_seiun.html

Japan's highest honour in science fiction, this award has a "Foreign Novel" category. The prize is originally presented at Japan's National Science Fiction Convention (Akicon) and then presented again at the World Science Fiction Convention.

SFWA Nebula Awards

http://www.sfwa.org/

Founded in 1965, the awards are sponsored by the Science Fiction Writers of America and are presented in a number of categories, including Best Novel, Novella, Novelette, and Short Story.

Smithbooks/*Books in Canada* First Novel Award. *See* **Amazon.ca/*Books in Canada* First Novel Award**

Spectrum Awards. *See* **Gaylactic Spectrum Awards**

The Stephen Leacock Memorial Medal for Humour

http://www.leacock.ca/awards.html

Established in 1947, this annual award is presented by The Stephen Leacock Association for the best book of humour written by a Canadian.

The Sunburst Award for Canadian Literature of the Fantastic

http://www.sunburstaward.org/

Named after Phyllis Gotlieb's first novel, this award is generally referred to as The Sunburst. It was established in 2001 by the Sunburst Award Committee and is presented annually for the best work of speculative fiction (novel or short story).

Thomas Head Raddall Atlantic Fiction Award. *See* **Atlantic Writing Awards**

Timothy Findley Award. *See* **The Writers' Trust of Canada Awards**

Torgi Literary Awards

http://www.cnib.ca/library/awards/Torgi/

These are Canada's only alternative-format book awards and are presented by the Canadian National Institute for the Blind in six categories: CNIB-produced Fiction, Non-fiction, Tiny Torgi Audio, Tiny Torgi PrintBraille, and Partner-produced Fiction and Non-fiction. It is a Readers' Choice Award and is meant to recognize all those who make alternative-format books possible, including the authors themselves.

Toronto Book Awards

http://www.city.toronto.on.ca/book_awards/

These awards were established in 1974 by Toronto City Council to honour authors of books of literary or artistic merit that evoke a sense of Toronto.

Translation Prize. *See* Quebec Writers' Federation Awards

Trillium Book Award

http://www.culture.gov.on.ca/english/culdiv/cultind/trillium.htm

Established in 1987 by the Ontario government to recognize excellence, the award is open to works in any genre.

VanCity Women's Book Prize

http://www.bcbookworld.com/vancity/

This is a jointly sponsored award, established in 1992 by VanCity Credit Union, Vancouver Public Library, and the B.C. Ministry of Community, Aboriginal and Women's Services to recognize the best book pertaining to women's issues.

Vancouver Book Award. *See* City of Vancouver Book Award

The W. O. Mitchell Book Prize. *See* City of Calgary W. O. Mitchell Book Prize

The W. O. Mitchell Literary Prize. *See* The Writers' Trust of Canada Awards

WHSmith Literary Award

http://www.whsmithplc.com/grp/welcome.htm

Established in 1959, this award is presented annually to an author from the United Kingdom, the Commonwealth, or the Republic of Ireland whose work is judged to make the most significant contribution to literature.

The William F. Crawford—IAFA Fantasy Award

http://wiz.cath.vt.edu/iafa/

Granted by the International Association for the Fantastic in the Arts, this award is given to the best first fantasy novel published in the previous eighteen months. It is usually referred to as the Crawford Award.

The Winifred Holtby Memorial Prize

http://62.73.167.70/prizes/holtby.php

Established in 1967 by the Royal Society of Literature, this award is presented annually for the best regional novel of the year. In 2003, this prize was replaced by the Royal Society of Literature Ondaatje Prize.

The Winterset Award

http://www.wintersetinsummer.ca/award.htm

Established in 2000 by author Richard Gwyn in memory of his wife, author Sandra Fraser-Gwyn, a vocal advocate of Newfoundland's arts scene, this award honours a work of outstanding literary merit in any genre. The annual literary prize is named after Fraser-Gwyn's childhood home.

World Fantasy Awards

http://www.worldfantasy.org/awards

Established in 1975 and presented annually by the World Fantasy Convention, this prize acknowledges excellence in fantasy writing.

Writers' Federation of Nova Scotia Awards

http://www.writers.ns.ca/competitions.html

This writers' organization administers various competitions for writing in the Atlantic region, which come under the umbrella of the Atlantic Writing Awards. The fiction award is the Thomas Head Raddall Atlantic Fiction Award. However, there are additional awards offered to Atlantic writers. *See* Atlantic Writing Awards.

The Writers' Trust of Canada Awards

http://www.writerstrust.com/

An association whose purpose is to celebrate and support Canadian writers, the Writers' Trust offers one prize for fiction (The Rogers Writers' Trust Fiction Prize) and several prizes for a writer's work and/or contribution to Canada's literary achievement.

The Marian Engel Award began in 1986, named in honour of the award-winning author of *Bear*, and is awarded to a female Canadian for her work to date and for her expected future contribution to Canadian literature.

The Writers' Trust of Canada's Matt Cohen Prize—in Celebration of a Writing Life was established in 2001, after the untimely death of Matt Cohen. It is for a lifetime of distinguished work by a Canadian writer, in either poetry or prose, in English or French.

The Rogers Writers' Trust Fiction Prize was established in 1997 to recognize Canadian writers of exceptional talent for the year's best novel or short story collection.

The W. O. Mitchell Literary Prize was first granted in 1998 to a writer who has produced an outstanding body of work, has acted during his or her career as a mentor for writers, and has published a work of fiction or had a new stage play produced during the three-year period specified for each competition.

The Writers' Trust of Canada's Timothy Findley Award was inaugurated in 2002 to recognize a body of work by a Canadian male. This *oeuvre* is to comprise no fewer than three books of literary merit that are predominantly fiction.

Appendix 3

Canadian Publishers and Publishing

Over the last number of years, the Canadian publishing scene, like publishing in many countries, has undergone a number of changes. While there are flourishing independents, many of the large publishers are Canadian branches of multinationals. The other market influence that is seen is the number of books that arrive in the marketplace from abroad, especially from Britain and the United States. The companies listed here are the primary publishers of Canadian authors and titles.

Cormorant Books
http://www.cormorantbooks.com

This company publishes literary mainstream fiction, works of fiction, translations, and creative non-fiction. Titles by a number of award-winning authors, including Nino Ricci (*Lives of the Saints*), Neil Bissoondath (*Doing the Heart Good*), and Edward O. Phillips (*Buried on Sunday*), have come out of this publishing house. The company Web site contains author information, links to author Web sites, review excerpts, awards information, and book club guides for selected titles. The company posts its current catalogue on the site in a downloadable format.

The Douglas & McIntyre Publishing Group
http://www.douglas-mcintyre.com

Established in 1971, Douglas & McIntyre Publishing Group consists of three imprints: Douglas & McIntyre, Greystone Books, and Groundwood Books. The Douglas & McIntyre imprint focuses on First Nations art and culture, literary fiction, popular memoir, Canadian issues and politics, and other non-fiction, publishing approximately twenty-five new books each year. The company has published the work of notable Canadian authors such as Wayson Choy and Fred Stenson. The imprint spotlights British Columbia culture in particular; however, many of the publications address issues relevant to all Canadians. The Web site contains company information, author biographies, and catalogues.

HarperCollinsCanada Ltd.

http://www.harpercollins.ca

HarperCollinsCanada Ltd. was created in 1989 through the merging of Harper & Row and the British publisher Collins. Authors published include such renowned writers as Sharon Butala, Thomas King, Andrew Pyper, and Greg Hollingshead. In addition, the company has two imprints. The first is the literary hardcover imprint, HarperFlamingoCanada, which has published works such as Barbara Gowdy's *The White Bone*, Timothy Findley's *Pilgrim,* and Bonnie Burnard's *A Good House.* The second is PerennialCanada, a literary paperback division publishing the work of Timothy Findley, Margaret Visser, Barbara Gowdy, Sharon Butala, James Raffan, and Rosemary Sullivan. Web site features include author information, electronic newsletters, and book club information.

House of Anansi Press

http://www.anansi.ca

This company was founded in 1967 by writers Dennis Lee and Dave Godfrey, with the intent of finding and developing Canada's great new writers of literary fiction, poetry, and non-fiction. The company has a commitment to maintaining a significant backlist, accumulated since the house was founded thirty-five years ago. Initially started as a small press with a mandate to publish only Canadian writers, it quickly gained attention for publishing significant authors such as Margaret Atwood, Matt Cohen, Michael Ondaatje, and Erin Mouré, as well as George Grant and Northrop Frye. In the industry the company is known to be a publisher of poetry and experimental fiction as well as works in translation. Information available on the Web site includes new releases, author information, and links of literary interest (author Web sites, prizes, writing festivals, and more).

Literary Press Group of Canada

http://www.lpg.ca

This non-profit association of Canadian-owned and -operated book publishers, established in 1975 and incorporated in November 1995, works to represent the interests of this group of small presses. Its purpose is to foster, promote, and support them in their goal to publish original literature and non-fiction by writers of all backgrounds who offer Canadians a true reflection of themselves. Some of the member publishers of this association are Beach Holme Publishing, Coach House Books, Coteau Books, Goose Lane Editions, NeWest Press, The Porcupine's Quill, and Turnstone Press. Over the years, these small presses have published the work of such authors as Margaret Atwood, and Michael Ondaatje. The association's Web site provides contact information and links to the Web sites of its members.

McArthur & Company Publishing Limited

http://www.mcarthur-co.com

Canadian-owned and -operated, this company was established in 1998 when Time Warner closed Little, Brown Canada. McArthur & Company is a publisher and distributor of quality Canadian and international fiction and non-fiction for adults and children, based in Toronto. Canadian authors published by the company include Nancy Huston (Giller Award nominee), Marsha Boulton (Leacock Award winner), Rosemary Aubert (Arthur Ellis Award winner), Kate Pullinger, Lisa Appignanesi, Rosemary Sullivan, David Rotenberg, and John Brady, among others. International authors published by McArthur include Maeve Binchy, Joanna Trollope, Bryce Courtenay, Vikram Seth, and Rosie Thomas. Resources available via the Web site include catalogues and news alerts.

McClelland & Stewart Ltd

http://www.mcclelland.com

In 2006 this company will celebrate its centenary anniversary. M & S produces roughly 100 new titles a year, including works from such fiction writers as Margaret Atwood, Alistair MacLeod, Rohinton Mistry, Alice Munro, and Jane Urquhart. The company also produces the classic New Canadian Library series that celebrates the country's literary achievements, ranging from Thomas Chandler Haliburton's *The Clockmaker* (1836), to Susanna Moodie's *Roughing It in the Bush* (1852), to L. M. Montgomery's *Anne of Green Gables* (1908). In 2000, McClelland & Stewart gifted 75 percent of the company to the University of Toronto as a way "to safeguard a great Canadian institution, a vital part of Canada's cultural heritage" for years to come.

Penguin Canada

http://www.penguin.ca

Penguin Group (Canada) publishes approximately 100 titles of crime, mystery, and general non-fiction and is moving towards literary fiction as well. Titles are published under the Viking Canada imprint, paperbacks as Penguin Canada, and children's books under the Puffin Canada imprint. The company Web site contains sample chapter excerpts, reading guides, and electronic newsletters.

Raincoast Books

http://www.raincoast.com

Raincoast Books is a Canadian publisher and distributor based in Vancouver, producing a wide range of fiction and non-fiction titles for adults and children and acting as the Canadian distributor for over forty national and international publishers. Some of the authors represented by this company are Nick Bantock (Griffin & Sabine Series) and Governor General's Literary Award nominee Colin McAdam (*Some Great Thing*); in addition, this company handles the publishing of the Harry Potter Series for Canadian distribution.

Random House of Canada

http://www.randomhouse.ca

Random House of Canada, established in 1944 as the Canadian distributor of Random House Books, established its own Canadian publishing program in 1986. Under the umbrella of the parent company, there are a number of imprints including Doubleday Canada, Vintage, Seal (a mass market division publishing both Canadian and international authors), and Alfred A. Knopf Canada. Knopf Canada publishes both literary fiction and non-fiction. One exciting initiative of this company is to publish and promote emerging authors through a program called "The New Face of Fiction." This program has been responsible for launching the careers of such authors as Ann-Marie MacDonald, Gail Anderson-Dargatz, Shauna Singh Baldwin, and Mary Lawson. The Web site features electronic newsletters, book excerpts, and information for book groups (http://www.bookclubs.ca), with reading guides, resources, and more.

Thomas Allen & Son, Ltd.

http://www.thomas-allen.com

Established in 1888, this company is the oldest family-owned and -operated agency-publisher in Canada, serving the Canadian book trade for more than eight decades. The recently launched division, Thomas Allen Publishers, publishes books by Natalee Caple, Austin Clarke, Sylvia Fraser, Cynthia Holz, Larissa Lai, Keith Maillard, Leon Rooke, Shyam Selvadurai, Cordelia Strube, and David Gilmour. Resources available on the company Web site include reading group guides and chapter excerpts.

References

Cambridge Companion to Canadian Literature, The. 2004. Edited by Eva-Marie Kröller. Cambridge University Press, 2004.

Canada. Statistics Canada. 2003, May 26. "The People. Books." Available at http://142.206.72.67/02/02f/02f_005d_e.htm (accessed March 2005).

Canadian Crime Fiction: An Annotated Comprehensive Bibliography of Canadian Crime Fiction from 1817 to 1996, and Biographical Dictionary of Canadian Crime Writers, with an Introductory Essay on the History and Development of Canadian Crime Writing. 1996. Compiled by David Skene-Melvin; assisted by Norbert Spehner. Battered Silicon Dispatch Box.

Encyclopedia of Literature in Canada. 2002. Edited by W. H. New. University of Toronto Press.

Fonseca, Anthony J., and June Michele Pulliam. 2003. *Hooked on Horror: A Guide to Reading Interests in Horror Fiction.* 2d ed. Libraries Unlimited.

Foran, Charles. 2002. "As Canadian as . . ." *The Globe and Mail*, October 19, D 5-6.

Herald, Diana Tixier. 1999. *Fluent in Fantasy: A Guide to Reading Interests.* Libraries Unlimited.

———. 2000. *Genreflecting.* 5th ed. Libraries Unlimited.

Herald, Diana Tixier, and Bonnie Kunzel. 2002. *Strictly Science Fiction: A Guide to Reading Interests.* Libraries Unlimited.

Hutchison, Don. 2001. *Wild Things Live There: The Best of Northern Frights.* Mosaic Press.

Lowry, Glen. 2005, Spring. Home Page. Syllabi. English 103 Canadian Literature. Available at http://www.glenlowry.ca/103_0501.html (accessed March 2005).

Merril, Judith. 1995. "History and Definition of Science Fiction." *Grolier Multimedia Encyclopaedia.* Available at http://alcor.concordia.ca/~talfred/sf-def.htm (accessed July 2005).

Northern Frights V. 2004. Edited by Don Hutchison. Mosaic Press.

Pearl, Nancy. 1999. *Now Read This: A Guide to Mainstream Fiction, 1978–1998.* Libraries Unlimited.

———. 2002. *Now Read This II: A Guide to Mainstream Fiction, 1990–2001.* Libraries Unlimited.

Ramsdell, Kristin. 2001. *Romance Fiction: A Guide to the Genre.* Libraries Unlimited.

The Readers' Advisor's Companion. 2001. Edited by Kenneth D. Shearer and Robert Burgin. Libraries Unlimited.

Ross, Catherine Sheldrick, and Mary K. Chelton. 2001. "Reader's Advisory: Matching Mood and Material." *Library Journal* (February 1): 52–55.

Saricks, Joyce G. 2001. *The Readers' Advisory Guide to Genre Fiction*. American Library Association.

Saricks, Joyce G., and Nancy Brown. 1997. *Readers' Advisory Service in the Public Library*. 2d ed. American Library Association.

Sawyer, Robert J. 1997, December. [Interview] in "Crime Writers of Canada." *Fingerprints*. Available at http://www.sfwriter.com/arcwc.htm (accessed July 2005).

Smith, Stephen. 2001. "Who's Taught, Who's Not," The Disappearing Canon: What Happened to CanLit's Classics?" *Quill & Quire* (November): 17.

Taylor, Charles. 1977. *Six Journeys: A Canadian Pattern*. Anansi.

Wilson, Edmund. 2005, February 1. "Edmund Wilson Quotes." *ThinkExist.com Quotations*. Available at http://en.thinkexist.com/quotes/edmund_wilson/ (accessed March 2005).

Author/Title Index

Boldface page numbers indicate the location of the main entry for that author, that title, or its translation, as well as titles within a series. Series titles are underscored, and boldface numbers indicate the location of the main entry for that series.

Subject Index

About the Authors

SHARRON SMITH is the Readers' Advisory Librarian at the Kitchener Public Library (Ontario, Canada); and holds a Master of Library Science degree from the University of Western Ontario. In addition to overseeing the provision of Readers' Advisory services, she is also responsible for the collection development of fiction resources throughout the library system. She currently chairs the Region of Waterloo's One Book, One Community committee, one of the first community reading campaigns in Canada. Sharron is a regular presenter of readers' advisory programs at the Ontario Library Association annual conference and has presented readers' advisory training across Canada. She is the chair of the Ontario Public Library Association's Readers' Advisory Committee, a member of the RUSA CODES Readers' Advisory Committee and writes a regular readers' advisory column for the Ontario Library Association's magazine ACCESS.

MAUREEN O'CONNOR has worked in the public library system, providing reference and readers' advisory for over thirty years, in both Toronto and Brampton, Ontario. She reviewed fiction and provided content for BookBrowser and conducts workshops in readers' advisory at the regional and provincial level. She also conducts workshops on readers' advisory with her co-author, Sharron Smith. Maureen initiated and moderates the Canadian Readers' Advisory Listserv, RA_Talk; she also leads book discussion groups and has done the same with Sharron Smith at a National Conference. Maureen is available to provide workshops, either alone, or in conjunction with Sharron Smith, on Canadian fiction (mainstream and genre), readers' advisory principles and practice, online and print readers' advisory materials, book discussion groups, and more.